# Design it Yourself
# Graphic Workshop

## A Step-by-Step Guide
## CHUCK GREEN

GLOUCESTER MASSACHUSETTS

ROCKPORT PUBLISHERS

First published in the United States of America by
Rockport Publishers, Inc.
33 Commercial Street
Gloucester, Massachusetts 01930-5089
Telephone: (978) 282-9590
Fax: (978) 283-2742
www.rockpub.com

Library of Congress Cataloging-in-Publication Data available

ISBN-13: 978-1-59253-348-0
ISBN-10: 1-59253-348-5

10 9 8 7 6 5 4 3 2 1

Design: Chuck Green

Printed in China

## Acknowledgments

A designer is a composer and arranger. We take the words, photographs, artwork, and typefaces created by others and assemble them into something that we hope is worthy of their efforts. To all those who contributed, I thank you.

Thanks, too, to the folks at Rockport Publishers for allowing me the creative freedom to take their vision for the Design-It-Yourself series and make it my own. I am especially grateful to Winnie Prentiss and Kristin Ellison.

Finally, thanks to my wife, Leslie, and sons Jeffrey and Robert, for supplying the support and energy that has allowed me to weave another small thread into the ever-growing fabric of ideas.

# Contents

INTRODUCTION

# This is not a design *theory* book— it is a design *instruction* book.

A design theory book examines abstract concepts such as contrast, symmetry, and white space, under the assumption that if you learn to think the thoughts of a designer, you will be a designer.

I'm not sure it's that easy. In my opinion, the capacity to visualize and compose is influenced by more than theory. Some mix of natural talent and experience seems to play a significant enough role that I doubt many of us could get the desired result by simply understanding a premise.

I propose an entirely different approach—to demonstrate how one designer does it.

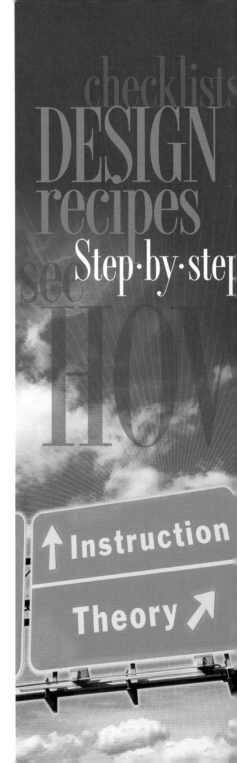

# Introduction

You and I will tackle a real project from the initial idea to the final printed piece—and I'm going to tell you how I handle each detail every step of the way. Think of it as a cookbook. Instead of discussing the history of the stove and the intricacies of milling flour, I'm going to show you how to bake a cake. And if I've done my job, following one of my design recipes will result in a logo, letterhead, business card, and newsletter that looks and sells as if it were designed by a pro.

## Who this book is for

The Design-It-Yourself series is written primarily for "non-designers," in layman's language, and endeavors to include all the information necessary to produce real-world, professional-quality results. Everyone, of course, is a designer in the sense that they make artistic judgments about everything from the clothes they wear to the way they decorate the rooms they live in. By "non-designer," I simply mean those who don't make their living at it.

But even chefs use cookbooks. I hope even an experienced designer will profit from seeing how another designer navigates familiar territory. I'm a much better designer for having studied my colleagues' work—their justification for making subtle choices, the tips and tricks they use in everyday production, and the resources they tap for the details they don't handle in-house.

## How to use it

This book is divided into two sections, each containing two parts, a Step-by-Step Design guide and a Design Guide. Section 1, part 1, beginning on page 9, covers the steps necessary to research, design, and produce a logo and incorporate it into a letterhead, business card, and envelope. We discuss how to create a name, write a benefits-oriented tag line, and how to choose the right tools and most effective resources. It includes eight ways to design a logo and shows you how to add important functionality to your business cards and letterheads. Section 2, part 1, beginning on page 159, discusses newsletters—how to establish your mission, define your audience, develop content, and choose the right tools and the most effective resources. Both parts even help you find a commercial printer and choose the right paper to print your letterhead and newsletters on.

I suggest you read through both sections' Part 1 start to finish before beginning your project, then use the checklist included with each step as a guide. The checklists summarize the key points and are coded to the text so you can easily review the details as necessary.

Section 1, part 2, beginning on page 53, features twenty-five Design Recipes and section 2, part 2, beginning on page 201, features thirteen Design Recipes, each including in-depth, detailed information about designing a logo, letterhead, business card, envelope, and newsletter using different styles, typefaces, and color schemes. Each recipe includes page layouts and dimensions, typeface names and sizes, specific color suggestions, even the sources of graphics and photography. And, because they are created specially for the Design-It-Yourself series, you are free to copy any recipe in whole or in part to create your own materials.

## What you need

This book is not about a particular software program and does not require a specific computer system. Most of the projects are easiest to produce using a desktop publishing program such as QuarkXPress, Adobe InDesign, Adobe PageMaker, or Microsoft Publisher. The other software you will need depends on the recipes you choose to follow. Some of the logos require a drawing program such as Adobe Illustrator, Macromedia FreeHand, or CorelDRAW; or an image editing program such as Adobe Photoshop or Jasc Software's Paint Shop Pro. Program suggestions are listed throughout.

## Continue the discussion at www.designiy.com

Want to share your side of the experience? I've established a place for you and other readers to share your insights and experiences about the Design-It-Yourself series: www.designiy.com. In addition to posting selected comments from readers, I'll keep you current on the latest resources and upcoming titles in the series.

This, of course, is just the beginning of what is possible. As more and more of us learn to master today's powerful design-oriented software programs, the appreciation of good design, based on honest marketing principles, will increase dramatically. I hope, in some small way, what you find here furthers that outcome.

Chuck Green
chuckgreen@designiy.com

# Logos, Letterheads, and Business Cards

## SECTION 1, PART 1
## Step-by-Step Design

STEP 1

# Establish Your Mission

Your logo is your organization's strategic center of gravity—the foundation on which your letterhead, business card, and envelope are built. It deserves an investment of significant thought and effort. Design it well, and in the months and years to come, it will help arouse the curiosity of your prospects, build your image in the minds of customers, and provide a symbolic rallying point for your organization.

For the purposes of this book, *a logo is defined as the combination of a name, a symbol, and a short tag line.* The sum of the parts identifies at a glance the nature of your product or service, transmits the benefit of using it, and defines your attitude about it. It is the first step of building a brand.

The brand, as advertising pioneer David Ogilvy put it, is a "product's personality... its name, its packaging, its price, the style of its advertising, and above all, the nature of the product itself." Your logo is an important part of that brand. Your customers and prospects will see it over and over again on everything you produce. As advertising and marketing themes ebb and flow, your logo is the visual anchor that holds the ship steady.

**Do some big-picture thinking**

The first step toward designing a logo is to establish a mission—to define what you hope to accomplish and determine how you will go about it. This takes some big-picture thinking.

**1.1** Start by *identifying the target*—are you selling a product, a service, or a cause? Though many an organization uses its reputation and attitude to do its selling, it is important to remember that customers buy benefits, not companies. From the outset, you need to determine if you should invest your resources in creating a logo for a specific product, service, or cause; for the organization that sells it; or both.

A consumer products company such as Frito-Lay, for example, sells many different products—Doritos, Ruffles, Lay's, and others—all of which have their own identity. It's obvious that, on the consumer front, they spend far more on the identities of individual products than they do on the Frito-Lay name. A legal firm or a custom-home builder typically does just the opposite—it focuses on establishing a favorable image of its company name.

**1.2** Next, *pinpoint your audience.* Obviously, to sell something to someone, you have to know who they are and how to reach them. At one extreme, you might have a single, easy-to-reach audience; at the other, different audiences for each product or service that are reached in a variety of ways.

**1.3** Though the name of this book is *Design-it-Yourself,* that doesn't mean you have to wear all the hats. It is a good idea, early on, to clearly *define your role* in the process. Maybe you are confident about your ability to create a symbol but have a terrible time deciding on a palette of colors. If that's the case, by all means, enlist some help. You may even go so far as to take the preliminary research and planning steps and hire someone else to complete the project using this book as your guide.

**1.4** Now, too, is the time to *determine how and where your logo will be used.*

*Size*—If your logo will be used at a very small size, you'll need to keep it simple. If it will be used in a retail environment, it may need to be readable from four or five feet away.

*Number of colors*—Your logo should work well in color and in black and white; you don't want to be forced to print your invoices or Yellow Pages ad in multiple colors.

*Where it is used*—Logos are imprinted on machinery, painted on the sides of trucks, and branded on the backsides of cattle. Though you can't anticipate all the places it will be used, it pays to make a list of the probable uses and determine how they affect the design. Here are a few:

| | |
|---|---|
| Yellow Pages | Packaging |
| Newspapers | Signage |
| Magazines | Marketing giveaways |
| TV | CDs |
| Webs | Clothing |

**1.5** The design process requires subjective judgments about matters of taste. Trying to gain the consensus of a group often leads to a homogeneous design that lacks the passion that makes a logo memorable. To expedite the process and avoid conflict, *appoint the decision-makers* before you begin. Choose people who best understand the organization and its style—people who are comfortable making aesthetic decisions and whose design and marketing sense you most trust.

**1.6** *Establish a budget*—not every nickel and dime, but a realistic, general figure. Include the cost of time, software, and outside services such as printing.

**1.7** Finally, *set a schedule.* At a minimum, allow:

| | |
|---|---|
| 4 | hours for research |
| 8 | hours to create a name |
| 4 | hours to write a defining phrase |
| 8 | hours to design a logo |
| 4 | hours to layout a letterhead |
| 2 | hours to layout a business card |
| 1 | hour to layout an envelope |
| 10 | working days for printing |

**Step 1: MISSION CHECKLIST**

| | |
|---|---|
| **1.1** | Identify the target |
| **1.2** | Pinpoint your audience |
| **1.3** | Define your role |
| **1.4** | Determine how and where your logo will be used |
| **1.5** | Appoint the decision-makers |
| **1.6** | Establish a budget |
| **1.7** | Set a schedule |

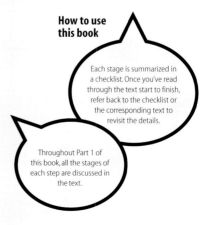

**How to use this book**

Each stage is summarized in a checklist. Once you've read through the text start to finish, refer back to the checklist or the corresponding text to revisit the details.

Throughout Part 1 of this book, all the stages of each step are discussed in the text.

STEP 2

# Do Some Research

Once you know where you're headed, you need to figure out how to get there. That takes research—about your competition, your customers, and what you need to do to stand out from the crowd. While some of this may seem excessive, I assure you that developing a good map up front will save you miles of backtracking later on. I learned this lesson the hard way: I decided to skip the research step in a rush to design an ad for a client on a tight deadline. They liked my solution and pointed out that their primary competitor must have liked it, too—it had run a nearly identical ad several months earlier.

This is not an unusual problem. Designers and writers often come up with similar ideas and layouts because, as a result of their research, they come to similar conclusions.

To compete effectively, you need to know as much as possible about the other players and the field of play.

**2.1** Start your research by *pinpointing your competition*. Find out as much as you can about them and their history. History is important because you may be able to avoid some of the mistakes they made early on. And don't limit yourself to local competitors. Even if you only operate in one region of the country, check out what others are doing elsewhere. Stiffer completion in another region may offer more advanced examples of how to top your rivals.

**2.2** Next, *assemble your competitors' materials*. This once-daunting task is easier now that so many organizations have sites on the World Wide Web. There is a huge amount of extraordinarily valuable competitive information available—you have only to seek it out. Read everything you can get your hands on, and see how competitors answer the same questions you are asking yourself about mission, style, customer relations, and so on.

**2.3** Now *study your customer*. Remember that business is not a "we" thing—it's a "they" thing. The most important principle for any organization to establish is the benefit of its products or services to its prospects and customers.

Everything you do, from the design of your logo to the layout of your invoices, should be focused on one thing— customer benefits. Step into your customer's shoes now, and stay there until you retire.

Don't hesitate to ask customers directly. What first attracted them to your products and services? What brought them back a second time? Surveying customers is the highest form of flattery. It means you value their opinion and appreciate that they have a perspective of your organization that you do not.

**2.4** With these basics under your belt, you can go about *collecting effective examples* of concepts, designs, and color schemes of the logos, letterheads, and business cards of other organizations. Not just in your field, but any material that catches your eye. Collect enough of them and you will begin to see a trend—the typefaces you find most attractive, the page layouts that look most professional, the colors that attract you, and so on.

Immerse yourself in the details—the more you know, the more confident you will be about the solutions you uncover.

## Step 2: RESEARCH CHECKLIST

- [ ] **2.1** Pinpoint your competition
- [ ] **2.2** Assemble your competitors' materials
- [ ] **2.3** Study your customer
- [ ] **2.4** Collect effective examples (concepts, designs, colors)

Who?
What?
Where?
When?
Why?

STEP 3

# Create a Name

Naming is simple. Naming is complex.

It is said that truly great abstract painters must learn to paint realistically before they can paint a valid abstraction. In naming, you must understand the complexity of your subject before you can simplify it.

Organizations that specialize in naming make it look easy. Take, for example, Solutia®, the name of a chemical business dreamed up by Addison and Metaphor Name Consultants, or Hewlett-Packard's printer family DeskJet®, named by Lexicon Branding, Inc.—two powerful names that make the benefits of complex services and products simple to understand.

The name of your organization is critical in itself and fundamental to its logo. The problem is, few small businesses can afford the tens of thousands of dollars it costs to pay naming experts to develop it. The alternative? Design-it-Yourself.

**3.1** Review the research you created in Step 2 and *collect the naming tools* necessary for the brainstorming session below. You'll need a good dictionary and thesaurus—something more complete than the standard tools included with your word processor. Another helpful resource, *The Random House Word Menu,* offers comprehensive lists of words organized in very specific subject classes.

**3.2** There are many ways to combine words and ideas into names. You can derive them from historical ideas and from foreign language words, or even invent new words altogether. But, generally speaking, it is to your advantage to start with a name that says what it means—Airbus, for example, makes aircraft, and Frigidaire, refrigerators. If the name is hazy, you will forever be explaining the meaning via your advertising and marketing efforts.

The most straightforward way to go about naming is to combine two or three ideas into a one- or two-word name. You can simply add whole words together as in QuickBooks, or abbreviate words and add them together as in FedEx.

To create your unique name, start by *compiling a brainstorming list.* Make one column for each of the benefits you have identified. For example, a delivery company that promises fast delivery to a nationwide audience might start with columns for words associated with delivery, nationwide, and speed. Find as many positive words as possible and list them, then begin to experiment with combinations of words from each column. There are hundreds, if not thousands, of possibilities.

| NATIONWIDE | SPEEDY | DELIVERY |
|---|---|---|
| central | express | dispatch |
| federal | fast | launch |
| focal | quick | send |
| national | rapid | ship |
| network | rush | transfer |

This is just one of many ways to name your organization. For more naming ideas and guidelines, visit www.designiy.com

**3.3** *Wait twenty-four hours, and then filter your list.* Put your list aside and return after a day or two with a fresh perspective. Judge the names against a specific list of merits, which might include:

  I  Is not neutral or negative

  I  Is not difficult to spell or pronounce

  I  Does not have to be seen or heard to be understood

  I  Does not play off another organization's identity

  I  Is not too cute or too funny

  I  Is not an acronym

  I  Does not use the names of people or places

  I  Does not use slang or offensive language

  I  Does not limit future growth

**3.4** Next, *choose the two or three strongest ideas and create a rationale for them.* The rationale is a paragraph of text that summarizes your perspective on the name. Ask others to read it after they have seen the name to help you gauge if they got a similar impression.

**3.5** The naming world is replete with stories of names that work well in one language but are nonsensical or offensive in another. If any of your prospects communicate in another language, you should work with a language expert to *check for language conflicts.*

**3.6** At this stage, before you invest any more time and money, you should *do a preliminary trademark check*

to determine if the name you are pursuing can be protected. Without a trademark, you could spend a huge amount of energy building a brand that belongs to someone else. At a minimum, do a search for the word or phrase on an Internet search engine and search the Trademark Electronic Search System (TESS) at www.uspto.gov/web/menu/search.html

**3.7** Once you have had a chance to sleep on it, *choose a name and test the market.* Testing could be as casual as gathering the reactions of a few colleagues and customers, or as formal as organizing a focus group of neutral prospects. The more extensive the survey and complete the opinions, the better.

**3.8** Finally, once you have a firm decision, you should *legally secure the name* by applying for a trademark. The United States Patent and Trademark Office defines a trademark as "a word, phrase, symbol or design, or combination of words, phrases, symbols or designs, which identifies and distinguishes the source of the goods or services of one party from those of others. A service mark is the same as a trademark except that it identifies and distinguishes the source of a service rather than a product.... Normally, a mark for goods appears on the product or on its packaging, while a service mark appears in advertising for the services."

The Trademark Electronic Business Center is a one-stop source for all online trademark searching, filing, and follow-up (www.uspto.gov). If you need answers to specific trademark questions or want to know more about trademarks in general, consult an attorney or contact the Trademark Assistance Center at 800-786-9199. Another good perspective is offered in the pages of *Trademark: Legal Care for Your Business & Product Name,* (NOLO Press, 1999).

**Step 3: NAMING CHECKLIST**

☐ **3.1** Collect your tools

☐ **3.2** Make a brainstorming list

☐ **3.3** Wait 24 hours and revisit your list

☐ **3.4** Choose names and create rationales

☐ **3.5** Check for language conflicts

☐ **3.6** Do a preliminary trademark check

☐ **3.7** Choose a name and test the market

☐ **3.8** Legally secure your name

STEP 4

# Write a Defining Phrase

The most important part of any design is the message it sends. Your logo, in addition to a visual image and the name of your organization, should include a five- to fifteen-word phrase that defines what you do and the benefit of your product or service to your customer.

For a small business, a defining phrase is better than a slogan or a tag line. Slogans and tag lines are so-called attention-getters that very often do not plainly declare what a company does.

A slogan such as "Just do it," for example, is successful for a company such as Nike because it spends millions of dollars repeating the message in its advertising. A small business such as a photo lab or a day care center doesn't get that kind of exposure and is better off getting right to the point.

**4.1** There are two components to a successful defining phrase. The first *defines your market*. This is especially important if your organization's name does not spell out the business you're in. The name "Delta Corporation" doesn't tell you what the company does, but the names "Delta Faucet Company" and "Delta Air Lines" are abundantly clear.

**4.2** The second component of your phrase should express the most important benefits of using your product or service. To do it, *translate features to benefits*—an extremely important distinction. Features describe your products or services from your organization's viewpoint; benefits describe them from your customer's perspective.

A "me"-oriented defining phrase is more effective when stated in terms of the customer. Visa could have used one like, "Our credit cards are accepted around the world," but instead they chose the more powerful, "Visa—It's everywhere you want to be." Apple could have claimed "the highest-quality computers" but opted instead to offer "The power to be your best." A "large selection" is a feature—"see all models in one place" is a benefit.

**4.3** Next, *list the benefits in order of importance*. Our first inclination is to advertise as many benefits as possible in the hope that everyone will find something that compels them to take action. But too many messages muddy the water—especially in the confines of a fifteen-word phrase. Keep it as simple as and as focused as possible.

For example, the top benefits of a hypothetical copier retailer might be:

1. They offer a lowest-price guarantee
2. They have the area's largest selection
3. They support and service everything they sell twenty-four hours a day, seven days a week

**4.4** The ideal defining phrase includes a "hook"—the combination of benefits that establishes the important difference between you and your competition. In advertising, it is sometimes called the unique selling proposition. To *identify the hook*, combine two or more of the top benefits. If that doesn't demonstrate the distinct difference, or if your benefits are much the same as your competitor's, study their marketing materials and focus on a benefit they do not promote.

**4.5** Next, *condense your ideas into a five- to fifteen-word phrase*. In this case it might be: "Lexington's largest copier showroom and guaranteed lowest prices, backed by 24/7 support and service." Too boring? Clever is good if it doesn't get in the way. It is far better to have a less-exciting defining phrase than a line that twenty percent of your prospects don't understand.

**4.6** Finally, *test your defining phrase with customers*. The true test of whether you have a good phrase is to ask someone who doesn't know anything about your business if, by reading it, they can name the type of business you are in and the benefits you have defined. One difficulty of writing and producing your own marketing materials is that you are very close to the action—at times, too close to see the message clearly. Run your defining phrase by a few customers to hear their reactions and suggestions.

**Step 4: PHRASE CHECKLIST**

**4.1** Define your market

**4.2** Translate features (me) to benefits (you)

**4.3** List benefits in order of importance

**4.4** Identify the hook

**4.5** Condense it to five to fifteen words

**4.6** Test your defining phrase with customers

STEP 5

# Choose a Logo Style

A brash man in a Hawaiian shirt will be treated differently than a soft-spoken man in a tailored business suit. *How* they are treated depends on where they wear what and who is making the judgment.

It's the same with an organization. Dress your organization in the style of the audience it hopes to attract. Get a sense of what appeals to them and adopt a demeanor they relate to. Want to attract young, affluent, technology workers? As a whole, they respond to a different style than middle-aged factory workers.

For the purposes of this book, *style is defined as the visual and emotional mood of your organization. It is the combination of the message, how it is presented, the images used to illustrate it, the stance of the layout, and the choices of typefaces and color.*

Why choose a style? From the first moment they meet your organization, prospective customers begin to form an opinion of it. You can take a passive role by allowing them to form their own opinions, or you can use your style to influence it.

**5.1** Your choice of style, like all your other marketing decisions, should be made from the customer's point of view. *Study the research* you gathered about who your prospects are, the benefits they seek, and what turns them on or off.

**5.2** Style is another way to draw distinctions between your organization and its competition. *Reexamine how your organization presents itself*—its message, illustrations, and layouts. What style would set your organization apart stylistically?

**5.3** Too often, today's advertising experts use negative or controversial messages under the guise of attracting the attention of prospects.

One postcard, for example, showed a young bride seated in a limousine next to an elderly man. The thought balloon above her head showed a bare-chested young man and a headline that read: "Why not love *and* money?"

While the approach might appeal to some, it is guaranteed to offend others. Savvy communicators *build on a positive message*. Why risk repelling a single prospect if you can achieve the same goal without offending anyone?

**5.4** Once you have a clear idea of where your competitors stand, you can *choose a style that fits*. That, of course, doesn't mean you should try to make your organization something it is not—sheep in wolves' clothing stand a good chance of being devoured.

The second part of this book, beginning on page 53, presents twenty-five different ways to handle the visual side of your style—combinations of layout, color, and type. The designs were created specifically for the Design-it-Yourself series. You are free to copy any recipe in whole or in part to produce your own materials. The only restriction is that you cannot trademark the copied design.

## Step 5: STYLE CHECKLIST

- **5.1** Study the research
- **5.2** Reexamine how your organization presents itself
- **5.3** Build on a positive message
- **5.4** Choose a style that fits

STEP 6

# Choose Your Tools

It wasn't long ago that the headline shown above cost $12 to set. That's right, as recently as the 1980s it was not unusual for a designer to pay $4 or more per word to have headline-sized words set on a machine called a Typositor. The words were cranked out, letter by letter, on strips of photographic paper, trimmed, lined up, cemented to a paste-up board, and burnished down. Designing something as simple as a letterhead was expensive and time-consuming, and it required significant mechanical skills.

Today, the financial and mechanical barriers are all but gone. With a personal computer and some specialized software, you wield creative potential that was not even dreamed of those few short years ago. The idea that designers are designers only if they devote their career to it is fast becoming as outmoded as the idea that you must drive full-time to be considered a driver.

**6.1** *Choose a desktop publishing program.* Most of the Design-it-Yourself projects are easiest to produce using a desktop publishing (DTP) program such as Adobe InDesign, Adobe PageMaker, QuarkXPress, or Microsoft Publisher. They offer the ideal venue for combining the text you create in your word processor and the graphics you create with a draw or paint program into the files needed by a commercial printer.

The primary difference between a DTP program and a word processing program is the ease and precision with which text can be formatted, graphics can be imported and manipulated, color can be applied and edited, and output can be controlled. If you are going to produce your own print materials, a desktop publishing program is a wise investment.

**6.2** *Choose a drawing program.* There are two basic categories of computer graphics—"draw," for creating line art, and "paint," for creating photograph-like images. Draw graphics, also referred to as "vector" or "object-oriented," are created using objects such as lines, ovals, rect-angles, and curves. The primary advantage of a draw file is that it is smaller than a paint file and can be sized very large or very small at the maximum quality the printer is able to produce.

A few of the most popular programs for creating and editing draw graphics are Adobe Illustrator, Macromedia FreeHand, and CorelDRAW. The most common draw file formats are Encapsulated PostScript (EPS) files and Windows Metafiles (WMF).

**6.3** *Choose a paint program.* Paint images, also referred to as "raster" or "bit-mapped," are divided into a grid of tens of thousands of tiny rectangles called pixels. Each pixel can be a different color or shade of gray. The primary advantage of a paint file is that it can represent a much more complex range of colors and shades than a draw file. The downside is

the larger you plan to print the image, the larger the file size.

Two of the most popular programs for creating and editing paint graphics are Adobe Photoshop and Jasc Software's Paint Shop Pro. The most common paint file formats are Joint Photographic Experts Group (JPEG or JPG) and Tagged-Image File Format (TIFF or TIF).

**6.4** *Choose a standard.* The design world speaks primarily in PostScript, a language that allows your software to talk to output devices such as desktop printers. Almost all commercial printers require that the files you send them are PostScript compatible—meaning they include the information necessary to be translated to the printers' software and ultimately their presses. Many of the best fonts and clip art collections are only available in PostScript format.

If you plan to create your own print materials, buy programs that produce PostScript output and a PostScript-compatible printer or add PostScript hardware/software to the printer you already own (check with your printer's manufacturer for details).

**6.5** *Choose a computer system.* It is said that you should choose software before you choose hardware. Nowhere is this more true than when you are working with graphics. Though Apple's Macintosh line has long been the platform of choice for the professional design community, PCs are gaining acceptance. All the programs mentioned are available in both Mac and Windows versions, and the program features and keystrokes are almost identical.

Perhaps the best gauge of the system you'll need is the software manufacturer's recommended hardware requirements. From the programs you plan to use, take the one that requires the most memory and CPU horsepower, and base your purchase on those recommendations.

**Step 6: Tools Checklist**

**6.1** Choose a desktop publishing program

**6.2** Choose a drawing program

**6.3** Choose a paint program

**6.4** Choose a standard

**6.5** Choose a computer system

STEP 7

# Design a Logo

Though it often looks as if the designer conceived and produced a logo just as you see it, that rarely happens. Design is an evolutionary process. One idea leads to another; one image sparks an idea for the next. Solutions are found in the mixing of image and typographic elements—sizing, shaping, adjusting the proximity of one object to another, and so on. If you come up with an initial idea that you like, push it to the next level. It is that exploration that makes an ordinary design exceptional.

Starting from scratch is just one way to design a logo. On pages 24 though 35 you'll see how to design a logo using clip art, typefaces, photographs, symbols, and other design elements. But there are some preliminary rules that apply to designing just about any type of logo.

**7.1** The first stage of creating a logo is to *collect the visual puzzle pieces*. These are the images that best illustrate the benefits you define. If, for example, you are designing a logo for a home

inspection company, make a list of all the images that might apply to homes and those that are associated with inspection.

Stuck for ideas? See what others have done. Clip art collections and illustration web sites show how professional illustrators approach just about any subject you can think of. You can also visit the U. S. Patent and Trademark Office Trademark Electronic Search System (TESS) at www.uspto.gov to search for the trademarks of competitors to see how they handle the same subject.

**7.2** The goal is to create a logo that visually defines the benefit of doing business with your organization. With that in mind, *merge the images from your list into unique visual ideas.* It is mingling the two that makes your logo one-of-a-kind.

Don't worry about creating fancy, finished drawings. Scribble as many different ideas as possible, visualizing your organization from as many different angles as possible. Take at least two or three hours to experiment, and don't settle for less than five strong ideas.

**7.3** Now, *wait twenty-four hours, then do some weeding.* Don't peek—you need a day or two to regain a fresh perspective. An idea that seemed right at first may seem totally misplaced. And the idea that was an afterthought might be worth pursuing. Eliminate ideas that others are using, are dated, or are clichéd. You may also want to ask for the opinion of one or two others involved in the process.

**7.4** If you need another brainstorming session, have at it. If you've got some strong possibilities, choose the two or three strongest ideas and *produce preliminary artwork using one of the techniques* described on pages 24 though 35. The objective is to produce artwork that is close to finished-looking, but it is not necessary to make it technically perfect.

**7.5** Next, *add the organization's name.* Typefaces have personalities— some are quiet and reserved; others stand out in a crowd. Adding a typeface to a logo pulls it in the direction of that personality. When you're done, take another break and return after twenty-four hours with a clear perspective.

**7.6** The next stage is to *test the effectiveness of the design.* Show your ideas to colleagues and at least two or three people who know little or nothing about your business. Get their reactions and gauge how effective your efforts have been. Don't make the mistake of showing weak ideas along with those you consider strong. It is not out of the realm of possibility for a decision-maker to choose a weak design that you will then have to talk them out of.

**7.7** Now, *choose and finalize the design.* Weigh the pros and cons of each design, consider the feedback you've gathered, consult your decision-makers, and select the winning design. As with the name you chose, you'll have to determine if your idea can be trademarked. Produce the finished artwork.

**7.8** Finally, *create usage guidelines,* a simple document that describes how and where the logo may be used. It is for use by your own organization and for anyone outside the organization that might have occasion to reproduce your logo. Large organizations go so far as to layout every conceivable way the logo might be used and to dictate every detail. Depending on how widely your logo will be used, and even if it is nothing more than a reminder for yourself, the guidelines might include:

Color values
Minimum sizes
Permission for use
Resolution restrictions
Legal notice
Typefaces used

## Step 2: LOGO DESIGN CHECKLIST

- [ ] **7.1** Collect the visual puzzle pieces
- [ ] **7.2** Merge the images into unique visual ideas
- [ ] **7.3** Wait twenty-four hours, then do some weeding
- [ ] **7.4** Produce preliminary artwork using one of the techniques
- [ ] **7.5** Add the organization's name
- [ ] **7.6** Test the effectiveness of the design
- [ ] **7.7** Choose and finalize the design
- [ ] **7.8** Create usage guidelines

STEP 8

## Choose a Technique
# Custom Logos

There are many ways to design a logo. Since this book speaks in large part to non-designers, it focuses on techniques that begin with a preexisting image: clip art, photographs, or silhouettes. If, however, you have some basic drawing skills or the patience to learn, designing a logo from scratch does allow you the most creative freedom.

No matter which technique you decide to pursue, it's important to understand the value of draw and paint software programs (see *Choose Your Tools,* page 20). They are logo laboratories—the ideal places to conduct visual experiments. With them, you can apply effects that make even the simplest of images interesting. Shown here, in column one, are some of the many effects possible with most draw programs. In a paint program, you can apply photographic effects such as those in column two.

Draw—Stretch    Paint—Shadow

Draw—Reflect    Paint—Colorize

Draw—Skew    Paint—Pastel Filter

Draw—Rotate    Paint—Tranparency

Draw—Distort    Paint—Radial Blur

Draw—Twirl Filter    Paint—Wave Distort

### What you need
Breaking apart draw artwork and editing the pieces requires a draw program such as Adobe Illustrator, CorelDRAW, or Macromedia FreeHand. Editing and adding effects to photographic images requires a paint or digital imaging program such as Adobe Photoshop or Jasc Software's Paint Shop Pro.

Once you've developed a sound, basic idea, open the appropriate software program and start experimenting. Be sure it is an idea worth pursuing—it can take hours to find the right combination of effects to make your design one-of-a-kind.

The illustration demonstrates just a few of the stages of one idea from the most basic idea (top left) to the finished design (bottom right). In reality, it is quite common to create many variations in order to find the one that works.

Start with a sound idea.

Refine the basic shapes.

Create a bold variation.

The shapes are thinned down slightly.

Would a chimney make the image more recognizable?

The height of the logo is stretched slightly.

Other variations are tried.

The image is distorted to give it perspective.

Text and color are added.

SOURCE Illustration: Clock from *Everyday Objects 2* by PhotoDisc, 800-979-4413, 206-441-9355, www.photodisc.com, © CMCD, all rights reserved.

STEP 8

## Choose a Technique
# Clip Art Logos

Clip art has overcome its inferiority complex. It was once considered junk art—little decorations pasted on advertisements. Today, talented professionals produce reams of eye-catching, thought-provoking images that are every bit a powerful as those commissioned from illustrators by clients for ten times the cost.

If you can get beyond one significant barrier, a clip art illustration can make a great logo. That barrier is protection—it is doubtful whether even a drastically altered clip art image can be trademarked. Though that certainly prevents a large organization from creating a clip art logo, it does not necessarily preclude a small one from doing so. A local plumbing-and-heating contractor, a small accounting firm, and a citywide real-estate operation probably don't need a trademarked logo.

**Use the illustration as is**
Sometimes the illustration already says what you want it to say. In this case, creating a logo is a matter of cropping the bold border and integrating the name. A second square with a simple row of triangles is added and colors pulled from the illustration are applied.

**Combine two or more illustrations**
Another way to arrive at a unique solution is to combine two images that are drawn in a similar style. In this case, two literal images—binoculars to represent the search, and pyramids to represent the destination—are combined on a rectangular shape and a complement of type. The whole is greater than the sum of its parts.

**Use a piece of an illustration**
Still another way to use clip art is to pull a small piece from a larger illustration. Since simplicity is often the goal of a logo, isolating a piece of a complex image is a good solution. Though many logos rely on subtle meanings, there's nothing wrong with being literal. Here, using an ornate chair to represent an antiques seller is an obvious—but effective—solution.

**What you need**
Breaking apart draw artwork and editing the pieces requires a draw program such as Adobe Illustrator, CorelDRAW, or Macromedia FreeHand.

If you take the clip art route, remember that when you purchase clip art and royalty-free photographs, you buy the right to use the images; you do not own them. Be sure to read license agreements carefully—they can differ significantly from company to company. Make it clear to everyone involved that the illustration is from a clip art collection and it is possible someone will see the same basic image used elsewhere.

These logos were all created from off-the-shelf clip art collections. Creating your version is a process of experimentation—deciding on an idea, finding the right illustrations, and choosing a compatible type style.

SOURCES Illustrations: Apples, binoculars, pyramids from *Task Force Image Gallery* by NVTech, 800-387-0732, 613-727-8184, www.nvtech.com, © NVTech, all rights reserved; chair: *Designer's Club* by Dynamic Graphics, 800-255-8800, 309-688-8800, www.dgusa.com, © Dynamic Graphics, all rights reserved.

Typefaces: "ORCHARDS" Raleigh Gothic, 888-988-2432, 978-658-0200, www.agfamonotype.com; "Sampler" (center) Copperplate Gothic 33BC, "Expeditions" Willow, "Sampler" (bottom) Bickham Script, "Antiques" Caslon Regular, Adobe Systems, Inc., 800-682-3623, www.adobe.com/type.

STEP 8

## Choose a Technique
# All-Type Logos

A typeface is like a language—some have a slight accent in a familiar tongue; others coin a dialect all their own.

Type is the designer's secret weapon. Your organization's name set in one or two carefully chosen typefaces is a fast, easy solution to creating a professional-looking logo. It does not, of course, show what your organization does, but if you choose the typefaces carefully, the finished logo provides a distinct personality.

**Use the typeface as is**
Sometimes a typeface is so well designed that you are better using it as is, without any modifications. What makes it work as a logo is the addition of a second, complementary typeface—typically a complex or bold face for the main expression, "Sampler River," and a simpler face for the supportive expression, "INN."

**Fit the words together**
Another simple technique is to set all the words in one or two typefaces and size each word to reflect its importance. The words are then fitted together like puzzle pieces. Making one word capitals and lowercase and another all caps adds a second level of emphasis and visual interest.

**Use contrast**
You can also use the differences between faces to create an interesting, all-type logo. Try using the contrast between intricate and simple, bold and light, condensed and extended, serif and sans serif, and so on. (Serif letters have "feet," sans serif do not. See page 37 for examples.)

**What you need**
Draw programs such as Adobe Illustrator, CorelDRAW, and Macromedia FreeHand allow you to covert type to line art. They provide powerful tools for fine-tuning size, adjusting alignment, adding color, distorting shapes, and so on.

SOURCES Typefaces: "River" Bickham Script, "INN" Copperplate Gothic 33BC, "Forge" Franklin Gothic Heavy, "SAMPLER…Fitness" Frutiger Light, Adobe Systems, Inc., 800-682-3623, www.adobe.com/type; "SPA" Giza-SevenSeven, Font Bureau, 617-423-3770, www.fontbureau.com.

It is critically important to pay close attention to the spacing between words and individual letters. Though most computer fonts compensate for the spacing (kerning) between letters, some do not do it well. For example, at the top (left) is the word "alignment" as it was typed. Below it is a version that shows the same word after the spacing has been tightened. You can see where to add and subtract space by squinting at the letters and by equalizing the space between the shapes.

As with people, personality is in the eye of the beholder. To the right are a few faces and one opinion of the qualities they represent.

Airy typeface
Raleigh Gothic

Bookish typeface
Century Expanded

Brash typeface
Impact

Clean typeface
Myriad Multiple Master 830BL, 700SE

Delicate typeface
Bodega Sans Light

Dynamic typefac
Frutiger 95 Ultra Black

Elegant typeface
Bickham Script

Funny typefa
Postino

Graceful typeface
Racer

Historical typeface
Caslon

Technical typeface
Cachet Bold

Thunderous typ
Giza Seven-Seven

TRADITIONAL TYPEFA
Charlemagne

Whimsical typeface
Galahad

SOURCES Typefaces: Raleigh Gothic, Bodega Sans Light, Cachet Bold, Charlemagne, Galahad, AGFA/Monotype, 888-988-2432, 978-658-0200, www.agfamonotype.com; Century Expanded, Impact, Myriad Multiple Master 830BL 700SE, Frutiger 95 Ultra Black, Bickham Script, Postino, Racer, Caslon, Adobe Systems, Inc., 800-682-3623, www.adobe.com/type; Giza-SevenSeven, Font Bureau, 617-423-8770, www.fontbureau.com.

STEP 8

## Choose a Technique
# Photo Logos

Photographs are convincing. We are so accustomed to seeing realistic images in the context of everyday life that when you combine a photo with your organization's name, it is sometimes more believable and compelling than stylized artwork.

Photographic logos have another thing going for them—they are uncommon. And when you do something unexpected, you attract interest and attention.

### Use the photograph as is
Some photographs say what needs to be said without embellishment. It could be the photograph itself or a combination of the photograph and the text that makes the point.

### Combine two or more images
Merging two or more photographs or a photograph and a drawing allows you to redirect the idea. Removing the arrow and adding a lightbulb changes this photograph of a road sign into a metaphor for a bright idea.

### Use a custom photograph
A photograph of your specific product or service is, perhaps, the most effective way to create a photographic logo. Visualize the result of working with your organization and reduce it to a simple expression.

### Color not required
A simple photographic logo can be just as effective in black and white.

### What you need
Breaking apart draw artwork and editing the pieces requires a draw program such as Adobe Illustrator, CorelDRAW, or Macromedia FreeHand. Editing and adding effects to photographic images requires a paint or digital imaging program such as Adobe Photoshop or Jasc Software's Paint Shop Pro.

Using an off-the-shelf photograph presents the same problem as using clip art—it typically cannot be trademarked. That's because when you purchase royalty-free photographs or clip art, you buy the right to use the images; you do not own them. Be sure to read license agreements carefully—they can differ significantly from company to company.

Unlike clip art, though, there is a realistic alternative that allows you to protect your logo—you can shoot the photograph yourself or commission a professional photographer to shoot one for you.

In the end, you'll have to decide if a photographic logo is a good alternative. If, for example, you will regularly use your logo at very small sizes, a photographic logo might be impractical.

SOURCES Illustrations: Typewriter, banana from *Metaphorically Speaking* by PhotoDisc, 800-979-4413, 206-441-9355, www.photodisc.com, © CMCD, all rights reserved; road sign from PhotoDisc, 800-979-4413, 206-441-9355, www.photodisc.com, © CMCD, all rights reserved; light bulb from *Universal Symbols* by Image Club Clip Art, 800-661-9410, 403-294-3195, www.eyewire.com, © Image Club Graphics, all rights reserved; home © J.R. Walker & Company, all rights reserved. Typefaces: "Comedy" Postino, "zone" Impact, Adobe Systems, Inc., 800-682-3623, www.adobe.com/type; "Homes" Bodega Serif Medium, AGFA/Monotype, 888-988-2432, 978-658-0200, www.agfamonotype.com.

STEP 8

## Choose a Technique
# Symbol Logos

Symbols, signs, and icons—we've been using them for all of recorded history. Well-conceived visual images transmit information quickly and effectively.

To be accurate, the images shown here are icons—images that suggest their meaning. A symbol is defined as a visible image of something that is invisible—for example, an hourglass represents the idea of time. A sign is a shorthand device that stands for something else, such as the @ sign, which stands for "at."

**Add a symbol to the name**
A symbol can be subtle. In this case, a leaf is added as if it were growing from a letter in the name, suggesting a connection with nature.

**Combine two or more symbols**
Mixing images results in new meanings. When a sun is combined with a snowflake, the result is hot and cold—in this case to represent heating and air-conditioning.

**Use a picture font**
There are many sources for symbols, signs, and icons, but one of the best is a picture font. You install a picture font like any other typeface, but when you type, instead of a character for each keystroke, you type pictures.

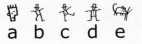

SOURCE Illustrations: Deer, rider, from Petroglyph font by Judith Sutcliffe.

 **What you need**
Breaking apart draw artwork and editing the pieces requires a draw program such as Adobe Illustrator, CorelDRAW, or Macromedia FreeHand.

=

 =

 =

Where do you find simple, symbolic images? In addition to the obvious places—in clip art collections, picture fonts, and print resources—you will find many suitable images as part of larger illustrations.

When illustrators reduce an idea to clip art form, they often dramatically simplify small elements. Those pictures-within-pictures, blown up and refined, can often be used as is or as a catalyst for a new idea.

Can you trademark a symbol such as those shown here? Possibly. Be sure to read license agreements of the clip art and graphics you are using. Usage can differ significantly from company to company. In some cases, using a small portion of an image or drastically changing it may allow you to trademark your logo.

SOURCES Illustrations: Leaf, sun, snowflake from *Design Elements* by Ultimate Symbol, 800-611-4761, 914-942-0003, www.ultimatesymbol.com, © Ultimate Symbol, all rights reserved; cow from Good Dog Bones font by Fonthead Design, 302-479-7922, www.fonthead.com; Typefaces: "GROVE" Racer, "Plumbing" Myriad Regular, "Sampler" (bottom) Impact, Adobe Systems, Inc., 800-682-3623, www.adobe.com/type.

STEP 8

## Choose a Technique
# Silhouette Logos, Engraving Logos, and Beyond

The techniques described on the previous pages are a few of the most straightforward ways to design a logo. They are, by no means, the only possibilities. At the right are three more techniques: using a silhouette, an antique illustration, and the outline of an image.

By now, you see that design is not a process in which you begin with a clear idea of the end result in mind. It is, instead, a process of building on an idea and pursuing it until you find what you're looking for, or until you find another direction to go in. In some cases, one idea leads to the next, and you may find yourself abandoning one idea altogether and taking an entirely different course.

**Use a silhouette**
A silhouette illustration shows the shape of the subject minus the detail. That simplicity makes silhouettes particularly good for designing logos.

**Use an antique illustration**
Woodcuts and engravings culled from old books and magazines can be found in compilations published for the purpose of reusing them. Publishers such as Dover Publications offer compilations with varied constraints on use of the artwork.

**Use shapes and outlines**
Still another way to make something unique out of something common is to reduce it to simple shapes and outlines.

**What you need**
Editing drawings such as the skier and the microphone requires a draw program such as Adobe Illustrator, CorelDRAW, or Macromedia FreeHand. Editing and adding effects to photographic images requires a paint or digital imaging program such as Adobe Photoshop or Jasc Software's Paint Shop Pro.

No matter what technique you choose, these five design fundamentals apply:

First, *get beyond the first idea.* It's oh-so-tempting to think you have the solution on the first or second try. Don't fool yourself. It typically takes lots of thinking to develop a unique idea, and lots of visualizing to discover a compelling logo. Once convinced you're finished, try another approach, change a typeface, choose a different color, or adjust the relative size of one element to another.

Second, *use a delicate hand.* New designers tend to make text and graphics too big and/or too bold.

Third, *take a real-world view of work in progress.* Print out ideas and see what they look like on paper. Physical size and the computer monitor can dramatically affect the look and feel of the final piece.

Fourth, *heed opinions.* When should you abandon what you think is a good solution? When twenty percent of the people you show the name, logo, and defining phrase dislike it. When anyone has a rational reason to dislike it intensely. Or when a respected judge thinks it is unprofessional.

When it comes to aesthetic judgments, it doesn't matter whether your audience is wrong or right. Their opinions represent the tastes of others, and it rarely makes sense to adopt a stance that precipitates a battle.

Fifth, once you have what you think is a final design, *remove yourself from the process for at least twenty-four hours* to see the design from a new perspective. A fresh review often results in the refinements that yield the kind of logo that seems as if it were the obvious solution all along.

SOURCES Illustrations: Skier from *Simple Silhouettes,* microphone, video screen, from *Objects & Icons* by Image Club Clip Art, 800-661-9410, 403-294-3195, www.eyewire.com, © Image Club Graphics, all rights reserved; hiker from *1800 Woodcuts by Thomas Bewick and His School* from Dover Publications, Inc., www.doverpublications.com.

Typefaces: "SKI" Interstate UltraBlack, Font Bureau, 617-423-8770, www.fontbureau.com; "Outfitters" Latino Elongated, ITC 866-823-5828, www.itcfonts.com; "Media" Fruitiger 45 Light, Adobe Systems, Inc., 800-682-3623, www.adobe.com/type.

STEP 9

# Lay Out a Letterhead

Your letterhead is ground zero. The layout, typefaces, and colors you establish here dictate the design of all the pieces that follow—from your business cards and envelopes to your Web site and brochure.

Why the letterhead? Because it is typically used to present the most important one-on-one personal communications—introductions, proposals, requests, personal messages, and such—the written greetings and meetings that require you to look your best.

Designers and printers use PANTONE® formula guides to specify ink colors. This guide is for specifying process colors, there are others for specifying solid colors.

SOURCE
PANTONE formula guides, www.pantone.com;
© Pantone, Inc., all rights reserved.

The Sampler Group

A one-sentence "hook" benefit that describes your product or service

The Sampler Group
123 Example Boulevard, Suite 210
Your City, ST 12345 6789
987 654 3210
800 987 6543
987 654 3210 Fax
www.yourwebaddressz.com
E-mail info@youremailaddressz.com

## Serif Typefaces

Lorem ipsum dolor sit amet, consectetuer adipiscing elit, sed diam nonummy nibh euismod tincidunt ut laoreet dolore magna aliquam erat volutpat. Ut wisi enim ad minim veniam, quis nostrud exerci tation ullamcorper suscipit.
Caslon Regular

Lorem ipsum dolor sit amet, consectetuer adipiscing elit, sed diam nonummy nibh euismod tincidunt ut laoreet dolore magna aliquam erat volutpat. Ut wisi enim ad minim veniam, quis nostrud exerci tation.
Century Expanded

Lorem ipsum dolor sit amet, consectetuer adipiscing elit, sed diam nonummy nibh euismod tincidunt ut laoreet dolore magna aliquam erat volutpat. Ut wisi enim ad minim veniam, quis nostrud exerci tation ullamcorper suscipit lobortis nisl ut aliquip ex ea commodo consequat. Lorem
Garamond Light Condensed

Lorem Lorem ipsum dolor sit amet, consectetuer adipiscing elit, sed diam nonummy nibh euismod tincidunt ut laoreet dolore magna aliquam erat volutpat. Ut wisi enim ad minim veniam, quis nostrud exerci tation ullamcorper suscipit.
Minion Regular

## Sans Serif Typefaces

Lorem ipsum dolor sit amet, consectetuer adipiscing elit, sed diam nonummy nibh euismod tincidunt ut laoreet dolore magna aliquam erat volutpat. Ut wisi enim ad minim veniam, quis nostrud exerci tation ullamcorper.
Formata Light

Lorem ipsum dolor sit amet, consectetuer adipiscing elit, sed diam nonummy nibh euismod tincidunt ut laoreet dolore magna aliquam erat volutpat. Ut wisi enim ad minim veniam, quis nostrud exerci tation ullamcorper suscipit lobortis nisl ut aliquip ex ea.
Franklin Gothic Book Condensed

Lorem ipsum dolor sit amet, consectetuer adipiscing elit, sed diam nonummy nibh euismod tincidunt ut laoreet dolore magna aliquam erat volutpat. Ut wisi enim ad minim veniam, quis nostrud exerci tation.
Helvetica Regular

Lorem ipsum dolor sit amet, consectetuer adipiscing elit, sed diam nonummy nibh euismod tincidunt ut laoreet dolore magna aliquam erat volutpat. Ut wisi enim ad minim veniam, quis nostrud exerci tation ullamcorper.
Myriad Regular

SOURCES Type families: Caslon Regular, Century Expanded, Garamond Light, Condensed, Minion Regular, Formata Light, Helvetica Regular, Myriad Regular, Adobe Systems, Inc., 800-682-3623, www.adobe.com/type; Franklin Gothic Book Condensed, ITC, 866-823-5828, www.itcfonts.com.

**9.1** Before you layout your letterhead, you must first *define the elements* you plan to include on it. Beyond the name of the organization, the symbol, and the defining phrase, consider including:

Department/division name
Street address
Floor/suite/mail stop
Alternate P.O. box address
Zip+4/postal code
Country
Voice phone/extension number
Toll-free phone number
Fax number
E-mail address
Web site address
Office hours
Time zone
Pronunciation of unusual names

**9.2** Next, *choose a typeface* for the letterhead text (fig. B), one that complements the typeface you chose for your logo. If you use a serif face for the name, it often works well to use a sans serif typeface for the text. (Serif letters have "feet," sans serif letters do not.) In either case, because it is meant to play a supporting role, choose a typeface that has a simple form and is easy to read.

**9.3** With those basics defined, you're ready to *decide on the number of colors*. You first need to understand how commercial printers reproduce color. There are two ways to arrive at matching a specific color. You can choose a specific ink color that matches it, called a solid PANTONE® Color or you can combine four standard colors to match it as closely as possible, referred to as process colors.

There are over one thousand Solid PANTONE Colors. If, for example, you want bright orange, you would choose a color from a PANTONE formula guide (fig. A), a tool designed for just that purpose. You choose the exact color you want, provide the printer with the corresponding PANTONE Number, and they buy a

container of that ink and print your job using it.

The alternative method is to print the job using the four-color process. The process colors are cyan, magenta, yellow, and black (CMYK). This combination of colors can be screened to represent just about any color value across the spectrum. This method is best for printing color photographs and any other material that contains a range of colors that cannot be reproduced using two or three solid colors.

The limitation the four-color process is that it cannot reproduce some colors as vividly, and is typically more expensive than the solid color method.

The least expensive route is to print black or single solid color on white or colored stock (in printer's language, black is a color). If you're willing to spend a little more, you can print with two colors, typically black and one solid color. The general rule is the more colors you print, the more complex the printing press needed to print them, and the more your job will cost. The four-color process, generally speaking, is the most expensive.

For a comprehensive look at the printing process, get a copy of the *Pocket Pal Graphic Arts Production Handbook* by International Paper from Signet Inc., 800-654-3889, 901-387-5560, www.pocketpalstore.com.

**9.4** You should also *incorporate your preliminary paper choices in your design*. There is a complete discussion of paper beginning on page 46.

**9.5** Now that you have all the puzzle pieces—the information and the typefaces, and you have determined your color strategy—you're ready to *experiment with the layout*.

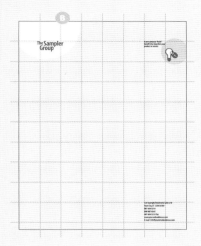

Take the elements and begin to move them around on the page. It's not necessary to create finished designs. Just shuffle the pieces to see what the possibilities are.

Once you have some potential solutions, print the pages out to see how well the designs work on paper. Designing on a computer screen can be deceiving. Type that looks just right on the screen is often too big at actual size. Printing your design early on keeps you from wasting time refining a design that still needs work.

**9.6** Once you know the basic layout, you should *build a grid* (fig. B) that will help you determine the final placement of the elements. A grid is a fundamental part of any layout that is often overlooked by non-designers. A grid is a series of invisible lines that keeps all the elements on the page lined up. The grid shown is nothing more than a series of columns. Desktop publishing, draw, and paint programs all have "guides" designed to be used for just this purpose.

**9.7** Before you finalize it, be sure to *test the design*. Prove its practicality by inserting the contents of a sample letter (fig. C). What might appear to be an excellent design can turn up with real problems when you start using it in the real world. Then fold it in thirds to insure that critical graphics and text are not affected by the creases.

**9.8** Finally, you should *refine the proportions* of all the elements on the page. Non-designers tend to make their designs too bold by making the images and the typefaces too large. Remember: It is the food on the plate that most interests the diner, not the plate itself. Likewise, your letterhead should enhance the experience of receiving the information—not overwhelm it.

## Step 9: LETTERHEAD CHECKLIST

- **9.1** Define the elements
- **9.2** Choose a typeface
- **9.3** Decide on the number of colors
- **9.4** Incorporate paper in the design
- **9.5** Experiment with the layout
- **9.6** Build a grid
- **9.7** Test the design
- **9.8** Refine the proportions

STEP 10

# Lay Out a Business Card

Don't be a formula thinker. Instead of doing things the way they have always been done, a smart designer challenges the premise of every project by asking three fundamental questions: What is its purpose? Why is it done the way it's done? And how can I do it more effectively?

**10.1** The first stage of designing a business card is to *choose a format*. Adopting the conventional 3.5-by-2-inch size (fig. A) is important if you hope your prospects will save your card in a business card binder or rotary file. If you use the standard size, by all means use

the back of the card. It is the ideal place for a more in-depth explanation of your services, a summary of your mission, or a space to jot down a message or product number.

But adopting the standard only means the finished size must be 3.5 by 2 inches. By adding panels and folds, you can create something more than a traditional calling card. The card in fig. B, for example, is a mini-brochure. In addition to a detachable business card, it includes a cover headline, a marketing message, and a photograph.

Fig. C shows some other possibilities. You might even consider something totally different such as printing your business card pre-cut to fit in a Rolodex.

**10.2** Like the letterhead, the next stage of designing a business card consists of *defining the elements* you plan to include on it. Beyond the basics, consider including:

PEOPLE
Name of person
(Nickname) in parentheses
Title
Affiliations
Professional/academic designations

PLACE
Pronunciation of unusual names
Department/division name
Organization street address
Floor/suite/mail stop
Alternate P.O. box address
City/state/state abbreviation
Zip+4/postal code
Country
Home street address

COMMUNICATION
Voice phone/extension number
Toll-free phone number
Mobile phone number
Pager number
Fax phone number
Home phone number
E-mail address
Web site address

DETAILS
Office hours
Time zone
Appointment fill-in
Map/directions

ORIENTATION
Name of organization
Defining phrase
Product/service categories
Resource info
Special offer
Invitation
Illustration/photo
Logo
Organizational affiliations

**10.3** The rest of the process is much like designing your letterhead. Use the same typefaces (see Step 9.2, *Choose a typeface*) with the possible addition of a typeface for headlines if the format you choose calls for them.

**10.4** In most cases, you will also repeat the colors you chose for the letterhead (see Step 9.3, *Decide on the number of colors*). The exception here is when you choose a different color scheme for each piece, as shown in fig. D.

**10.5** Next, repeat process of *experimenting with the layout* (Step 9.4). Move the elements around on the page, decide on a potential solution, and print the page out to see how well the design works on paper.

**10.6** Even a layout as small as a business card or a business card brochure should be *built on a grid*. When all of the elements line up, the design has an ordered look that cannot be achieved any other way.

**10.7** Before you finalize it, be sure to *test the design*. As you did with the letterhead, be sure critical text and graphics are not affected by folds and trimming.

**10.8** Finally, you should *refine the proportions* of all the elements on the page. Be sure the type is readable. Type smaller than six points high will be unreadable by many.

## Step 10: BUSINESS CARD CHECKLIST

- **10.1** Choose a format
- **10.2** Define the elements
- **10.3** Choose a typeface
- **10.4** Decide on the number of colors
- **10.5** Experiment with the layout
- **10.6** Build on a grid
- **10.7** Test the design
- **10.8** Refine the proportions

STEP 11

# Lay Out an Envelope

Don't underestimate the importance of your envelope. When you send unsolicited mail, in the moments between its arrival and the time your prospect decides what to do with it, your envelope is the most important marketing weapon in your arsenal.

You could print your envelopes one by one, as you need them, from a laser or inkjet printer, but commercial printing produces a far superior product. It allows you to print on any type of paper and sends the message that you are in business to stay.

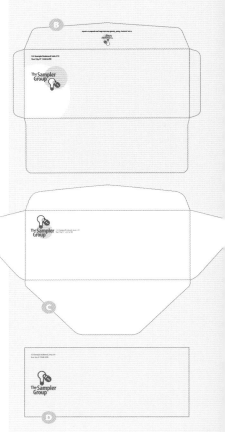

123 Example Boulevard, Suite 210
Your City, ST 12345 6789

**More information**
For a complete discussion of business mail regulations and downloadable resources, visit www.usps.com and select "Info," then "Business Mail 101."

**11.1** When it comes to envelopes, to a great degree, postal regulations influence the *format you choose*. Though just about any envelope can be mailed, the size, shape, proportions, weight, speed of delivery, and other issues dictate how much postage is necessary. Adding an additional ten cents to the standard first-class postage of one envelope may not seem like much, but over a period of years, an unusual design can cost hundreds, possibly thousands, of dollars more than a design that meets certain guidelines.

As of this writing, the United States Post Office (USPS) says that to qualify for first-class postage, an envelope must be "at least 3 1/2 inches high by 5 inches long by 0.007 inch thick and no more than 6 1/8 inches high by 11 1/2 inches long by 1/4 inch thick." Disproportionate sizes—envelopes that are unusually short and wide or tall and narrow and more or less square pieces—may also cost more because they tend to jam postal equipment. Using a standard 4.125-by-9.5-inch (#10) commercial business envelope is the best way to insure you qualify for the best rate.

**11.2** Printing envelopes is a bit more complicated than printing letterheads and business cards. In most cases, you print on envelopes that are already folded and glued in finished form (fig. A). If you design an envelope with an image that extends (bleeds) off the edge of the envelope (fig. B), the artwork must be printed on a flat sheet before it is assembled. This may make your design significantly more interesting, but it comes at a cost. Printing on a flat sheet could cost twice as much, or more, than using a finished envelope.

This side-seamed commercial envelope (fig. B) allows you to wrap your graphics around the back of the envelope more easily than does a standard version (fig. C).

If you use a finished envelope, keep the artwork a minimum of 0.25 inches from the edge.

**11.3** The next stage, as with the previous pieces, is to *define the elements*. In most cases, they are limited to your logo and return address. In some cases, you might also include your defining phrase, but including more might make your everyday correspondence look like a direct mail piece, which might result in it being discarded.

**11.4** For the rest of the process, you can follow the same steps used in developing your letterhead and business cards: Use the same typefaces used in Step 9.2, *Choose a typeface*.

**11.5** In most cases, you will also repeat the colors you chose for the letterhead (see Step 9.3, *Decide on the number of colors*). If you have a limited budget, the alternative is to print one color on a colored envelope, as shown in fig. D.

**11.6** Next, repeat the process of *experimenting with the layout* (Step 9.4). Move the elements around on the page, decide on a potential solution, and print the page to see how well the design works on paper.

**11.7** Even your envelope should be *built on a grid*. Be sure each element is in line.

**11.8** And, as always, be sure to *test the design*. Consider how the design will look with the addition of postage and an imprinted address or label.

**11.9** Finally, *refine the proportions* of all the elements on the page. The USPS has specific recommendations on how to type the name and address of the recipient to help speed the mailing process. In part, you should use black, uppercase letters in a 10- or 12-point, sans serif typeface. Type the name and address flush left, with the city, state, and zip code on one line. Use standard, two-letter state abbreviations and omit punctuation.

**Step 11: ENVELOPE CHECKLIST**

- **11.1** Choose a format
- **11.2** Choose a printing process
- **11.3** Define the elements
- **11.4** Choose a typeface
- **11.5** Decide on the number of colors
- **11.6** Experiment with the layout
- **11.7** Build on a grid
- **11.8** Test the design
- **11.9** Refine the proportions

STEP 12

# Find a Printer

You're only as good as your printer. No matter how well you plan and execute a smart, good-looking design, you must rely on the skills of a commercial printer to translate your computer files into a finished product. Finding a printer that is well-suited to the type of job you are printing, committed to producing a quality product, and willing to produce it for a reasonable price is a critical piece of the design-it-yourself puzzle.

**12.1** The first stage is to *find a printer with an offset lithographic press.* There are other methods of printing equal to the task, but offset lithography is, generally speaking, the best process for a one- to four-color job such as a letterhead, business card, or envelope. It can reproduce fine detail and big areas of color, and can print large-enough sheet sizes to allow you to extend (bleed) images and areas of color off the edges of the sheet.

SOURCE Illustration:
Photographs courtesy of
Printing Services, Inc.
Richmond, Virginia.

**12.2** When you first speak to the printer's representative, *explain the scope of the job* to determine if it fits within the printer's capabilities. Some printers specialize in printing one- and two-color work and are ill-equipped to print four-color process, others aren't interested in anything but large runs of four-color, and so on. A rule of thumb is avoid being the smallest job in a big shop or vice versa.

Expect to order at least 1,000 sheets of letterhead, 500 envelopes, and 500 business cards for each name. It is possible to print less, but the difference between printing fifty and five hundred impressions is insignificant—little more than the cost of the paper.

Be aware that it is not unusual for printers without the equipment to produce your job to accept it and broker it to a third party. Ask early on if the printer will be printing your project in-house. If they are sending it out, you may get a better price by going direct.

**12.3** *Verify that you and the printer are technically compatible.* Ask if the printer's prepress department supports the computer hardware and software you will use to produce the artwork, exactly how the files need to be set up, and how they charge for their services.

**12.4** Assuming all of the preliminary answers are to your liking, *ask to see some samples* of similar jobs the printer has produced. Look for good printing, not good design. The creative part of printing is normally in the client's hands, so a printer is more concerned with science than art. Check for bright, clean colors; for smooth, dense solid areas; for text and images that are focused and clear; and for images that are printed on the page squarely and in the correct position.

It also helps to show the printer an example of the quality you expect and the effects you are hoping to achieve. Take advantage of the expertise of veteran salespeople and their coworkers in the press room. They can provide a wealth of information and guidance.

**12.5** Find at least two printers that can handle your job and *request job estimates.* Estimates can vary widely from printer to printer. Some base them on strict estimating formulas; others adjust for how busy they are and, therefore, how eager they are to have your business. Most are willing to bargain.

The cost of printing is based on the amount of time the job ties up the press and the size of the press needed to print the job. The more complex the job, the more complex the press needed to print it. You normally get the best price on the smallest press that can handle your job.

To prepare an estimate, the printer will need some preliminary information: the form in which you will supply the artwork, the overall size of the piece, the finished/folded size, the number of colors on each surface, the preferred paper color and weight, the quantity, and how you want it finished, folded, bound, packaged and shipped.

**12.6** Finally, *review the printer's contract.* Many printers include a detailed contract with their estimate. Printing is a complex combination of product and service that presents many opportunities for misunderstanding. Be certain you understand the intricacies of the legalese.

STEP 13

# Choose Paper

Paper is a fundamental element of design. In the printing world, it is referred to as "stock." The impact of a letter, in particular, can be greatly enhanced by the quality of the stock it is printed on and the look and feel of the envelope in which it is delivered.

**13.1** Paper plays an important role in printing, but you should also incorporate the paper into the design process. To see what is possible, *request paper samples* from your printer or a local paper distributor. They can provide swatch books and printed samples of literally thousands of possible finishes, weights, and colors of paper available. A printer might narrow the selection to the brands that are most readily available— but insist on seeing at least five to ten different brands.

**13.2** The first consideration when selecting paper is to *choose the proper grade*. Though there are many different grades available, there are only two to concern yourself with for this type of project—bond or writing papers for letterheads and envelopes, and cover papers for business cards.

**13.3** The next consideration is to *choose the surface texture or finish of the paper*.

Generally speaking, letterhead, business cards, and envelopes are printed on uncoated stock, not the coated stock you typically see in magazines. Coated stock has a thin layer of clay-like substrate that creates a smooth, flat surface ideal for printing superfine detail such as photographs.

Uncoated stock ranges from rough to smooth with finishes such as "laid," a series of tiny ridges; pebbled; and smooth. Assuming the letterhead and envelopes will be printed on a laser or inkjet printer, any finish is acceptable as long as it is designated laser-compatible.

**13.4** Next, *choose the weight*. Typically, letterhead is printed on 20- to 28-lb bond stock. Check the documentation of the desktop printer that will be used to print on the letterhead and envelopes to determine the minimum and maximum weights it can accommodate.

Your business card should be printed on a more substantial weight stock that can withstand a significant amount of handling—in most cases a minimum 80-lb cover stock. The bond paper you use for the letterhead and envelopes will often have a matching cover stock for just this purpose.

Be aware that paper has a grain, much like a wooden board. The printer can show you how rigidity is affected by printing with—versus against—the grain.

**13.5** *The most obvious choice is color*. There is a seemingly endless rainbow of paper colors and a huge range of warm to cool whites. In some cases, the sheets are a consistent color; in other cases, a subtle, confetti-like mix of fibers provide various effects.

It is important to remember that ink color is affected by the color of paper. Yellow ink on white paper, for example, will look significantly different than yellow ink on a light shade of green.

Again, paper samples can help you envision the result of various combinations. Paper companies go to great expense creating samples that show how different inks and printing techniques affect their papers. Be sure to request samples from the printer and figure them into your preliminary design decisions.

**13.6** Be sure to *consider opacity*. Opacity is the property of paper that determines the degree to which a printed image shows through from one side of a sheet to the other. If the letterhead is not opaque enough, you might see enough of the image from the opposite side for it to be distracting. Your printer representative can help you gauge the amount of show-through likely from the paper you specify.

**13.7** Finally, *ask your printer for guidance*. They may discourage you from using a certain sheet for a particular job because of past experience, incompatibility with their equipment, availability, and so on. As long as they have given you a wide range of finishes, weights, and color to choose from, it is best to follow their recommendations.

## Step 13: PAPER CHECKLIST

- **13.1** Request paper samples
- **13.2** Choose the proper grade
- **13.3** Choose the finish
- **13.4** Choose the weight
- **13.5** Choose the color
- **13.6** Consider opacity
- **13.7** Ask your printer for guidance

**Some popular paper brands**

Fox River Paper Company: www.foxriverpaper.com
Fraser Papers: www.fraserpapers.com
French Paper Co.: www.mrfrench.com
Gilbert Paper: www.gilbertpaper.com
International Paper: www.internationalpaper.com
Mead Paper: www.meadpaper.com
Mohawk Paper: www.mohawkpaper.com

STEP 14

# Prepare for the Press

One of the most critical parts of printing does not involve a press at all—the prepress process.

Prepress is a general term used to describe the steps taken to prepare your project for printing. The printer takes the files you created along with the fonts and any images you linked to them and translates them to a form the shop's hardware and software understands. Among other things, prepress processes determine how to position each piece on the sheet, incorporate a slight overlap, or "trap," between colors that touch, and separate the colors for making individual plates.

You play an important part in the prepress process.

**14.1** First and foremost, you should *finalize and proofread the content.* Triple-check spelling and grammar, and determine that all the information necessary is included and correct. Then have someone else check it. You might be surprised how often a printer's clients leave issues unresolved in the rush to keep a job in progress. Changes once your job is in the printer's hands can be very costly.

**14.2** Next, *preflight your files.* "Preflighting" is the process of gathering together and reviewing all the elements necessary for the printer to translate what you create on your computer to their computer system—in most cases, printers use something other than conventional, off-the-shelf software. Most printers can provide you with a preflight checklist such as the one shown in fig. A.

Some desktop publishing programs have a preflight feature that aids in the process. At minimum, the printer will require the names and descriptions of the document files and any other image files linked to them, the name and version number of the software program used to produce them, and copies of the fonts used (check your font license agreement for restrictions).

**14.3** Before you hand over your files, be sure you and the printer *agree about who is responsible for what.* You, of course, are responsible for the content of your job, but you should also understand, for example, who is responsible for settings as obscure as the screen frequency or negative orientation.

**14.4** And lastly, be sure to *see and sign off on a proof* of your job before it is printed. A proof is a printout that should, as closely as possible, show the final result.

There are many different types of proofs. Some printers still provide a blueline (named for its monochrome blue color) made by exposing a film negative on a sheet of light-sensitive paper. It shows a highly accurate representation of what to expect from the printing process minus actual color. If you specify more than one or two colors, a color proof is sometimes required to approximate the colors you should expect. Today, though, in an ever-changing print marketplace, new and more accurate ways of proofing are available. Your printing representative can show you an example of the system they use.

In any case, your responsibility is the same—to recheck the proof thoroughly. Once you sign off on it, responsibility for everything shown on the proof is yours—even if it is the printer's mistake. Something as simple as a line break that eliminates or obscures an important phone number can undermine an entire project.

Use a red pen or pencil to circle errors and make notes. Are pages printed at the right size? Are the photographs, artwork, and text in the right places? Are the images and text clear and focused? Are the typefaces correct? Did special characters such as fractions and copyright marks translate correctly? Circle scratches, dust, and broken characters. And if there are significant changes, request a second proof.

**Step 14: PREPRESS CHECKLIST**

| | |
|---|---|
| **14.1** | Finalize and proofread the content |
| **14.2** | Preflight your files |
| **14.3** | Determine who is responsible for what |
| **14.4** | Review and sign off on a proof |

STEP 15

# Print and Proof It

Good printing is the absence of mistakes. The printer's proof you saw in the prepress process should have given you a good idea what your finished job would look like. So your final responsibility is to see that the results are a fair representation of what you approved.

There are two stages at which to intercept problems—during the printing process and after it is complete.

Many printers are receptive to, and in fact encourage, clients to *check their jobs at the beginning of the press run.* This is especially true if there is some part of the process that requires an aesthetic judgment—if you are using process colors, the press operator can often fine-tune the result by increasing or decreasing the intensity of individual colors. But remember, press time is expensive. If you choose to approve your job on press, be prepared to give clear directions and to make quick decisions. Check with your printing representative to see what their policy is and requirements are for press checks.

**Coverage**
Watch for inconsistent ink coverage—too little or too much.

**Mottle**
Check solid areas for mottle—uneven, spotty areas of ink.

**Registration and trapping**
All colors and shapes should be aligned, or registered, with great precision; and the nearly imperceptible overlap between colors, the trap, should be very precise.

**Pinholes and hickies**
A pinhole is the result of a hole in the printing plate negative. Erratically shaped hickies are caused by dirt or paper particles that adhere to the plate or rollers during printing.

**Skew**
A crooked or skewed image could be the result of a misaligned plate or careless trimming.

**Trimming**
Some of the most common problems occur after the job is printed. A page trimmed even slightly out of alignment can be drastically different.

**Ghosting**
A doubled or blurred image, termed "ghosting," is typically caused by a misapplication of ink on the rollers.

**15.1** Whether you are looking at a job in progress or one that is complete, the figures show a few of the most obvious problems to look for. Though a small portion of just about every job will be spoiled by one or more of them, attentive press workers should spot and discard problem sheets. And, though quality varies from printer to printer, most would agree that problems this extreme are not considered deliverable.

*Check your job in progress* and, afterward, question anything that is distinctly different than the proof you approved.

**15.2** Repeat the process by *rechecking your job when it is delivered*. Look at a representative sample of pieces from the beginning, middle, and end of the run. If the middle third of the job is spoiled, you don't want to discover it six months after the job is delivered.

**15.3** Next, *do a rough count* to determine if your got the quantity of pieces you paid for. Count a stack of one hundred pieces, measure the height of the stack, and roughly calculate if you are within ten percent of the quantity you ordered. Most printers consider ten percent over or under the amount you requested as acceptable. Therefore, if you need exactly 500 envelopes, be sure to tell the printer beforehand that anything less is unacceptable. Some printers expect you to pay extra for overruns unless you agree otherwise in advance.

**15.4** Finally, *negotiate an adjustment for printing problems*. If there are minor problems with your job, something even a meticulous reader would normally miss, you can request a reprint or ask for an adjustment of the price. If it is the printer's mistake, most are amenable to either option. If there are significant, obvious problems with your job, insist on a reprint. Though some readers might not notice a problem, it may cause others to judge your organization negatively.

## Step 15: PRINTING CHECKLIST

**15.1** Check your job in progress

**15.2** Recheck your job after it is delivered

**15.3** Do a rough count

**15.4** Negotiate an adjustment for printing problems

This layout requires three colors and, therefore, three printing plates: one for black, one for red, and one for orange.

# Logos, Letterheads, and Business Cards

## SECTION 1, PART 2
## Design Recipes

PART 2: DESIGN RECIPES

# How to Use the Recipes

Now it's time to put the step-by-step process to work. The pages that follow present a cookbook of style recipes for a wide variety of letterhead, business card, and envelope designs.

The first two pages of each recipe show the development of a logo and the overall style of the letterhead, business card, and envelope. The third and fourth pages provide a detailed recipe and list of ingredients of the designs.

Don't limit your thinking to using a logo idea only with the style it is paired with. Some logos will work just as well with several other styles.

Above all, remember this: These designs were created specifically for the Design-it-Yourself series—you are free to copy any recipe in whole or in part to produce your own materials. The only restriction is that you cannot trademark the copied design.

**A: Definition**
The recipe begins with an explanation of the thinking behind its particular style.

**B: The logo**
The large version of the logo reveals the details you might miss at a smaller size.

**C: Source links**
The caption next to the logo lists the source of illustrations; the caption to the right, the source of the type families.

**D: Software recommendations**
This caption lists the type of software required to create the artwork.

**E: Step-by-step design**
From top to bottom, these are the primary steps of executing the style.

**F: The result**
To demonstrate the end result, here is the suite of letterhead, business card, and envelope.

**G: Letterhead recipe**
This is the recipe for creating the letterhead. The rulers show measurements in inches, and the light gray guides pinpoint the position of the primary elements.

**H: Business card recipe**
This is a recipe for the front and back of the business card. Color that extends outside the bold gray outline means the color bleeds off the edge of the page.

**I: Envelope recipe**
This is the envelope recipe, in most cases, for a standard 4.125-by-9.5-inch (#10) commercial business envelope.

**J: The color palette**
All the projects are created using either four-color process or Solid PANTONE Colors (see Step 9.3). The palette identifies compostion of CMYK mixes or the PANTONE Number and tint values of the solid colors.

**K: The ingredients**
The type used in each recipe is keyed, by number, to this list of ingredients—it includes the name of the typeface, the point size, line spacing (when there is more than one line of the same typeface), alignment, and the point size of lines.

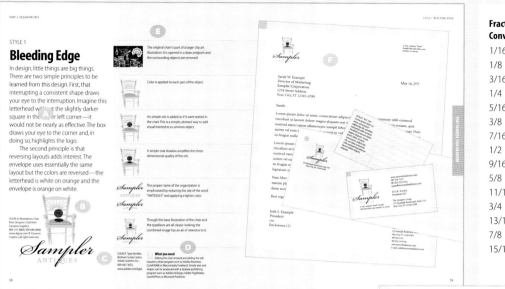

## Fraction = Decimal Conversion

| Fraction | | Decimal |
|---|---|---|
| 1/16 | = | 0.0625 |
| 1/8 | = | 0.125 |
| 3/16 | = | 0.1875 |
| 1/4 | = | 0.25 |
| 5/16 | = | 0.3125 |
| 3/8 | = | 0.375 |
| 7/16 | = | 0.4375 |
| 1/2 | = | 0.5 |
| 9/16 | = | 0.5625 |
| 5/8 | = | 0.625 |
| 11/16 | = | 0.6875 |
| 3/4 | = | 0.75 |
| 13/16 | = | 0.8125 |
| 7/8 | = | 0.875 |
| 15/16 | = | 0.9375 |

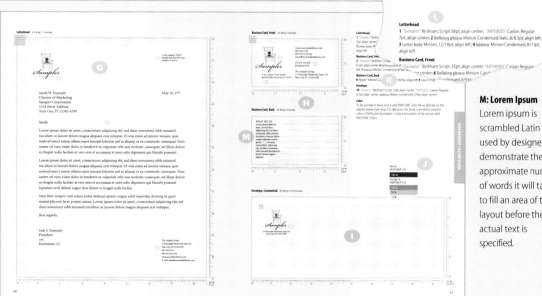

**M: Lorem Ipsum**

Lorem ipsum is scrambled Latin text used by designer's to demonstrate the approximate number of words it will take to fill an area of the layout before the actual text is specified.

**L: The ingredient details**

In this example, the number "2" points to the item; "Defining phrase" is the type of item; "Minion Condensed Italic" is the typeface;" 8/8.5pt" means 8-point type on 8.5 points of leading (the space between the baselines of two rows of type); and "align left" is the alignment—aligned left or right, centered, or justified. Several examples employ customizable Adobe Multiple Master (MM) fonts such as Myriad MM (see page 71, item 10). Settings such as "700bd, 300cn" following the typeface name, represent customized character weights and widths. See your Multiple Master documentation for details.

STYLE 1

# Bleeding Edge

In design, little things are big things. There are two simple principles to be learned from this design. First, that interrupting a consistent shape draws your eye to the interruption. Imagine this letterhead without the slightly darker square in the upper left corner—it would not be nearly as effective. The box draws your eye to the corner and, in doing so, highlights the logo.

The second principle is that reversing layouts adds interest. The envelope uses essentially the same layout but the colors are reversed—the letterhead is white on orange and the envelope is orange on white.

SOURCE Illustrations: Chair from *Designer's Club* from Dynamic Graphics 800-255-8800, 309-688-8800, www.dgusa.com, © Dynamic Graphics, all rights reserved.

The original chair is part of a larger clip art illustration. It is opened in a draw program and the surrounding objects are removed.

Color is applied to each part of the object.

An simple orb is added as if it were seated in the chair. This is a simple, abstract way to add visual interest to a common object.

A simple oval shadow amplifies the three-dimensional quality of the orb.

The proper name of the organization is emphasized by reducing the size of the word "ANTIQUES" and applying a lighter color.

Though the base illustration of the chair and the typefaces are all classic-looking, the combined image has an air of newness to it.

SOURCE Type families: Bickham Script, Caslon, Adobe Systems, Inc., 800-682-3623, www.adobe.com/type.

**? What you need**

Editing the chair artwork and adding the orb requires a draw program such as Adobe Illustrator, CorelDRAW, or Macromedia FreeHand. Simple text and shapes can be produced with a desktop publishing program such as Adobe InDesign, Adobe PageMaker, QuarkXPress, or Microsoft Publisher.

*Sampler*
ANTIQUES

*A one-sentence "hook"
benefit that describes your
product or service*

Sarah W. Example
Director of Marketing
Sampler Corporation
1234 Street Address
Your City, ST 12345-6789

May 16, 2???

Sarah:

Lorem ipsum dolor sit amet, consectetuer adipiscin... nonummy nibh euismod
tincidunt ut laoreet dolore magna aliquam erat v... im veniam, quis
nostrud exerci tation ullamcorper suscipit lobo... autem vel eum i... drerit in vul... quat. Duis
eu feugiat nulla...

Lorem ipsum ...
tincidunt ut la...
nostrud exerc...
autem vel eu...
eu feugiat n...
luptatum zz...

Nam liber ...
mazim pla...
diam non...

Best rega...

Josh S. Example
President
coc
Enclosures (2)

*WHAT WE DO*
Lorem ipsum dolor sit
amet, consectetuer
adipiscing elit, sed diam
nonummy nibh euismod
tincidunt ut laoreet dolore
magna aliquam. Lorem
ipsum dolor sit amet,
consectetuer adipiscing
elit, sed diam nonummy
nibh euismod tincidunt ut
laoreet dolore magna
aliquam.

*Sampler*
ANTIQUES
123 Example Boulevard, Suite 210
Your City, ST 12345 6789

www.yourwebaddressz.com
987 654 3210
987 654 3210 Fax
name@youremailaddressz.com

YOUR NAME
President/CEO

The Sampler Group
123 Example Boulevard, Suite 210
Your City, ST 12345 6789

*Sampler*
ANTIQUES
*A one-sentence "hook" benefit
that describes your product or service*

123 Example Boulevard, Suit...
Your City, ST 12345 6789
987 654 3210
987 654 3210 Fax
www.yourwebaddressz.com
E-mail info@youremailaddressz.com

57

A one-sentence "hook"
benefit that describes your
product or service

*Sampler*
ANTIQUES

Sarah W. Example
Director of Marketing
Sampler Corporation
1234 Street Address
Your City, ST 12345-6789

May 16, 2???

Sarah:

Lorem ipsum dolor sit amet, consectetuer adipiscing elit, sed diam nonummy nibh euismod
tincidunt ut laoreet dolore magna aliquam erat volutpat. Ut wisi enim ad minim veniam, quis
nostrud exerci tation ullamcorper suscipit lobortis nisl ut aliquip ex ea commodo consequat. Duis
autem vel eum iriure dolor in hendrerit in vulputate velit esse molestie consequat, vel illum dolore
eu feugiat nulla facilisis at vero eros et accumsan et iusto odio dignissim qui blandit praesent.

Lorem ipsum dolor sit amet, consectetuer adipiscing elit, sed diam nonummy nibh euismod
tincidunt ut laoreet dolore magna aliquam erat volutpat. Ut wisi enim ad minim veniam, quis
nostrud exerci tation ullamcorper suscipit lobortis nisl ut aliquip ex ea commodo consequat. Duis
autem vel eum iriure dolor in hendrerit in vulputate velit esse molestie consequat, vel illum dolore
eu feugiat nulla facilisis at vero eros et accumsan et iusto odio dignissim qui blandit praesent
luptatum zzril delenit augue duis dolore te feugait nulla facilisi.

Nam liber tempor cum soluta nobis eleifend option congue nihil imperdiet doming id quod
mazim placerat facer possim assum. Lorem ipsum dolor sit amet, consectetuer adipiscing elit, sed
diam nonummy nibh euismod tincidunt ut laoreet dolore magna aliquam erat volutpat.

Best regards,

Josh S. Example
President
coc
Enclosures (2)

The Sampler Group
123 Example Boulevard, Suite 210
Your City, ST 12345 6789
987 654 3210
987 654 3210 Fax
www.yourwebaddressz.com
E-mail info@youremailaddressz.com

## Business Card, Front   3.5 W by 2 H inches

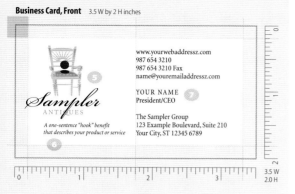

## Business Card, Back   3.5 W by 2 H inches

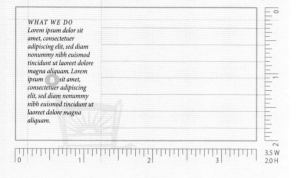

## Envelope, Commercial   9.5 W by 4.125 H inches

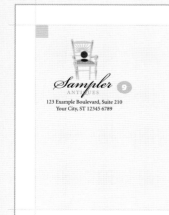

### Letterhead

**1** "Sampler" Bickham Script, 38pt, align center; "ANTIQUES" Caslon Regular, 7pt, align center; **2** Defining phrase Minion Condensed Italic, 8/8.5pt, align left; **3** Letter body Minion, 12/18pt, align left; **4** Address Minion Condensed, 8/11pt, align left

### Business Card, Front

**5** "Sampler" Bickham Script, 35pt, align center; "ANTIQUES" Caslon Regular, 6.5pt, align center; **6** Defining phrase Minion Condensed Italic, 7/8pt, align left; **7** Address Minion Condensed, 8/9pt, align left

### Business Card, Back

**8** "WHAT" Minion Condensed Italic, 8/9pt, align left; **Lines** 0.25pt

### Envelope

**9** "Sampler" Bickham Script, 35pt, align center; "ANTIQUES" Caslon Regular, 6.5pt, align center; Address Minion Condensed, 7/9pt, align center

### Color

To be printed in black and a solid PANTONE Color Ink as defined on the palette below (see Step 9.3). (Because this book is printed in process colors (CMYK), the illustration is only a simulation of the actual solid PANTONE Color Inks).

Red or
PANTONE® 193

| 100 % | |

Orange or
PANTONE® 152

| 100 % |
| 50 % |
| 15 % |

STYLE 2

# Border

Document design has a long history, and you rarely go wrong reviving classic examples. These layouts borrow from the designs of the early 1900s, when the founders' art was so revered.

Borders have long been used to establish the boundaries of a layout. Visual boundaries give you a barrier to break. Notice how pushing the flower bud beyond the border adds depth to the design.

There are many versions of classic typefaces such as Caslon. Originally designed by William Caslon in the early 1700s, this one was reinterpreted for Adobe by Carol Twombly. Beautiful!

SOURCES Illustrations: Flower bud from Caslon Ornaments typeface, Adobe Systems, Inc., 800-682-3623, www.adobe.com/type; berries from *Signature Series 4*, PhotoDisc, 800-979-4413, 206-441-9355, www.photodisc.com, © CMCD, all rights reserved.

A simple thick/thin border establishes the boundaries of the design.

An ornament accents the text. In this case, it is from the Caslon Ornaments typeface—a collection of decorative elements designed to match the personality of the Caslon type family.

A subtle gray-on-gray version of the ornament and oval is used to add the flavor of a watermark—the delicate mark visible when you hold fine paper up to a light.

The sum of simple changes, such as making the "S" slightly larger than the "A" and subtracting and adding space between characters, make this logo one-of-a-kind.

The finished logo looks simple, but is actually quite complex. Though it is easy to produce, it requires five different typefaces: Charlemagne, Caslon Regular, Regular Italic, Swash Italic, and Caslon Ornaments.

Surprise! The back of the business card presents the benefit of the business—beautiful, fresh produce. Imagine the impression of sending a letter with the business card enclosed so the first thing the reader sees is that benefit.

SOURCE Type families: Caslon, Charlemagne, Minion, Adobe Systems, Inc., 800-682-3623, www.adobe.com/type.

 **What you need**
Simple text and shapes can be produced with a desktop publishing program such as Adobe InDesign, Adobe PageMaker, QuarkXPress, or Microsoft Publisher.

*A one-sentence "hook" benefit that describes your product or service Lorem ipsum dolor sit amet, consectetuer adipiscing elit*

*Since 1976*

# SAMPLER

## PRODUCE

FRUIT
VEGETABLES
CHEESES
EGGS
FRUIT JUICES

Sarah W. Example
Director of Marketing
Sampler Corporation
1234 Street Address
Your City, ST 12345-6789

May 16, 2???

Sarah:

Lorem ipsum dolor sit amet, consectetuer adipiscing el
tincidunt ut laoreet dolore magna aliquam erat volutpa
nostrud
autem v
eu feugi

Lorem i
tincidun
nostrud
autem v
eu feugi
luptatum zzril delenit augue duis

Nam liber tempor cum soluta nobi
mazim placerat facer possim assum
diam nonummy nibh euismod tinci

Best regards,

Josh S. Example
President
coc
Enclosures (2)

*Since 1976*

# SAMPLER

## PRODUCE

123 Example Boulevard, Suite 210
Your City, ST 12345 6789

*Since 1976*

# SAMPLER

## PRODUCE

*A one-sentence "hook" benefit that describes your product or service Lorem ipsum dolor sit amet, consectetuer adipiscing elit*

YOUR NAME
*President/CEO*

www.yourwebaddressz.com
123 Example Boulevard, Suite 210, Your City, ST 12345 6789
Toll Free 800 987 6543 • Voice 987 654 3210 • Fax 987 654 3210
E-mail info@youremailaddressz.com

123 Example Boulevard, Suite 210, Your City, ST 12345 6789
Toll Free 800 987 6543 • Voice 987 654 3210 • Fax 987 654 3210 • E-mail info@youremailaddressz.com
www.yourwebaddressz.com

*A one-sentence "hook"*
*benefit that describes your*
*product or service Lorem*
*ipsum dolor sit amet,*
*consectetuer adipiscing elit*

*Since 1976*

# SAMPLER

PRODUCE

FRUIT
VEGETABLES
CHEESES
EGGS
FRUIT JUICES

May 16, 2???

Sarah W. Example
Director of Marketing
Sampler Corporation
1234 Street Address
Your City, ST 12345-6789

Sarah:

Lorem ipsum dolor sit amet, consectetuer adipiscing elit, sed diam nonummy nibh euismod tincidunt ut laoreet dolore magna aliquam erat volutpat. Ut wisi enim ad minim veniam, quis nostrud exerci tation ullamcorper suscipit lobortis nisl ut aliquip ex ea commodo consequat. Duis autem vel eum iriure dolor in hendrerit in vulputate velit esse molestie consequat, vel illum dolore eu feugiat nulla facilisis at vero eros et accumsan et iusto odio dignissim qui blandit praesent.

Lorem ipsum dolor sit amet, consectetuer adipiscing elit, sed diam nonummy nibh euismod tincidunt ut laoreet dolore magna aliquam erat volutpat. Ut wisi enim ad minim veniam, quis nostrud exerci tation ullamcorper suscipit lobortis nisl ut aliquip ex ea commodo consequat. Duis autem vel eum iriure dolor in hendrerit in vulputate velit esse molestie consequat, vel illum dolore eu feugiat nulla facilisis at vero eros et accumsan et iusto odio dignissim qui blandit praesent luptatum zzril delenit augue duis dolore te feugait nulla facilisi.

Nam liber tempor cum soluta nobis eleifend option congue nihil imperdiet doming id quod mazim placerat facer possim assum. Lorem ipsum dolor sit amet, consectetuer adipiscing elit, sed diam nonummy nibh euismod tincidunt ut laoreet dolore magna aliquam erat volutpat.

Best regards,


Josh S. Example
President
coc
Enclosures (2)

123 Example Boulevard, Suite 210, Your City, ST 12345 6789
Toll Free 800 987 6543 • Voice 987 654 3210 • Fax 987 654 3210 • E-mail info@youremailaddressz.com
www.yourwebaddressz.com

**Business Card, Front**  3.5 W by 2 H inches

**Business Card, Back**  3.5 W by 2 H inches

**Envelope, Commercial**  9.5 W by 4.125 H inches

### Letterhead

**1** Lines Thick 1pt, thin 0.25pt; **2** Defining phrase Caslon Regular Italic, 8/12pt, align left; **3** "S" Caslon Swash Italic, 12pt, align center; "ince" Caslon Regular Italic, 12pt, align center; "S" Charlemagne, 28pt, align center; "AMPLER" Charlemagne, 24pt, align center; "P" Caslon Regular, 12pt, align center; "RODUCE" Caslon Regular, 10pt, align center; Lines 0.25pt; align center; **4** List Caslon Regular, 6/12pt, align right; Lines 0.25pt; **5** Letter body Minion, 12/18pt, align left; **6** Address Caslon Regular, 8/11pt, align center

### Business Card, Front

**7** "S" Caslon Swash Italic, 10pt, align center; "ince" Caslon Regular Italic, 10pt, align center; "S" Charlemagne, 24pt, align center; "AMPLER" Charlemagne, 20pt, align center; "P" Caslon Regular, 10pt, align center; "RODUCE" Caslon Regular, 8.5pt, align center; Lines 0.25pt; **8** Defining phrase Caslon Regular Italic, 6/8pt, align right; **9** Name Caslon Regular, 7pt, align center; Title Caslon Regular Italic, 7pt, align center; Address Caslon Regular, 7/9pt, align center

### Envelope

**10** "S" Caslon Swash Italic, 12pt, align center; "ince" Caslon Regular Italic, 12pt, align center; "S" Charlemagne, 28pt, align center; "AMPLER" Charlemagne, 24pt, align center; "P" Caslon Regular, 12pt, align center; "RODUCE" Caslon Regular, 10pt, align center; Lines 0.25pt; Address Caslon Regular, 7/10pt; align center

### Color

Printed in black and tints of black as defined on the palette below. The back of the business card is printed in four-color process (see Step 9.3) using values of cyan, magenta, yellow, and black (CMYK). Actual color will vary.

Black

| 100% | |
|---|---|
| 20% | |
| 10% | |
| 5% | |

STYLE 3

# Boxes

Boxes—think outside them. Must a logo look like a logo? Only if you can't think beyond it. In this case, the defining phrase *is* the logo. After all, if you've invested the time to produce a compelling, customer-oriented benefit statement, why wouldn't you want it to take center stage?

Boxes are different than borders. Borders define boundaries, boxes encapsulate information.

Sampler defining phrase or mission statement. A one-paragraph "hook" benefit that describes your product or service.

This style, among the easiest to produce in this series, makes the all-important defining phrase (see page 18) the focus of attention.

A bold typeface is used for the initial cap and a light typeface for the text. If possible, begin your defining phrase with a visually interesting letter such as A, B, E, G, J, K, M, N, Q, R, S, or W.

The relative size of each element—the initial cap, defining phrase, and the organization's name—are increased and decreased until they fill the box with a minimum of white space.

The layouts of all three pieces play on the box theme. Various-sized boxes each contain a different information element—the organization's name, defining phrase, letter body, address, and so on.

Various tints of the solid color are used to differentiate each box from the others.

SOURCES Type families: Giza, Font Bureau, 617-423-8770, www.font bureau.com; Century Expanded, Franklin Gothic, Adobe Systems, Inc., 800-682-3623, www.adobe.com/type.

 **What you need**
Simple text and shapes can be produced with a desktop publishing program such as Adobe InDesign, Adobe PageMaker, QuarkXPress, or Microsoft Publisher.

**S**ampler defining phrase or mission statement: a one-paragraph "hook" benefit that describes your product or service

SAMPLER
LEGAL SERVICES

May 16, 2???

Sarah W. Example
Director of Marketing
Sampler Corporation
1234 Street Address
Your City, ST 12345-6789

Sarah:

Lorem ipsum dolor sit amet, co
tincidunt ut laoreet dolore ma
nostrud exerci tation ullamco
autem vel eum iriure dolor i
eu feugiat nulla facilisis at ve

Lorem ipsum dolor sit ame
tincidunt ut laore
nostrud exerci ta
autem vel eum i
eu feugiat nulla
luptatum zzril

Nam liber tem
mazim placera
diam nonummy

Best regards,

Josh S. Example
President
coc
Enclosures (2)

**S**ampler defining phrase or mission statement: a one-paragraph "hook" benefit that describes your product or service

SAMPLER
LEGAL
SERVICES

123 Example Boulevard, Suite 123
Your City, State 12345 6789

IMPORTANT

**YOUR NAME**
*President/CEO*

SAMPLER
LEGAL
SERVICES

**S**ampler defining phrase or mission statement: a one-paragraph "hook" benefit that describes your product or service

SAMPLER LEGAL SERVICES

123 Example Boulevard, Suite 123
Your City, State 12345 6789
Voice 987 654 3210  Fax 987 654 3210
info@emailaddressz.com
www.yourwebaddressz.com

**Sampler Legal Services**
123 Example Boulevard, Suite 123
Your City, State 12345 6789
Voice 987 654 3210  Fax 987 654 3210
info@emailaddressz.com
www.yourwebaddressz.com

**s**ampler defining phrase or mission statement: a one-paragraph "hook" benefit that describes your product or service

SAMPLER LEGAL SERVICES

May 16, 2???

Sarah W. Example
Director of Marketing
Sampler Corporation
1234 Street Address
Your City, ST 12345-6789

Sarah:

Lorem ipsum dolor sit amet, consectetuer adipiscing elit, sed diam nonummy nibh euismod tincidunt ut laoreet dolore magna aliquam erat volutpat. Ut wisi enim ad minim veniam, quis nostrud exerci tation ullamcorper suscipit lobortis nisl ut aliquip ex ea commodo consequat. Duis autem vel eum iriure dolor in hendrerit in vulputate velit esse molestie consequat, vel illum dolore eu feugiat nulla facilisis at vero eros et accumsan et iusto odio dignissim qui blandit praesent.

Lorem ipsum dolor sit amet, consectetuer adipiscing elit, sed diam nonummy nibh euismod tincidunt ut laoreet dolore magna aliquam erat volutpat. Ut wisi enim ad minim veniam, quis nostrud exerci tation ullamcorper suscipit lobortis nisl ut aliquip ex ea commodo consequat. Duis autem vel eum iriure dolor in hendrerit in vulputate velit esse molestie consequat, vel illum dolore eu feugiat nulla facilisis at vero eros et accumsan et iusto odio dignissim qui blandit praesent luptatum zzril delenit augue duis dolore te feugait nulla facilisi.

Nam liber tempor cum soluta nobis eleifend option congue nihil imperdiet doming id quod mazim placerat facer possim assum. Lorem ipsum dolor sit amet, consectetuer adipiscing elit, sed diam nonummy nibh euismod tincidunt ut laoreet dolore magna aliquam erat volutpat.

Best regards,

Josh S. Example
President
coc
Enclosures (2)

**Sampler Legal Services**
123 Example Boulevard, Suite 123
Your City, State 12345 6789
Voice 987 654 3210  Fax 987 654 3210
info@emailaddressz.com
www.yourwebaddressz.com

8.5 W
11 H

## Business Card, Front  3.5 W by 2 H inches

## Business Card, Back  3.5 W by 2 H inches

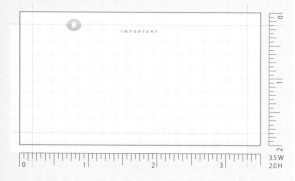

### Letterhead

**1** "S" Giza SevenSeven, 72pt, align left; Defining phrase Century Expanded, 12/14pt, align left; Organization Franklin Gothic Heavy, 5pt, align left; **2** Lines 0.25pt; **3** Letter body Minion, 12/18pt, align left; **4** Organization Franklin Gothic Heavy, 9pt, align left; Address Century Expanded, 9/14pt, align left

### Business Card, Front

**5** Name Franklin Gothic Heavy, 9pt, align left; Title Century Expanded Italic, 7/9pt, align left; Organization Franklin Gothic Heavy, 11/10pt, align left; **6** Lines 0.25pt; "S" Giza SevenSeven, 54pt; Defining phrase Century Expanded, 9/10.5pt, align left; Organization Franklin Gothic Heavy, 4pt, align left; **7** Address Century Expanded, 7/10pt, align left

### Business Card, Back

**8** Lines 0.5pt; "IMPORTANT" Franklin Gothic Heavy, 4pt, align left

### Envelope

**9** Lines 0.25pt; "S" Giza SevenSeven, 54pt; Defining phrase Century Expanded, 9/10.5pt, align left; Organization Franklin Gothic Heavy, 11/10pt, align left; **10** Address Century Expanded, 7/10pt, align left

### Color

To be printed in black and a solid PANTONE Color Ink as defined on the palette below (see Step 9.3). (Because this book is printed in process colors (CMYK), the illustration is only a simulation of the actual solid PANTONE Color).

Mustard Yellow or PANTONE® 123

| |
| --- |
| 100% |
| 30% |
| 15% |

## Envelope, Commercial  9.5 W by 4.125 H inches

s ampler defining phrase or mission statement: a one-paragraph "hook" benefit that describes your product or service

SAMPLER LEGAL SERVICES

123 Example Boulevard, Suite 123
Your City, State 12345 6789

9.5 W
4.125 H

STYLE 4

# Burst

The success of this style rides on a kind of subtle visual complexity.

A burst is nothing more than a star with a small center and lots of points. Printing it in a light tint in the background of your design lends the air of an official document similar to that of paper money or a stock certificate.

In contrast, the logo is simple and bold. Though an acronym (using the initial letter of each word in the name) is not the ideal way to name an organization, it is a common solution, and this is an attractive way to present it.

A one-sentence "hook" benefit that describes your product or service

Sampler
Fire Alarm
Systems

Note the small but significant difference between two similar typefaces. The background "S" is slightly bolder and sleeker. As in the previous style, if you're creating a type logo, it pays to search for the most interesting typefaces.

The initials are grouped on a four-box foundation. The same design would work with three letters, perhaps using the last box for the spelled out name.

Using a draw program, the parts of the letters that overlap the edges of the box are cut and removed.

The defining phrase paragraph and the company name are sized as if to fill invisible boxes on the top left and bottom right.

The burst is created using the polygon or star tool of your desktop publishing or drawing program. The only difference is that the star, instead of having the conventional five points, has 500 points.

SOURCES Type families: Interstate, Font Bureau, 617-423-8770, www.fontbureau.com; Minion, Myriad, Adobe Systems, Inc., 800-682-3623, www.adobe.com/type.

**What you need**
Simple text and shapes can be produced with a desktop publishing program such as Adobe InDesign, Adobe PageMaker, QuarkXPress, or Microsoft Publisher.

A one-sentence
"hook" benefit
that describes
your product
or service

Sampler
Fire Alarm
Systems

May 16, 2???

Sarah W. Example
Director of Marketing
Sampler Corporation
1234 Street Address
Your City, ST 12345-6789

Sarah:

Lorem ipsum dolor
tincidunt ut laoreet
nostrud exerci tatio
autem vel eum iriur
eu feugiat nulla faci

**CLASS A**
Lorem ipsum dolor sit
amet, consectetuer
adipiscing elit, sed diam
nonummy nibh euismod
tincidunt ut laoreet
dolore magna aliquam
erat volutpat. Ut wisi
enim ad minim ven
quis nostrud

**CLASS B**
Loremtation ullamcorper
suscipit lobortis nisl ut
aliquip ex ea commodo
consequat. Duis autem vel
eum iriure dolor in
hendrerit in vulputate
velit esse molestie

**CLASS C**
Lorem ipsum dolor sit
amet, consectetuer
adipiscing elit, sed diam
nonummy nibh euismod

mmy nibh euismod
minim veniam, quis
quat. Duis

123 Example Boulev
Your City, State 1234

www.yourwebaddressz.com
Voice 987 654 3210
Fax 987 654 3210

A one-sentence
"hook" benefit
that describes
your product
or service

Sampler
Fire Alarm
Systems

**YOUR NAME**
President/CEO

123 Example Boulevard
Your City, State 12345 6789
E-mail info@emailaddressz.com

Lorem ipsum dolor sit amet, con
tincidunt ut laoreet dolore magn
nostrud exerci tation ullamcorpe
autem vel eum iriure dolor in he
eu feugiat nulla facilisis at vero e
luptatum zzril delenit augue du

A one-sentence
"hook" benefit
that describes
your product
or service

Sampler
Fire Alarm
Systems

Nam liber tempor cum soluta n
mazim placerat facer possim as
diam nonummy nibh euismod

Best regards,

Josh S. Example
President
coc
Enclosures (2)

123 Example Boulevard,
Your City, State 12345 6789
Voice 987 654 3210
Fax 987 654 3210
www.yourwebaddressz.com
E-mail info@emailaddressz.com

A one-sentence
"hook" benefit
that describes
your product
or service

Sampler
Fire Alarm
Systems

May 16, 2???

Sarah W. Example
Director of Marketing
Sampler Corporation
1234 Street Address
Your City, ST 12345-6789

Sarah:

Lorem ipsum dolor sit amet, consectetuer adipiscing elit, sed diam nonummy nibh euismod tincidunt ut laoreet dolore magna aliquam erat volutpat. Ut wisi enim ad minim veniam, quis nostrud exerci tation ullamcorper suscipit lobortis nisl ut aliquip ex ea commodo consequat. Duis autem vel eum iriure dolor in hendrerit in vulputate velit esse molestie consequat, vel illum dolore eu feugiat nulla facilisis at vero eros et accumsan et iusto odio dignissim qui blandit praesent.

Lorem ipsum dolor sit amet, consectetuer adipiscing elit, sed diam nonummy nibh euismod tincidunt ut laoreet dolore magna aliquam erat volutpat. Ut wisi enim ad minim veniam, quis nostrud exerci tation ullamcorper suscipit lobortis nisl ut aliquip ex ea commodo consequat. Duis autem vel eum iriure dolor in hendrerit in vulputate velit esse molestie consequat, vel illum dolore eu feugiat nulla facilisis at vero eros et accumsan et iusto odio dignissim qui blandit praesent luptatum zzril delenit augue duis dolore te feugait nulla facilisi.

Nam liber tempor cum soluta nobis eleifend option congue nihil imperdiet doming id quod mazim placerat facer possim assum. Lorem ipsum dolor sit amet, consectetuer adipiscing elit, sed diam nonummy nibh euismod tincidunt ut laoreet dolore magna aliquam erat volutpat.

Best regards,

Josh S. Example
President
coc
Enclosures (2)

123 Example Boulevard
Your City, State 12345 6789
Voice 987 654 3210
Fax 987 654 3210
www.yourwebaddressz.com
E-mail info@emailaddressz.com

**Business Card, Front**  3.5 W by 2 H inches

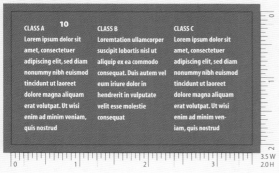

www.yourwebaddressz.com
Voice 987 654 3210
Fax 987 654 3210

A one-sentence
"hook" benefit
that describes
your product
or service

**SF**
**AS**

Sampler
Fire Alarm
Systems

YOUR NAME
President / CEO

123 Example Boulevard
Your City, State 12345 6789
E-mail info@emailaddressz.com

3.5 W
2.0 H

**Business Card, Back**  3.5 W by 2 H inches

**CLASS A**  **10**
Lorem ipsum dolor sit
amet, consectetuer
adipiscing elit, sed diam
nonummy nibh euismod
tincidunt ut laoreet
dolore magna aliquam
erat volutpat. Ut wisi
enim ad minim veniam,
quis nostrud

**CLASS B**
Loremtation ullamcorper
suscipit lobortis nisl ut
aliquip ex ea commodo
consequat. Duis autem vel
eum iriure dolor in
hendrerit in vulputate
velit esse molestie
consequat

**CLASS C**
Lorem ipsum dolor sit
amet, consectetuer
adipiscing elit, sed diam
nonummy nibh euismod
tincidunt ut laoreet
dolore magna aliquam
erat volutpat. Ut wisi
enim ad minim ven-
iam, quis nostrud

3.5 W
2.0 H

**Envelope, Commercial**  9.5 W by 4.125 H inches

123 Example Boulevard
Your City, State 12345 6789

A one-sentence
"hook" benefit
that describes
your product
or service

**SF**
**AS**

Sampler
Fire Alarm
Systems

9.5 W
4.125 H

### Letterhead

**1** Burst 500 points **2** Defining phrase Myriad Regular, 6/10pt, align left; **3** "SFAS" Interstate UltraBlack, 52pt; **4** Organization Myriad Regular, 10.5/10.5pt, align left; **5** Letter body Minion, 12/18pt, align left; **6** Address Myriad Regular, 7.5/10pt, align left

### Business Card, Front

**7** Address Myriad Regular, 7.5/10pt, align left; Title Myriad Regular, 7pt, align left; **8** Defining phrase Myriad Regular, 4.5/7pt, align left; "SFAS" Interstate UltraBlack, 39pt; **9** Organization Myriad Regular, 8.5/8.5pt, align left

### Business Card, Back

**10** Text Myriad Multiple Master (MM), 700bd, 300cn, 8/12pt, align left

### Envelope

**11** Address Myriad Regular, 7/9pt, align left; **12** "SFAS" Interstate UltraBlack, 39pt; Defining phrase Myriad Regular, 4.5/7pt, align left; Organization Myriad Regular, 8.5/8.5pt, align left

### Color

Printed in four-color process (see Step 9.3) using values of cyan, magenta, yellow, and black (CMYK) as defined on the color palette below. Actual color will vary.

Process Colors

| | | | |
|---|---|---|---|
| C0 | M100 | Y70 | K10 |
| C0 | M60 | Y100 | K0 |
| C60 | M70 | Y0 | K10 |
| C85 | M0 | Y35 | K20 |
| C30 | M0 | Y10 | K5 |

STYLE 5

# Circles

How do you represent a concept as abstract as intellectual property? By defining the term in its most literal form. Intellectual property is an idea—an invention, trademark, design, or artistic work. Therefore, what is the customer benefit of using a firm that offers protection of intellectual property? Simple: the protection of the client's ideas—idea security.

Start by identifying symbols that represent the concept of an idea—a question mark and a light bulb are two obvious choices. For security, how about a safe or a lock? Combine two—a lock and a light bulb—and the result is a simple, effective icon.

SOURCE Illustrations: Light bulb, lock from *Universal Symbols* by Image Club Clip Art, 800-661-9410, 403-294-3195, www.eyewire.com, © Image Club Graphics, all rights reserved.

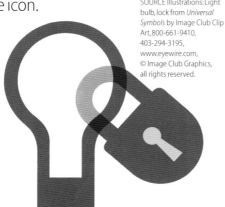

Two simple symbols in a draw/vector file format: The light bulb represents ideas, and the lock represents security. (See *Symbol Logos* on page 32.)

Reducing the size of the lock to roughly 75 percent makes the "idea" bulb the anchoring element. Rotating it and overlapping the edge of the bulb results in a third idea: idea security.

Dividing the artwork allows you to edit individual elements. The black outlines show that the images are now divided into ten individual shapes.

Applying different screen values of the same color adds a sense of transparency. Where paths cross, colors darken. When one shape is behind the other (the top of the lock is behind the edge of the bulb), the shape behind is lighter.

**The Sampler Group**

**The Sampler Group**

Reducing the size of "The" and fitting the words together forms a simple but effective wordmark. (See *All-Type Logos* on page 28.)

**The Sampler Group**

Adding a circle pulls the elements together. These curved shapes work well with a circle. If your logo is square or rectangular, a square or rectangular background shape may work best.

SOURCE Type families: Myriad, Minion, Adobe Systems, Inc., 800-682-3623, www.adobe.com/type.

 **What you need**

Breaking apart draw/vector artwork and editing the pieces requires a draw program such as Adobe Illustrator, CorelDRAW, or Macromedia FreeHand. Simple text and shapes can be produced with a desktop publishing program such as Adobe InDesign, Adobe PageMaker, QuarkXPress, or Microsoft Publisher.

# The Sampler Group

May 16, 2???

Sarah W. Example
Director of Marketing
Sampler Corporation
1234 Street Address
Your City, ST 12345-6789

Sarah:

Lorem ipsum dolor sit amet, consectet
tincidunt ut laoreet dolore magn
nostrud e
autem
eu feu

Lorem
tincidu
nostrud
autem ve
eu feugia
luptatum

Nam liber t
mazim plac
diam nonun

Best regards,

Josh S. Example
President
coc
Enclosures (2)

## The Sampler Group

www.yourwebaddressz.com

987 654 3210
800 987 6543
987 654 3210 Fax
name@youremailaddressz.com

**YOUR NAME**
President/CEO

*A one-sentence "hook" benefit that describes your product or service*

The Sampler Group
123 Example Boulevard
Suite 210
Your City, ST 12345 6789

123 Example Boulevard, Suite 210
Your City, ST 12345 6789

## The Sampler Group

ipsum dolor sit amet, consectetuer
adipiscing elit, sed diam nonummy nibh euismod
tincidunt ut laoreet dolore magna aliquam.

- Service list – Lorem ipsum dolor sit amet
- Service list – Eonsectetuer adipiscing elit, sed diam nonummy nibh euismod tincidunt
- Service list – Ut laoreet dolore magna

The Sampler Group

The Sampler Group
123 Example Boulevard, Suite 210
Your City, ST 12345 6789
987 654 3210
800 987 6543
987 654 3210 Fax
www.yourwebaddressz.com
E-mail info@youremailaddressz.com

**The Sampler Group** ①

*A one-sentence "hook" benefit that describes your product or service* ②

May 16, 2???

Sarah W. Example
Director of Marketing
Sampler Corporation
1234 Street Address
Your City, ST 12345-6789

③

Sarah:

Lorem ipsum dolor sit amet, consectetuer adipiscing elit, sed diam nonummy nibh euismod tincidunt ut laoreet dolore magna aliquam erat volutpat. Ut wisi enim ad minim veniam, quis nostrud exerci tation ullamcorper suscipit lobortis nisl ut aliquip ex ea commodo consequat. Duis autem vel eum iriure dolor in hendrerit in vulputate velit esse molestie consequat, vel illum dolore eu feugiat nulla facilisis at vero eros et accumsan et iusto odio dignissim qui blandit praesent.

Lorem ipsum dolor sit amet, consectetuer adipiscing elit, sed diam nonummy nibh euismod tincidunt ut laoreet dolore magna aliquam erat volutpat. Ut wisi enim ad minim veniam, quis nostrud exerci tation ullamcorper suscipit lobortis nisl ut aliquip ex ea commodo consequat. Duis autem vel eum iriure dolor in hendrerit in vulputate velit esse molestie consequat, vel illum dolore eu feugiat nulla facilisis at vero eros et accumsan et iusto odio dignissim qui blandit praesent luptatum zzril delenit augue duis dolore te feugait nulla facilisi.

Nam liber tempor cum soluta nobis eleifend option congue nihil imperdiet doming id quod mazim placerat facer possim assum. Lorem ipsum dolor sit amet, consectetuer adipiscing elit, sed diam nonummy nibh euismod tincidunt ut laoreet dolore magna aliquam erat volutpat.

Best regards,

Josh S. Example
President
coc
Enclosures (2)

The Sampler Group
123 Example Boulevard, Suite 210
Your City, ST 12345 6789
987 654 3210
800 987 6543
987 654 3210 Fax
www.yourwebaddressz.com
E-mail  info@youremailaddressz.com
④

## Business Card, Front  3.5 W by 2 H inches

The**Sampler**
Group

www.yourwebaddressz.com

987 654 3210
800 987 6543
987 654 3210 Fax
name@youremailaddressz.com

YOUR NAME
President/CEO

The Sampler Group
123 Example Boulevard
Suite 210
Your City, ST 12345 6789

*A one-sentence "hook"
benefit that describes your
product or service*

```
|''''|''''|''''|''''|''''|''''|''''|''''|''''|''''|''''|   3.5 W
0            1            2            3                     2.0 H
   .25                 1.75
```

## Business Card, Back  3.5 W by 2 H inches

WHAT WE DO
Lorem ipsum dolor sit amet, consectetuer
adipiscing elit, sed diam nonummy nibh euismod
tincidunt ut laoreet dolore magna aliquam.

- Service list – Lorem ipsum dolor sit amet
- Service list – Eonsectetuer adipiscing elit, sed diam
  nonummy nibh euismod tincidunt
- Service list – Ut laoreet dolore magna

The**Sampler**
Group

```
|''''|''''|''''|''''|''''|''''|''''|''''|''''|''''|''''|   3.5 W
0            1            2            3                     2.0 H
```

## Envelope, Commercial  9.5 W by 4.125 H inches

123 Example Boulevard, Suite 210
Your City, ST 12345 6789

The**Sampler**
Group

```
|''''|''''|''''|''''|''''|''''|''''|''''|''''|''''|''''|''''|''''|''''|''''|''''|''''|''''|''''|   9.5 W
0      1      2      3      4      5      6      7      8      9                                   4.125 H
   .375
```

---

### Letterhead

**1** "The" Myriad Multiple Master (MM), 700bd, 300cn, 18pt; "Sampler" Myriad MM, 700bd, 300cn, 26pt; **2** Defining phrase Myriad MM Italic, 400 weight, 500 width, 8/11pt, align left; **3** Letter body Minion, 12/18pt, align left; **4** Address Myriad MM, 400 weight, 500 width, 8/10pt, align left

### Business Card, Front

**5** "The" Myriad MM, 700bd, 300cn, 18pt; "Sampler" Myriad MM, 700bd, 300cn, 26pt; **6** Name/Title Myriad MM, 400 weight, 500 width, 8/10pt, align left; Defining phrase Myriad MM Italic, 400 weight, 500 width, 8/10pt, align left; **7** Address Myriad MM, 400 weight, 500 width, 8/11pt, align left

### Business Card, Back

**8** "WHAT" Myriad MM, 400 weight, 500 width, 8/11pt, align left; Text Myriad MM Italic, 400 weight, 500 width, 9/11pt, align left; **9** "The" Myriad MM, 700bd, 300cn, 13pt; "Sampler" Myriad MM, 700bd, 300cn, 18pt

### Envelope

**10** Address Myriad MM, 400 weight, 500 width, 8/11pt; **11** "The" Myriad MM, 700bd, 300cn, 12pt; "Sampler" Myriad MM, 700bd, 300cn, 17pt, align left

### Color

To be printed in black and a solid PANTONE Color Ink as defined on the palette below (see Step 9.3). (Because this book is printed in process colors (CMYK), the illustration is only a simulation of the actual solid PANTONE Color).

Violet or
PANTONE® 265

| 100% |
| 75% |
| 40% |
| 20% |
| 10% |

STYLE 6

# Comics

Being funny is serious business. When appropriate, humor is an effective way to win people to your way of thinking. The challenge is to determine if a funny or lighthearted logo and letterhead scheme projects an appropriate image for your organization. Only you can make that judgment.

If you do opt for this approach, insist on first-class artwork. Like a stand-up comic, you should not venture on stage without proven, professional material.

SOURCES Illustrations: Cartoons from *Task Force Image Gallery* by NVTech, 800-387-0732, 613-727-8184, www.nvtech.com, © NVTech, all rights reserved; spiral background from *Design Elements* by Ultimate Symbol, 800-611-4761, 914-942-0003, www.ultimatesymbol.com, © Ultimate Symbol, all rights reserved.

The style centers around a real comic book typeface called WildAndCrazy from Comic Book Fonts, a masterful group of real comic book illustrators. Using something that looks somewhat like a comic typeface won't cut it.

The quality of the illustrations must be strong enough to carry the design. These are bright, colorful, and well executed. Using a different character on each layout maximizes the overall effect.

The radiating background pattern adds movement to the logo. The original artwork is stretched to give it perspective.

Adding a yellow tint to the background of the letterhead and business card makes the speech balloons and the character's eyes pop off the page.

SOURCES Type families: WildAndCrazy, Comic Book Fonts, www.comicbookfonts.com; Minion, Myriad, Adobe Systems, Inc., 800-682-3623, www.adobe.com/type.

 **What you need**

Combining multiple pieces of artwork requires a draw program such as Adobe Illustrator, CorelDRAW, or Macromedia FreeHand. Simple text and shapes can be produced with a desktop publishing program such as Adobe InDesign, Adobe PageMaker, QuarkXPress, or Microsoft Publisher.

www.yourwebaddressz.com
Voice 987 654 3210
Fax 987 654 3210

YOUR NAME
President/CEO

123 Example Boulevard
Your City, State 12345 6789
E-mail info@emailaddressz.com

**SAMPLER CENTER**
*NUTRITION THERAPY FOR CHILDREN*

A one-paragraph "hook" benefit that describes your product or service

**SAMPLER CENTER**
*NUTRITION THERAPY FOR CHILDREN*

*DOLOR SIT AMET, CONSEC TETUER*

123 Example Boulevard
Your City, State 12345 6789

**SAMPLER CENTER**
*NUTRITION THERAPY FOR CHILDREN*

A one-paragraph "hook" benefit that describes your product or service

May 16,

Sarah W. Example
Director of Marketing
Sampler Corporation
1234 Street Address
Your City, ST 12345-6789

Sarah:

Lorem ipsum dolor sit amet, consectetuer adipis
tincidunt ut laoreet dolore magna aliquam erat
nostrud exerci tation ullamcorper suscipit lobo
autem vel eum iriure dolor in hendrerit in vul
eu feugiat nulla facilisis at vero eros et accuma

Lorem ipsum dolor sit amet, consectetuer ad
tincidunt ut laoreet dolore magna aliquam e
nostrud exerci tation ullamcorper suscipit l
autem vel eum iriure dolor in hendrerit in
eu feugiat nulla facilisis at vero eros et ac
luptatum zzril delenit augue duis dolore t

Nam liber tempor cum soluta nobis eleifend option congue nihil imperdie
mazim placerat facer possim assum. Lorem ipsum dolor sit amet, consectetuer adipiscing elit, se
diam nonummy nibh euismod tincidunt ut laoreet dolore magna aliquam erat volutpat.

Best regards,

Josh S. Example
President
coc
Enclosures (2)

A one-paragraph "hook" benefit that describes your product or service

123 Example Boulevard,
Your City, State 12345 6789
Voice 987 654 3210
Fax 987 654 3210
www.yourwebaddressz.com
E-mail info@emailaddressz.com

SAMPLER
CENTER
NUTRITION
THERAPY FOR
CHILDREN

May 16, 2???

Sarah W. Example
Director of Marketing
Sampler Corporation
1234 Street Address
Your City, ST 12345-6789

Sarah:

Lorem ipsum dolor sit amet, consectetuer adipiscing elit, sed diam nonummy nibh euismod tincidunt ut laoreet dolore magna aliquam erat volutpat. Ut wisi enim ad minim veniam, quis nostrud exerci tation ullamcorper suscipit lobortis nisl ut aliquip ex ea commodo consequat. Duis autem vel eum iriure dolor in hendrerit in vulputate velit esse molestie consequat, vel illum dolore eu feugiat nulla facilisis at vero eros et accumsan et iusto odio dignissim qui blandit praesent.

Lorem ipsum dolor sit amet, consectetuer adipiscing elit, sed diam nonummy nibh euismod tincidunt ut laoreet dolore magna aliquam erat volutpat. Ut wisi enim ad minim veniam, quis nostrud exerci tation ullamcorper suscipit lobortis nisl ut aliquip ex ea commodo consequat. Duis autem vel eum iriure dolor in hendrerit in vulputate velit esse molestie consequat, vel illum dolore eu feugiat nulla facilisis at vero eros et accumsan et iusto odio dignissim qui blandit praesent luptatum zzril delenit augue duis dolore te feugait nulla facilisi.

Nam liber tempor cum soluta nobis eleifend option congue nihil imperdiet doming id quod mazim placerat facer possim assum. Lorem ipsum dolor sit amet, consectetuer adipiscing elit, sed diam nonummy nibh euismod tincidunt ut laoreet dolore magna aliquam erat volutpat.

Best regards,

Josh S. Example
President
coc
Enclosures (2)

A one-paragraph "hook" benefit that describes your product or service

123 Example Boulevard,
Your City, State 12345 6789
Voice 987 654 3210
Fax 987 654 3210
www.yourwebaddressz.com
E-mail  info@emailaddressz.com

May 16, 2???

## Business Card, Front   3.5 W by 2 H inches

## Business Card, Back   3.5 W by 2 H inches

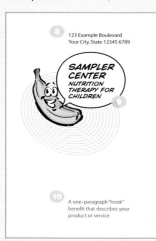

## Envelope, Commercial   9.5 W by 4.125 H inches

### Letterhead

**1** Lines 1.75pt; **Organization** WildAndCrazy, 16/18pt, align left; "NUTRI-TION" WildAndCrazy, 11/13pt, align left; **2** Letter body Minion, 12/18pt, align left; **3** Defining phrase Myriad Regular, 7.5/10pt, align left; **Address** Myriad Regular, 7.5/10pt, align left

### Business Card, Front

**4** Phone/Address/Name Myriad Regular, 8/10pt, align left; **Title** Myriad Regular, 7/10pt, align left; **5** Lines 1pt; **Organization** WildAndCrazy, 12/14pt, align left; "NUTRITION" WildAndCrazy, 9/10pt, align left; **6** Defining phrase Myriad Regular, 7/9pt, align left

### Business Card, Back

**7** Lines 1pt; **Organization** WildAndCrazy, 7/9pt, align left

### Envelope

**8** Address Myriad Regular, 7/9pt, align left; **9** Lines 1pt; **Organization** WildAndCrazy, 11/12pt, align left; "NUTRITION" WildAndCrazy, 7/8pt, align left; **10** Defining phrase Myriad Regular, 7/9pt, align left

### Color

Printed in four-color process (see Step 9.3) using values of cyan, magenta, yellow, and black (CMYK) as defined in the clip art and on the color palette below. Actual color will vary.

Process Colors

| C0 | M80 | Y100 | K0 | C0 |
|----|-----|------|----|----|
| C0 | M10 | Y40  | K0 |    |
| C0 | M0  | Y10  | K0 |    |

STYLE 7

# Corners

For this style, the logo is pushed into the corner and off the edge of the page. Why? Because designing it that way is a little unexpected. And that is one sure way to attract attention—by showing your audience something they might not have pictured themselves.

Do something unexpected with the logo. Change any of the four basic elements used to design it—the box, the clip art image, the typeface, or the color—and you've added something new to the idea.

How do you make clip art images unique? By adding two or three together. The basic artwork for these logos is nothing more than a combination of two or more simple images.

The artwork is sized and rotated to comfortably fill the space reserved for the type. Solid color and tints are applied and the portions of the image that extend beyond the edge of the box are removed.

SAMPLER INDUSTRIAL LIGHTING

The no-frills typeface is used to spell the name of the organization in three strips. You can add or subtract strips to accommodate your organization's name.

This and several other projects are printed using two colors—black and one solid color. By using the solid color and two or three different tints, you add a sense that there are more than two colors.

It is an easily adaptable design that can be used with a variety of different image combinations.

SOURCE Illustrations: Compass rose, bulbs, branches, from *Design Elements* by Ultimate Symbol, 800-611-4761, 914-942-0003, www.ultimate symbol.com, © Ultimate Symbol, all rights reserved.

SOURCES Type families: OCR-A, AGFA/Monotype, 888-988-2432, 978-658-0200, www.agfamono type.com; Franklin Gothic, Minion, Adobe Systems, Inc., 800-682-3623, www.adobe.com/type.

**What you need**
Breaking apart draw/vector artwork and editing the pieces requires a draw program such as Adobe Illustrator, CorelDRAW, or Macromedia FreeHand. Simple text and shapes can be produced with a desktop publishing program such as Adobe InDesign, Adobe PageMaker, QuarkXPress, or Microsoft Publisher.

May 16, 2???

Sarah W. Example
Director of Marketing
Sampler Corporation
1234 Street Address
Your City, ST 12345-6789

Sarah:

Lorem ipsum dolor sit amet, consec
tincidunt ut laoreet dolore magna a
nostrud exerci tation ullamcorper s
autem vel eum iriure dolor in henc
eu feugiat nulla facilisis at vero erc

Lorem ipsum dol   it amet, consectetuer ad
tincidunt ut laor
nostrud exerci ta
autem vel eum                                    sim qui blandit praesent
eu feugiat nulla
luptatum zzril                                   nperdiet doming id quod

Nam liber ter                                    consectetuer adipiscing elit, sed
mazim place                                      aliquam erat volutpat.
diam nonummy nibh euismod

Best regards,

Josh S. Example
President
coc
Enclosures (2)

A one-sentence
"hook" benefit that
describes your
product or service

**SAMPLER INDUSTRIAL LIGHTING**

Furniture Mart, 4th Floor
123 Example Boulevard
Your City, ST 12345 6789

**WHAT WE DO**
Lorem ipsum dolor sit amet, consectetuer
adipiscing elit, sed diam nonummy nibh euis sit amet
ut laoreet dolore magna aliquam.

- Service list – Lorem ipsum dolor sit amet nibh euis
- Service list – Ipsum consectetuer adipiscing elit
  nonummy nibh euismod tincidunt
- Service list – Ut laoreet dolore magna
- Service list – Ipsum dolor sit amet nibh euis

A one-sentence "hook" benefit that describes your product or service

YOUR NAME
President/CEO
www.yourwebaddressz.com
987 654 3210
987 654 3210 Fax
name@emailaddressz.com
Furniture Mart, 4th Floor
123 Example Boulevard
Your City, ST 12345 6789

Furniture Mart, 4th Floor
123 Example Boulevard
Your City, ST 12345 6789
987 654 3210
987 654 3210 Fax
www.yourwebaddressz.com
E-mail info@emailaddressz.com

SAMPLER
INDUSTRIAL
LIGHTING

May 16, 2???


Sarah W. Example
Director of Marketing
Sampler Corporation
1234 Street Address
Your City, ST 12345-6789


Sarah:

Lorem ipsum dolor sit amet, consectetuer adipiscing elit, sed diam nonummy nibh euismod tincidunt ut laoreet dolore magna aliquam erat volutpat. Ut wisi enim ad minim veniam, quis nostrud exerci tation ullamcorper suscipit lobortis nisl ut aliquip ex ea commodo consequat. Duis autem vel eum iriure dolor in hendrerit in vulputate velit esse molestie consequat, vel illum dolore eu feugiat nulla facilisis at vero eros et accumsan et iusto odio dignissim qui blandit praesent.

Lorem ipsum dolor sit amet, consectetuer adipiscing elit, sed diam nonummy nibh euismod tincidunt ut laoreet dolore magna aliquam erat volutpat. Ut wisi enim ad minim veniam, quis nostrud exerci tation ullamcorper suscipit lobortis nisl ut aliquip ex ea commodo consequat. Duis autem vel eum iriure dolor in hendrerit in vulputate velit esse molestie consequat, vel illum dolore eu feugiat nulla facilisis at vero eros et accumsan et iusto odio dignissim qui blandit praesent luptatum zzril delenit augue duis dolore te feugait nulla facilisi.

Nam liber tempor cum soluta nobis eleifend option congue nihil imperdiet doming id quod mazim placerat facer possim assum. Lorem ipsum dolor sit amet, consectetuer adipiscing elit, sed diam nonummy nibh euismod tincidunt ut laoreet dolore magna aliquam erat volutpat.

Best regards,



Josh S. Example
President
coc
Enclosures (2)

A one-sentence
"hook" benefit that
describes your
product or service

Furniture Mart, 4th Floor
123 Example Boulevard
Your City, ST 12345 6789
987 654 3210
987 654 3210 Fax
www.yourwebaddressz.com
E-mail  info@emailaddressz.com

**Business Card, Front**  3.5 W by 2 H inches

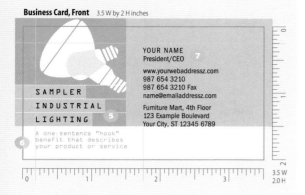

YOUR NAME
President/CEO  **7**

www.yourwebaddressz.com
987 654 3210
987 654 3210 Fax
name@emailaddressz.com

S A M P L E R
I N D U S T R I A L
L I G H T I N G  **5**

A one-sentence "hook"
benefit that describes
your product or service  **6**

| | | | | | | |
0  1  2  3  3.5 W  2.0 H

**Business Card, Back**  3.5 W by 2 H inches

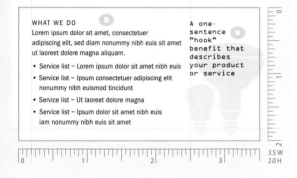

WHAT WE DO  **8**
Lorem ipsum dolor sit amet, consectetuer
adipiscing elit, sed diam nonummy nibh euis sit amet
ut laoreet dolore magna aliquam.

- Service list – Lorem ipsum dolor sit amet nibh euis
- Service list – Ipsum consectetuer adipiscing elit
  nonummy nibh euismod tincidunt
- Service list – Ut laoreet dolore magna
- Service list – Ipsum dolor sit amet nibh euis
  iam nonummy nibh euis sit amet

A one-
sentence
"hook"  **9**
benefit that
describes
your product
or service

0  1  2  3  3.5 W  2.0 H

**Envelope, Commercial**  9.5 W by 4.125 H inches

  **10**

S A M P L E R
I N D U S T R I A L
L I G H T I N G

Furniture Mart, 4th Floor
123 Example Boulevard
Your City, ST 12345 6789

A one-sentence
"hook" benefit that  **11**
describes your
product or service

0  1  2  3  4  5  6  7  8  9  9.5 W  4.125 H

### Letterhead

**1** Lines 0.4pt; Organization OCR-A Regular, 9/15pt, align left; **2** Letter body Minion, 12/18pt, align left; **3** Defining phrase OCR-A Regular, 8/11pt, align left; **4** Address Franklin Gothic Book, 8/12pt, align left

### Business Card, Front

**5** Lines 0.5pt; Organization OCR-A Regular, 9/15pt, align left; **6** Defining phrase OCR-A Regular, 7/7pt, align left; **7** Address Franklin Gothic Book, 8/9pt, align left

### Business Card, Back

**8** "WHAT" Franklin Gothic Book, 8/11pt, align left; **9** Defining phrase OCR-A Regular, 8/9pt, align left

### Envelope

**10** Lines 0.35pt; Organization OCR-A Regular, 9/15pt, align left; Address Franklin Gothic Book, 7/9pt, align left; **11** Defining phrase OCR-A Regular, 7/10pt, align left

### Color

To be printed in black and a solid PANTONE Color Ink as defined on the palette below (see Step 9.3). (Because this book is printed in process colors (CMYK), the illustration is only a simulation of the actual solid PANTONE Color).

Light Olive or
PANTONE® 5845

| |
|---|
| 100% |
| 60% |
| 30% |

STYLE 8

# Experimental

This layout breaks all the rules: The Z-folded letterhead and window envelope eliminate the need for a mailing label. The business card is designed to fit a rotary file. And every other aspect of the design—from the way the information is organized to the signature block on the right-hand column—flies in the face of convention.

Hopefully, it will cause you to question why we do things the way we've always done them and encourage you to rethink your letterhead, business card, and envelope.

SOURCE Illustrations: Penguin from *Designer's Club* from Dynamic Graphics 800-255-8800, 309-688-8800, www.dgusa.com, © Dynamic Graphics, all rights reserved.

The letter is designed to be Z-folded so that the return and recipient's addresses show through the windows in the envelope. How much time and money will you save if you don't have to address an envelope?

Moving the address information to the left leaves a big space for your logo and defining phrase.

A clip art illustration is combined with a series of lines to give a sense of motion.

The design of the letterhead and rotary card use a windowpane grid to visually organize and present the information.

Lots of organizations would profit from offering its business card in the form of a rotary card. Your commercial printer can arrange to have it die-cut in the correct shape.

Tints are a cost-effective way to make a two-color layout far more visually interesting.

SOURCE Type families: Minion, Myriad, Adobe Systems, Inc., 800-682-3623, www.adobe.com/type.

 **What you need**

Breaking apart draw/vector artwork and editing the pieces requires a draw program such as Adobe Illustrator, CorelDRAW, or Macromedia FreeHand. Simple text and shapes can be produced with a desktop publishing program such as Adobe InDesign, Adobe PageMaker, QuarkXPress, or Microsoft Publisher.

Sampler Refrigeration
123 Example Boulevard
Your City, State 12345 6789

A one-paragraph "hook"
benefit that describes
your product or service

Sampler Refrigeration
123 Example Boulevard
Your City, State 12345 6789
OR
Post Office Box 12345
Your City, State 12345 6789

**Sampler
Refrigeration**

Sarah W. Example
Sampler Corporation
1234 Street Address
Your City, ST 12345-6789

Voice 987 654 3210
Fax 987 654 3210

Sarah Anne:   Lorem ipsum dolor sit amet, consectetuer adipiscing elit, sed diam
nonummy nibh e[...] ut laoreet dolore magna
[...]eniam, quis nostrud
[...] ut aliquip ex ea
[...]re dolor in hendrerit
[...]lore eu
[...]odio
[...]gue duis

May 16, 2???

Best regards,

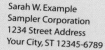

Josh S. Example
PRESIDENT
exam@emailaddressz.com

ABOUT SAMPLER
REFRIGERATION Lorem ipsum
dolor sit amet, consectetuer
adipiscing elit[...]

[...]scing elit, sed
[...]lore magna
[...]quis nostrud
[...]uip ex ea
[...]r in hendrerit

in vulputat[...]it [...]te [...]
feugiat nulla facilis[...]

A one paragraph "hook"
benefit that describes
your product or service

**Sampler
Refrigeration**

Sampler Refrigeration
123 Example Boulevard
Your City, State 12345 6789

**1**

**3** A one-paragraph "hook"
benefit that describes
your product or service

Sampler Refrigeration
123 Example Boulevard
Your City, State 12345 6789
OR
Post Office Box 12345
Your City, State 12345 6789

**5**

**4** **Sampler Refrigeration**

Sarah W. Example
Sampler Corporation
1234 Street Address
Your City, ST 12345-6789

**2**

Voice 987 654 3210
Fax 987 654 3210

**6**

Sarah Anne:

Lorem ipsum dolor sit amet, consectetuer adipiscing elit, sed diam nonummy nibh euismod tincidunt ut laoreet dolore magna aliquam erat volutpat. Ut wisi enim ad minim veniam, quis nostrud exerci tation ullamcorper suscipit lobortis nisl ut aliquip ex ea commodo consequat. Duis autem vel eum iriure dolor in hendrerit in vulputate velit esse molestie consequat, vel illum dolore eu feugiat nulla facilisis at vero eros et accumsan et iusto odio dignissim qui blandit praesent luptatum zzril delenit augue duis dolore te feugait nulla facilisi.

Lorem ipsum dolor sit amet, consectetuer adipiscing elit, sed diam nonummy nibh euismod tincidunt ut laoreet dolore magna aliquam erat volutpat. Ut wisi enim ad minim veniam, quis nostrud exerci tation ullamcorper suscipit lobortis nisl ut aliquip ex ea commodo consequat. Duis autem vel eum iriure dolor in hendrerit in vulputate velit esse molestie consequat, vel illum dolore eu feugiat nulla facilisis at vero eros et accumsan et iusto odio dignissim qui blandit praesent luptatum zzril delenit augue duis dolore te feugait nulla facilisi.

Nam liber tempor cum soluta nobis eleifend option congue nihil imperdiet doming id quod mazim placerat facer possim assum. Lorem ipsum dolor sit amet, consectetuer adipiscing elit, sed diam nonummy nibh euismod tincidunt ut laoreet dolore magna aliquam erat volutpat.

**7**

**www.yourwebaddressz.com**

**8**

May 16, 2???

**9**

Best regards,

Josh S. Example
PRESIDENT
exam@emailaddressz.com

**10**

ABOUT SAMPLER
REFRIGERATION Lorem ipsum
dolor sit amet, consectetuer
adipiscing elit, sed diam
nonummy nibh euismod
tincidunt ut laoreet dolore
magna aliquam erat volutpat.

ABOUT Mr. EXAMPLE Ut wisi
enim ad minim veniam, quis
nostrud exerci tation
ullamcorper suscipit lobortis
nisl ut aliquip ex ea commodo
consequat. Duis autem vel
eum iriure dolor in hendrerit
in vulputate velit esse
molestie consequat.

**11**

8.5 W
11 H

## Business Card, Front   4 W by 2.625 H inches

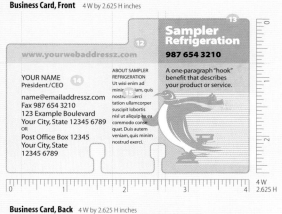

## Business Card, Back   4 W by 2.625 H inches

| CONVERSIONS TABLE A | CONVERSIONS TABLE B | CONVERSIONS TABLE C | CONVERSIONS TABLE D |
|---|---|---|---|
| 123567 > 890123 | 123567 > 890123 | 123567 > 890123 | 123567 > 890123 |
| 123567 > 890123 | 123567 > 890123 | 123567 > 890123 | 123567 > 890123 |
| 123567 > 890123 | 123567 > 890123 | 123567 > 890123 | 123567 > 890123 |
| 123567 > 890123 | 123567 > 890123 | 123567 > 890123 | 123567 > 890123 |
| 123567 > 890123 | 123567 > 890123 | 123567 > 890123 | 123567 > 890123 |
| 123567 > 890123 | 123567 > 890123 | 123567 > 890123 | 123567 > 890123 |
| 123567 > 890123 | 123567 > 890123 | 123567 > 890123 | 123567 > 890123 |

### Letterhead

**1** Return address Myriad Regular, 11/14pt, align left; **2** Send to address Myriad Regular, 11/14pt, align left; **3** Defining phrase Myriad Regular, 11/12pt, align left; **4** "Sampler" Myriad Multiple Master (MM), 830bl, 700se, 20pt, align left; "Refrigeration" Myriad MM, 830bl, 700se, 18pt, align left; **5** Address Myriad Regular, 9/10pt, align left; "OR" Myriad Regular, 6pt, align left; **6** Phone Myriad Regular, 9/10pt, align left; **7** Letter body Myriad Regular, 12/18pt, align left; **8** Web address Myriad MM, 830bl, 700se, 18pt, align left; **9** Date/salutation Myriad Regular, 12pt, align left; **10** Name Myriad Regular, 12pt, align left; "PRESIDENT" Myriad Regular, 9/12pt, align left; **11** "ABOUT" Myriad Regular, 9/10pt, align left

### Business Card, Front

**12** Web address Myriad MM, 830bl, 700se, 10pt; **13** "Sampler" Myriad MM, 830bl, 700se, 17pt, align left; "Refrigeration" Myriad MM, 830bl, 700se, 14pt, align left; Phone Myriad MM, 830bl, 700se, 10pt, align left; Defining phrase Myriad Regular, 8/9pt, align left; **14** "NAME"/address Myriad Regular, 9/10pt, align left; Title Myriad Regular, 8pt, align left; "OR" Myriad Regular, 6pt, align left; **15** "ABOUT" Myriad Regular, 6/8pt, align left; **16** "CONVERSIONS" Myriad MM, 830bl, 700se, 7.5/7.5pt, align left; Numbers Myriad Regular, 7.5/12.5pt, align left

### Envelope

**17** Defining phrase Myriad Regular, 11/12pt, align left; "Sampler" Myriad MM, 830bl, 700se, 20pt, align left; "Refrigeration" Myriad MM, 830bl, 700se, 18pt, align left

### Color

To be printed in black and a solid PANTONE Color Ink as defined on the palette below (see Step 9.3). (Because this book is printed in process colors (CMYK), the illustration is only a simulation of the actual solid PANTONE Color).

Sky Blue or PANTONE® 550

| |
|---|
| 100% |
| 75% |
| 60% |
| 50% |
| 25% |
| 15% |

## Envelope, Commercial   8.875 W by 3.875 H inches

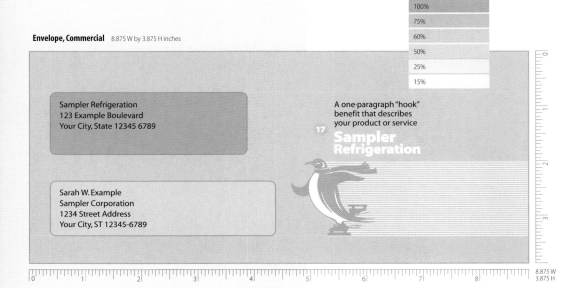

STYLE 9

# Floating Objects

Everything on this layout is floating. Overlapping and offsetting the layers of type used to create the logo is a simple way to create the illusion of depth. Increasing the size of each instrument from top to bottom amplifies it.

When you include this many elements in a design, it is important to keep the background objects subtle. Too much contrast between the background and the instruments would make your letter difficult to read.

A drawing program is used to stack the four layers of the logo. The weight of the line that surrounds each letter (stroke weight) is adjusted to create the outlines.

A simple overlay of lines provides a background on which to position the logo.

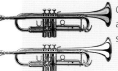

Color is removed from the instrument clip art and the black lines are changed to a tint of the solid green spot color.

Increasing the size of the instruments from top to bottom creates the illusion of depth— larger images are closer, smaller images are farther away.

A one-paragraph "hook" benefit that describes your product or service

SOURCE Illustrations: Instruments from *Task Force Image Gallery* by NVTech, 800-387-0732, 613-727-8184, www.nvtech.com, © NVTech, all rights reserved.

SOURCES Type families: Giza, Font Bureau, 617-423-8770, www.fontbureau.com; Minion, Myriad, Adobe Systems, Inc., 800-682-3623, www.adobe.com/type.

**What you need**

Breaking apart draw/vector artwork and editing the pieces requires a draw program such as Adobe Illustrator, CorelDRAW, or Macromedia FreeHand. Simple text and shapes can be produced with a desktop publishing program such as Adobe InDesign, Adobe PageMaker, QuarkXPress, or Microsoft Publisher.

**SAMPLER MUSIC**

A one-paragraph "hook" benefit that describes your product or service

Sarah W. Example
Director of Marketing
Sampler Corporation

May 16, 2???

**SAMPLER MUSIC**

A one-paragraph "hook" benefit that describes your product or service

**YOUR NAME**
President/CEO

EXAMPLE MALL  123 Example Boulevard, Your City, State 12345 6789
Voice 987 654 3210    Fax 987 654 3210
www.yourwebaddressz.com    E-mail info@emailaddressz.com

amet, con...
adipiscing elit, sed diam
nonummy nibh euismod
tincidunt ut laoreet
dolore magna aliquam
erat volutpat. Ut wisi
enim ad minim veniam,
quis nostrud.

...dipiscing elit, sed diam nonummy nibh euismod ...rat volutpat. Ut wisi enim ad minim veniam, quis ...bortis nisl ut aliquip ex ea commodo consequat. Duis ...lputate velit esse molestie consequat, vel illum dolore ...an et iusto odio dignissim qui blandit praesent.

...ipiscing e... ...nibh euismod ...volutp...
...rper suscipit lobortis ni...

autem vel eum iriure dolor in hendrerit in vulputate...
eu feugiat nulla facilisis at vero eros et accumsan et
luptatum zzril delenit augue duis dolore te feugait

Nam liber tempor cum soluta nobis eleifend optio...
mazim placerat facer possim assum. Lorem ipsum...
diam nonummy nibh euismod tincidunt ut laore...

Best regards,

Josh S. Example
President
coc
Enclosures (2)

**SAMPLER MUSIC**

A one-paragraph "hook" benefit that describes your product or service

EXAMPLE MALL
123 Example Boulevard
Your City, State 12345 6789

EXAMPLE MALL  123 Example Boulevard, Your City, State 12345 6789
Voice 987 654 3210    Fax 987 654 3210    www.yourwebaddressz.com    E-mail info@emailaddressz.com

S A M P L E R
# MUSIC

A one-paragraph "hook" benefit that describes
your product or service

May 16, 2???

Sarah W. Example
Director of Marketing
Sampler Corporation
1234 Street Address
Your City, ST 12345-6789

Sarah:

Lorem ipsum dolor sit amet, consectetuer adipiscing elit, sed diam nonummy nibh euismod
tincidunt ut laoreet dolore magna aliquam erat volutpat. Ut wisi enim ad minim veniam, quis
nostrud exerci tation ullamcorper suscipit lobortis nisl ut aliquip ex ea commodo consequat. Duis
autem vel eum iriure dolor in hendrerit in vulputate velit esse molestie consequat, vel illum dolore
eu feugiat nulla facilisis at vero eros et accumsan et iusto odio dignissim qui blandit praesent.

Lorem ipsum dolor sit amet, consectetuer adipiscing elit, sed diam nonummy nibh euismod
tincidunt ut laoreet dolore magna aliquam erat volutpat. Ut wisi enim ad minim veniam, quis
nostrud exerci tation ullamcorper suscipit lobortis nisl ut aliquip ex ea commodo consequat. Duis
autem vel eum iriure dolor in hendrerit in vulputate velit esse molestie consequat, vel illum dolore
eu feugiat nulla facilisis at vero eros et accumsan et iusto odio dignissim qui blandit praesent
luptatum zzril delenit augue duis dolore te feugait nulla facilisi.

Nam liber tempor cum soluta nobis eleifend option congue nihil imperdiet doming id quod
mazim placerat facer possim assum. Lorem ipsum dolor sit amet, consectetuer adipiscing elit, sed
diam nonummy nibh euismod tincidunt ut laoreet dolore magna aliquam erat volutpat.

Best regards,

Josh S. Example
President
coc
Enclosures (2)

EXAMPLE MALL 123 Example Boulevard, Your City, State 12345 6789
Voice 987 654 3210   Fax 987 654 3210   www.yourwebaddressz.com   E-mail info@emailaddressz.com

**Business Card, Front** 3.5 W by 2 H inches

**Business Card, Back** 3.5 W by 2 H inches

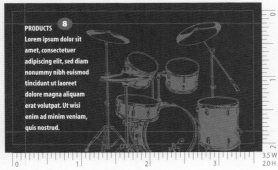

**Envelope, Commercial** 9.5 W by 4.125 H inches

### Letterhead

**1** "SAMPLER" Interstate UltraBlack, 13.5pt, align center; "MUSIC" Giza SevenSeven, 54pt, align center; **2** Defining phrase Myriad Regular, 7/8pt, align center; **3** Letter body Minion, 12/18pt, align left; **4** "EXAMPLE" Myriad Regular, 6/10.5pt, align center; Address Myriad Regular, 7.5/10.5pt, align center

### Business Card, Front

**5** "SAMPLER" Interstate UltraBlack, 9pt, align center; "MUSIC" Giza SevenSeven, 35pt, align center; Defining phrase Myriad Regular, 5/6pt, align center; **6** Name Myriad Regular, 8pt, align center; Title Myriad Regular, 7pt, align center; **7** "EXAMPLE" Myriad Regular, 6/10pt, align center; Address Myriad Regular, 7.5/10pt, align center

### Business Card, Back

**8** Text Myriad Multiple Master (MM), 700bd, 300cn, 8/12pt, align left

### Envelope

**9** "SAMPLER" Interstate UltraBlack, 9pt, align center; "MUSIC" Giza SevenSeven, 35pt, align center; Defining phrase Myriad Regular, 5/6pt, align center; **10** "EXAMPLE" Myriad Regular, 6/10.5pt, align center; Address Myriad Regular, 7/10.5pt, align center

### Color

To be printed in black and a solid PANTONE Color Ink as defined on the palette below (see Step 9.3). (Because this book is printed in process colors (CMYK), the illustration is only a simulation of the actual solid PANTONE Color).

Dark Green or
PANTONE® 555

| |
|---|
| 100% |
| 70% |
| 35% |
| 20% |
| 15% |

Warm Gray or
PANTONE® 406

| |
|---|
| 100% |
| 50% |

Black

| |
|---|
| 75% |
| 60% |

STYLE 10

# Flowchart

This is a "non-logo" logo. The closest thing to a conventional logo is the rectangle that holds the company name. Used alone, it is something less than exciting, but when combined with other brightly colored boxes and arrows, the overall effect is both interesting and versatile.

The same idea could easily be adapted to a brochure, signage, and packaging—each different from the next, incorporating the various angles of the marketing message.

The idea of a flowchart is almost universally understood and ideal for any organization that follows a series of steps to a solution.

To ensure they complement each other, the colors are a consecutive series from a standard color wheel.

The colors, tinted backgrounds, and borders visually punctuate the difference between one element and the next.

Note the differences between the rough and finished type. "Sampler" is reduced slightly, space is added between the letters of "SYSTEMS," and the space between lines and individual letters is tightened.

The name of the organization and the flowchart box form the logo. It is the one element that remains the same relative shape and size throughout the design.

Inserting "you" on each piece emphasizes your recognition of the fact that clients are the cornerstone of every business.

SOURCE Type families: Franklin Gothic, Minion, Adobe Systems, Inc., 800-682-3623, www.adobe.com/type.

**What you need**

The easiest way to create, position, and color these arrows, boxes, and text is a draw/vector program such as Adobe Illustrator, CorelDRAW, or Macromedia FreeHand. Simple text and shapes can be produced with a desktop publishing program such as Adobe InDesign, Adobe PageMaker, QuarkXPress, or Microsoft Publisher.

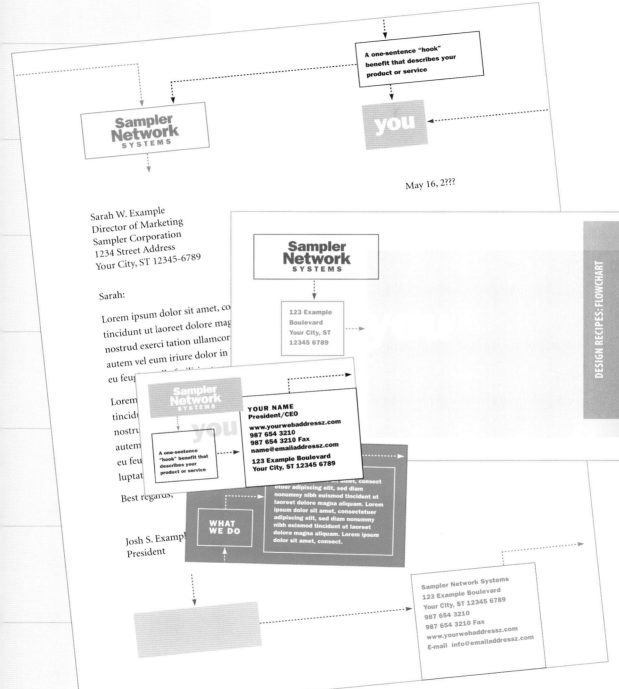

A one-sentence "hook" benefit that describes your product or service

**you**

May 16, 2???

Sarah W. Example
Director of Marketing
Sampler Corporation
1234 Street Address
Your City, ST 12345-6789

Sarah:

Lorem ipsum dolor sit amet, co
tincidunt ut laoreet dolore mag
nostrud exerci tation ullamcor
autem vel eum iriure dolor in
eu feug

Lorem
tincidu
nostru
autem
eu feu
luptat

Best regards,

Josh S. Exampl
President

123 Example
Boulevard
Your City, ST
12345 6789

**YOUR NAME**
President/CEO
www.yourwebaddressz.com
987 654 3210
987 654 3210 Fax
name@emailaddressz.com
123 Example Boulevard
Your City, ST 12345 6789

A one-sentence "hook" benefit that describes your product or service

amet, consect
etuer adipiscing elit, sed diam
nonummy nibh euismod tincidunt ut
laoreet dolore magna aliquam. Lorem
ipsum dolor sit amet, consectetuer
adipiscing elit, sed diam nonummy
nibh euismod tincidunt ut laoreet
dolore magna aliquam. Lorem ipsum
dolor sit amet, consect.

**WHAT WE DO**

Sampler Network Systems
123 Example Boulevard
Your City, ST 12345 6789
987 654 3210
987 654 3210 Fax
www.yourwebaddressz.com
E-mail info@emailaddressz.com

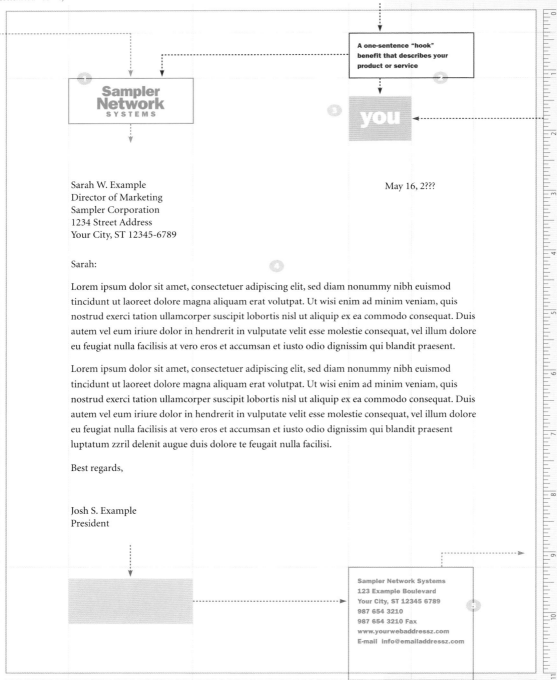

A one-sentence "hook" benefit that describes your product or service

Sampler
Network
SYSTEMS

you

Sarah W. Example                                    May 16, 2???
Director of Marketing
Sampler Corporation
1234 Street Address
Your City, ST 12345-6789

Sarah:

Lorem ipsum dolor sit amet, consectetuer adipiscing elit, sed diam nonummy nibh euismod
tincidunt ut laoreet dolore magna aliquam erat volutpat. Ut wisi enim ad minim veniam, quis
nostrud exerci tation ullamcorper suscipit lobortis nisl ut aliquip ex ea commodo consequat. Duis
autem vel eum iriure dolor in hendrerit in vulputate velit esse molestie consequat, vel illum dolore
eu feugiat nulla facilisis at vero eros et accumsan et iusto odio dignissim qui blandit praesent.

Lorem ipsum dolor sit amet, consectetuer adipiscing elit, sed diam nonummy nibh euismod
tincidunt ut laoreet dolore magna aliquam erat volutpat. Ut wisi enim ad minim veniam, quis
nostrud exerci tation ullamcorper suscipit lobortis nisl ut aliquip ex ea commodo consequat. Duis
autem vel eum iriure dolor in hendrerit in vulputate velit esse molestie consequat, vel illum dolore
eu feugiat nulla facilisis at vero eros et accumsan et iusto odio dignissim qui blandit praesent
luptatum zzril delenit augue duis dolore te feugait nulla facilisi.

Best regards,

Josh S. Example
President

Sampler Network Systems
123 Example Boulevard
Your City, ST 12345 6789
987 654 3210
987 654 3210 Fax
www.yourwebaddressz.com
E-mail  info@emailaddressz.com

8.5 W
11 H

## Business Card, Front  3.5 W by 2 H inches

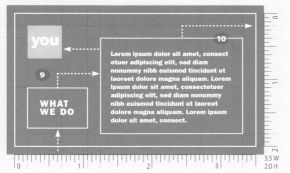

**YOUR NAME**
President/CEO

www.yourwebaddressz.com
987 654 3210
987 654 3210 Fax
name@emailaddress.com

123 Example Boulevard
Your City, ST 12345 6789

A one-sentence "hook" benefit that describes your product or service

3.5 W
2.0 H

## Business Card, Back  3.5 W by 2 H inches

you

10

Lorem ipsum dolor sit amet, consect etuer adipiscing elit, sed diam nonummy nibh euismod tincidunt ut laoreet dolore magna aliquam. Lorem ipsum dolor sit amet, consectetuer adipiscing elit, sed diam nonummy nibh euismod tincidunt ut laoreet dolore magna aliquam. Lorem ipsum dolor sit amet, consect.

9

WHAT
WE DO

3.5 W
2.0 H

## Envelope, Commercial  9.5 W by 4.125 H inches

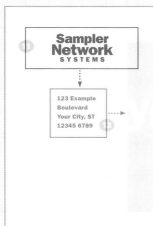

**Sampler Network** SYSTEMS

123 Example Boulevard
Your City, ST 12345 6789

9.5 W
4.125 H

### Letterhead

**1** Lines 0.9pt; "Sampler" Franklin Gothic Heavy, 17pt, align center; "Network" Franklin Gothic Heavy, 20pt, align center; "SYSTEMS" Franklin Gothic Heavy, 9pt, align center; **2** Defining phrase Franklin Gothic Heavy, 8/12pt, align left; **3** "you" Franklin Gothic Heavy, 28pt; **4** Letter body Minion, 12/18pt, align left; **5** Address Franklin Gothic Heavy, 8/12pt, align left

### Business Card, Front

**6** Lines 0.9pt; Organization "Sampler" Franklin Gothic Heavy, 13pt, align center; "Network" Franklin Gothic Heavy, 15pt, align center; "SYSTEMS" Franklin Gothic Heavy, 7pt, align center; **7** Defining phrase Franklin Gothic Heavy, 6/8pt, align left; "you" Franklin Gothic Heavy, 32pt; **8** Address Franklin Gothic Heavy, 8/9pt, align left

### Business Card, Back

**9** "you" Franklin Gothic Heavy, 18pt; "WHAT" Franklin Gothic Heavy, 10pt, align left; **10** Lines 0.9pt; Text Franklin Gothic Heavy, 7/8pt, align left

### Envelope

**11** Lines 0.9pt; "Sampler" Franklin Gothic Heavy, 17pt, align center; "Network" Franklin Gothic Heavy, 20pt, align center; "SYSTEMS" Franklin Gothic Heavy, 9pt, align center; **12** Address Franklin Gothic Heavy, 8/12pt, align left; "you" Franklin Gothic Heavy, 60pt

### Color

Printed in four-color process (see Step 9.3) using values of cyan, magenta, yellow, and black (CMYK) as defined on the color palette below. Actual color will vary.

Process Colors

| C0 | M50 | Y100 | K0 |
|----|-----|------|-----|
| C0 | M25 | Y50 | K0 |
| C0 | M100 | Y70 | K10 |
| C15 | M20 | Y0 | K3 |
| C60 | M70 | Y0 | K10 |
| C25 | M10 | Y0 | K0 |
| C85 | M35 | Y0 | K0 |
| C35 | M0 | Y5 | K2 |
| C75 | M0 | Y15 | K5 |
| C12 | M0 | Y5 | K3 |

STYLE 11

# Form

A well-designed form effectively organizes lots of information. The same principles can be applied to your letterhead, business card, and envelope.

The goal is to create an feeling of both elegance and organization—an image that might also be appropriate for an accounting or legal firm, a Web designer, a consultant, and so on.

Each cell of the form holds an important tidbit of information—the mission or defining phrase, the date the organization was founded, affiliations, a list of products and services, and the phone, fax, and street, Web site and e-mail addresses.

### SAMPLER JEWELERS

The spot color and a tint of that color is added to a simple black and white jewel icon.

The background for the jewel is a heart-shaped, diamond-cut illustration colored with a subtle tint of the same spot color.

The icons from several different sources are centered on a solid circle to make them look as if they were designed for just this purpose.

The "S" is slightly larger than the "AMPLER"—a simple but important detail.

S A

To play on the form theme, a list of the company's products and services is listed as if they might be checked off.

SOURCES Illustrations: Gem, page, from *Objects & Icons* from Image Club Clip Art, 800-661-9410, 403-294-3195, www.eyewire.com, © Image Club Graphics, all rights reserved; heart, mail, phone, from *Design Elements* by Ultimate Symbol, 800-611-4761, 914-942-0003, www.ultimatesymbol.com, © Ultimate Symbol, all rights reserved.

SOURCE Type families: Caslon, Franklin Gothic, Minion, Adobe Systems, Inc., 800-682-3623, www.adobe.com/type.

**What you need**

Breaking apart draw/vector artwork and editing the pieces requires a draw program such as Adobe Illustrator, CorelDRAW, or Macromedia FreeHand. Simple text and shapes can be produced with a desktop publishing program such as Adobe InDesign, Adobe PageMaker, QuarkXPress, or Microsoft Publisher.

DESIGN RECIPES: FORM

**MISSION**

A one-sentence "hook" benefit that describes your product or service

SAMPLER JEWELERS

SINCE 1978

Founding Member
National Association of
Jewelry Samplers

Precious Stones
Pearls
Fine Watches
Engagement Rings
Wedding Bands
Gold & Silver Jewelry
Estate Jewelry
Repairs, Restorations & Appraisals
Custom Remounting
Original Designs

May 16, 2???

Sarah W. Example
Director of Marketing
Sampler Corporation
1234 Street Address
Your City, ST 12345-6789

Sarah:

Lorem ipsum dolor sit amet, consectetuer adipiscing elit, sed diam nonummy nibh euismod tincidunt ut laoreet dolore ma... at volutpat. Ut wisi enim ad minim veniam, quis ...ortis nisl ut aliquip ex ea commodo ...putate velit esse ...n et iusto odio ...

luptat...

Nam ...

mazim... nihil i... diam nonummy nibh euismod tincidunt ut laoreet dolore magna a...

Best regards,

Josh S. Example
President
coc
Enclosures (2)

**IMPORTANT**

SAMPLER JEWELERS

www.yourwebaddressz.com

Precious Stones · Pearls · Fine Watches
Engagement Rings · Wedding Bands
Gold & Silver Jewelry · Estate Jewelry
Repairs, Restorations & Appraisals
Custom Remounting · Original Designs

A one-sentence "hook" benefit that describes your product or service

**YOUR NAME**
PRESIDENT

123 Example Boulevard
Your City, State 12345 6789

Voice 987 654 3210

Fax 987 654 3210

info@emailaddressz.com

SAMPLER JEWELERS

123 Example Boulevard
Your City, State 12345 6789

**ADDRESS**
123 Example Boulevard
...ur City, State 12345 6789

**VOICE**
987 654 3210

**FAX**
987 654 3210

**WEB SITE**
www.yourwebaddressz.com

**E-MAIL**
info@emailaddressz.com

A one-sentence "hook" benefit that describes your product or service

S A M P L E R   J E W E L E R S

Founding Member
National Association of
Jewelry Samplers

☐ Precious Stones
☐ Pearls
☐ Fine Watches
☐ Engagement Rings
☐ Wedding Bands
☐ Gold & Silver Jewelry
☐ Estate Jewelry
☐ Repairs, Restorations & Appraisals
☐ Custom Remounting
☐ Original Designs

May 16, 2???

Sarah W. Example
Director of Marketing
Sampler Corporation
1234 Street Address
Your City, ST 12345-6789

Sarah:

Lorem ipsum dolor sit amet, consectetuer adipiscing elit, sed diam nonummy nibh euismod tincidunt ut laoreet dolore magna aliquam erat volutpat. Ut wisi enim ad minim veniam, quis nostrud exerci tation ullamcorper suscipit lobortis nisl ut aliquip ex ea commodo consequat. Duis autem vel eum iriure dolor in hendrerit in vulputate velit esse molestie consequat, vel illum dolore eu feugiat nulla facilisis at vero eros et accumsan et iusto odio dignissim qui blandit praesent.

Lorem ipsum dolor sit amet, consectetuer adipiscing elit, sed diam nonummy nibh euismod tincidunt ut laoreet dolore magna aliquam erat volutpat. Ut wisi enim ad minim veniam, quis nostrud exerci tation ullamcorper suscipit lobortis nisl ut aliquip ex ea commodo consequat. Duis autem vel eum iriure dolor in hendrerit in vulputate velit esse molestie consequat, vel illum dolore eu feugiat nulla facilisis at vero eros et accumsan et iusto odio dignissim qui blandit praesent luptatum zzril delenit augue duis dolore te feugait nulla facilisi.

Nam liber tempor cum soluta nobis eleifend option congue nihil imperdiet doming id quod mazim placerat facer possim assum. Lorem ipsum dolor sit amet, consectetuer adipiscing elit, sed diam nonummy nibh euismod tincidunt ut laoreet dolore magna aliquam erat volutpat.

Best regards,

Josh S. Example
President

**ADDRESS**
123 Example Boulevard
Your City, State 12345 6789

**VOICE**
987 654 3210

**FAX**
987 654 3210

**WEB SITE**
www.yourwebaddressz.com

**E-MAIL**
info@emailaddressz.com

## Business Card, Front  3.5 W by 2 H inches

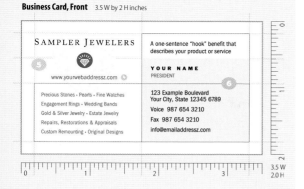

## Business Card, Back  3.5 W by 2 H inches

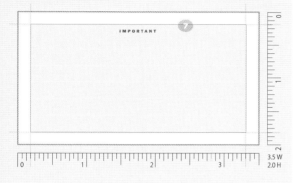

### Letterhead

**1** "MISSION" Franklin Gothic Roman Bold, 4pt, align left; Defining phrase Franklin Gothic Book Condensed, 8/10pt, align left; "S" Adobe Caslon Regular, 11pt, align center; "AMPLER" Adobe Caslon Regular, 9pt, align center; **2** Lines 0.25pt; "SINCE" Franklin Gothic Roman Bold, 4pt, align right; "Founding" Franklin Gothic Book Condensed, 8/10pt, align right; "Precious" Franklin Gothic Book Condensed, 6/12pt, align center; **3** Letter body Minion, 12/18pt, align left; **4** "ADDRESS" Franklin Gothic Roman Bold, 4pt, align center; Address Franklin Gothic Book Condensed, 8/10pt, align center

### Business Card, Front

**5** "S" Adobe Caslon Regular, 9.5pt, align center; "AMPLER" Adobe Caslon Regular, 7.5pt, align center; Web Address Franklin Gothic Book Condensed, 7/8pt, align center; Lines 0.25pt; "Precious" Franklin Gothic Book Condensed, 7/8pt, align left; **6** Defining phrase Franklin Gothic Book Condensed, 8/10pt, align left; Name Franklin Gothic Roman Bold, 5pt, align left; Title Franklin Gothic Book Condensed, 6pt, align left; Address Franklin Gothic Book Condensed, 7/11pt, align left

### Business Card, Back

**7** "IMPORTANT" Franklin Gothic Roman Bold, 4pt, align center; Lines 0.25pt

### Envelope

**8** "S" Adobe Caslon Regular, 10pt; "AMPLER" Adobe Caslon Regular, 8pt, align center; Address Franklin Gothic Book Condensed, 6/8pt, align center

### Color

To be printed in black and a solid PANTONE Color Ink as defined on the palette below (see Step 9.3). (Because this book is printed in process colors (CMYK), the illustration is only a simulation of the actual solid PANTONE Color).

Teal or
PANTONE® 569

| |
|---|
| 100% |
| 50% |
| 35% |
| 10% |
| 5% |

## Envelope, Commercial  9.5 W by 4.125 H inches

STYLE 12

# Horizontal Bar

Want to witness the real power of design? Do you doubt that if this organization used the Border Style on page 61, your impression would be significantly different?

This style is modern and progressive, while the Border Style has a historical, traditional look and feel. It's not the case of one being better than the other—it simply serves to demonstrate how style helps define your organization.

If you can't put your finger on the attitude a particular design portrays, survey your audience.

The church photograph is scanned in grayscale. The rotated and cropped version looks as if you are zooming in on the subject with a hand-held camera.

The original color image is converted to black and white and cropped to match the size, shape, and feel of the church photograph.

The sans serif typeface builds on the progressive attitude of the photographs. A traditional serif typeface such as Caslon or a script such as Bickham (see page 29) would change the look completely.

No space is wasted. Printing the back of your business card only costs a little more but gives you twice as much usable space. In this case, a valuable addition is a map that pinpoints the church's location.

SOURCE Illustrations: Church/steeple from author; stained glass from *ClickArt 200,000* from Broderbund, available from software retailers worldwide, © T/Maker, all rights reserved.

SOURCE Type families: Berthold Akzidenz-Grotesk, Minion, Adobe Systems, Inc., 800-682-3623, www.adobe.com/type.

**What you need**

Creating artwork for the map requires a draw program such as Adobe Illustrator, CorelDRAW, or Macromedia FreeHand. Editing photographic images requires a paint or digital imaging program such as Adobe Photoshop or Jasc Software's Paint Shop Pro. Simple text and shapes can be produced with a desktop publishing program such as Adobe InDesign, Adobe PageMaker, QuarkXPress, or Microsoft Publisher.

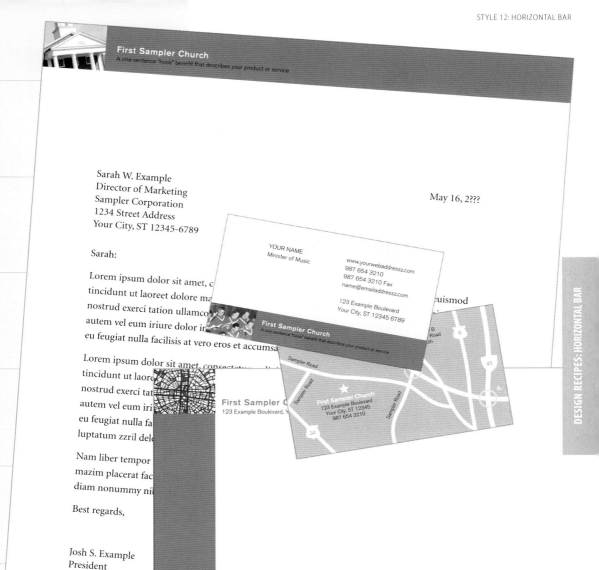

**First Sampler Church**
A one-sentence "hook" benefit that describes your product or service

Sarah W. Example
Director of Marketing
Sampler Corporation
1234 Street Address
Your City, ST 12345-6789

May 16, 2???

Sarah:

Lorem ipsum dolor sit amet, c
tincidunt ut laoreet dolore ma
nostrud exerci tation ullamco
autem vel eum iriure dolor in
eu feugiat nulla facilisis at vero eros et accumsa

Lorem ipsum dolor sit amet, consectetu
tincidunt ut laor
nostrud exerci tat
autem vel eum iri
eu feugiat nulla fa
luptatum zzril del

Nam liber tempor
mazim placerat fac
diam nonummy ni

Best regards,

Josh S. Example
President
coc
Enclosures (2)

YOUR NAME
Minister of Music

www.yourwebaddressz.com
987 654 3210
987 654 3210 Fax
name@emailaddressz.com

123 Example Boulevard
Your City, ST 12345 6789

**First Sampler Church**
A one-sentence "hook" benefit that describes your product or service

**First Sampler C**
123 Example Boulevard, Y

Sampler Road

**First Sampler Church**
123 Example Boulevard
Your City, ST 12345
987 654 3210

**First Sampler Church**
A one-sentence "hook" benefit that describes your product or service

Sarah W. Example                                    May 16, 2???
Director of Marketing
Sampler Corporation
1234 Street Address
Your City, ST 12345-6789

Sarah:

Lorem ipsum dolor sit amet, consectetuer adipiscing elit, sed diam nonummy nibh euismod tincidunt ut laoreet dolore magna aliquam erat volutpat. Ut wisi enim ad minim veniam, quis nostrud exerci tation ullamcorper suscipit lobortis nisl ut aliquip ex ea commodo consequat. Duis autem vel eum iriure dolor in hendrerit in vulputate velit esse molestie consequat, vel illum dolore eu feugiat nulla facilisis at vero eros et accumsan et iusto odio dignissim qui blandit praesent.

Lorem ipsum dolor sit amet, consectetuer adipiscing elit, sed diam nonummy nibh euismod tincidunt ut laoreet dolore magna aliquam erat volutpat. Ut wisi enim ad minim veniam, quis nostrud exerci tation ullamcorper suscipit lobortis nisl ut aliquip ex ea commodo consequat. Duis autem vel eum iriure dolor in hendrerit in vulputate velit esse molestie consequat, vel illum dolore eu feugiat nulla facilisis at vero eros et accumsan et iusto odio dignissim qui blandit praesent luptatum zzril delenit augue duis dolore te feugait nulla facilisi.

Nam liber tempor cum soluta nobis eleifend option congue nihil imperdiet doming id quod mazim placerat facer possim assum. Lorem ipsum dolor sit amet, consectetuer adipiscing elit, sed diam nonummy nibh euismod tincidunt ut laoreet dolore magna aliquam erat volutpat.

Best regards,


Josh S. Example
President
coc
Enclosures (2)

## Business Card, Front  3.5 W by 2 H inches

YOUR NAME
Minister of Music

www.yourwebaddressz.com
987 654 3210
987 654 3210 Fax
name@emailaddressz.com

123 Example Boulevard
Your City, ST 12345 6789

**First Sampler Church**
A one sentence "hook" benefit that describes your product or service

3.5 W
2.0 H

## Business Card, Back  3.5 W by 2 H inches

Sampler Road
Sampler Road
123
Sampler Road
Sampler Road
Exit 45 B
Sampler Road
South
6
45
★
**First Sampler Church**
123 Example Boulevard
Your City, ST 12345
987 654 3210
34

3.5 W
2.0 H

## Envelope, Commercial  9.5 W by 4.125 H inches

**First Sampler Church**
123 Example Boulevard, Your City, ST 12345 6789

9.5 W
4.125 H

---

### Letterhead

**1** Organization Berthold Akzidenz-Grotesk Medium, 10pt, align left; Defining phrase Berthold Akzidenz-Grotesk Light, 7pt, align left; **2** Letter body Minion, 12/18pt, align left; **3** Address Berthold Akzidenz-Grotesk Light, 7/10pt, align left

### Business Card, Front

**4** Name Berthold Akzidenz-Grotesk Light, 7/10pt, align left; **5** Address Berthold Akzidenz-Grotesk Light, 7/10pt, align left; **6** Organization Berthold Akzidenz-Grotesk Medium, 7.5pt, align left; Defining phrase Berthold Akzidenz-Grotesk Light, 5.25pt, align left

### Business Card, Back

**7** Organization Berthold Akzidenz-Grotesk Medium, 6pt, align center; Text Berthold Akzidenz-Grotesk Light, 6/7pt, align left

### Envelope

**8** Organization Berthold Akzidenz-Grotesk Medium, 10pt, align left; Address Berthold Akzidenz-Grotesk Light, 7pt, align left

### Color

To be printed in black and a solid PANTONE Color Ink as defined on the palette below (see Step 9.3). (Because this book is printed in process colors (CMYK) the illustration is only a simulation of the actual solid PANTONE Color).

Steel Blue or
PANTONE® 652

100%
50%
10%

STYLE 13

# Lines

A design grid is an invisible series of lines used as the framework of a layout (see Step 9.6). This style uses grid-like lines as the foundation of the design itself. They are not only decorative; they form spaces for each information element.

This bright, fresh-looking photograph makes a great "non-logo" logo. The life jacket is a symbol of water and also promotes water safety. But the reason it works well is because it's an unexpected solution.

The grid is slightly taller than it is wide to better accommodate the photograph. Adjust yours to match the shape of your visual.

**A one-paragr
hook benefit t
describes you
product or ser
lorem ipsum
sit amet, con
adipiscing el**

The type in all the cells is equidistant from the corner—at least one whole letterspace away. Space is added between lines of type to make the paragraph fit the space top to bottom.

A line pattern is used to decorate the front and back of the business card. The kind of simple change that makes each piece—letterhead, business card, and envelope—unique.

A slight shadow is added to the life jacket to raise it off the page.

SAMPLER
MARINA

A bold typeface is used to emphasize the importance of the defining phrase.

A one-paragraph
hook benefit that
describes your
product or service
lorem ipsum dolo
sit amet, consecr
adipiscing elit

SAMPLER
MARINA

SOURCE Illustration: Life jacket from CMCD *Everyday Objects 2* from PhotoDisc, 800-979-4413, 206-441-9355, www.photo disc.com, © CMCD, all rights reserved.

SOURCES Type families: Minion, Myriad, Adobe Systems, Inc., 800-682-3623, www.adobe.com/type.

**What you need**
Editing photographic images requires a paint or digital imaging program such as Adobe Photoshop or Jasc Software's Paint Shop Pro. Simple text, lines, and shapes can be produced with a desktop publishing program such as Adobe InDesign, Adobe PageMaker, QuarkXPress, or Microsoft Publisher.

May 16, 2???

Sarah W. Example
Director of Marketing
Sampler Corporation
1234 Street Address
Your City, ST 12345-6789

Sarah:

Lorem ipsum dolor sit amet, consectetuer adipiscing elit, sed diam nonummy nibh euismod tincidunt ut laoreet dolore magna aliquam erat volutpat. Ut wisi enim ad minim veniam, quis nostrud exerci tation ullamcorper suscipit lobortis nisl ut aliquip ex ea commodo consequat. Duis autem vel eum iriure dolor in hendrerit in vulputate velit esse molestie con eu feugiat nulla facilisis at vero eros et accumsan et iusto odio dignissim qu

Lorem ipsum dolor sit amet, consectetuer adipiscing elit, sed diam nonumm tincidunt ut laoreet dolore magna aliquam erat volutpat. Ut wisi nostrud exerci tation ullamcorper suscipit lobortis nisl ut aliqu autem vel eum iriure dolor in hendrerit in vulputate velit esse eu feugiat nulla facilisis at vero eros et accumsan et iusto odi luptatum zzril delenit augue duis dolore te feugait nulla

Nam liber tempor cum soluta nobis eleifend mazim placerat facer possim assum. L iam nonummy nibh euismod

st regards,

Example
nt

es (2)

SAMPLER MARINA
123 Example Boulevard
Suite 123
Your City, State 12345 6789
Voice 987 654 3210
Fax 987 654 3210
www.yourwebaddressz.com
E-mail  info@emailaddressz.com

May 16, 2???

Sarah W. Example
Director of Marketing
Sampler Corporation
1234 Street Address
Your City, ST 12345-6789

**A one-paragraph
hook benefit that
describes your
product or service
lorem ipsum dolor
sit amet, consec
adipiscing elit**
SAMPLER MARINA

Sarah:

Lorem ipsum dolor sit amet, consectetuer adipiscing elit, sed diam nonummy nibh euismod tincidunt ut laoreet dolore magna aliquam erat volutpat. Ut wisi enim ad minim veniam, quis nostrud exerci tation ullamcorper suscipit lobortis nisl ut aliquip ex ea commodo consequat. Duis autem vel eum iriure dolor in hendrerit in vulputate velit esse molestie consequat, vel illum dolore eu feugiat nulla facilisis at vero eros et accumsan et iusto odio dignissim qui blandit praesent.

Lorem ipsum dolor sit amet, consectetuer adipiscing elit, sed diam nonummy nibh euismod tincidunt ut laoreet dolore magna aliquam erat volutpat. Ut wisi enim ad minim veniam, quis nostrud exerci tation ullamcorper suscipit lobortis nisl ut aliquip ex ea commodo consequat. Duis autem vel eum iriure dolor in hendrerit in vulputate velit esse molestie consequat, vel illum dolore eu feugiat nulla facilisis at vero eros et accumsan et iusto odio dignissim qui blandit praesent luptatum zzril delenit augue duis dolore te feugait nulla facilisi.

Nam liber tempor cum soluta nobis eleifend option congue nihil imperdiet doming id quod mazim placerat facer possim assum. Lorem ipsum dolor sit amet, consectetuer adipiscing elit, sed diam nonummy nibh euismod tincidunt ut laoreet dolore magna aliquam erat volutpat.

Best regards,


Josh S. Example
President
coc
Enclosures (2)

8.5 W
11 H

## Business Card, Front · 3.5 W by 2 H inches

A one-paragraph hook benefit that describes your product or service lorem ipsum dolor sit amet, consec adi

YOUR NAME
President / CEO

SAMPLER MARINA
123 Example Boulevard
Your City, State 12345 6789

E-mail  info@emailaddressz.com
www.yourwebaddressz.com
Voice 987 654 3210, Fax 987 654 3210

3.5 W
2.0 H

## Business Card, Back · 3.5 W by 2 H inches

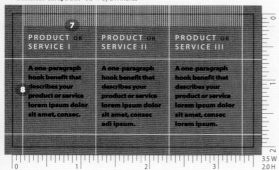

PRODUCT OR
SERVICE I

A one-paragraph hook benefit that describes your product or service lorem ipsum dolor sit amet, consec.

PRODUCT OR
SERVICE II

A one-paragraph hook benefit that describes your product or service lorem ipsum dolor sit amet, consec adi ipsum.

PRODUCT OR
SERVICE III

A one-paragraph hook benefit that describes your product or service lorem ipsum dolor lorem ipsum.

3.5 W
2.0 H

## Envelope, Commercial · 9.5 W by 4.125 H inches

123 Example
Boulevard, Suite 123
Your City, State
12345 6789

SAMPLER
MARINA

A one-paragraph
hook benefit that
describes your
product or service
lorem ipsum dolor
sit amet, consec
adipiscing elit
SAMPLER MARINA

9.5 W
4.125 H

### Letterhead

**1** Organization/Address Myriad Regular, 8/13pt, align left; Lines 0.5pt;
**2** Defining phrase Myriad Multiple Master (MM), 830bl, 700se, 11/12.5pt, align left; "SAMPLER" Myriad Regular, 9pt, align left; **3** Letter body Minion, 12/18pt, align left

### Business Card, Front

**4** Defining phrase Myriad MM, 830bl, 700se, 7/10pt, align left; Lines 0.5pt;
**5** Name Myriad Regular, 8pt, align left; Title Myriad Regular, 7pt, align left;
**6** Organization/Address Myriad Regular, 8/10pt, align left

### Business Card, Back

**7** "PRODUCT" Myriad Regular, 8/10pt, align left; "OR" Myriad Regular, 6pt, align left; **8** Lines 0.5pt; Text Myriad MM, 830bl, 700se, 7/10pt, align left

### Envelope

**9** Lines .5pt; Address Myriad Regular, 7/10pt, align left; **10** Organization Myriad Regular, 8/11pt, align left; Defining phrase Myriad MM, 830bl, 700se, 7/8pt, align left; "SAMPLER" Myriad Regular, 6pt, align left

### Color

Printed in four-color process (see Step 9.3) using values of cyan, magenta, yellow, and black (CMYK) as defined on the color palette below. Actual color will vary.

Process Colors

| | | | |
|---|---|---|---|
| C5 | M75 | Y100 | K0 |
| C0 | M60 | Y80 | K0 |
| C0 | M25 | Y35 | K0 |

DESIGN RECIPES:LINES

STYLE 14

# Opposing Elements

Convention suggests we group elements together—if nothing else, certainly the logo artwork and the organization's name.

Most of the logos explored in this book follow that convention. But there's something to be said for exploring the idea of opposing elements. It adds interest and can be used to draw attention to a specific area of the page.

On this letterhead, the logo is on the left and the name is opposite on the right. On the business card, the logo is offset from all the text. It is a small distinction but worth considering.

**Sampler**Kennels

The cat is from a picture font. Instead of typing characters, each key of a picture font produces a different picture. Because the characters are often used at small sizes, they're good germs for logo design ideas.

A simple shape is added to give the image a boundary and weight.

A combination of very bold and very light typeface weights adds emphasis to one word or the other.

Sampler**Kennels**  **Sampler**Kennels

The lighter word is stretched slightly to compensate for the difference in the width of the letters. Lighter weights of type are typically more condensed than bolder weights.

The back of the business card is put to good use. In this case, a floor plan of the kennel's guest accommodations.

SOURCE Illustrations:
Cat from Dick & Jane font from DsgnHaus, Inc., 800-942-9110, 203-367-1993, www.fonthaus.com.

SOURCE Type families: Fruitger, Minion, Adobe Systems, Inc., 800-682-3623, www.adobe.com/type.

**What you need**
Breaking apart draw/vector artwork and editing the pieces requires a draw program such as Adobe Illustrator, CorelDRAW, or Macromedia FreeHand. Simple text and shapes can be produced with a desktop publishing program such as Adobe InDesign, Adobe PageMaker, QuarkXPress, or Microsoft Publisher.

A one-paragraph "hook" benefit that describes your product or service

**Sampler**Kennels

May 16, 2???

Sarah W. Example
Director of Marketing
Sampler Corporation
1234 Street Address
Your City, ST 12345-6789

Sarah:

Lorem ipsum dolor sit amet, consectetuer ad
tincidunt ut laoreet dolore magna aliquam e
nostrud exerci tation ullamcorper suscipit lo
autem vel eum iriure dolor in hendrerit in vu
eu feugiat nulla facilisis at v

Lorem ipsum dolor sit am
tincidunt ut laoreet dolor
nostrud exerci tation ulla
autem vel eum iriure do
eu feugiat nulla facilisis
luptatum zzril delenit

Nam liber tempor cu
mazim placerat face
diam nonummy nih

Best regards,

Josh S. Example
President
coc
Enclosures (2)

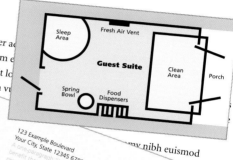

Guest Suite — Sleep Area · Fresh Air Vent · Clean Area · Porch · Spring Bowl · Food Dispensers

123 Example Boulevard
Your City, State 12345 6789
A one-paragraph "hook"
benefit that describes your
product or service

...my nibh euismod

**Sampler**Kennels

123 Exampl...
Your City, State 12345 6...
www.yourwebaddressz.com
E-mail info@emailaddressz.com

**Sampler**Kennels

May 16, 2???

Sarah W. Example
Director of Marketing
Sampler Corporation
1234 Street Address
Your City, ST 12345-6789

Sarah:

Lorem ipsum dolor sit amet, consectetuer adipiscing elit, sed diam nonummy nibh euismod tincidunt ut laoreet dolore magna aliquam erat volutpat. Ut wisi enim ad minim veniam, quis nostrud exerci tation ullamcorper suscipit lobortis nisl ut aliquip ex ea commodo consequat. Duis autem vel eum iriure dolor in hendrerit in vulputate velit esse molestie consequat, vel illum dolore eu feugiat nulla facilisis at vero eros et accumsan et iusto odio dignissim qui blandit praesent.

Lorem ipsum dolor sit amet, consectetuer adipiscing elit, sed diam nonummy nibh euismod tincidunt ut laoreet dolore magna aliquam erat volutpat. Ut wisi enim ad minim veniam, quis nostrud exerci tation ullamcorper suscipit lobortis nisl ut aliquip ex ea commodo consequat. Duis autem vel eum iriure dolor in hendrerit in vulputate velit esse molestie consequat, vel illum dolore eu feugiat nulla facilisis at vero eros et accumsan et iusto odio dignissim qui blandit praesent luptatum zzril delenit augue duis dolore te feugait nulla facilisi.

Nam liber tempor cum soluta nobis eleifend option congue nihil imperdiet doming id quod mazim placerat facer possim assum. Lorem ipsum dolor sit amet, consectetuer adipiscing elit, sed diam nonummy nibh euismod tincidunt ut laoreet dolore magna aliquam erat volutpat.

Best regards,


Josh S. Example
President
coc
Enclosures (2)

Voice 987 654 3210
Fax 987 654 3210
123 Example Boulevard
Your City, State 12345 6789
www.yourwebaddressz.com
E-mail info@emailaddressz.com

## Business Card, Front 3.5 W by 2 H inches

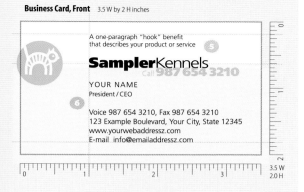

A one-paragraph "hook" benefit
that describes your product or service

**Sampler**Kennels
Call 987 654 3210

YOUR NAME
President / CEO

Voice 987 654 3210, Fax 987 654 3210
123 Example Boulevard, Your City, State 12345
www.yourwebaddressz.com
E-mail info@emailaddressz.com

3.5 W
2.0 H

## Business Card, Back 3.5 W by 2 H inches

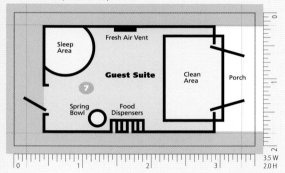

Sleep Area
Fresh Air Vent
**Guest Suite**
Clean Area
Porch
Spring Bowl
Food Dispensers
7

3.5 W
2.0 H

## Envelope, Commercial 9.5 W by 4.125 H inches

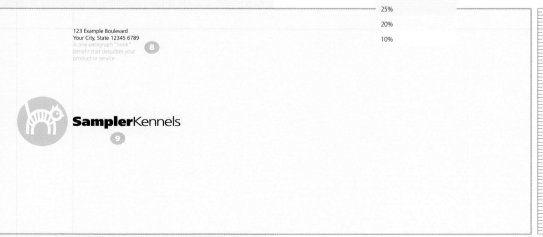

123 Example Boulevard
Your City, State 12345 6789
A one-paragraph "hook"
benefit that describes your
product or service
8

**Sampler**Kennels
9

9.5 W
4.125 H

### Letterhead

**1** Defining phrase Frutiger 45 Light, 7/8pt, align left; **2** "Sampler" Frutiger 95 UltraBlack, 20pt; "Kennels" Frutiger 45 Light, 20pt; **3** Letter body Minion, 12/18pt, align left; **4** Address Frutiger 45 Light, 7.5/10pt, align left

### Business Card, Front

**5** Defining phrase Frutiger 45 Light, 7/8pt, align left; "Sampler" Frutiger 95 UltraBlack, 16pt; "Kennels" Frutiger 45 Light, 16pt; "Call" Frutiger 45 Light, 8pt; Phone number Frutiger 95 UltraBlack, 13pt; **6** Name Frutiger 45 Light, 8pt, align left; Title Frutiger 45 Light, 7pt, align left; Address Frutiger 45 Light, 8/10pt, align left

### Business Card, Back

**7** Text Frutiger 45 Light, 7/8pt, align left or center; Title Frutiger 95 UltraBlack, 8pt, align center

### Envelope

**8** Address Frutiger 45 Light, 7/9pt, align left; Defining phrase Frutiger 45 Light, 7/9pt, align left; **9** "Sampler" Frutiger 95 UltraBlack, 17pt; "Kennels" Frutiger 45 Light, 17pt

### Color

To be printed in black and a solid PANTONE Color Ink as defined on the palette below (see Step 9.3). (Because this book is printed in process colors (CMYK), the illustration is only a simulation of the actual solid PANTONE Color).

Lime Green or
PANTONE® 382

| | |
|---|---|
| 100% | |
| 50% | |
| 25% | |
| 20% | |
| 10% | |

STYLE 15

# Outlines

For this style, the logo is the layout. The only element on the letterhead other than the address is the single horizontal line that visually separates the logo from the letter. The business card and envelope don't even need that.

The layout is plain because the logo is so visually complex. The outlines not only spell out the name of the organization, they pronounce the products and services it sells. In this case, good design is as much about restraint as it is about excess.

**Display**
Display

A drawing program is used to remove the fill color from the words and to thicken the outline (stroke) of each letter.

**Sound**
**VIDEO**
**projection**

Words that describe the organization's products and services are added to the background. To increase the visual interest, some are capitalized, some are all caps, and some are all lowercase.

Various tones and colors are added to the background words. In each case, the tone for these supporting elements are significantly lighter than the name. Some words are enlarged, and others are reduced.

The words are assembled like a puzzle. Taking the time to experiment with how each word fits a particular space is what makes this technique work.

SAMPLER Display

SOURCE Type families: Frutiger, Minion, Adobe Systems, Inc., 800-682-3623, www.adobe.com/type.

**What you need**
Creating the outlines requires a draw program such as Adobe Illustrator, CorelDRAW, or Macromedia FreeHand. Simple text and shapes can be produced with a desktop publishing program such as Adobe InDesign, Adobe PageMaker, QuarkXPress, or Microsoft Publisher.

A one-sentence "hook"
benefit that describes
your product or service

Sarah W. Example
Director of Marketing
Sampler Corporation
1234 Street Address
Your City, ST 12345-6789

May 16, 2???

Sarah:

Lorem ipsum dolor sit amet, consectetuer adipiscing elit, sed diam nonummy
tincidunt ut laoreet dolore magna aliquam
nostrud exerci

autem

eu feug

Lorem i

tincidur        123 Example Boulevard
                Your City, ST 12345 6789
nostrud

autem ve

eu feugia                                    A one-sentence "hook"
                                             benefit that describes your
luptatum                                     product or service

                     YOUR NAME               www.yourwebaddressz.com
Nam liber            President/CEO           987 654 3210
                                             987 654 3210 Fax
mazim pla                                    name@emailaddressz.com
                                             123 Example Boulevard
diam nonu                                    Your City, ST 12345 6789

Best regards

                                             Product Five
                                             Product Six
                                             Product Seven
Josh S. Exampl                               Product Eight
President                                    Product Nine
coc                                          Product Ten
Enclosures (2)

123 Example Boulevard, Your City, ST 12345 6789
987 654 3210   987 654 3210 FaX   www.yourwebaddressz.com   E-mail info@emailaddressz.com

DESIGN RECIPES: OUTLINES

113

SAMPLER
**Display**

Sarah W. Example                                    May 16, 2???
Director of Marketing
Sampler Corporation
1234 Street Address
Your City, ST 12345-6789

Sarah:

Lorem ipsum dolor sit amet, consectetuer adipiscing elit, sed diam nonummy nibh euismod tincidunt ut laoreet dolore magna aliquam erat volutpat. Ut wisi enim ad minim veniam, quis nostrud exerci tation ullamcorper suscipit lobortis nisl ut aliquip ex ea commodo consequat. Duis autem vel eum iriure dolor in hendrerit in vulputate velit esse molestie consequat, vel illum dolore eu feugiat nulla facilisis at vero eros et accumsan et iusto odio dignissim qui blandit praesent.

Lorem ipsum dolor sit amet, consectetuer adipiscing elit, sed diam nonummy nibh euismod tincidunt ut laoreet dolore magna aliquam erat volutpat. Ut wisi enim ad minim veniam, quis nostrud exerci tation ullamcorper suscipit lobortis nisl ut aliquip ex ea commodo consequat. Duis autem vel eum iriure dolor in hendrerit in vulputate velit esse molestie consequat, vel illum dolore eu feugiat nulla facilisis at vero eros et accumsan et iusto odio dignissim qui blandit praesent luptatum zzril delenit augue duis dolore te feugait nulla facilisi.

Nam liber tempor cum soluta nobis eleifend option congue nihil imperdiet doming id quod mazim placerat facer possim assum. Lorem ipsum dolor sit amet, consectetuer adipiscing elit, sed diam nonummy nibh euismod tincidunt ut laoreet dolore magna aliquam erat volutpat.

Best regards,

Josh S. Example
President
coc
Enclosures (2)

## Business Card, Front
3.5 W by 2 H inches

## Business Card, Back
3.5 W by 2 H inches

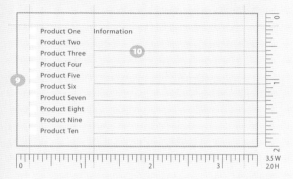

## Envelope, Commercial
9.5 W by 4.125 H inches

### Letterhead
**1** "SAMPLER" Frutiger 95 UltraBlack, 9pt; "Display" Frutiger 95 UltraBlack, 36pt, 1pt outline; "projection" Frutiger 95 UltraBlack, 15pt, 0.5pt outline; "Sound" Frutiger 95 UltraBlack, 60pt, 0.5pt outline; "VIDEO" Frutiger 95 UltraBlack, 18pt, 0.5pt outline; **2** Defining phrase Frutiger 45 Light, 7/9pt, align left; **3** Line 0.5pt; **4** Letter body Minion, 12/18pt, align left; **5** Address Frutiger 45 Light, 8/10pt, align left

### Business Card, Front
**6** Name Frutiger 45 Light, 7/10pt, align left; **7** Defining phrase Frutiger 45 Light, 7/8pt, align left; Address Frutiger 45 Light, 7/10pt, align left; **8** "SAMPLER" Frutiger 95 UltraBlack, 6.5pt; "Display" Frutiger 95 UltraBlack, 26pt, 0.75pt outline; "projection" Frutiger 95 UltraBlack, 9pt, .36pt outline; "Sound" Frutiger 95 UltraBlack, 43pt, 0.36pt outline; "VIDEO" Frutiger 95 UltraBlack, 13pt, 0.36pt outline

### Business Card, Back
**9** List Frutiger 55 Roman, 7/12pt, align left; **10** "Information" Frutiger 55 Roman, 7pt, align left; Lines 0.25pt

### Envelope
**11** "SAMPLER" Frutiger 95 UltraBlack, 7.5pt; "Display" Frutiger 95 UltraBlack, 30pt, 0.85pt outline; "projection" Frutiger 95 UltraBlack, 12.75pt, 0.43pt outline; "Sound" Frutiger 95 UltraBlack, 51pt, 0.43pt outline; "VIDEO" Frutiger 95 UltraBlack, 15pt, 0.43pt outline; **12** Address Frutiger 45 Light, 7/10pt, align left

### Color
To be printed in black and a solid PANTONE Color Ink as defined on the palette below (see Step 9.3). (Because this book is printed in process colors (CMYK), the illustration is only a simulation of the actual solid PANTONE Color).

Violet or
PANTONE® 265

| 100% |
| --- |
| 20% |

Sea Blue
PANTONE® 293

| 100% |
| --- |
| 50% |
| 20% |
| 10% |

STYLE 16

# Photographs

When you think about designing a logo, a photograph is probably not the first solution that comes to mind. That is what makes the style so enticing.

A photograph adds something to a design that a drawing cannot—evidence. It gives the reader a sense that they are witnessing the benefit of using your organization with their own eyes.

Would you visit a resort that is unwilling to show you a photograph of its facilities? Or buy a deck from a builder who shows no examples? If your story is enhanced by visual evidence, a photograph is a persuasive way to provide it.

The strips are assembled in a paint program. Each is a separate piece of artwork and is added to the layout like a long, thin photograph.

Because the photographs will be used at such a small size, close-up pictures-within-pictures are selected, and the outside is cropped away.

The color palette is created by selecting areas of color from the photographs.

Type is added to the strips in a coordinated color.

*Sampler*

SOURCE Illustrations:
Home photographs from
*Home Comforts* from
PhotoDisc, 800-979-4413,
206-441-9355,
www.photo disc.com,
© PhotoDisc, all rights
reserved.

SOURCE Type families:
Bickham Script,
Frutiger, Minion,
Adobe Systems, Inc.,
800-682-3623,
www.adobe.com/type.

**What you need**
Editing photographic images requires a paint or digital imaging program such as Adobe Photoshop or Jasc Software's Paint Shop Pro. Simple text and shapes can be produced with a desktop publishing program such as Adobe InDesign, Adobe PageMaker, QuarkXPress, or Microsoft Publisher.

Sarah W. Example
Director of Marketing
Sampler Corporation
1234 Street Address
Your City, ST 12345-6789

May 16, 2???

Sarah:

Lorem ipsum
tincidunt ut la
nostrud exerc
autem vel eum
eu feugiat null

Lorem ipsum d
tincidunt ut lac
nostrud exerci
autem vel eum
eu feugiat nulla
luptatum zzril d

Nam liber tempo
mazim placerat f
diam nonummy

Best regards,

Josh S. Example
President
coc
Enclosures (2)

A one-sentence "hook" benefit that describes your product or service

*Sampler*
REAL ESTATE

Sarah W. Example                                              May 16, 2???
Director of Marketing
Sampler Corporation
1234 Street Address
Your City, ST 12345-6789

Sarah:

Lorem ipsum dolor sit amet, consectetuer adipiscing elit, sed diam nonummy nibh euismod tincidunt ut laoreet dolore magna aliquam erat volutpat. Ut wisi enim ad minim veniam, quis nostrud exerci tation ullamcorper suscipit lobortis nisl ut aliquip ex ea commodo consequat. Duis autem vel eum iriure dolor in hendrerit in vulputate velit esse molestie consequat, vel illum dolore eu feugiat nulla facilisis at vero eros et accumsan et iusto odio dignissim qui blandit praesent.

Lorem ipsum dolor sit amet, consectetuer adipiscing elit, sed diam nonummy nibh euismod tincidunt ut laoreet dolore magna aliquam erat volutpat. Ut wisi enim ad minim veniam, quis nostrud exerci tation ullamcorper suscipit lobortis nisl ut aliquip ex ea commodo consequat. Duis autem vel eum iriure dolor in hendrerit in vulputate velit esse molestie consequat, vel illum dolore eu feugiat nulla facilisis at vero eros et accumsan et iusto odio dignissim qui blandit praesent luptatum zzril delenit augue duis dolore te feugait nulla facilisi.

Nam liber tempor cum soluta nobis eleifend option congue nihil imperdiet doming id quod mazim placerat facer possim assum. Lorem ipsum dolor sit amet, consectetuer adipiscing elit, sed diam nonummy nibh euismod tincidunt ut laoreet dolore magna aliquam erat volutpat.

Best regards,

Josh S. Example
President
coc
Enclosures (2)

Sampler Real Estate
123 Example Boulevard
Your City, ST 12345 6789
987 654 3210
987 654 3210 Fax
www.yourwebaddressz.com
E-mail  info@emailaddressz.com

## Business Card, Front 3.5 W by 2 H inches

## Business Card, Back 3.5 W by 2 H inches

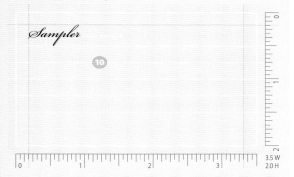

## Envelope, Commercial 9.5 W by 4.125 H inches

### Letterhead

**1** "Sampler" Bickham Script, 60pt; **2** Defining phrase Frutiger 95 UltraBlack, 6/7.5pt, align left; **3** "REAL" Frutiger 95 UltraBlack, 8pt, align left; **4** Letter body Minion, 12/18pt, align left; **5** Address Frutiger 45 Light, 8/10pt, align left

### Business Card, Front

**6** "Sampler" Bickham Script, 33pt; **7** Defining phrase Frutiger 95 UltraBlack, 6/7pt, align left; **8** Name Frutiger 45 Light, 7/8pt, align left; **9** Address Frutiger 45 Light, 7/8.5pt, align left

### Business Card, Back

**10** "Sampler" Bickham Script, 24pt; "REAL" Frutiger 95 UltraBlack, 4pt; Lines 0.5pt

### Envelope

**11** "Sampler" Bickham Script, 36pt; **12** "REAL" Frutiger 95 UltraBlack, 7pt; Address Frutiger 45 Light, 7/9pt, align left

### Color

Printed in four-color process (see Step 9.3) using values of cyan, magenta, yellow, and black (CMYK) as defined on the color palette below. Actual color will vary.

| Process Colors | | | |
|---|---|---|---|
| C0 | M45 | Y60 | K0 |
| C0 | M30 | Y50 | K0 |
| C0 | M10 | Y20 | K0 |
| C0 | M15 | Y50 | K0 |
| C0 | M7 | Y25 | K0 |
| C10 | M10 | Y50 | K10 |
| C5 | M5 | Y20 | K0 |

STYLE 17

# Products

Everyone has a product, whether it's a physical product or, as in this case, objects that represent an intangible.

Showing your product provides evidence of its value and a unique way to visualize your organization.

This is how you might present a service. A manufacturer could use the same style to present photographs of its best-selling product or feature a different product on each its letterhead, business card, and envelope.

The original photograph is cleaned up and brightened in a paint program. This photograph was shot on a white sheet of paper using a digital camera. If you don't have the equipment or the desire to do it yourself, commission a photograph by a professional photographer. Many photographers have the skill not only to shoot the picture but to compose it in an attractive way using special lighting, effects, and props.

This photograph is posterized in the paint program—it reduces the number of colors, resulting in a photograph that has the color quality of a painting.

**Sampler Writer's & Editor's WORKSHOP**

**Sampler Writer's & Editor's WORKSHOP**

A one-paragraph "hook" benefit that describes your product or service

The words of the name are typed out in a drawing program, and each is individually reduced to fit the with of a hypothetical box. Then space is added between the lines of the defining phrase to produce a visual element of the same relative size and weight.

*Hand writing fonts* stet

The word "stet" is created using a typeface that simulates handwriting. It is a proofreader's mark that means "let it stand." To a writer or editor, the meaning is obvious; for the uninitiated, it adds a little mystery to the design.

SOURCE
Illustration:
Marker/pens
from author.

SOURCES Type families:
Emmascript, DsgnHaus,
Inc., 203-367-1993,
www.fonthaus.com;
Franklin Gothic, Minion,
Adobe Systems, Inc.,
800-682-3623,
www.adobe.com/type.

 **What you need**
Editing photographic images requires a paint or digital imaging program such as Adobe Photoshop or Jasc Software's Paint Shop Pro. Simple text and shapes can be produced with a desktop publishing program such as Adobe InDesign, Adobe PageMaker, QuarkXPress, or Microsoft Publisher.

## Sampler Writer's & Editor's WORKSHOP

A one-para-graph "hook" benefit that describes your product or service

www.yourwebaddressz.com
Sampler Writer's & Editor's Workshop
123 Example Boulevard, Suite 123
Your City, State 12345 6789
Voice 987 654 3210
Fax 987 654 3210
E-mail info@emailaddressz.com

May 16, 2???

Sarah W. Example
Director of Marketing
Sampler Corporation
1234 Street Address
Your City, ST 12345-6789

Sarah:

Lor... ...psum dolo... ...nonummy nibh euismod
ti... ...ree... ...n ad minim veniam, quis
...a commodo consequat.

...tal...

nostr...

Duis autem v...

illum dolore eu feug...

blandit praesent luptatum z...

Nam liber tempor cum soluta nobis el...

mazim placerat facer possim assum. ...

sed diam nonummy nibh euismod tin...

Best regards,

Josh S. Example
President
coc
Enclosures (2)

www.yourwebaddressz.com
Voice 987 654 3210
Fax 987 654 3210

YOUR NAME
President/CEO

Sampler Writer's & Editor's Workshop
123 Example Boulevard
Your City, State 12345 6789
E-mail info@emailaddressz.com

### Sampler Writer's & Editor's WORKSHOP

A one-para-graph "hook" benefit that describes your product or service

Sampler Writer's
& Editor's Workshop
123 Example
Boulevard, Suite 123
Your City, State
12345 6789

PROOFREADERS' MARKS

**Sampler Writer's & Editor's WORKSHOP**

A one-paragraph "hook" benefit that describes your product or service

www.yourwebaddressz.com
Sampler Writer's & Editor's Workshop
123 Example Boulevard, Suite 123
Your City, State 12345 6789
Voice 987 654 3210
Fax 987 654 3210
E-mail  info@emailaddressz.com

Sarah W. Example
Director of Marketing
Sampler Corporation
1234 Street Address
Your City, ST 12345-6789

May 16, 2???

Sarah:

Lorem ipsum dolor sit amet, consectetuer adipiscing elit, sed diam nonummy nibh euismod tincidunt ut laoreet dolore magna aliquam erat volutpat. Ut wisi enim ad minim veniam, quis nostrud exerci tation ullamcorper suscipit lobortis nisl ut aliquip ex ea commodo consequat. Duis autem vel eum iriure dolor in hendrerit in vulputate velit esse molestie consequat, vel illum dolore eu feugiat nulla facilisis at vero eros et accumsan et iusto odio dignissim qui blandit praesent luptatum zzril delenit augue duis dolore te feugait nulla facili.

Lorem ipsum dolor sit amet, consectetuer adipiscing elit, sed diam nonummy nibh euismod tincidunt ut laoreet dolore magna aliquam erat volutpat. Ut wisi enim ad minim veniam, quis nostrud exerci tation ullamcorper suscipit lobortis nisl ut aliquip ex ea commodo consequat. Duis autem vel eum iriure dolor in hendrerit in vulputate velit esse molestie consequat, vel illum dolore eu feugiat nulla facilisis at vero eros et accumsan et iusto odio dignissim qui blandit praesent luptatum zzril delenit augue duis dolore te feugait nulla facili.

Nam liber tempor cum soluta nobis eleifend option congue nihil imperdiet doming id quod mazim placerat facer possim assum. Lorem ipsum dolor sit amet, consectetuer adipiscing elit, sed diam nonummy nibh euismod tincidunt ut laoreet dolore magna aliquam erat volutpat.

Best regards,

Josh S. Example
President
coc
Enclosures (2)

*stet*

## Business Card, Front
3.5 W by 2 H inches

www.yourwebaddressz.com
Voice 987 654 3210
Fax 987 654 3210

YOUR NAME
President / CEO

Sampler Writer's & Editor's Workshop
123 Example Boulevard
Your City, State 12345 6789
E-mail info@emailaddressz.com

**Sampler Writer's & Editor's WORKSHOP**
A one-para-graph "hook" benefit that describes your product or service

*stet*

3.5 W
2.0 H

## Business Card, Back
3.5 W by 2 H inches

### PROOFREADERS' MARKS

| | | | | | | | | |
|---|---|---|---|---|---|---|---|---|
| *lc* | Lorem ipsum | *fr* | Adipiscing elit | *lc* | Lorem ipsum |
| stet | Sit amet | *tr* | Diam nonummy | stet | Sit amet |
| wf | Consectetuer | ][ | Euismod tinci | wf | Consectetuer |
| ⌒ | Adipiscing | *sp* | Ut laoreet dol | ⌒ | Adipiscing |
| ⋁ | Diam nonummy | # | Magna aliqua | ⋁ | Diam nonummy |
| caps | Euismod | *M* | Volutpat | caps | Euismod |
| x | Ut laoreet | *ital* | Enim ad mini | x | Ut laoreet |

3.5 W
2.0 H

## Letterhead
**1** Line 0.5pt; "Sampler" Franklin Gothic Heavy, 21pt, align justified; "Writer's" Franklin Gothic Heavy, 23pt, align justified; "& Editor's" Franklin Gothic Heavy, 19pt, align justified; "WORKSHOP" Franklin Gothic Heavy, 14pt, align justified; **2** Defining phrase Franklin Gothic Heavy, 11/10.5pt, align left; **3** Address Franklin Gothic Book, 7/9pt, align left; **4** Letter body Franklin Gothic Book, 12/18pt, align left; **5** "Stet" Emmascript, 28pt

## Business Card, Front
**6** Line 0.5pt; Address/Name Franklin Gothic Book, 8/10pt, align left; Title Franklin Gothic Book, 7/10pt, align left; **7** "Sampler" Franklin Gothic Heavy, 13.5pt, align justified; "Writer's" Franklin Gothic Heavy, 15pt, align justified; "& Editor's" Franklin Gothic Heavy, 12pt, align justified; "WORKSHOP" Franklin Gothic Heavy, 9pt, align justified; **8** Defining phrase Franklin Gothic Heavy, 7/7pt, align left; **9** "Stet" Emmascript, 14pt

## Business Card, Back
**10** "PROOFREADERS'" Franklin Gothic Heavy, 9pt, align left; **11** Marks Emmascript, 15pt; **12** Text Franklin Gothic Demi, 8/14pt, align left

## Envelope
**13** Line 0.5pt; "Sampler" Franklin Gothic Heavy, 17pt, align justified; "Writer's" Franklin Gothic Heavy, 18.5pt, align justified; "& Editor's" Franklin Gothic Heavy, 15pt, align justified; "WORKSHOP" Franklin Gothic Heavy, 11pt, align justified; **14** Defining phrase Franklin Gothic Heavy, 9/9pt, align left; **15** Address Franklin Gothic Book, 7/8.5pt, align left; **16** "Stet" Emmascript, 28pt

## Color
Printed in four-color process (see Step 9.3) using values of cyan, magenta, yellow, and black (CMYK) as defined on the color palette below. Actual color will vary.

Process Colors

| C0 | M30 | Y90 | K0 |
|---|---|---|---|
| C60 | M10 | Y0 | K30 |

## Envelope, Commercial
9.5 W by 4.125 H inches

**Sampler Writer's & Editor's WORKSHOP**
A one-para-graph "hook" benefit that describes your product or service
Sampler Writer's & Editor's Workshop 123 Example Boulevard, Suite 123 Your City, State 12345 6789

*stet*

9.5 W
4.125 H

STYLE 18

# Rectangles

If you use rectangles to divide your letter from your logo, your logo from your organization's name, and your organization's name from its defining phrase, what will your reader focus on? The circle.

It is a design mainstay—when you build your design on a consistent pattern of shapes, the shape that breaks the pattern becomes the focal point.

The logo is nothing more than a simple light bulb and burst.

To ensure the colors complement each other, they are chosen as a consecutive series from a standard color wheel.

Where the gray, teal, and violet rectangles overlap, two more rectangular shapes are formed. By making the outside shapes lighter, you create a sense of transparency.

The circle breaks the border of the box on which it is positioned.

SAMPLER STUDIO
**ideas**

The name of the organization is typed in all capital letters. The word "idea" is not a part of the name but part of its logo—a design element meant to shout the benefit of the organization.

The type butts up to the edge of the color precisely.

SOURCE Illustration:
Light bulb from Dick &
Jane font from DsgnHaus,
Inc., 203-367-1993,
www.fonthaus.com.

SOURCE Type families:
Franklin Gothic, Minion,
Adobe Systems, Inc.,
800-682-3623,
www.adobe.com/type.

 **What you need**
Breaking apart draw/vector artwork and editing the pieces requires a draw program such as Adobe Illustrator, CorelDRAW, or Macromedia FreeHand. Simple text and shapes can be produced with a desktop publishing program such as Adobe InDesign, Adobe PageMaker, QuarkXPress, or Microsoft Publisher.

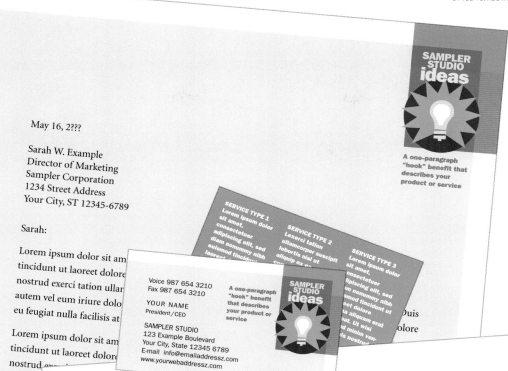

May 16, 2???

Sarah W. Example
Director of Marketing
Sampler Corporation
1234 Street Address
Your City, ST 12345-6789

Sarah:

Lorem ipsum dolor sit am
tincidunt ut laoreet dolore
nostrud exerci tation ullan
autem vel eum iriure dolo
eu feugiat nulla facilisis at

Lorem ipsum dolor sit am
tincidunt ut laoreet dolore
nostrud exe
autem ve
eu feugia
luptatum

Nam liber
mazim pla
diam nonu

Best regards,

Josh S. Examp
President
coc
Enclosures (2)

A one-paragraph
"hook" benefit that
describes your
product or service

**SERVICE TYPE 1**
Lorem ipsum dolor
sit amet,
consectetuer
adipiscing elit, sed
diam nonummy nibh
euismod tincidunt

**SERVICE TYPE 2**
Lexerci tation
ullamcorper suscipit
lobortis nisl ut
aliquip ex

**SERVICE TYPE 3**
Lorem ipsum dolor
sit amet,
consectetuer
adipiscing elit, sed
am nonummy nibh
smod tincidunt ut
et dolore
a aliquam erat
a. Ut wisi
d minim ven-
s nostru

Voice 987 654 3210
Fax 987 654 3210

A one-paragraph
"hook" benefit
that describes
your product or
service

**YOUR NAME**
President / CEO

SAMPLER STUDIO
123 Example Boulevard
Your City, State 12345 6789
E-mail info@emailaddressz.com
www.yourwebaddressz.com

SAMPLER
STUDIO
123 Example
Boulevard
Your City, State
12345 6789

A one-
paragraph
hook benefit
that describes
your product
or service

SAMPLER STUDIO
123 Example Boulevard
Your City, State 12345 6789
Voice 987 654 3210
Fax 987 654 3210
www.yourwebaddressz.com
info@emailaddressz.com

May 16, 2???

Sarah W. Example
Director of Marketing
Sampler Corporation
1234 Street Address
Your City, ST 12345-6789

Sarah:

Lorem ipsum dolor sit amet, consectetuer adipiscing elit, sed diam nonummy nibh euismod tincidunt ut laoreet dolore magna aliquam erat volutpat. Ut wisi enim ad minim veniam, quis nostrud exerci tation ullamcorper suscipit lobortis nisl ut aliquip ex ea commodo consequat. Duis autem vel eum iriure dolor in hendrerit in vulputate velit esse molestie consequat, vel illum dolore eu feugiat nulla facilisis at vero eros et accumsan et iusto odio dignissim qui blandit praesent.

Lorem ipsum dolor sit amet, consectetuer adipiscing elit, sed diam nonummy nibh euismod tincidunt ut laoreet dolore magna aliquam erat volutpat. Ut wisi enim ad minim veniam, quis nostrud exerci tation ullamcorper suscipit lobortis nisl ut aliquip ex ea commodo consequat. Duis autem vel eum iriure dolor in hendrerit in vulputate velit esse molestie consequat, vel illum dolore eu feugiat nulla facilisis at vero eros et accumsan et iusto odio dignissim qui blandit praesent luptatum zzril delenit augue duis dolore te feugait nulla facilisi.

Nam liber tempor cum soluta nobis eleifend option congue nihil imperdiet doming id quod mazim placerat facer possim assum. Lorem ipsum dolor sit amet, consectetuer adipiscing elit, sed diam nonummy nibh euismod tincidunt ut laoreet dolore magna aliquam erat volutpat.

Best regards,

Josh S. Example
President
coc
Enclosures (2)

SAMPLER STUDIO
123 Example Boulevard
Your City, State 12345 6789
Voice 987 654 3210
Fax 987 654 3210
www.yourwebaddressz.com
info@emailaddressz.com

8.5 W
11 H

## Business Card, Front  3.5 W by 2 H inches

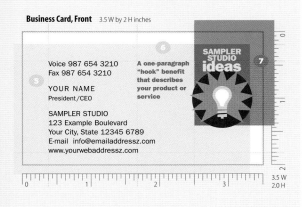

Voice 987 654 3210
Fax 987 654 3210

A one-paragraph "hook" benefit that describes your product or service

YOUR NAME
President/CEO

SAMPLER STUDIO
123 Example Boulevard
Your City, State 12345 6789
E-mail info@emailaddressz.com
www.yourwebaddressz.com

```
0          1          2          3          3.5 W
                                              2.0 H
```

## Business Card, Back  3.5 W by 2 H inches

**SERVICE TYPE 1**
Lorem ipsum dolor sit amet, consectetuer adipiscing elit, sed diam nonummy nibh euismod tincidunt ut laoreet dolore magna aliquam erat volutpat. Ut wisi enim ad minim veniam, quis nostrud

**SERVICE TYPE 2**
Lexerci tation ullamcorper suscipit lobortis nisl ut aliquip ex ea commodo consequat. Duis autem vel eum iriure dolor in hendrerit in vulputate velit esse molestie consequat

**SERVICE TYPE 3**
Lorem ipsum dolor sit amet, consectetuer adipiscing elit, sed diam nonummy nibh euismod tincidunt ut laoreet dolore magna aliquam erat volutpat. Ut wisi enim ad minim ven-iam, quis nostrud

```
0          1          2          3          3.5 W
                                              2.0 H
```

## Envelope, Commercial  9.5 W by 4.125 H inches

SAMPLER
STUDIO
123 Example
Boulevard
Your City, State
12345 6789

A one-paragraph hook benefit that describes your product or service

```
0     1     2     3     4     5     6     7     8     9     9.5 W
                                                            4.125 H
```

### Letterhead

**1 Organization** Franklin Gothic Heavy, 12/13pt, align center; **"ideas"** Franklin Gothic Heavy, 24pt, align center; **2 Defining phrase** Franklin Gothic Heavy, 8/10pt, align center; **3 Letter body** Minion, 12/18pt, align left; **4 Address** Franklin Gothic Book, 7.5/10pt; align left

### Business Card, Front

**5 Phone/Name/Address** Franklin Gothic Book, 8/10pt, align left; **Title** Franklin Gothic Book, 7pt, align left; **6 Defining phrase** Franklin Gothic Heavy, 7/9pt, align left; **7 Organization** Franklin Gothic Heavy, 9/7pt, align center; **"ideas"** Franklin Gothic Heavy, 17pt, align center

### Business Card, Back

**8 Text** Franklin Gothic Heavy, 7/9pt, align left

### Envelope

**9 Address** Franklin Gothic Book, 7.5/10pt, align left; **10 Defining phrase** Franklin Gothic Heavy, 7.5/10pt, align left; **11 Organization** Franklin Gothic Heavy, 9/7pt, align center; **"ideas"** Franklin Gothic Heavy, 17pt, align center

### Color

Printed in four-color process (see Step 9.3) using values of cyan, magenta, yellow, and black (CMYK) as defined on the color palette below. Actual color will vary.

**Process Colors**

| C0 | M0 | Y4 | K10 |
| C95 | M0 | Y40 | K0 |
| C70 | M0 | Y30 | K0 |
| C25 | M0 | Y15 | K0 |
| C60 | M50 | Y0 | K0 |
| C50 | M40 | Y0 | K0 |
| C0 | M10 | Y75 | K0 |
| C0 | M0 | Y50 | K5 |
| C0 | M100 | Y70 | K10 |
| C0 | M50 | Y85 | K0 |

STYLE 19

# Scribbles

Those years of scribbling and doodling in idle moments are about to pay off.

Scribbles make great logos. They portray a relaxed, lighthearted attitude that may not be appropriate for a law firm or an elegant hotel, but perfectly suited to hundreds of other types of organizations.

The key to success is to find a natural artist. If you can't do it yourself, recruit someone with particularly good handwriting. Sometimes even children can invent natural, free-form scribbles that make excellent logos.

SOURCE Illustrations:
Wine glass, clock, match,
by the author.

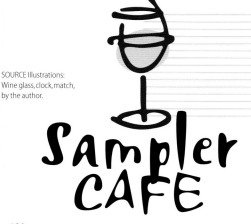

Start by brainstorming ideas. Using a fountain pen on color laserjet paper produces very fluid, thin and thick strokes.

Settle on an object and draw it at least twenty-five times. The trick is to draw it small (roughly one-inch square) and rapidly, using as few strokes as necessary. Return after a couple of hours and see if you've created a winner.

This version is a scan of the original that was traced in a drawing program. The oval focuses the eye on the contents of the glass, and the horizontal lines add an interesting background.

The typeface should emphasize the effect you're trying to achieve. The top typeface is fun, the middle version is more traditional, and the bottom is almost elegant.

The lines from the logo are repeated on the background of the business card. Subtle changes on each piece—the letterhead, business card, and envelope—improve the combined effect.

Take advantage of the space on the back of your business card. Valuable information encourages your prospect to keep it on hand—in this case, the recipe for the cafe's signature cocktail.

SOURCE Type families:
Airstream, Frutiger,
Minion, Adobe Systems,
Inc., 800-682-3623,
www.adobe.com/type.

### What you need

Scanning and editing your scribbles requires a paint or digital imaging program such as Adobe Photoshop or Jasc Software's Paint Shop Pro. Simple text and shapes can be produced with a desktop publishing program such as Adobe InDesign, Adobe PageMaker, QuarkXPress, or Microsoft Publisher.

Sarah W. Example
Director of Marketing
Sampler Corporation
1234 Street Address
Your City, ST 12345-6789

May 16, 2???

Sarah:

Lorem ipsum dolor sit amet, consectetuer adipiscing elit, sed diam nonummy nibh euismod tincidunt ut laoreet dolore magna aliquam erat volutpat. Ut wisi enim ad minim veniam, quis nostrud exerci tation ullamcorper suscipit lobortis nisl ut aliquip ex ea commodo consequat. Duis autem vel eum iriure dolor in hendrerit in vulputate velit esse molestie consequat, vel illum dolore eu feugiat nulla facilisis at vero eros et accumsan et iusto odio dignissim qui blandit praesent.

Lorem ipsum dolor sit amet, consectetuer adipiscing elit, sed diam nonummy nibh euismod tincidunt ut laoreet dolore magna aliquam erat volutpat. Ut wisi enim ad minim veniam, quis nostrud exerci tation ullamcorper suscipit lobortis nisl ut aliquip ex ea commodo consequat. Duis autem vel eum iriure dolor in hendrerit in vulputate velit esse molestie consequat, vel illum dolore eu feugiat nulla facilisis at vero eros et accumsan et iusto odio dignissim qui blandit praesent luptatum.

Nam liber tempor cum soluta nobis eleifend option congue nihil imperdiet doming id quod mazim placerat facer possim assum. Lorem ipsum dolor sit amet, consectetuer adipiscing elit, sed diam nonummy nibh euismod tincidunt ut laoreet dolore magna aliquam erat volutpat.

Best regards,

Josh S. Example
President
coc
Enclosures (2)

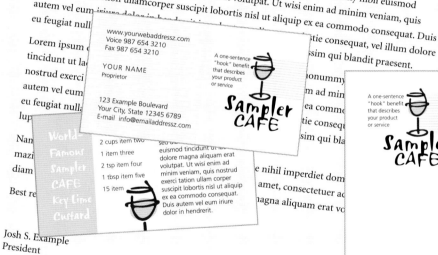

A one-sentence
"hook" benefit
that describes
your product
or service

Sarah W. Example                                    May 16, 2???
Director of Marketing
Sampler Corporation
1234 Street Address
Your City, ST 12345-6789

Sarah:

Lorem ipsum dolor sit amet, consectetuer adipiscing elit, sed diam nonummy nibh euismod
tincidunt ut laoreet dolore magna aliquam erat volutpat. Ut wisi enim ad minim veniam, quis
nostrud exerci tation ullamcorper suscipit lobortis nisl ut aliquip ex ea commodo consequat. Duis
autem vel eum iriure dolor in hendrerit in vulputate velit esse molestie consequat, vel illum dolore
eu feugiat nulla facilisis at vero eros et accumsan et iusto odio dignissim qui blandit praesent.

Lorem ipsum dolor sit amet, consectetuer adipiscing elit, sed diam nonummy nibh euismod
tincidunt ut laoreet dolore magna aliquam erat volutpat. Ut wisi enim ad minim veniam, quis
nostrud exerci tation ullamcorper suscipit lobortis nisl ut aliquip ex ea commodo consequat. Duis
autem vel eum iriure dolor in hendrerit in vulputate velit esse molestie consequat, vel illum dolore
eu feugiat nulla facilisis at vero eros et accumsan et iusto odio dignissim qui blandit praesent
luptatum zzril delenit augue duis dolore te feugait nulla facilisi.

Nam liber tempor cum soluta nobis eleifend option congue nihil imperdiet doming id quod
mazim placerat facer possim assum. Lorem ipsum dolor sit amet, consectetuer adipiscing elit, sed
diam nonummy nibh euismod tincidunt ut laoreet dolore magna aliquam erat volutpat.

Best regards,


Josh S. Example
President
coc
Enclosures (2)

123 Example Boulevard
Your City, State 12345 6789
Voice 987 654 3210
Fax 987 654 3210
www.yourwebaddressz.com
E-mail  info@emailaddressz.com

**Business Card, Front**  3.5 W by 2 H inches

www.yourwebaddressz.com
Voice 987 654 3210
Fax 987 654 3210

YOUR NAME
Proprietor

123 Example Boulevard
Your City, State 12345 6789
E-mail info@emailaddressz.com

A one-sentence
"hook" benefit
that describes
your product
or service

3.5 W
2.0 H

**Business Card, Back**  3.5 W by 2 H inches

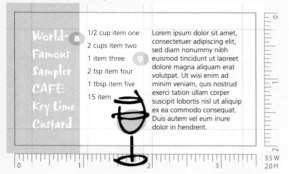

World-
Famous
Sampler
CAFE
Key Lime
Custard

1/2 cup item one
2 cups item two
1 item three
2 tsp item four
1 tbsp item five
15 item

Lorem ipsum dolor sit amet, consectetuer adipiscing elit, sed diam nonummy nibh euismod tincidunt ut laoreet dolore magna aliquam erat volutpat. Ut wisi enim ad minim veniam, quis nostrud exerci tation ullam corper suscipit lobortis nisl ut aliquip ex ea commodo consequat. Duis autem vel eum iriure dolor in hendrerit.

3.5 W
2.0 H

## Letterhead

**1** "Sampler" Airstream, 30pt, align center; "CAFE" Airstream, 24pt, align center; Defining phrase Frutiger 45 Light, 7/9pt, align left; **2** Lines 0.5pt; **3** Letter body Minion 12/18pt, align left; **4** Address Frutiger 45 Light, 7.5/10pt, align left

## Business Card, Front

**5** Address Frutiger 45 Light, 8/10pt, align left; Title Frutiger 45 Light, 7pt, align left; **6** Defining phrase Frutiger 45 Light, 6/8pt, align left; **7** "Sampler" Airstream, 27pt, align center; "CAFE" Airstream, 21pt, align center; Lines 0.5pt

## Business Card, Back

**8** Headline Frutiger 45 Light, 14/19pt, align left; **9** Ingredients Frutiger 45 Light, 7.5/14pt, align left; Recipe Frutiger 45 Light, 7.5/9pt, align left

## Envelope

**10** Defining phrase Frutiger 45 Light, 6/8pt, align left; "Sampler" Airstream, 27pt, align center; "CAFE" Airstream, 21pt, align center; Lines 0.5pt; **11** Address Frutiger 45 Light, 8/10pt, align left

## Color

To be printed in black and a solid PANTONE Color Ink as defined on the palette below (see Step 9.3). (Because this book is printed in process colors (CMYK), the illustration is only a simulation of the actual solid PANTONE Color).

Lemon Green or
PANTONE® 458

| 100% |
| 50% |
| 30% |

**Envelope, Commercial**  9.5 W by 4.125 H inches

A one-sentence
"hook" benefit
that describes
your product
or service

Sampler
CAFE

123 Example Boulevard
Your City, State 12345 6789

9.5 W
4.125 H

STYLE 20

# Shadows

Paint programs make using subtle shadows, with all types of artwork, practical. And those shadows have a significant impact on the desktop publishing world: They add a third dimension to conventional two-dimensional layouts. A simple shadow can create the illusion of an object floating above the page or, as shown here, cut into the surface.

On these layouts, the photographs are the visual center around which the name, defining phrase, and address orbit. Rather than repeat the same photograph on all three pieces, the scope of the organization is expanded by featuring a different image on each.

The shadow is created in a paint program using a photograph that is cropped and sized to fit the layout.

A black angle shape is added to a layer above the photograph.

The angle shape is blurred.

The opacity of the angle layer is adjusted to lighten it.

And the final image is cropped to size and saved.

The back of the card lists all the locations the tour company visits—information that encourages the prospect to keep it on hand.

SOURCES Illustrations: Landscapes from *US Landmarks and Travel* from PhotoDisc, 800-979-4413, 206-441-9355, www.photodisc.com, © CMCD, all rights reserved; map from *Task Force Image Gallery* by NVTech, 800-387-0732, 613-727-8184, www.nvtech.com, © NVTech, all rights reserved.

SOURCE Type families: Iris, Minion, Myriad, Adobe Systems, Inc., 800-682-3623, www.adobe.com/type.

### What you need

Editing photographic images requires a paint or digital imaging program such as Adobe Photoshop or Jasc Software's Paint Shop Pro. Creating artwork for the map requires a draw program such as Adobe Illustrator, CorelDRAW, or Macromedia FreeHand. Simple text and shapes can be produced with a desktop publishing program such as Adobe InDesign, Adobe PageMaker, QuarkX-Press, or Microsoft Publisher.

SAMPLER TOURS

A one-paragraph "hook" benefit that describes your product or service

123 Example Boulevard
Suite 100
Your City, State 12345 6789
Voice 987 654 3210
Fax 987 654 3210
www.yourwebaddressz.com
info@emailaddressz.com

May 16, 2???

Sarah W. Example
Director of Marketing
Sampler Corporation
1234 Street Address
Your City, ST 12345-6789

Sarah:

ing elit, sed diam nonummy nibh euismod
isi enim ad minim veniam, quis
mmodo consequat. Duis
illum dolore

Lorem ipsu

tincidunt

nostrud e

autem v

eu feug

SAMPLER TOURS

123 Example
Boulevard, Suite 100
Your City, State
12345 6789

A one-paragraph "hook"
benefit that describes
your product or service

Lore

tinc

no

a

www.yourwebaddressz.com
Voice 987 654 3210
Fax 987 654 3210

SAMPLER TOURS

YOUR NAME
President / CEO

123 Example Boulevard,
Your City, State 12345 6
E-mail info@emailaddr

A one-paragraph
"hook" benefit that
describes your

TOP DESTINATIONS
Lorem ipsum
amet, consectetuer
adipiscing elit, sed diam
nonummy nibh euismod
tincidunt ut laoreet
dolore magna aliquam
erat volutpat. Ut wisi
enim ad minim veniam,
quis nostrud.

Lorem ipsum 1
Consectetuer 2
Sed diam 3
Nonummy nibh 4
Euismod tinci 5
Dolore magna 6
Aliquam erat 7
Volutpat ut wisi 8
Enim ad 9

diam nonu

Best regards,

Josh S. Example
President
coc
Enclosures (2)

SAMPLER
TOURS

A one-paragraph
"hook" benefit that
describes your
product or service

123 Example Boulevard
Suite 100
Your City, State 12345 6789
Voice 987 654 3210
Fax 987 654 3210
www.yourwebaddressz.com
info@emailaddressz.com

May 16, 2???

Sarah W. Example
Director of Marketing
Sampler Corporation
1234 Street Address
Your City, ST 12345-6789

Sarah:

Lorem ipsum dolor sit amet, consectetuer adipiscing elit, sed diam nonummy nibh euismod tincidunt ut laoreet dolore magna aliquam erat volutpat. Ut wisi enim ad minim veniam, quis nostrud exerci tation ullamcorper suscipit lobortis nisl ut aliquip ex ea commodo consequat. Duis autem vel eum iriure dolor in hendrerit in vulputate velit esse molestie consequat, vel illum dolore eu feugiat nulla facilisis at vero eros et accumsan et iusto odio dignissim qui blandit praesent.

Lorem ipsum dolor sit amet, consectetuer adipiscing elit, sed diam nonummy nibh euismod tincidunt ut laoreet dolore magna aliquam erat volutpat. Ut wisi enim ad minim veniam, quis nostrud exerci tation ullamcorper suscipit lobortis nisl ut aliquip ex ea commodo consequat. Duis autem vel eum iriure dolor in hendrerit in vulputate velit esse molestie consequat, vel illum dolore eu feugiat nulla facilisis at vero eros et accumsan et iusto odio dignissim qui blandit praesent luptatum zzril delenit augue duis dolore te feugait nulla facilisi.

Nam liber tempor cum soluta nobis eleifend option congue nihil imperdiet doming id quod mazim placerat facer possim assum. Lorem ipsum dolor sit amet, consectetuer adipiscing elit, sed diam nonummy nibh euismod tincidunt ut laoreet dolore magna aliquam erat volutpat.

Best regards,


Josh S. Example
President
coc
Enclosures (2)

**Business Card, Front** 3.5 W by 2 H inches

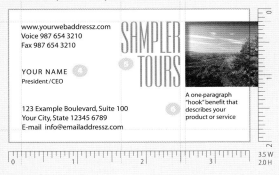

www.yourwebaddressz.com
Voice 987 654 3210
Fax 987 654 3210

SAMPLER
TOURS

YOUR NAME
President/CEO

123 Example Boulevard, Suite 100
Your City, State 12345 6789
E-mail info@emailaddressz.com

A one-paragraph
"hook" benefit that
describes your
product or service

3.5 W
2.0 H

**Business Card, Back** 3.5 W by 2 H inches

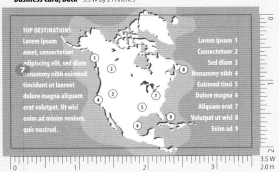

TOP DESTINATIONS
Lorem ipsum
amet, consectetuer
adipiscing elit, sed diam
nonummy nibh euismod
tincidunt ut laoreet
dolore magna aliquam
erat volutpat. Ut wisi
enim ad minim veniam,
quis nostrud.

Lorem ipsum 1
Consectetuer 2
Sed diam 3
Nonummy nibh 4
Euismod tinci 5
Dolore magna 6
Aliquam erat 7
Volutpat ut wisi 8
Enim ad 9

3.5 W
2.0 H

**Envelope, Commercial** 9.5 W by 4.125 H inches

SAMPLER
TOURS

123 Example
Boulevard, Suite 100
Your City, State
12345 6789

A one-paragraph "hook"
benefit that describes
your product or service

9.5 W
4.125 H

## Letterhead

**1** Organization Iris, 48/35pt, align right; Defining phrase Myriad Regular, 7/8pt, align right; **2** Address Myriad Regular, 7/9pt, align left; **3** Letter body Minion, 12/18pt, align left

## Business Card, Front

**4** Address Myriad Regular, 8/10pt, align left; Title Myriad Regular, 7pt, align left; **5** Organization Iris, 50/37pt, align right; **6** Defining phrase Myriad Regular, 7/8pt, align left

## Business Card, Back

**7** Address Myriad Multiple Master (MM), 700bd, 300cn, 8/12pt, align left; Numbers Myriad MM, 700bd, 300cn, 6pt, align center

## Envelope

**8** Organization Iris, 48/35pt, align right; **9** Defining phrase Myriad Regular, 7/8pt, align right; **10** Address Myriad Regular, 7/8pt, align left

## Color

Printed in four-color process (see Step 9.3) using values of cyan, magenta, yellow, and black (CMYK) as defined on the color palette below. Actual color will vary.

Process Colors

| | | | |
|---|---|---|---|
| C50 | M15 | Y0 | K0 |
| C0 | M55 | Y75 | K0 |
| C40 | M15 | Y0 | K0 |
| C50 | M20 | Y0 | K0 |
| C15 | M35 | Y75 | K5 |

STYLE 21

# Simplicity

Seals are the definition of simplicity. Historians tell us they are among the first design artifacts, reaching back to centuries before the birth of Christ. They have been used throughout the ages, stamped in clay, wax, and ink as the authenticating signature and proof of their owner's authority.

Today seals still are used for both practical and ceremonial purposes. The random shape and three-dimensional effect of this version imitates an imprint in sealing wax.

Because the seal will be used at a small size, the artwork must be simple, bold, and easily recognizable. The original apple here was simplified and centered within a circle.

The sealing wax is a free-form outline.

The sealing wax outline is filled with the desired color and a second, black copy for a shadow is positioned beneath it.

The three-dimensional effect is nothing more than three copies of the same artwork slightly offset—the light version up and to the left; the black shadow, down and to the right.

That seal layer is sandwiched with the sealing wax layer to create the finished seal.

A simple edge highlight is made by duplicating the sealing wax shape.

SOURCE Illustrations:
Apple from *Designer's Club* from Dynamic Graphics 800-255-8800, 309-688-8800, www.dgusa.com
© Dynamic Graphics, all rights reserved.

SOURCE Type families:
Caslon, Minion, Adobe Systems, Inc., 800-682-3623, www.adobe.com/type.

**What you need**

Drawing the shape of the seal and editing the apple artwork requires a draw program such as Adobe Illustrator, CorelDRAW, or Macromedia FreeHand. Simple text and shapes can be produced with a desktop publishing program such as Adobe InDesign, Adobe PageMaker, QuarkXPress, or Microsoft Publisher.

SAMPLER CIDER MILLS
SINCE 1823

Sarah W. Example                                                        May 16, 2???
Director of Marketing
Sampler Corporation
1234 Street Address
Your City, ST 12345-6789

Sarah:

Lorem ipsum dolor sit amet, consectetue
tincidunt ut laoreet dolore magna aliqua
nostrud exerci tation ullamcorper suscip
autem vel eum iriure dolor in hendrerit
eu feugiat nulla facilisis at vero eros et ad

Lorem ipsum dolor sit amet, consectetue
tincidunt ut laoreet dolore magna aliqua
nostrud exerci tation ullan
autem vel eum iriure dolo
eu feugiat nulla facilisis at
luptatum zzril delenit augu

Nam liber tempor cum sol
mazim placerat facer possi                                              g elit, sed
diam nonummy nibh euis

Best regards,


Josh S. Example
President
coc
Enclosures (2)

SAMPLER CIDER MILLS
123 Example Boulevard
Your City, ST 12345 6789

IMPORTANT

SINCE 1823

A one-sentence
"hook" benefit that
describes your
product or service

SAMPLER CIDER MILLS

YOUR NAME
President/CEO

Voice 987 654 3210   Fax 987 654 3210   www.yourwebaddressz.com
E-mail info@emailaddressz.com
123 Example Boulevard, Your City, State 12345 6789

*A one-sentence "hook" benefit that describes your product or service*

123 Example Boulevard, Your City, State 12345 6789
Voice 987 654 3210   Fax 987 654 3210   www.yourwebaddressz.com   E-mail info@emailaddressz.com

DESIGN RECIPES: SIMPLICITY

**SAMPLER CIDER MILLS**
SINCE 1823

Sarah W. Example                                                        May 16, 2???
Director of Marketing
Sampler Corporation
1234 Street Address
Your City, ST 12345-6789

Sarah:

Lorem ipsum dolor sit amet, consectetuer adipiscing elit, sed diam nonummy nibh euismod tincidunt ut laoreet dolore magna aliquam erat volutpat. Ut wisi enim ad minim veniam, quis nostrud exerci tation ullamcorper suscipit lobortis nisl ut aliquip ex ea commodo consequat. Duis autem vel eum iriure dolor in hendrerit in vulputate velit esse molestie consequat, vel illum dolore eu feugiat nulla facilisis at vero eros et accumsan et iusto odio dignissim qui blandit praesent.

Lorem ipsum dolor sit amet, consectetuer adipiscing elit, sed diam nonummy nibh euismod tincidunt ut laoreet dolore magna aliquam erat volutpat. Ut wisi enim ad minim veniam, quis nostrud exerci tation ullamcorper suscipit lobortis nisl ut aliquip ex ea commodo consequat. Duis autem vel eum iriure dolor in hendrerit in vulputate velit esse molestie consequat, vel illum dolore eu feugiat nulla facilisis at vero eros et accumsan et iusto odio dignissim qui blandit praesent luptatum zzril delenit augue duis dolore te feugait nulla facilisi.

Nam liber tempor cum soluta nobis eleifend option congue nihil imperdiet doming id quod mazim placerat facer possim assum. Lorem ipsum dolor sit amet, consectetuer adipiscing elit, sed diam nonummy nibh euismod tincidunt ut laoreet dolore magna aliquam erat volutpat.

Best regards,


Josh S. Example
President
coc
Enclosures (2)

*A one-sentence "hook" benefit that describes your product or service*

123 Example Boulevard, Your City, State 12345 6789
Voice 987 654 3210    Fax 987 654 3210    www.yourwebaddressz.com    E-mail info@emailaddressz.com

**Business Card, Front**  3.5 W by 2 H inches

**Business Card, Back**  3.5 W by 2 H inches

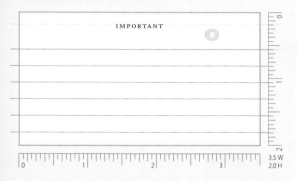

**Envelope, Commercial**  9.5 W by 4.125 H inches

### Letterhead

**1** "S" Adobe Caslon Swash Italic, 10pt, align center; "AMPLER" Adobe Caslon Expert, 10pt, align center; "SINCE" Adobe Caslon Expert, 9pt, align center; **2** Line 0.25pt; **3** Letter body Minion, 12/18pt, align left; **4** Defining phrase Adobe Caslon Regular Italic, 8/12pt, align center; Address Adobe Caslon Regular, 8/11pt, align center

### Business Card, Front

**5** Line 0.25pt; "SINCE" Adobe Caslon Expert, 8pt, align left; **6** "S" Adobe Caslon Swash Italic, 8.5pt, align center; "AMPLER" Adobe Caslon Expert, 8.5pt, align center; Defining phrase Adobe Caslon Italic, 8/9pt, align left; **7** Name Adobe Caslon Regular, 8/9pt, align center; Address Adobe Caslon Regular, 8/10pt, align center

### Business Card, Back

**8** "IMPORTANT" Adobe Caslon Expert, 9pt, align center; Lines 0.25pt

### Envelope

**9** "S" Adobe Caslon Swash Italic, 8.5pt, align center; "AMPLER" Adobe Caslon Expert, 8.5pt, align center

### Color

To be printed in black and a solid PANTONE Color Ink as defined on the palette below (see Step 9.3). (Because this book is printed in process colors (CMYK), the illustration is only a simulation of the actual solid PANTONE Color).

Burgundy or
PANTONE® 187

100 %

50 %

STYLE 22

# Stack

Who's to say that a letterhead has to be eleven inches tall—every desktop printer can print an 8.5-by-14-inch sheet. This letterhead easily folds to fit a standard #10 envelope, and it provides twenty-five percent more space for little or no cost. Stacking a standard letterhead on top of an 8.5-by-3.5-inch extension makes simple sense.

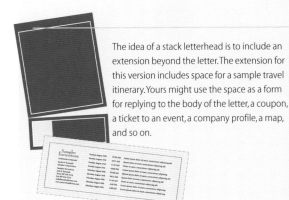

The idea of a stack letterhead is to include an extension beyond the letter. The extension for this version includes space for a sample travel itinerary. Yours might use the space as a form for replying to the body of the letter, a coupon, a ticket to an event, a company profile, a map, and so on.

The illustration is extracted from an old advertising sign found in a clip art collection. With a full-featured paint program and some practice, it is possible to add and remove objects and type, and to change colors. The result of learning to use such a program is you can repurpose beautifully executed illustrations, one of which may satisfy your need perfectly.

A typeface is chosen to match the flavor of the illustration. "Sampler" is reduced slightly so the "E" and "S" don't touch.

**What you need**

Editing the camel illustration requires a paint or digital imaging program such as Adobe Photoshop or Jasc Software's Paint Shop Pro. Simple text and shapes can be produced with a desktop publishing program such as Adobe InDesign, Adobe PageMaker, QuarkXPress, or Microsoft Publisher.

*Sampler*
*Excursions*

*A one-paragraph "hook"
benefit that describes
your product or service*

*Dallas, Texas, USA
Sydney, Australia
London, England*

May 16, 2???

Sarah W. Example
Director of Marketing
Sampler Corporation
1234 Street Address
Your City, ST 12345-6789

Sarah:

Lorem ipsum dolor sit amet, consectetuer adipisci
tincidunt ut laoreet dolore magna aliquam erat vo
nostrud exerci tation u          init lobortis
autem vel eum iriure
eu feugiat nulla facili

Lorem ipsum dolor
tincidunt ut laoreet
nostrud exerci tati
autem vel eum iri
eu feugiat nulla f
luptatum zzril d

Nam liber temp
mazim placera
diam nonum

Best regards

Josh S. Example
President
coc
Enclosures (2)

*Sampler*
*Excursions*

*A one-
paragraph
"hook" benefit
that describes
your product
or service
Lorem ipsum*

123 Example Boulevard
Your City, State 12345 6789

TRAVEL IDEAS

www.yourwebaddressz.com
Voice 987 654 3210
Fax 987 654 3210

*Sampler*
*Excursions*

*A one-
paragraph
"hook" benefit
that describes
your product
or service
Lorem ipsum*

YOUR NAME
President / CEO

123 Example Boulevard
Your City, State 12345 6789
E-mail  info@emailaddressz.com

123 Example Boulevard, Your City, State 12345 6789
Voice 987 654 3210   Fax 987 654 3210   E-mail  info@emailaddressz.com   www.yourwebaddressz.com

*Sampler*
*Excursions*

ITINERARY SUMMARY
Sarah W. Example
Sampler Corporation

| | | |
|---|---|---|
| Sunday, August 25th | 07:00 AM | Lorem ipsum dolor sit amet, consectetuer adipiscing elit |
| Sunday, August 25th | 10:15 AM | Ipsum dolor sit amet, consectetuer adipiscing elit |
| Sunday, August 25th | 11:45 AM | Dolor sit amet, consectetuer adipiscing elit |
| Sunday, August 25th | 04:00 PM | Lorem ipsum dolor sit amet, consectetuer adipiscing |
| Monday, August 26th | 07:00 AM | Slorem ipsum dolor sit amet, consectetuer adipiscing elit |
| 26th | 10:15 AM | Ipsum dolor sit amet, consectetuer adipiscing elit |

# Sampler Excursions

Dallas, Texas, USA
Sydney, Australia
London, England

*A one-paragraph "hook"
benefit that describes
your product or service*

Sarah W. Example
Director of Marketing
Sampler Corporation
1234 Street Address
Your City, ST 12345-6789

May 16, 2???

Sarah:

Lorem ipsum dolor sit amet, consectetuer adipiscing elit, sed diam nonummy nibh euismod tincidunt ut laoreet dolore magna aliquam erat volutpat. Ut wisi enim ad minim veniam, quis nostrud exerci tation ullamcorper suscipit lobortis nisl ut aliquip ex ea commodo consequat. Duis autem vel eum iriure dolor in hendrerit in vulputate velit esse molestie consequat, vel illum dolore eu feugiat nulla facilisis at vero eros et accumsan et iusto odio dignissim qui blandit praesent.

Lorem ipsum dolor sit amet, consectetuer adipiscing elit, sed diam nonummy nibh euismod tincidunt ut laoreet dolore magna aliquam erat volutpat. Ut wisi enim ad minim veniam, quis nostrud exerci tation ullamcorper suscipit lobortis nisl ut aliquip ex ea commodo consequat. Duis autem vel eum iriure dolor in hendrerit in vulputate velit esse molestie consequat, vel illum dolore eu feugiat nulla facilisis at vero eros et accumsan et iusto odio dignissim qui blandit praesent luptatum zzril delenit augue duis dolore te feugait nulla facilisi.

Nam liber tempor cum soluta nobis eleifend option congue nihil imperdiet doming id quod mazim placerat facer possim assum. Lorem ipsum dolor sit amet, consectetuer adipiscing elit, sed diam nonummy nibh euismod tincidunt ut laoreet dolore magna aliquam erat volutpat.

Best regards,

Josh S. Example
President
coc
Enclosures (2)

123 Example Boulevard, Your City, State 12345 6789
Voice 987 654 3210   Fax 987 654 3210   E-mail info@emailaddressz.com   www.yourwebaddressz.com

## Sampler Excursions

ITINERARY SUMMARY

Sarah W. Example
Sampler Corporation

Sampler Excursions
Josh S. Example
Voice 987 654 3210
Fax 987 654 3210
josh@emailaddressz.com
www.yourwebaddressz.com

| Sunday, August 25th | 07:00 AM | Lorem ipsum dolor sit amet, consectetuer adipiscing elit |
| Sunday, August 25th | 10:15 AM | Ipsum dolor sit amet, consectetuer adipiscing elit |
| Sunday, August 25th | 11:45 AM | Dolor sit amet, consectetuer adipiscing elit |
| Sunday, August 25th | 04:00 PM | Lorem ipsum dolor sit amet, consectetuer adipiscing |
| Monday, August 26th | 07:00 AM | Slorem ipsum dolor sit amet, consectetuer adipiscing elit |
| Monday, August 26th | 10:15 AM | Ipsum dolor sit amet, consectetuer adipiscing elit |
| Monday, August 26th | 11:45 AM | Dolor sit amet, consectetuer adipiscing elit |
| Monday, August 26th | 4:00 PM | Lorem ipsum dolor sit amet, consectetuer adipiscing |
| Monday, August 26th | 4:00 PM | Lorem ipsum dolor sit amet, consectetuer adipiscing |

## Business Card, Front  3.5 W by 2 H inches

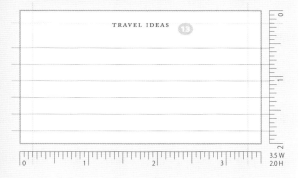

www.yourwebaddressz.com
Voice 987 654 3210
Fax 987 654 3210

YOUR NAME
President / CEO

123 Example Boulevard
Your City, State 12345 6789
E-mail  info@emailaddressz.com

Sampler
Excursions

*A one-paragraph "hook" benefit that describes your product or service Lorem ipsum*

## Business Card, Back  3.5 W by 2 H inches

TRAVEL IDEAS

## Envelope, Commercial  9.5 W by 4.125 H inches

Sampler
Excursions

*A one-paragraph "hook" benefit that describes your product or service Lorem ipsum*

123 Example Boulevard
Your City, State 12345 6789

### Letterhead

**1** Lines 1pt; "Dallas" Caslon Regular Italic, 9/10pt, align left; **2** "Sampler" Burlington, 22pt, align center; "Excursions" Burlington, 24pt, align center; **3** Defining phrase Caslon Regular Italic, 9/10pt, align left; **4** Letter body Minion, 12/18pt, align left; **5** Address Caslon Regular, 9/11pt, align center; **6** "Sampler" Burlington, 22pt, align center; "Excursions" Burlington, 24pt, align center; "ITINERARY" Caslon Regular, 7pt, align left; **7** "Sarah" Minion, 9/12pt, align left; **8** Text Minion, 9/17pt, align left

### Business Card, Front

**9** "www." Caslon Regular, 8/10pt, align left; **10** Name Caslon Regular, 7/10pt, align left; **11** Address Caslon Regular, 8/10pt, align left; **12** Defining phrase Caslon Regular Italic, 7/9pt, align left; "Sampler" Burlington, 17pt, align center; "Excursions" Burlington, 19pt, align center

### Business Card, Back

**13** "TRAVEL" Caslon Regular, 9pt, align center; Lines 0.25pt

### Envelope

**14** "Sampler" Burlington, 17pt, align center; "Excursions" Burlington, 19pt, align center; **15** Defining phrase Caslon Regular Italic, 7/9pt, align left; **16** Address Caslon Regular, 7/9pt, align left

### Color

Printed in four-color process (see Step 9.3) using values of cyan, magenta, yellow, and black (CMYK) as defined on the color palette below. Actual color will vary.

Process Colors

| C5 | M10 | Y20 | K0 |
|---|---|---|---|
| C100 | M45 | Y0 | K15 |
| C15 | M7.5 | Y0 | K0 |

STYLE 23

# Transparency

This style requires some real finesse with your paint program, but the results can be stunning.

A program such as Adobe Photoshop allows you to layer one image on top of another. It is possible then to change the opacity of a layer enough to see through it to the layers below. That single feature allows seemingly endless possibilities.

The logo below includes four layers.

The orange plant and sliced orange are extracted from the same illustration.

The sliced orange is the top layer of the logo.

The layer below the orange includes the shadow of the orange.

The next layer holds a semitransparent version of the plant illustration.

The bottom layer is the background.

For the business card, a simple white rectangle is on the layer above the illustration. The opacity of the rectangle is adjusted to reveal the illustration below.

The parts and pieces of illustrations are combined to create a second version of the logo for the envelope.

The space between the letters in the word "ORCHARDS" is increased to allow for the descending loop of the "p"—one of the small details that make the difference between a design that works and one that doesn't.

SOURCE Illustration:
Oranges from *Antique Botanical Illustrations VII*, From Visual Language, 888-702-8777, www.visuallanguage.com, © Visual Language, all rights reserved.

SOURCE Type families:
Bickham Script, Minion, Myriad, Adobe Systems, Inc., 800-682-3623, www.adobe.com/type.

**What you need**
Editing the illustration requires a paint or digital imaging program such as Adobe Photoshop or Jasc Software's Paint Shop Pro. Simple text and shapes can be produced with a desktop publishing program such as Adobe InDesign, Adobe PageMaker, QuarkXPress, or Microsoft Publisher.

*Samplerhaven*
ORCHARDS

A one-paragraph "hook"
benefit that describes
your product or service

May 16, 2???

Sarah W. Example
Director of Marketing
Sampler Corporation
1234 Street Address
Your City, ST 12345-6789

Sarah:

Lorem ipsum dolor sit amet, consectetue
tincidunt ut laoreet dolore magna aliqua
nostrud exerci tation ullamcorper suscip
autem vel eum iriure dolor in hendrerit
eu feugiat nulla facilisis at vero eros et a

Lorem ipsum dolor sit amet, consectetu
tincidunt ut laoreet dolore magna aliqu
nostrud exerci tation ullamcorper susci
autem vel eum iriure dolor in hendrerit
eu feugiat nulla facilisis at vero eros et accumsa
luptatum zzril delenit augu   dolore te fe

Nam liber tempor cum so
mazim placerat facer pos
diam nonummy nibh eu

Best regards,

Josh S. Example
President
coc
Enclosures (2)

*Samplerhaven*
ORCHARDS

123 Example Boulevard
Your City, State 12345 6789

A one-paragra
describe

*Samplerhaven*
ORCHARDS

YOUR NAME
President/CEO

Voice 987 654 3210    Fax 987 654 3210
www.yourwebaddressz.com    E-mail info@emailaddressz.com
123 Example Boulevard, Your City, State 12345 6789
A one-paragraph "hook" benefit that describes your product or service

123 Example Boulevard
Your City, State 12345 6789
Voice 987 654 3210
Fax 987 654 3210
www.yourwebaddressz.com
E-mail info@emailaddressz.com

A one-paragraph "hook" benefit that describes your product or service

May 16, 2???

Sarah W. Example
Director of Marketing
Sampler Corporation
1234 Street Address
Your City, ST 12345-6789

Sarah:

Lorem ipsum dolor sit amet, consectetuer adipiscing elit, sed diam nonummy nibh euismod tincidunt ut laoreet dolore magna aliquam erat volutpat. Ut wisi enim ad minim veniam, quis nostrud exerci tation ullamcorper suscipit lobortis nisl ut aliquip ex ea commodo consequat. Duis autem vel eum iriure dolor in hendrerit in vulputate velit esse molestie consequat, vel illum dolore eu feugiat nulla facilisis at vero eros et accumsan et iusto odio dignissim qui blandit praesent.

Lorem ipsum dolor sit amet, consectetuer adipiscing elit, sed diam nonummy nibh euismod tincidunt ut laoreet dolore magna aliquam erat volutpat. Ut wisi enim ad minim veniam, quis nostrud exerci tation ullamcorper suscipit lobortis nisl ut aliquip ex ea commodo consequat. Duis autem vel eum iriure dolor in hendrerit in vulputate velit esse molestie consequat, vel illum dolore eu feugiat nulla facilisis at vero eros et accumsan et iusto odio dignissim qui blandit praesent luptatum zzril delenit augue duis dolore te feugait nulla facilisi.

Nam liber tempor cum soluta nobis eleifend option congue nihil imperdiet doming id quod mazim placerat facer possim assum. Lorem ipsum dolor sit amet, consectetuer adipiscing elit, sed diam nonummy nibh euismod tincidunt ut laoreet dolore magna aliquam erat volutpat.

Best regards,


Josh S. Example
President
coc
Enclosures (2)

123 Example Boulevard
Your City, State 12345 6789
Voice 987 654 3210
Fax 987 654 3210
www.yourwebaddressz.com
E-mail info@emailaddressz.com

**Business Card, Front** 3.5 W by 2 H inches

**Business Card, Back** 3.5 W by 2 H inches

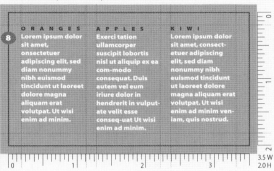

### Letterhead

**1** "Samplerhaven" Bickham Script, 60pt; "ORCHARDS" Myriad 800bl, 700se, 18pt; **2** Defining phrase Myriad Regular, 9/10pt, align left; **3** Letter body Minion, 12/18pt, align left; **4** Address Myriad Regular, 7.5/10pt, align left

### Business Card, Front

**5** "Samplerhaven" Bickham Script, 38pt; "ORCHARDS" Myriad 800bl, 700se, 8pt; **6** Name Myriad Regular, 8pt, align center; Title Myriad Regular, 7pt, align center; **7** Address Myriad Regular, 7/9pt, align center; Defining phrase Myriad Regular, 6pt, align center

### Business Card, Back

**8** "ORANGES" Myriad 800bl, 700se, 6pt, align left; Text Myriad 800bl, 700se, Bold, 7/9pt, align left

### Envelope

**9** "Samplerhaven" Bickham Script, 34pt; "ORCHARDS" Myriad 800bl, 700se, 7pt; Address Myriad Regular, 7/8pt, align center; **10** Defining phrase Myriad Regular, 6/7pt, align center

### Color

Printed in four-color process (see Step 9.3) using values of cyan, magenta, yellow, and black (CMYK) as defined on the color palette below. Actual color will vary.

**Envelope, Commercial** 9.5 W by 4.125 H inches

Process Colors

| C0 | M45 | Y80 | K0 |
| --- | --- | --- | --- |
| C20 | M75 | Y95 | K10 |

STYLE 24

# Type

Who needs illustrations when you've got beautiful typefaces? And filters?

A filter is a feature within most draw and paint software that allows you to apply special effects to the images, lines, shapes, and text that you create and edit within the program.

In a paint program, you can, for example, change a photograph into something more reminiscent of a pastel drawing. In a drawing program, you can take a simple rank of horizontal lines, as shown here, and use a twirl filter to turn it into a wave.

Color instead of space is used to divide the words in the name.

In a drawing program, a twirl filter is applied to a series of horizontal lines to create the backgrounds.

**Graphic Design >**

A list of products and services is added along the path above the bottom wave.

A map is used to pinpoint the organization's location.

**SamplerCopyCenter**

SOURCE Typeface: Franklin Gothic, Minion, Myriad, Adobe Systems, Inc., 800-682-3623, www.adobe.com/type.

**What you need**

Creating wave lines, text along a path, and the map requires a draw program such as Adobe Illustrator, CorelDRAW, or Macromedia FreeHand. Simple text and shapes can be produced with a desktop publishing program such as Adobe InDesign, Adobe PageMaker, QuarkXPress, or Microsoft Publisher.

www.yourwebaddressz.com
**Sampler**Copy**Center**

May 16, 2???

Sarah W. Example
Director of Marketing
Sampler Corporation
1234 Street Address
Your City, ST 12345-6789

Sarah:

Lorem ipsum dolor sit amet, conse
tincidunt ut laoreet dolore magna
nostrud exerci tation ullamcorpe
autem vel eum iriure dolor in he
eu feugiat nulla facilisis at vero

Lorem ipsum dolor sit amet, c
tincidunt ut laoreet dolore m
nostrud ex
autem vel
eu feugiat
luptatum

Nam libe
mazim
diam n

Best regards,

Josh S. Example
President
coc
Enclosures (2)

**Sampler**Copy**Center**
123 Example Boulevard, Your City, State 12345 6789

**Graphic Design > Copies > Binding > Laminating > Banners > Exhibits >**

www.yourwebaddressz.com
**Sampler**Copy**Center**

YOUR NAME          123 Example Boulevard
President / CEO        Your City, State 12345 6789
                            Voice 987 654 3210
                            Fax 987 654 3210
                            E-mail  info@emailaddressz.com

Graphic Design > Copies > Binding > Laminating > Banners > Exhibits > Pick-Up Service > Bulk Mailing > C

**Sampler**Copy**Center**
123 Example Boulevard
Your City, ST 12345
987 654 3210

Exit 45 B
Sampler Road
South
6
45
34

123 Example Boulevard, Your City, State 12345 6789
Voice 987 654 3210  Fax 987 654 3210
E-mail  info@emailaddressz.com

**raphic Design > Copies > Binding > Laminating > Banners > Exhibits > Pick-Up Service > Bulk Mailing > Col**

www.yourwebaddressz.com
**SamplerCopyCenter**

Sarah W. Example                                  May 16, 2???
Director of Marketing
Sampler Corporation
1234 Street Address
Your City, ST 12345-6789

Sarah:

Lorem ipsum dolor sit amet, consectetuer adipiscing elit, sed diam nonummy nibh euismod
tincidunt ut laoreet dolore magna aliquam erat volutpat. Ut wisi enim ad minim veniam, quis
nostrud exerci tation ullamcorper suscipit lobortis nisl ut aliquip ex ea commodo consequat. Duis
autem vel eum iriure dolor in hendrerit in vulputate velit esse molestie consequat, vel illum dolore
eu feugiat nulla facilisis at vero eros et accumsan et iusto odio dignissim qui blandit praesent.

Lorem ipsum dolor sit amet, consectetuer adipiscing elit, sed diam nonummy nibh euismod
tincidunt ut laoreet dolore magna aliquam erat volutpat. Ut wisi enim ad minim veniam, quis
nostrud exerci tation ullamcorper suscipit lobortis nisl ut aliquip ex ea commodo consequat. Duis
autem vel eum iriure dolor in hendrerit in vulputate velit esse molestie consequat, vel illum dolore
eu feugiat nulla facilisis at vero eros et accumsan et iusto odio dignissim qui blandit praesent
luptatum zzril delenit augue duis dolore te feugait nulla facilisi.

Nam liber tempor cum soluta nobis eleifend option congue nihil imperdiet doming id quod
mazim placerat facer possim assum. Lorem ipsum dolor sit amet, consectetuer adipiscing elit, sed
diam nonummy nibh euismod tincidunt ut laoreet dolore magna aliquam erat volutpat.

Best regards,


Josh S. Example
President
coc
Enclosures (2)

123 Example Boulevard, Your City, State 12345 6789
Voice 987 654 3210  Fax 987 654 3210
E-mail  info@emailaddressz.com

Graphic Design > Copies > Binding > Laminating > Banners > Exhibits > Pick-Up Service > Bulk Mailing > Color

**Business Card, Front**  3.5 W by 2 H inches

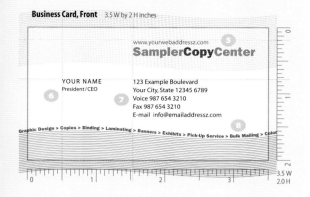

**Business Card, Back**  3.5 W by 2 H inches

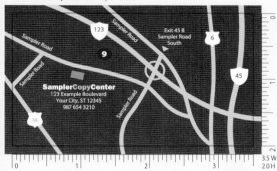

**Envelope, Commercial**  9.5 W by 4.125 H inches

## SamplerCopyCenter ⑩
123 Example Boulevard, Your City, State 12345 6789

Graphic Design > Copies > Binding > Laminating > Banners > Exhibits > Pick-Up Service > Bulk Mailing > Color ⑪

**Letterhead**

**1** Web Address Myriad Regular, 9pt, align left; Organization Franklin Gothic Heavy, 18pt, align left; **2** Letter body Minion, 12/18pt, align left; **3** Address Myriad Regular, 9/11pt, align left; **4** Defining Phrase Franklin Gothic Heavy, 18pt

**Business Card, Front**

**5** Web Address Myriad Regular, 6.75pt, align left; Organization Franklin Gothic Heavy, 13.5pt, align left; **6** Name Myriad Regular, 7pt, align left; Title Myriad Regular, 6pt, align left; **7** Address Myriad Regular, 7/9pt, align left; Title Myriad Regular, 6pt, align left; **8** Defining Phrase Franklin Gothic Heavy, 5pt

**Business Card, Back**

**9** Organization Franklin Gothic Heavy, 8pt, align center; Text Myriad Regular, 6/7pt, align center; Route Numbers Myriad Regular, 7pt

**Envelope**

**10** Organization Franklin Gothic Heavy, 18pt, align left; Address Myriad Regular, 7pt, align left; **11** Defining Phrase Franklin Gothic Heavy, 12pt

**Color**

To be printed in black and a solid PANTONE Color Ink as defined on the palette below (see Step 9.3). (Because this book is printed in process colors (CMYK), the illustration is only a simulation of the actual solid PANTONE Color).

Red or
PANTONE® 185

| 100% |
| 60% |
| 40% |
| 25% |

Black

| 100% |
| 50% |
| 15% |

STYLE 25

# Vertical Bar

Bars of color—vertical or horizontal— serve the same purpose: They anchor the page.

It is important to note on this and on similar styles that placing the foundation graphics on the right of the page keeps the letter as the center of attention. Remember, the primary purpose of a letterhead, business card, and envelope is to communicate information. The style of your materials should complement, never overwhelm, that message.

SOURCE Illustration: figure by the author.

The figure is created from a series of simple lines and circles.

Copies of the figure are stacked in a flock formation.

The formation is slightly distorted and rotated into position, and color is added.

To create a shadow, a copy of the formation is pasted behind the original and colored with a tint of the solid blue.

**Sampler**
Employment

The name is made up of contrasting bold and light typefaces. The longest word is reduced to fit the same width as the other. Changing "Employment" to the bold face would reverse the emphasis.

SOURCE Type families: Franklin Gothic, Minion, Myriad, Adobe Systems, Inc., 800-682-3623, www.adobe.com/type.

 **What you need**
Creating the figure requires a draw program such as Adobe Illustrator, CorelDRAW, or Macromedia FreeHand. Simple text and shapes can be produced with a desktop publishing program such as Adobe InDesign, Adobe PageMaker, QuarkXPress, or Microsoft Publisher.

**Sampler**
Employment

A one-sentence "hook"
benefit that describes your
product or service lorem
ipsum dolor sit amet ipsum
dolor sit amet

May 16, 2???

Sarah W. Example
Director of Marketing
Sampler Corporation
1234 Street Address
Your City, ST 12345-6789

Sarah:

Lorem ipsum dolor sit amet, consectetuer adipiscing elit, sed diam nonummy nibh euismod
tincidunt ut laoreet dolore magna aliquam erat volutpat. Ut wisi enim ad minim veniam, quis
nostrud exerci tation ullamcorper suscipit lobortis n____ quip ex ea commodo consequat. Duis
autem vel eum iriure dolor in hendrerit in vulputate ____ ____umsan et ___ dolore
eu feugiat nulla

Lorem ipsum d
tincidunt ut la____
nostrud exerci ____
autem vel eun____
eu feugiat nu____
luptatum zzr____

Nam liber te____
mazim plac____
diam nonu____

Best regar____

Josh S. E____
Presiden____
coc
Enclosures (2)

www.yourwebaddressz.com
Voice 987 654 3210
Fax 987 654 3210

**Sampler**
Employment

YOUR NAME
President / CEO

123 Example Boulevard
Your City, State 12345 6789
info@emailaddressz.com

A one
sentence
"hook"
benefit that
describes
your product
or service
lorem ipsum
dolor sit
amet,
ipsum dolor
sit amet

**Sampler**
Employment
123 Example Boulevard
Your City, State 12345 6789

| JOBS | MISSION |
|---|---|
| 1 Lorem ipsumo | Lorem ipsum dolor sit amet, consectetuer adipiscing elit, |
| 2 Dolor sit ametpt | sed diam nonummy nibh euismod tincidunt ut laoreet |
| 3 Sconsectetuer | dolore magna aliquam erat volutpat. Ut wisi enim ad |
| 4 Jadipiscing elite | minim veniam, quis nostrud lorem ipsum dolor sit amet, |
| 5 Lsed diammod | consectetuer adipiscing elit, sed |
| 6 Dnonummy | diam nonummy nibh euismod |
| 7 Snibh euismod | tincidunt ut laoreet dolore |
| 8 Dtincidunt elite | magna aliquam erat |
| 9 Slaoreet dolore ip | veniam, quis nostrud. |

www.yo____
info@emailaddressz.com

Sampler
Employment

A one-sentence "hook"
benefit that describes your
product or service lorem
ipsum dolor sit amet ipsum
dolor sit amet

May 16, 2???

Sarah W. Example
Director of Marketing
Sampler Corporation
1234 Street Address
Your City, ST 12345-6789

Sarah:

Lorem ipsum dolor sit amet, consectetuer adipiscing elit, sed diam nonummy nibh euismod
tincidunt ut laoreet dolore magna aliquam erat volutpat. Ut wisi enim ad minim veniam, quis
nostrud exerci tation ullamcorper suscipit lobortis nisl ut aliquip ex ea commodo consequat. Duis
autem vel eum iriure dolor in hendrerit in vulputate velit esse molestie consequat, vel illum dolore
eu feugiat nulla facilisis at vero eros et accumsan et iusto odio dignissim qui blandit praesent.

Lorem ipsum dolor sit amet, consectetuer adipiscing elit, sed diam nonummy nibh euismod
tincidunt ut laoreet dolore magna aliquam erat volutpat. Ut wisi enim ad minim veniam, quis
nostrud exerci tation ullamcorper suscipit lobortis nisl ut aliquip ex ea commodo consequat. Duis
autem vel eum iriure dolor in hendrerit in vulputate velit esse molestie consequat, vel illum dolore
eu feugiat nulla facilisis at vero eros et accumsan et iusto odio dignissim qui blandit praesent
luptatum zzril delenit augue duis dolore te feugait nulla facilisi.

Nam liber tempor cum soluta nobis eleifend option congue nihil imperdiet doming id quod
mazim placerat facer possim assum. Lorem ipsum dolor sit amet, consectetuer adipiscing elit, sed
diam nonummy nibh euismod tincidunt ut laoreet dolore magna aliquam erat volutpat.

Best regards,

Josh S. Example
President
coc
Enclosures (2)

123 Example Boulevard,
Your City, State 12345 6789
Voice 987 654 3210
Fax 987 654 3210
www.yourwebaddressz.com
info@emailaddressz.com

## Business Card, Front  3.5 W by 2 H inches

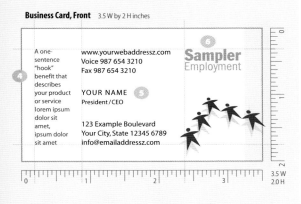

A one-sentence "hook" benefit that describes your product or service lorem ipsum dolor sit amet, ipsum dolor sit amet

www.yourwebaddressz.com
Voice 987 654 3210
Fax 987 654 3210

**Sampler**
Employment

YOUR NAME
President / CEO

123 Example Boulevard
Your City, State 12345 6789
info@emailaddressz.com

3.5 W
2.0 H

## Business Card, Back  3.5 W by 2 H inches

JOBS
1 Lorem ipsumo
2 Dolor sit ametpt
3 Sconsectetuer
4 Jadipiscing elite
5 Lsed diammod
6 Dnonummy
7 Snibh euismod
8 Dtincidunt elite
9 Slaoreet dolore ip

MISSION
Lorem ipsum dolor sit amet, consectetuer adipiscing elit, sed diam nonummy nibh euismod tincidunt ut laoreet dolore magna aliquam erat volutpat. Ut wisi enim ad minim veniam, quis nostrud lorem ipsum dolor sit amet, consectetuer adipiscing elit, sed diam nonummy nibh euismod tincidunt ut laoreet dolore magna aliquam erat veniam, quis nostrud.

3.5 W
2.0 H

## Envelope, Commercial  9.5 W by 4.125 H inches

**Sampler**
Employment
123 Example Boulevard
Your City, State 12345 6789

9.5 W
4.125 H

### Letterhead
**1** "Sampler" Franklin Gothic Bold Condensed, 25pt, align left; "Employment" Franklin Gothic Book Condensed, 18.5pt, align left; Defining Phrase Myriad Regular, 7/10pt, align left; **2** Letter body Minion, 12/18pt, align left; **3** Address Myriad Regular, 7/10pt, align left

### Business Card, Front
**4** Defining Phrase Myriad Regular, 7/9pt, align left; **5** Address Myriad Regular, 8/10pt, align left; Title Myriad Regular, 7pt, align left; **6** "Sampler" Franklin Gothic Bold Condensed, 18pt, align left; "Employment" Franklin Gothic Book Condensed, 13pt, align left

### Business Card, Back
**7** "JOBS" Myriad Multiple Master (MM), 700bd, 300cn, 8/12.5pt, align left; **8** "MISSION" Myriad MM, 700bd, 300cn, 8/12pt, align left

### Envelope
**9** "Sampler" Franklin Gothic Bold Condensed, 22pt, align left; "Employment" Franklin Gothic Book Condensed, 15.5pt, align left; Address Myriad Regular, 7/9pt, align left

### Color
To be printed in black and a solid PANTONE Color Ink as defined on the palette below (see Step 9.3). (Because this book is printed in process colors (CMYK), the illustration is only a simulation of the actual solid PANTONE Color).

Deep Blue or
PANTONE® 286

| |
|---|
| 100% |
| 50% |
| 20% |
| 10% |

# Newsletters

## SECTION 2, PART 1
# Step-by-Step Design

STEP 1

# Establish Your Mission

"Newsletter" is an ambiguous term. The words "news" and "letter" point to its origins but no longer adequately describe the scope or potential of today's hybrid publications. Contemporary newsletters serve many functions and take many forms.

For the purposes of this book, a newsletter is defined as *a condensed periodical used to communicate specialized editorial information*. "Condensed" means it is shorter than the average newspaper or magazine and provides lots of information in limited space. "Periodical" means it is published regularly. "Specialized" means it focuses not on a broad subject area such as finance, but on a subject-within-a-subject, such as real estate finance—not on organizations in general, but a specific organization.

"Editorial information" means articles as opposed to purely marketing-oriented content. The difference between a newsletter and a brochure, for example, is that a newsletter includes information of value to the reader whether they buy your idea, product, service, or not.

That definition is where the similarity between newsletters ends—or at least it should. The best newsletters develop their own personalities through the way they talk, the way they look, and the unique mix of reader-oriented benefits they offer. They instruct, entertain, solve problems, offer useful opinions and insights, recommend resources, inspire action, and are a reliable source. You might even consider the best of them a respected colleague or friend in fixed form.

Publishing an effective newsletter is not an easy job. Even in its simplest form, it requires a significant commitment: a clearly defined goal, a thorough understanding of your reader, a meticulous plan, and the skills and resources necessary to execute it. Anything less could end up doing your product, your service, or your cause more harm than good.

**1.1** The first step of such a considerable journey is to *choose a destination*. Where are you heading? What's your goal in publishing your newsletter? There are some obvious destinations: to sell a product or service, to promote a cause, to develop your client base or membership, or perhaps even to develop a group of people who are willing to pay for your information.

There are also some important provisos. First, be sure your goal requires a long-term relationship. There is little sense in using a newsletter to sell products or services that constitute a one-time purchase. Think of a newsletter as a friendship instead of a one-time meeting.

Second, before you begin, be sure that you have the will to persevere. If your business makes it difficult to meet deadlines, if you're not sure you will have the time, or you can't depend on others to help, a less ambitious vehicle might be more realistic.

Next, be sure your publication's subject matter is important to your prospective subscriber. Excellent content and expert execution will not interest an uninterested reader. Your topic must be significant in their eyes.

Finally, be sure you're in shape for the journey. A sedentary person who attempts a marathon without the necessary training is going to encounter great pain. Publishing a monthly eight-page newsletter without adequate resources, skills, and stamina exacts a cost.

**1.2** That destination will help you *choose a model*. There are three basic types: If your mission is to market your product, service, or ideas, the vehicle is a *promotional newsletter*. The reader benefit of a promotional newsletter is that it educates them about a certain area of interest and provides solutions, some of which come in the form of your products, services, or your way of thinking.

If the mission is to build rapport with your audience, the answer is a *relationship newsletter*. Its benefit is to inform the reader about a group to which they belong or might consider joining. It promotes the group's shared philosophy,

a calendar of events, notices of meetings, individual and group milestones, member profiles, and so on.

If you want to sell information for profit, the vehicle is an *expert newsletter*. What makes an expert letter different from its counterparts is that it is sold for a profit. The benefits are far more clear-cut—information, statistics, advice, and instruction—for the price of a subscription.

There are, of course, no absolutes in the newsletter-publishing world; your newsletter may well include components of all three.

**1.3** Finally, *define how you will measure your success*. How will you know your newsletter is building toward success or that it has arrived—from your point of view and from the reader's? Be specific, writing from the reader's perspective, instead of setting a blanket goal such as educating clients about your manufacturing process. Incorporate a means to prove they are learning. From your perspective, instead of projecting a goal of increasing sales, set a goal to increase out-of-state orders by ten percent.

**Step 1: MISSION CHECKLIST**

| | 1.1 | Choose a destination |

| | 1.2 | Choose a model |

| | 1.3 | Define how you will measure success |

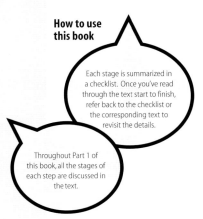

**How to use this book**

Each stage is summarized in a checklist. Once you've read through the text start to finish, refer back to the checklist or the corresponding text to revisit the details.

Throughout Part 1 of this book, all the stages of each step are discussed in the text.

STEP 2

# Do Some Research

If you don't have the time or budget to do some research, you don't have the time or budget to create a newsletter. To compete effectively, you need to know as much as possible about your competition, your supporters, and the field of play.

**2.1** Start your research by *identifying your competition*—organizations in the same business—especially those reaching a similar audience with a newsletter. Don't make the mistake of assuming your idea is so unique that no one else could possibly be doing the same thing. Discovering a significant competitor late in the game can be costly.

SOURCE Illustrations: Orange from *Everyday Objects 1* by CMCD, Apple from *Image Club ArtRoom, Sketches On The Town*, 800-661-9410, 403-294-3195, www.eyewire.com.

Search for rivals and find out as much as you can about them and their history. History is important because you may be able to avoid some of the mistakes they have made. And don't limit yourself to local competitors. Even if you operate in just one region of the country, check out what others are doing elsewhere. Studying how stiff competition alters a market in another area may offer insights for leapfrogging competition locally.

**2.2** Next, *collect your competitors' marketing materials*. This once-daunting task is easier now that so many organizations have sites on the World Wide Web. There is a huge amount of extraordinarily valuable competitive information available—you have only to use an online search engine. Some organizations even provide conventional newsletter issues or issue samples in a form you can download and print. Read everything you can get your hands on to see how competitors attempt to move their audience to action.

**2.3** The next critical piece of research involves *creating a reader profile:* identifying and outlining who you think will read and support your publication. Do it in the form of a list of attributes that classifies the readers you already have and those you hope to attract. Following are some of the possible characteristics from which to choose your demographics.

*Personal characteristics* classify readers by gender, age, marital status, and style preferences for everything from the type of clothing they wear to the colors they prefer.

*Financial status* might include income, spending habits, specific dollar amounts spent on particular products and services, and so on.

*Professional and personal affiliations* such as employment status, memberships, and formal and informal associations with business and private groups may prove valuable.

In some cases the *location* of where the reader lives or works is significant.

*Special interests* such as preferences in entertainment or dining, the reader's health status, hobbies, and the like are pivotal in defining interest.

An accurate reader profile can lead you to other prospects. If, for example, you find that a significant number of your readers are volleyball players, you might construe that people who play volleyball are good prospects. Making assumptions, of course, entails risk. Before you acquire a list of 5,000 volleyball players, test a representative sample to exercise your theory.

Don't hesitate to survey prospects directly—done right, asking their opinion can be the highest form of flattery. It telegraphs you value their opinion and appreciate the fact that they have a perspective you and your organization do not.

**2.4** With a basic picture of who the reader is, you need to *identify the degree of reader interest*.

Just because, for example, you purchase a palette of cardboard boxes from a local supplier does not necessarily make you a prospect for a box-industry newsletter. You might have a passing interest in saving money on box purchases or box recycling, but chances are you won't devote thirty minutes a month reading about it.

Be realistic—is your subject one that lends itself to newsletter-length information and frequency? Could you realistically create interest with a first-class publication? If the answer is not a resounding yes, your dollars may be better spent with a periodic direct-mail letter campaign, a series of informational fliers, or a benefits-oriented brochure.

You might also consider motives for why readers might lend their support. Do they have a significant interest in the subject and/or a compelling reason to read about it? Do they stand to save significant time, money, or energy by consuming the information in your newsletter? Will they gain some other important benefit? Are they likely to take the prescribed actions?

**2.5** Once you understand who your prospects are, you can begin to *research sources of names*. The importance of access to lists of qualified and prospective readers cannot be overstated. It alone does not ensure success, but the absence of such sources guarantees failure.

Your first most obvious source is your house list—your existing list of members, clients, customers, prospects, inquiries, visitors, e-mail contacts, colleagues, and so on. You might also arrange to buy or trade lists with a noncompeting organization that is in contact with the same audience. If you publish a newsletter for teachers, for example, you may arrange to swap lists with a teacher's organization.

Second, you can rent or buy lists of people or organizations that have purchased consumer or business products. There are many sources for such lists. Standard Rates and Data Service (SRDS), a well-respected provider of media rates and data to the advertising industry, publishes the Direct Marketing List Source, a source of more than 35,000 lists from 200-plus market classifications—from air conditioning to welding. The company's publication (available in some libraries and at www.SRDS.com) details the organization and audience the list represents, reveals information such as ranges of the amounts they spent, the ratio of females to males, and the usage basics such as cost and who to contact for more information.

You can also rent or buy lists that are compiled from general sources such as the Yellow Pages, the names and addresses of people who live within a specific zip code, organizations that have some affiliation with the federal government, and so on. The key to building a list is to continually seek sources of names that match some characteristics of your reader profile.

If you intend to build a completely new audience, you'll need to do extensive research and develop a complete reader profile. If you are developing a full-fledged, paid-subscription publication, more formal research may be called for. Research conducted by a firm that specializes in information gathering through direct mail questionnaires, telephone surveys, or focus groups may provide more reliable results.

**2.6** With these basics under your belt, you can go about *collecting effective examples of newsletters* published by other organizations. Search for ideas at all levels—content, design, layout configuration, color, paper, type, illustrations, and so on. Not just in your field but any material that catches your eye. Collect enough of them and you will begin to discover similarities—compelling content, unusual benefits, the typefaces you find most attractive, the page layouts that look most professional, the colors that attract you, and so on.

Another way to acquire samples is to use Adobe's PDF Search Web at http://searchpdf.adobe.com. It allows you to type in a search term such as "newsletter" along with a word or phrase that describes your area of interest and locate Adobe Acrobat Portable Document Format (PDF) files of newsletters from all over the Web. You can then view and print them using the free-of-charge Adobe Acrobat Reader.

**2.7** Your final research objective is to *gather mailing information and expertise*. Why address the final step of newsletter publishing at such an early stage? Because mailing regulations can significantly affect a newsletter's content, design, weight, and so on.

Mailing preparation and postage can command a significant percentage of your budget. To qualify for U.S. Postal Service's periodical postage rates, for example, regulations governing such things as publication frequency, continuity, purpose, and content must be understood and followed. If you were to save ten cents per piece on 750 pieces mailed once a month, you'd save $4,500 over a five-year period, a handsome return for a few hours of legwork.

For a complete overview of designing and mailing periodicals, start by reviewing the "Eligibility" section of the "Domestic Mail Manual" (DMM) at the USPS Postal Explorer at http://pe.usps.gov/, or visit your local post office. Then consult a mailing services expert—you'll find them listed in the Yellow Pages under "mailing services." For more about the process, see *Step 14: Mail It,* page 198.

Do not leave research for later. After launching a newsletter, finding out about a significant competitor, realizing that your readers are not sufficiently interested, learning that a list you assumed was available isn't, or concluding that the cost of renting a particular list puts it beyond reach can all be showstoppers. Immerse yourself in the details of getting to know your competition, your readers, and the process—the more you know, the more confident you will be about the content you create and the development process.

## Step 2:  RESEARCH CHECKLIST

☐ **2.1**  Identify your competition

☐ **2.2**  Collect your competitors' marketing materials

☐ **2.3**  Create a reader profile

☐ **2.4**  Identify the degree of reader interest

☐ **2.5**  Research sources of names

☐ **2.6**  Collect effective newsletter examples

☐ **2.7**  Gather mailing information and expertise

Who?
What?
Where?
When?
Why?

STEP 3

# Create a Plan

Every successful product, service, or idea does one of two things for its consumer— it provides pleasure or eases pain—and some do both. That simple proposition is known as a customer benefit. Explaining and communicating it is what marketing is all about.

The problem is, millions, perhaps billions of marketing dollars are wasted each year disguising those benefits with witty advertising headlines, vague analogies, and ambiguous images. They are hidden among lists of features and data and concealed within descriptions of an organization's history, employees, and systems.

To create a successful newsletter, or for that matter, a successful *anything*, you must uncover, express, and communicate those benefits. Think in big-picture terms. Throw out your preconceptions about newsletters and how they are typically used, and focus on creating a hybrid publication that speaks to your unique circumstance. See *Jolt Your Thinking*, on the next page.

**3.1** Start by *creating a list of the customer benefits* in order of their importance. For example, the top three benefits a hypothetical retailer offers its customers might be: a lowest-price guarantee, the area's largest equipment selection, and support and service for what they sell twenty-four hours a day, seven days a week.

The benefits a professional organization offers its members might be: opportunities to network with colleagues, access to local and national industry information, and links to unusual or unexpected resources.

For supporters of a charitable organization: a venue for solving a specific problem, a place of service, and an opportunity to become educated about associated issues.

For users of a particular software program: a vehicle for learning to use specific features, a forum for understanding advanced functions, and a place for getting a behind-the-scenes look at the software publisher.

Take time to articulate every benefit you can—an obscure, tenth-level advantage to a small group of prospects could result in an idea that entices a whole class of readers.

**3.2** Next, *translate benefits into articles.* A newsletter, simply put, is a medium for providing benefits in the form of words and pictures. To build a foundation for your publication you have only to translate your list of benefits to the working elements of a newsletter. For example, a low-price guarantee might translate into a feature about equipment costs and financing. Local and national industry information translates to an insider column by a respected expert. A place of service could take the form of regular profiles of its volunteers. And an understanding of advanced software program functions might translate to an issue-by-issue focus on each primary software function.

**3.3** This is also the time to *develop a rough marketing plan* to promote your newsletter. Ask and answer a few general questions: How will you market your newsletter? How will you distinguish it from its competition? What are the top venues for reaching prospective readers? What is the best way to demonstrate its benefits? What other ways can you use your newsletter and the reputation it develops to generate income?

In some cases, you should consider enlisting sponsors and/or advertisers. Is there a noncompeting product, service, or cause that is interested in the same audience? If so, you can defray costs, perhaps even turn a profit by selling advertising space or enlisting ongoing sponsorship.

You'll find books about developing marketing plans on the shelves of any library. But if you are looking for an excellent, solid overview of commonsense marketing—get the most recent edition of the standard that started a marketing revolution: *Guerrilla Marketing: Secrets for Making Big Profits from Your Small Business,* by Jay Levinson (Houghton Mifflin, 1998).

**3.4** In the end, you must *calculate the risks* of any project. If good research, thorough analysis, careful planning, big budgets, and skillful execution guaranteed success, lofty manufacturers, service providers, and institutions would never fail. They, of course, can provide volumes of evidence attesting to the fact that even the best intentions and the most perfect execution can elude success. The planning, design, and publication of a successful newsletter, like anything else, requires an indefinable confluence of the right audience, information, design, timing, and talent. Don't let anyone tell you differently.

### Jolt Your Thinking

When you travel a road over and over it develops a rut—a well-worn path of least resistance. The same is true with publishing and marketing. Jaded thinking envisions a newsletter as a certain size and shape with a certain type of content. Once you've created a few, it's easy to forget their true purpose and why and how they work. It's easier to simply repeat a formula.

Good designers and marketers avoid ruts—they carve new roads to different places. You do it with "jolt thinking"—thinking that questions the basic premise—the what, why, and how of doing something. It challenges you to examine your mission, strategy, and execution of a project by posing and answering three basic questions:

1. What is the purpose?

2. Why is it done the way it's done?

3. How can I do it more effectively?

### Step 3: **PLANNING CHECKLIST**

**3.1**  Create a list of customer benefits

**3.2**  Translate benefits into articles

**3.3**  Develop a marketing plan

**3.4**  Calculate the risks

STEP 4

# Choose a Format

The results of the first three steps—a well-conceived goal, informed understanding, and a clear plan—are the foundation of a newsletter. It's time to envision what you plan to build.

**4.1** 4.1 Based on the editorial model you chose in *Step 1.2: Choose a model,* page 161—a promotional newsletter, a relationship newsletter, or an expert newsletter—the next step is to *select a page configuration.*

The only limitation of the size, shape, and arrangement of your newsletter is your preconceptions.

**Step 4: FORMAT CHECKLIST**

| | |
|---|---|
| **4.1** | Select a page configuration |
| **4.2** | Plot the content |
| **4.3** | Determine the frequency of publication |

The newsletter's namesake is news in letter form—typically 8.5 by 11 inches folded in half or in thirds as a self-mailer or to fit a conventional business envelope. If you need a bit more space you can use a standard legal sheet—8.5 by 14 inches. You can fit just as much information on a standard page in one-column letter form as you can in three columns.

Most of us probably picture a newsletter as a *booklet*—one or more 11 by 17 inch pages folded in half to 8.5 by 11 inches. Some other common booklet sizes are a 8.5 by 11 inches folded to 5.5 by 8.5 inches, and a tabloid booklet: a 17 by 22 inch folded to 11 by 17 inches. Booklets, of course, often include more than four pages. You can add as many four-page signatures (the folded sheet) as are necessary and practical.

If you want the advantages of a newsletter with less preparation and cost, consider using a postcard format. See *Style 9: Postcard,* page 268. Using both sides of a 4.25 by 6 inches to 6 by 9 inch card will accommodate a surprising amount of information. Less content means less preparation.

Beyond letters, booklets, and post-cards there are plenty of ways to make your newsletter unique. Custom-folds are an easy way to organize and present your information in an out-of-the-ordinary way—Z-folds, M-folds, gatefolds, roll-folds, accordion-folds, and many others.

**4.2** Although it's difficult to determine before you begin creating actual articles and illustrations, this is a good time to decide just how broad a range of information your publication will cover—to *plot the content*.

First, look at the scope in terms of the subject. How broadly will you cover the themes you are developing? Remember, a newsletter is "specialized," focusing on a subject-within-a-subject—instead of farming, aquatic farming.

At one extreme, a church newsletter, for example, might simply offer a calendar of events and a few paragraphs about programs and church business. At the other extreme is a comprehensive production that touches all aspects of church life, including articles by clergy, staff, and lay-leaders; contact information; a calendar; events information; missions focus; membership news; a financial report; letters to the editor; a Bible verse to cut out and put on the refrigerator; a list of recommended Web links; and so on.

Second, look at the scope in terms of the number of pages. Assuming you can fit roughly 500 to 800 words per page, consider how many pages you intend to fill and how many articles and other forms of content it will take to fill them. The simple church newsletter would likely fit on the front and back of a single sheet while the more comprehensive version could easily take eight or more pages.

Consider this—adding pages later on is a sign of success to your readers. Biting off more than you can chew at the beginning and having to cut back may be a letdown.

**4.3** Finally, *determine the frequency of publication*. The theory is simple: The more frequently you publish, the more visible you are to your audience. Every organization cannot, however, justify publishing a sixteen-page letter twice a month.

Do a commonsense analysis. Determine frequency on the basis of whether your publication is free or paid—most paid publications are published at least once a month. Another factor to consider is whether the information is time sensitive. Take into consideration how many other venues you have for maintaining interest in your theme, and how often readers will be receptive to paying attention.

STEP 5

# Choose a Newsletter Style

Each of us develops two types of style: a style of thinking and a style of expression. Our style of thinking shows up in what we choose to talk about, the way we emphasize our points, our tone of voice, level of self-confidence, and so on. Our style of expression manifests itself in our choice of colors, the clothes we wear, the car we drive, the music we appreciate, and so forth. Everyone has it—an absence of overt style is a style in itself.

A publication exhibits the same sensibilities—the design is the expression and the words are the thinking. Why commit to a style? From the first moment they meet your organization, prospective customers begin to form an opinion of it. You can take a passive role by allowing them to form their own opinions, or you can use your style to influence it.

**5.1** Your choice of style, like all your other marketing decisions, should be made from the customer's point of view. *Review the research* you gathered about who your prospective readers are, the benefits they seek, and what turns them on or off. Study what attracts them to other products they buy and other causes they embrace. Read the magazines they read, study their workplace, become acquainted with the relevant facts.

**5.2** Style is another way to *play on the differences between you and your competition.* Stylistic clues are found everywhere in an organization's corporate environment, its advertising and marketing materials, the makeup of its workforce, its geographical location, the color scheme of its logo, the attitude of its management, and so on.

**5.3** In any case, *match the style to your organization*—don't try to make it something it is not. Sheep in wolves' clothing stand a good chance of being devoured.

Consider two examples. Organization one manufactures signs, has a gregarious owner, and works in a casual, upbeat environment. Its readers are typically young marketing professionals and the owners of small to medium-size business-es. Organization two works to prevent spousal abuse, has a Ph.D. serving as its director, and a very businesslike office environment. This organization's readers are associated with shelters, hospitals, and law enforcement.

The style of the newsletters they publish should be quite different. Organization one might choose a style that expresses its creative product—a casual voice, four-color printing using bold typefaces, bright colors, and whimsical illustrations. Organization two might speak in a more sober voice and present a frugal two-color format, with serif typefaces, clean photographs, and a realistic style of illustration.

**5.4** With those thoughts in mind, you're ready to formally *establish a voice*. Sober and serious, casual and credible, or something in between—make it a conscious decision. In any case, speak like a person and not like a term paper. Initiate a conversation with your readers and develop a relationship. Speak to them one-on-one as you would in person, and they will come to consider your publication a message from a friend rather than a formal communication with an anonymous author.

**5.5** There are as many defini-tions of design as there are designers. For the purposes of this book, design is defined as the process of arranging elements and information on a page in a way that improves its communication. How readable the text is and how well the artwork illustrates the ideas set forth is every bit as important as the overall look and feel of the page. Designers, in short, should be as concerned about function as they are about form.

The second part of this book, beginning on page 50, presents thirteen different design recipes from which to *choose a layout style.* You can combine styles, or you can choose part of a style you like and add your own touches. The designs were created specifically for the Design-it-Yourself series. You are free to copy any recipe in whole or in part to produce your own materials. The only restriction is that you cannot assume ownership of the copied design.

**5.6** Too often, today's advertis-ing experts use negative or controversial messages under the guise of attracting the attention of a product's prospective buyers. Savvy communicators *build on the positive.* Why risk repelling a single person if you can achieve the same goal without offending anyone?

**Step 5: STYLE CHECKLIST**

☐ **5.1** Review the research

☐ **5.2** Play on the differences between you and your competition

☐ **5.3** Match the style to your organization

☐ **5.4** Establish a voice

☐ **5.5** Choose a layout style

☐ **5.6** Build on the positive

STEP 6

# Define the Steps and Stages

With a basic format and style in mind, it's time to do a big-picture assessment of what it will take to produce your newsletter—how much it will cost, how long it will take, and how many people will be necessary to make it all happen. Making that assessment now will help prevent surprises later.

Budgets, schedules, and workforces are interdependent—an ample budget, lots of help, and a lengthy schedule produces a different set of expectations than a thin budget, few hands, and a tight schedule. On pages 174 and 175, a production planning form shows basic tasks that need to be performed and space for specifying a person, a schedule, and a budget for each stage. The list is designed to flesh out potential problems. As you make your designations and estimates, you'll be forced to deal with many of the issues that will present themselves throughout the process.

Start with the categories you know the answers to. If, for example, you know you only have a certain number of dollars to commit to the project, start allocating those dollars to specific categories. If, on the other hand, you have a schedule limitation, begin to allocate a time for each process and see how those limitations increase the cost and the number of people necessary to complete the project.

Don't attempt to budget to the last hour and dime—make broad estimates on the first go-round, then fine-tune your answers as the project evolves.

**6.1** Don't mistake the meaning of *Design-it-Yourself*. It does not mean you must wear all the hats in the design, editing, and production of your newsletter. In fact, for a full-blown publication, expecting to produce all the parts single-handedly is probably downright unrealistic. For that reason, it pays to take the time, early on, to clearly outline your role in the process. You might, for example, be willing to tackle the design and production of your newsletter but prefer to rely on others to provide the content. If that's the case, by all means enlist help. You may even go so far as to take the preliminary research and planning steps and hire others to complete the project using this book as a guide.

Use the "Who will do it?" column to *identify your team*. Pinpoint the role or roles you will play and the players necessary to complete the other tasks. For a simple newsletter in postcard form (see page 268), all the roles above could conceivably be accomplished by one person. A thirty-two-page monthly publication, on the other hand, could easily require a full-time staff of four or five.

There are eleven major roles to be played in the production of a typical newsletter. Don't confuse roles with job descriptions—different organizations might divide up the editor's role, for example, in different ways—editor, managing editor, editorial director, assistant editor, contributing editor, and so on. The descriptions below summarize general responsibilities.

The *publisher* is the sponsor. Publishers establish the purpose and goals of the publication, manage its financial and editorial course, and help other players make broad-ranging decisions.

The *editor* typically organizes and manages the action. Editors plan and dictate the type of content that goes into the publication, find the right people to do the right things, and make and manage assignments. Editors are into the big picture and small details. They read and edit content to ensure that it meets the objectives of the publication and matches the publication's personality.

The *writer* is a composer. Whether they are employed by the publisher or write on a freelance basis, writers are charged with researching and writing articles of a specific length on assigned subjects. They must understand the broad goals of the publication and translate each piece into a vehicle for pursuing them.

The *designer's* responsibility is to translate written information into the form that best communicates it to the reader. Designers use type, layout, and illustration like writers use words to dress the publication in a way that sends the appropriate signals to the reader—instilling confidence, exuding style, and communicating effectively.

The *production artist* takes the plans and builds the house. These computer graphics people place, scale, compose, move, format, and edit the elements into a cohesive layout, shepherd it through the proofing process, and prepare it for printing.

The *illustrator*—artist or photographer—creates the images that express ideas, realities, or style and mood in a way words cannot. These artists provide bold visual headlines and quiet aesthetic details that draw readers in and help them to absorb information on the fly.

The *legal expert* protects the enterprise. These people develop a model, file the forms, extract the permissions, and research and register the copyrights and trademarks that keep the publication from unwarranted legal exposure.

The *printer* is part engineer and part artist. Printing vendors endeavor to strike a balance between the publisher's budget, the editor's schedule, and the designer's vision. The printer's job is to take one copy and turn it into 10,000 with no discernible difference between copy 73 and copy 6,899.

The *distributor* controls the outcome. If a newsletter is destined for the wrong reader or delivered to the wrong address, the party's over. The distributor develops and manages the mailing list, prepares each piece for shipping, and troubleshoots delivery.

The *promoter* leads the cheers. Through advertising and public relations, promoters broadcast the benefits of the publication, its reputation, and authority to prospective readers and to forums that connect with prospective readers.

The *administrator* runs the mill. Administrators develop and maintain the physical systems, do the accounting, meet the professional needs of the players—in short, allow for everything else to happen.

**6.2** The schedule is dependent on how complex your newsletter will be and how many people are involved. Use the "How long will it take?" column to *rough out a schedule*—not every minute and hour, but rough figures to help you assess whether you are headed toward a realistic goal. Your situation will vary based on what you are proposing, but here's a rough idea of the amount of time it might take to produce a typical page.

| | |
|---|---|
| 0.5 | hour to plan the issue |
| 2–5 | hours to write the copy |
| 0.5 | hour to edit the copy and layout |
| 1.5 | hours to lay out the page, including positioning and formatting type, finding and placing illustrations, and arranging the elements to fit |
| 10 | working days for printing |
| 2 | days for mail preparation |
| 5 | working days for delivery |

**6.3** Use the "How much will it cost?" column to *estimate costs*. Rates for production talents and services vary widely. The fees of a technical writer for a high-end business publication and a contributor to a local charitable organization's newsletter are incongruent. Prices for printing in a suburban community are often significantly different from its urban counterpart. Suffice it to say, you'll need to do some homework here—to find out how much local vendors and potential contributors charge. Don't try to account for every nickel and dime, but do develop a realistic range of prices.

**Production Planning Form**

| Task | Who will do it?<br>(title/name) | How long will it take?<br>(hours/days) | How much will it cost?<br>(dollar amounts) |
|---|---|---|---|
| **Editor** | | | |
| Choose > Format | | | |
| Plan > Content mix | | | |
| Plan > Editorial calendar | | | |
| Develop > Content model | | | |
| Develop > Proofing process | | | |
| Develop/choose > Newsletter name | | | |
| Develop > Defining phrase | | | |
| Develop/manage > Schedule | | | |
| Make/manage > Assignments | | | |
| Manage > Vendor contracts, permissions forms, usage forms | | | |
| Edit > Content | | | |
| **Content Developer** | | | |
| Write > Original articles | | | |
| Acquire > Freelance articles | | | |
| Acquire > Stock articles | | | |
| Acquire > Previously published articles | | | |
| Create > Illustrations > Photographs | | | |
| Acquire > Stock/royalty-free photographs | | | |
| Create > Illustrations > Artwork | | | |
| Acquire > Stock/royalty-free artwork | | | |
| Proofread/correct > Content | | | |
| **Designer** | | | |
| Choose > Style (grid, layout, color, typefaces, illustrations) | | | |
| Create > Nameplate and initial design | | | |
| Make/manage > Ongoing design decisions | | | |
| Create > Advertisement designs | | | |
| Choose > Paper stock | | | |
| **Production Artist** | | | |
| Create > Page layout | | | |
| Insert > Content | | | |
| Insert > Advertisements | | | |
| Proof/correct > Content | | | |
| | | | |
| | | | |

**Production Planning Form**

| Task | Who will do it? (title/name) | How long will it take? (hours/days) | How much will it cost? (dollar amounts) |
|---|---|---|---|
| **Legal expert** | | | |
| Create > Vendor contracts, forms for permissions, content proofing | | | |
| Register > Copyright, ISSN, mailing permit, nameplate trademark | | | |
| Create > Masthead content | | | |
| Review > Printing contract | | | |
| Evaluate > Insurance | | | |
| **Printing Coordinator/Printer** | | | |
| Search/choose > Printer | | | |
| Manage > Prepress document prep and preflighting | | | |
| Manage > Prepress proofing | | | |
| Manage > Printing | | | |
| Manage > Postpress proofing | | | |
| **Distributor** | | | |
| Develop/manage > Mailing list | | | |
| Determine/manage > Postage | | | |
| Manage > Mailing (labeling, applying postage, folding, sealing, stuffing, delivery to mailer) | | | |
| **Promoter** | | | |
| Develop/manage > Promotion programs | | | |
| **Administrator** | | | |
| Budget > Miscellaneous costs (phone, deliveries, software/hardware, media) | | | |
| Process > Payments (freelancers, vendors, printer) | | | |
| Determine/manage > Subscriptions | | | |
| Determine/manage > Sponsorships | | | |
| Determine/manage > Advertising | | | |
| **Other** | | | |
| | | | |
| | | | |
| | | | |
| | | | |
| | | | |
| | | | |

STEP 7

# Choose Your Tools

In the early 1980s, the production of raw type and illustrations for a typical eight-page newsletter might have gone something like this: The text was typed on a typewriter and marked up for typesetting by a production artist. The marked up sheets of paper were sent across town to an art studio or printer equipped with a computerized typesetting machine and a skilled typesetter. The text was retyped into the system and formatted as the artist specified.

The typesetting might have taken six hours of typing and formatting at $75 per hour. Headlines would have been set separately for $4 a word on another typesetting machine called a Typositor. Photographic prints were sized and shot on a graphic arts camera using a special screen negative so the finished image reproduced on a printing press. At $450 for the text, $200 for headlines, and another $200 for darkroom work, the materials for a single issue cost $850—just materials, not writing, not editing, not design, not production, not printing.

Today, you no longer have to be a corporate powerhouse to publish a professional-quality newsletter. The software necessary to complete the entire process without leaving your chair costs less than that single issue those few short years ago. For the first time in history, the success of your enterprise is dictated more by the quality of your information than by the depth of your pockets. This fact has profoundly altered the very concept of publishing.

**7.1** *Your first investment should be in a desktop publishing (DTP) program.* Most of the Design-it-Yourself projects are easiest to produce using a program such as Adobe InDesign, Adobe PageMaker, QuarkXPress, or Microsoft Publisher. They offer the ideal venue for combining the text you create in your word processor and the graphics you create with a draw or paint program into the files needed by a commercial printer.

There are significant differences between most desktop publishing programs and their word-processing counterparts. Most DTP programs are based on a pasteboard—pages sit on a background, onto which you can move text and graphics within reach until you need them.

On the page, you place, arrange, and manage multiple frames filled with text or graphics. Though word processing programs also support text boxes and the placement of graphics, they are typically used to create a string of pages—add a paragraph to page 2, and it affects page 5. When you format a page in a DTP program, each page can be laid out quite differently, and moving elements on one page does not automatically affect the others.

Plus, a DTP program has more precise, intuitive tools for formatting text, importing and manipulating graphics, applying and editing color, and producing output for a commercial printer.

**7.2** To create line art for your newsletter, *you'll need a drawing program*. There are two basic categories of computer graphics—"draw," for creating line art, and "paint," for creating photograph-like images. Draw graphics, also referred to as "vector" or "object-oriented," are created using objects such as lines, ovals, rectangles, and curves. The primary advantages of a draw file are that it can be sized very large or very small without losing print quality, and that draw file sizes are generally smaller than those of paint files.

Many clip art illustrations are created in draw formats. With a draw program such as Adobe Illustrator, Macromedia FreeHand, or CorelDRAW, you can use parts and pieces of clip art illustrations or create and edit your own. The most common draw file formats are Encapsulated PostScript (EPS) files and Windows Metafiles (WMF).

**7.3** To edit photographs and other paint illustrations *you'll need a paint program*. Paint images, also referred to as "raster" or "bit-mapped," are divided into a grid of thousands of tiny rectangles called pixels. Each pixel can be a different color or shade of gray. The primary advantage of a paint file is that it can represent a much more complex range of colors and shades than a draw file. The down side is the larger you plan to print the image, the larger the file size.

Programs such as Adobe Photoshop and Jasc Software's Paint Shop Pro are used to create and edit paint graphics. With one of these programs you can change, touch up, and combine photographs and other types of images, adjust attributes such as contrast and brightness, and apply a seemingly endless variety of effects and filters. The most common paint file formats are Joint Photographic Experts Group (JPEG or JPG) and Tagged-Image File Format (TIFF or TIF).

**7.4** *Anticipate file sharing.* The design world speaks primarily inPostScript, a language that allows your software to talk to output devices such as desktop printers. Almost all commercial printers require that the files you send them are PostScript compatible—meaning they include the information necessary to be translated to the printers' software and ultimately their presses. Many of the best fonts and clip art collections are available only in PostScript format.

If you plan to create your own print materials, buy programs that produce PostScript output and a PostScript-compatible printer, or add PostScript hardware/software to the printer you already own (check with your printer's manufacturer for details).

Another way to prepare files for distribution to a commercial printer or even online is to use Adobe Acrobat to produce files in the Portable Document Format (PDF). PDF files contain all the fonts, graphics, and printing information needed to view and print the document.

**7.5** *Choose a computer system.* It is said that you should choose software before you choose hardware. Nowhere is this more true than when you are working with graphics. Though Apple's Macintosh line has long been the platform of choice for the professional design community, PCs too are now widely used. All the programs mentioned are available in both Mac and Windows versions, and the program features and keystrokes are almost identical.

Perhaps the best gauge of the system you'll need is the software manufacturer's "recommended" hardware requirements versus the "minimum" requirements. From the programs you plan to use, identify the one that requires the most memory and CPU horsepower, and base your purchase on those recommendations.

**Step 7: TOOLS CHECKLIST**

- **7.1** Choose a desktop publishing program
- **7.2** Choose a drawing program
- **7.3** Choose a paint program
- **7.4** Anticipate file sharing
- **7.5** Choose a computer system

STEP 8

# Create a Name, a Defining Phrase, and a Nameplate

Your newsletter's nameplate is a statement, a standard, and a brand. It's a statement of purpose, a standard that reflects or establishes the visual style of the publication, and a visual brand that readers will grow to recognize.

**8.1** The first stage of creating a nameplate is to *develop a name*. In the case of a newsletter the name incorporates information from any of five different categories—the newsletter's publisher, audience, subject matter, primary reader benefit, or a modifier. Generally speaking, it is to your advantage to create a name that says what it means, or you will forever be explaining its meaning via your advertising and marketing efforts.

Begin by compiling a brainstorming list. Divide a sheet into several sections—the publisher, audience, reader benefit, and a modifier—as shown below, and list as many relevant terms as you can conjure up. For example, the list for a newsletter that teaches builders how to sell homes might look like this:

| | |
|---|---|
| Publisher | Sampler Group |
| Audience | Builders |
| Subject | Marketing homes |
| Benefit 1 | Selling success |
| Benefit 2 | Profits |
| Benefit 3 | Marketing strategy |
| Modifier | How-to |

The modifier is a generic term for the many ways you can describe intent, frequency, importance, and so on. Some examples: advisor, alert, bulletin, currents, digest, forum, hotline, how-to, letter, monitor, monthly, news, newsletter, outlook, quarterly, report, review, talk, trends, update, and weekly.

Use your brainstorming list to experiment with combinations. The goal is to create a name that states the benefit of the newsletter to the reader and then fills in as many of the who, what, where, when, and why blanks as possible. Even the short list above presents many possibilities.

Sampler's Home Seller Strategies
Sampler's Builder Profits
Sampler's How-To Market Homes
Sampler's Builder Marketing
Sampler's Home Marketing Forum
Sampler's Successful Builder

Once you have a name and before you invest any more time and money, do a preliminary trademark check to determine if the name you are pursuing can be protected. Without a trademark, you could spend a significant amount of money and energy building a brand that belongs to someone else. At a minimum, do a search for the word or phrase on an Internet search engine and search the Trademark Electronic Search System (TESS) at www.uspto.gov/web/menu/search.html.

**8.2** The next stage is to *create a five- to fifteen-word defining phrase* (fig. A, below) that lays out the full scope of the newsletter. Not an attention-getting slogan or advertising tagline, but a clear statement of purpose. A slogan such as "All the News That's Fit to Print" may be appropriate for *The New York Times*, but a small enterprise that doesn't get that kind of exposure is better off getting right to the point with a defining phrase such as "News, events, opinion, and resources for New Yorkers." Clever is only good if it doesn't get in the way of communicating the message.

Include as much information as possible—the publisher, audience, subject, reader benefit, and a modifier. For the builder marketing publication above, the tagline might be "The builder's guide to home-selling success."

**8.3** Use the name and defining phrase to *design the nameplate* (fig. B, below)—the logo-like banner that typically appears at the top of page one. Since you have already chosen a newsletter style from Part 2 of this book, designing yours should be easy. You have only to translate your words into nameplate form.

You'll find many nameplate examples and much discussion about them in Part 2 of this book, beginning on page 201.

**8.4** Finally, *test your message*. The true test of whether your name, defining phrase, nameplate, or for that matter any other type of communication, works is to present it to someone who doesn't know anything about your organization, and see if that person can tell what you are trying to accomplish. Does your material communicate its intended message to that stranger? One complication of writing and designing is that you are very close to the action—at times, too close to gauge its effect clearly. Find people whose opinion you respect and invite their reactions and suggestions.

**Step 8: NAME CHECKLIST**

- [ ] **8.1** Develop a name
- [ ] **8.2** Create a defining phrase
- [ ] **8.3** Design the nameplate
- [ ] **8.4** Test your message

An example of how to design a new nameplate (left) from an existing design recipe (right). See *Style 4: Icons,* page 228, for recipe details.

STEP 9

# Compose the Content

Good content may survive a poor design, but the best design cannot overcome poor content.

**9.1** Even if you intend to generate most of your material internally, *developing a set of writer's guidelines* is a good way to start the process. Typically offered to contributors by magazine and book publishers, guidelines answer all of the questions a writer with little or no knowledge of your publication might ask. Even if you intend to solicit an article only periodically from someone within your organization, composing guidelines can help you flesh out ideas you might not otherwise consider.

Some of the common issues guidelines address are:

> The subject/theme of the publication
> A statement of editorial style
> Who to contact
> The action it is hoped the reader will take
> The type of information featured
> Subjects and angles that attract readers
> The appropriate writing style
> How much is paid
> What rights are purchased
> How submissions are made
> Specific articles being pursued
> Recent articles published

At this stage, especially if you will be working with lots of writers and/or complex topics, you might also identify a style book or manual to follow. A style manual sets forth a set of rules regarding the usage of words—punctuation, abbreviations, distinctive treatments, documentation, and so on. Some also deal with related topics such as book layout and general printing and production. When an issue such as the correct way to use parentheses arises, everyone involved can turn to the same source for answers. An excellent example is *The Chicago Manual of Style, 14th Edition* (The University of Chicago Press, 1993).

**9.2** Plan and execute, gather reactions, revise the plan, and execute again—that is the formula for succeeding at virtually anything. The trick is to document the plan exactly so you know where and how to make the sweeping changes and subtle adjustments that reactions dictate. The best way to start developing newsletter content is to *plan the content mix*. What types of materials will you be producing and how much real estate will you devote to each area of interest?

Want to see how others do it? Deconstruct the best newsletters, newspapers, and magazines you can find and diagram the types of material they include. Chart out the number of words or proportion of space they reserve for various types of content. Base your initial plan on what you considered an interesting, balanced mix, then tweak the formula as you begin to gather responses.

Divide your publication into the number of page spreads you plan to use and diagram the mix of content you plan to present. Example of types of content include:

Acknowledgments
Advertising
Announcements
Calendars
Case studies
Checklists
Columns written by regulars or guests
Condensations
Discussion transcripts
Event coverage
Excerpts
Fiction
Forecasts
How-to articles
Interviews of groups or individuals
Letters/submissions from readers
Listings
News coverage
News releases
Opinion
Profiles of organizations or individuals
Questions and answers
Quotations
Reprints from other publications or online
Resource lists
Results
Reviews
Serializations
Sidebars
Statistical data
Surveys and results
Synopses

**9.3** Based on your newly defined content mix, *plan the editorial calendar*. Take a sheet of paper divide it into the number of issues you plan to produce over the first year and list the major articles and supplemental information you intend to publish. For now, just do a rough projection—later you can produce a detailed version from which the editor can make assignments. The calendar helps you see how much information it will be necessary to generate. Don't be surprised if you need to adjust how comprehensively you cover the topics, reevaluate the frequency with which you plan to publish, or adjust the newsletter's format or number of pages.

**9.4** When you get to the stage of writing articles it pays to *develop content formulas*. A formula is an article outline. It can be general or explicit, but if you are generating lots of material, it's a valuable tool. Here, for example, is what a formula for a how-to article might look:

| | |
|---|---|
| [Headline] | Your action will result in this benefit |
| [Credit] | Author |
| [1] | Establish the mood |
| [2] | Summarize the article |
| [3] | Map the subject |
| [4] | Detail the benefits |
| [5] | Explain how it looks from the reader's angle |
| [6] | Show how it works |
| [7] | Demonstrate the steps |
| [8] | Provide sources of materials |
| [9] | Provide more information |
| [10] | Restate the summary |
| [Link] | Name of author, author's e-mail address, Web link for more information |

**9.5** Once you have a good handle on the stages above, you're ready to *produce original content*.

This book does not pretend to instruct you in an art as diverse and complex as writing. If you or the people you will enlist have not written for publication, there are many excellent books on myriad writing methods: technical, instructional, journalistic, marketing, and so on.

Do consider this: There is a big difference between gathering information and writing. If you find it necessary to ask nonwriters to write, it may be better to frame your request in the form of a request for information than as a request for finished articles. You can even do it via forms and questionnaires. If, for example, you intend to produce articles about people within your organization who are celebrating employment milestones, you may find it more productive to request the person's name, division, years of service, proudest professional moment, and such, rather than asking their supervisor to "write a short article about Elaine's tenth anniversary."

Using freelance writers is an added expense, but people who are accustomed to producing cogent copy on diverse subjects—using a wide variety of sources—will pay for themselves in the time and stress they save you. A good writer can also shorten the write, edit, and rewrite process to just one or two cycles.

One more note about original content: Insisting that writers write to fit a layout "to the word" belittles the importance of content. A flexible design should accommodate a 525-word article as well as it does a 480-word article.

**9.6** It is not necessary to generate original content for every element of every issue of your publication. Some elements—the nameplate, masthead, mailing indicia, and so on—will be repeated from issue to issue. But you should also consider *acquiring stock and previously published content.*

Most established organizations have previously published material from reports, presentations, marketing materials, news releases, and so on that may fit as is or after some light editing to translate it into the newsletter's context.

You can also track down free material from professional organizations, associations, the government and other public institutions, and organizations that promote related products, services, and causes.

You can also buy previously published materials from subject experts. Most magazines, for example, buy only one-time rights to the articles they publish. That means after the contracted time of exclusivity, you could negotiate an agreement with the writer to reprint the same article for a fee. Writers, obviously, are eager for you to repurpose material because they realize a profit. You may even find an article that doesn't quite fit and hire the author to rewrite a version that fits your newsletter's context exactly. You can create a very effective newsletter by purchasing a single feature article by a respected subject expert for each issue of your publication and generating material that supports and supplements it.

**9.7** Doing it yourself, using freelance writers, and repurposing content of other kinds requires that you *develop forms and contracts.* For more about the legal issues of creating a newsletter, see *Get a Legal Checkup,* page 33.

**9.8** Part of the editor's job is to *make and manage assignments.* Doing so requires a good scheduling form to track who is to produce what by when. The more clearly defined your expectations are, the more likely they are to be met. Some writers like a general assignment where they build the article from scratch. At the other extreme are those who would prefer a detailed outline that spells out exactly where you're headed. The better your system for making assignments, the easier they will be to manage.

**9.9** Before a final edit, take the time to *compile the content and prepare the file.* Translating all of the text into a single word processing program and file allows the editor to see everything together for the first time. This is important from the conceptual standpoint to determine if the ideas as a whole flow well together, and from a practical standpoint to see if the text will fit the layout.

Because text is reformatted when it is placed in the desktop publishing program, before or after final content editing, take time to remove all but the most basic text formatting. In most cases it is best to use just one typeface, one font size, one alignment (align left), and to remove extra spacing, tabs, and special attributes such as bolding.

The publishing world is different than the business typing world—instead of two spaces following a period, use just one. In most cases, instead of underlines, use italics. Instead of two hyphens, use a long em dash (—). Instead of straight inch marks ("), use open (") and close (") quotation marks. Instead of a straight foot mark ('), use an apostrophe ('). And use tabs and alignment settings, not spaces, to indent or center text.

**9.10** The final stage of development is to *edit and proof the content.* The content, no matter where it originates, must be edited to speak in the publication's voice (see *Step 5.4: Establish a voice,* page 21). The editor either established that voice or is well acquainted with it. Editors read the copy and review the illustrations to ensure that they are presented by the same authority. They check that the information matches what was assigned, that it accurately represents the publications style and views, and that it is copyedited and technically correct—the grammar, spelling, and punctuation are correct, copyrights are noted, the address has the correct zip code, and so on.

### Get a Legal Checkup

Publishers large and small heed the axiom: Ignorance of the law is no defense. Be sure you have a clear understanding of your legal rights before you publish anything. This book does not pretend to provide legal counsel, but rather offers a general overview of what is involved and some resources for pursuing remedies.

Consult a lawyer, legal expert, or a definitive guide:

- To help you understand your legal responsibility and limit your liability for the comments and claims you make about individuals and organizations, products and services, statistics and data, and so on.

- To develop the contracts and the simple agreements used to formalize the relationship between your publication and researchers, writers, illustrators, photographers, printers, list brokers and list maintenance providers, and so on.

- To obtain and archive model releases (agreements with people who appear in photographs you publish).

- To review the license agreements tendered by providers of stock and royalty-free artwork and photography, fonts, software, and so on.

- To register, employ, and/or provide notice of copyrights of the content you generate and the copyrights of content created by others. For more information visit www.loc.gov/copyright, or call 202-707-9100 to order forms and publications.

- To register, employ, and/or provide notice of the trademark of your newsletter's name and the trademarks owned by others. For more information, visit www.uspto.gov/main/trademarks.htm, or call 800-786-9199 to order forms and publications.

- To register, employ, and/or provide notice of an International Standard Serial Number (ISSN), a free-of-charge code that identifies your newsletter as a serialized publication. It is used by librarians, publishers, suppliers, and others to identify it and as a vehicle for exchanging information about it. For more information visit www.issn.org.

- To register, employ, and/or provide notice of a mailing permit indicia that allows you to mail your publication at a discounted price.

- Your publication may require legal syntax that is not mentioned here. Be sure to have a lawyer or appropriate legal expert review and approve your publication before you print it.

STEP 10

# Illustrate the Message

Pictures speak louder than words, and illustrations speak louder than pictures. Fill your newsletter with illustrations—not decorations, but photographs, artwork, and diagrams that clarify your message and transmit your publication's style.

**10.1** With the advent of digital cameras and powerful editing software, perhaps the easiest way to illustrate your publication is to *shoot custom photographs.* Remember, illustrations are more than pictures; they are pictures that, ideally, make your message more understandable. A head-and-shoulders photograph of a person works, but a shot of the same person in the place your article describes works better.

Advertising pioneer David Ogilvy once said, "The kind of photographs which work hardest are those which arouse the reader's curiosity. He glances at the photograph and says to himself, 'What goes on here?' Then he reads your story to find out." You can compose illustrative photographs, too.

Instead of a child holding a doll to illustrate child abuse, show the child standing in the shadow of an adult. Instead of a head-and-shoulders shot of the newly appointed coach, pose her juggling a volleyball, basketball, and baseball. Rather than a straight, smile-for-the-camera shot of accountants around a meeting table, pose them in front of a vault door.

If you don't want to shoot photographs yourself but you need a customized shot, consider hiring a photographer to shoot them for you. Some photographers charge an hourly rate, and some charge by the project. Be sure to understand who owns the rights to the specified and future use of the photographs you commission. Some photographers will assign all rights to you, others want to retain them, but most will negotiate.

**10.2** If you don't have the time for shooting your own photographs, there are plenty of places to *acquire stock and royalty-free photographs.* Generally speaking, stock photographs are licensed for specific uses. The license is based on criteria such as the type of publication it appears in and the number of copies that are printed. On the other hand, once you pay the license fee for a royalty-free photograph, you can use it just about any way and anywhere you want.

In either case, stock or royalty-free images, you only license the use of the image, you do not own the copyright. Be sure to read the fine print of any license agreement so there are no surprises after you have your newsletter printed.

There are many excellent sources of stock and royalty-free photographs on the World Wide Web. Some examples include www.corbis.com, www.creatas.com, www.eyewire.com, www.gettyworks.com, and www.tonystone.com.

**10.3** *Creating custom artwork* is not quite as simple as shooting a custom photograph but it can do something a photograph has a harder time doing—it can express the intangible. You can illustrate an article on dog obedience training using a drawing of a dog dressed in gentleman's finery or show an artist's sketch of your latest product before it is even manufactured.

If you don't personally have a talent for drawing, commission an illustration by a professional illustrator. You simply find an artist whose style you admire, negotiate a price, and provide them with the specifics of what you want. There are plenty of Web sites where you can browse examples of work by many different illustrators using a diversity of styles. Good examples are www.workbook. com and www.creative-hotlist.com. You can also look through magazines, newspapers, and Web sites to find the names of illustrators and track them down through the publications.

You can also take apart and reassemble parts and pieces of clip art illustrations to represent ideas for which they were not originally intended. This is easy to do using the type of draw programs described in *Step 7.2: Choose a Drawing Program,* page 177. Combining a drawing of a snowflake with a drawing of the sun, for example, produces a new illustration that represents heating and cooling or seasonal change.

**10.4** Which leads us to *using stock illustrations and clip art*. Stock illustration, like stock photography, is licensed for use in specific situations. Stock illustrations and photography are considered by some to be a step up from clip art. The theory is that a stock illustration, many of which are originally commissioned by a client for a specific project, is given more thought and care than a clip art illustration created in the hope that someone might buy it.

You'll find excellent samples of stock illustration and photography at www.blackbook.com.

The flip side of that thinking is why clip art was once the outcast class of the illustration world. The perception was, because clip art was created specifically for resale, it was not equal to the artwork created for client projects. Today, much extremely well-conceived and -executed illustration is created as clip art. You can buy it by the piece or as a part of a collection. Two stellar clip art sources are Dynamic Graphics at www.dgusa.com and Image Club at www.eyewire.com.

You can also find clip art in book form. For decades, Dover Publications and others have been publishing the books from which art was originally "clipped" and pasted on the pages being prepared for printing—hence the term "clip art." Dover, at www.doverpublications.com, remains a particularly good source for compilations of antique engravings, silhouettes, and drawings.

Finally, there are many good sources of specialty illustrations such as maps from Map Resources at www.mapresource.com, government and military clip art from One Mile Up at www.onemileup.com, beautifully intricate borders, initials, and ornaments from Aridi Computer Graphics at www.aridi.com, and health and medical subjects from LifeArt at www.lifeart.com.

**10.5** Do you have a tough idea to visualize? *Do some illustration brainstorming*. There are lots of Web sites that feature stock and royalty-free graphics and photography for sale—graphics and photography that visualize ideas. They are obviously a great way to find and purchase the rights to specific images, but they can also double as a creative tool. Next time you're stuck for ideas, visit one of these sites and search for words associated with the concept to see how other artists have illustrated the same idea. Do not steal ideas; use them as seeds for growing your own.

**Step 10: ILLUSTRATION CHECKLIST**

- **10.1** Shoot custom photographs
- **10.2** Acquire stock and royalty-free photographs
- **10.3** Create custom artwork
- **10.4** Acquire stock illustrations and clip art
- **10.5** Do some illustration brainstorming

STEP 11

# Assemble the Pieces

Eleven steps into the process and you're just now getting to the most obvious and, arguably, the most fun part of designing a newsletter—bringing the pages to life. Using the format you decided on in *Step 4: Choose a Format*, page 168, and the style you chose in *Step 5: Choose a Style*, page 170, you can begin to recreate the basic page layouts in your desktop publishing program.

**11.1** Before you can execute the design recipes in Part 2 of the book, you'll need to *select and purchase the associated fonts* or choose similar fonts from your own arsenal.

All fonts are not created equal. Those developed by the leading type foundries—names such as Adobe, Berthold, Font Bureau, International Typeface Corporation (ITC), and Linotype—are, generally speaking, designed by premier type designers, past and present,

**Serif Typefaces**

Lorem ipsum dolor sit amet, consectetue adipiscing elit, sed diam nonummy nibh tincidunt ut laoreet dolore magna aliqua volutpat. Ut wisi enim ad minim veniam
Caslon Regular

Lorem ipsum dolor sit amet, consect adipiscing elit, sed diam nonummy ni euismod tincidunt ut laoreet dolore r aliquam erat volutpat. Ut wisi enim a
Century Expanded

Lorem ipsum dolor sit amet, consectetuer adipiscir diam nonummy nibh euismod tincidunt ut laoree magna aliquam erat volutpat. Ut wisi enim ad mir veniam, quis nostrud exerci tation ullamcorper sus
Garamond Light Condensed

Lorem Lorem ipsum dolor sit amet, cons adipiscing elit, sed diam nonummy nibh tincidunt ut laoreet dolore magna aliqua volutpat. Ut wisi enim ad minim veniam
Minion Regular

**Sans Serif Typefaces**

Lorem ipsum dolor sit amet, consectetu adipiscing elit, sed diam nonummy nib euismod tincidunt ut laoreet dolore ma aliquam erat volutpat. Ut wisi enim ad
Formata Light

Lorem ipsum dolor sit amet, consectetuer ad elit, sed diam nonummy nibh euismod tincic laoreet dolore magna aliquam erat volutpat. enim ad minim veniam, quis nostrud exerci
Franklin Gothic Book Condensed

Lorem ipsum dolor sit amet, consect adipiscing elit, sed diam nonummy n euismod tincidunt ut laoreet dolore m aliquam erat volutpat. Ut wisi enim ac
Helvetica Regular

Lorem ipsum dolor sit amet, consectetu adipiscing elit, sed diam nonummy nib euismod tincidunt ut laoreet dolore ma aliquam erat volutpat. Ut wisi enim ad r
Myriad Regular

and translated into electronic form by people who have a deep understanding of and profound respect for the art of typography. Many of the free fonts you download online or that are included by the hundreds with inexpensive software packages are knock-offs of originals. They often are not as well designed or are simply not very good software in the way they calculate the space between different combinations of characters, print on the page, and so on.

Check up front with the printer that will be reproducing your newsletter to determine whether they would prefer a specific font software format—PostScript, TrueType, or OpenType.

If you opt to use a font other than that recommended in the design recipe, be prepared to alter the amount of text you project to fit on a page. Different fonts take up different amounts of space.

**11.2** Turn to the design recipe style you chose in *Step 5: Choose a Style*, page 170, and begin building your newsletter template by *establishing the page size and grid*. Each recipe includes everything you need—the page size, the margins, the number of columns, the gutter (space between columns), and various other guides that divide the page proportionally. Together, those elements form a "grid"—an invisible foundation on which to position all of the elements you place on the page. Aligning as much as possible to the grid provides a sense of visual order and stability that is difficult to achieve any other way. Desktop publishing programs have "guides" you can position for just this purpose.

**11.3** With a framework developed, begin to recreate and *place the foundation elements*—the nameplate, masthead, running heads, and page numbers—and establish, if necessary, a mailing area.

The nameplate is the logo-like banner you created in *Step 8.3: Design the Nameplate*, page 179—it typically appears at the top of page one. The masthead is the block of information that defines the publication, posts legal information, identifies the publisher and the key contributors, and provides contact information (see *The Masthead*, right ). The running heads are the text and graphics repeated on most pages to remind the reader where they are—the publication name, the page number, perhaps the subject of the publication or its defining phrase, and so on. The page numbers are typically on the top or bottom outside edge of the page. And a mailing area (if your newsletter is a self-mailer), the area where the postage or mailing indicia, return address, and address label are displayed.

**11.4** Once those pieces are in place, begin to *place the text*. If it was compiled and prepared as described in *Step 9.9: Prepare the File*, page 182, the process is easy. Be sure the content is in finished form—it is useless to lay out and illustrate text that has not yet been edited, proofed, and signed off on.

Don't be concerned about exactly where it is first placed, just get it into the publication, then apply the attributes of the most widely used format—the size and style of the text.

The person in charge of assembling the elements of the layout should understand how to create, edit, and apply styles. The styles feature is among the most powerful features of a desktop publishing program and is relatively easy to learn. Styles control all the attributes of a paragraph of text such as its typeface, its size, whether it is bold, italic, all caps, or underlined, and whether the paragraph is indented, has extra space above or below it, is hyphenated, and if it is aligned right, left, centered, or justified.

**The Masthead**

The masthead is a newsletter's passport. Mailing regulations, laws, affiliations, and customs all present newsletter publishers with requirements for entry into the various jurisdictions of publishing. The postal service, for example, requires certain information for preferred rates; laws dictate standards for certain types of information, such as financial data; and a sponsor may require its beneficiary to post a particular disclaimer.

The masthead is an area of the newsletter, often enclosed within a bordered box, that is a repository of much of that information. Generally speaking, your newsletter's masthead should include some or all of the following:

> Publication title
> Defining phrase
> Publisher
> Titles and names of editors, writers, contributors, staff
> Statement of purpose
> Office of publication address, phone, fax, Web, e-mail
> Editorial office address, phone, fax, Web, e-mail
> Publication's Internet address
> Information/instructions regarding back issues, subscriptions, advertising, sponsorship, membership, nonprofit status
> Legal disclaimer
> Copyright notice
> Trademark notice
> ISSN code or USPS number
> Issue date, volume, number
> Statement of frequency
> Contribution guidelines
> Postmaster change of address notice
> Reprint/copying guidelines
> Forwarding information
> Miscellaneous postal information

Whether you apply a style to one or one hundred different paragraphs of text, you only have to edit the style to change the formatting of every occurrence of the style throughout the document. In future issues of your publication they make formatting fast and easy.

Take the time to format one paragraph of text and create a style for each different paragraph in the design recipe—one for headlines, one for subheads, one for captions, one for the author's byline, and so on. With those styles created you can apply formatting to all the text by simply clicking on a paragraph and applying a style.

After you format the text, you can begin to move the pieces around. Use the content mix plan you developed in *Step 9: Compose the Content*, page 180, to divide the various types of content up and place them on the designated pages. If you did not create a formal plan, confer with the editor to determine the flow of the publication.

**11.5** Once you have a rough layout, you can begin to *place illustrations*. Text comes first because photographs and artwork generally can be sized to fit the space available. Since the text is in finished form, enlarging an illustration to fill space or reducing it to allow for more text is preferable to going back to the writing/editing stages.

**11.6** If your newsletter includes more than one color, (black is a color in printing terms), it is at this stage that you *apply color*. But first, you need to understand how commercial printers reproduce color.

There are two ways to arrive at matching a specific color. You can choose a specific ink color that matches it, called a solid PANTONE® Color, or you can combine four standard colors to match it as closely as possible, referred to as process colors.

There are over 1,000 solid PANTONE Colors. If, for example, you want bright orange, you would choose a color from a PANTONE formula guide (left). After you have choosen the exact color you want, you provide the printer with the corresponding PANTONE number. They buy a container of that ink and print your job with it.

The alternative method is to print the job using the four-color process. The process colors are cyan, magenta, yellow, and black (CMYK). This combination of colors can be screened to represent just about any color value across the spectrum. This method is best for printing color photographs and other material that contain a range of colors that cannot be reproduced using two or three solid colors.

The limitation of the four-color process is that it cannot reproduce some colors as vividly and is typically more expensive than the solid color method.

The least expensive route is to print black or a single solid color on white or colored stock. If you're willing to spend a little more, you can print with two colors, typically black and one solid color. The general rule is the more colors you print, the more complex the printing press needs to be to print them, and the more your job will cost. The four-color process, generally speaking, is the most expensive.

**11.7** With all the elements roughly in place you're ready to *adjust elements*. Layout and design are all about details. Artists often spend hours simply moving elements around on pages to see what works best. You have the advantage of an established design recipe, but you still need to make aesthetic judgments about how the different elements of your layout work together.

A few layout tips: One, use a delicate hand—new designers tend to make text and graphics too big and/or too bold. Keep your layout simple and delicate.

Two, print sample pages early and often. It's difficult to judge how well a layout is working until you see the pages printed out at actual size—a typeface or illustration that looks good on the screen often looks very different at actual size. If the pages will be folded, fold them. If they will be printed on an unusual paper, print it on that paper. Review the results and make adjustments.

Three, build in time to allow your finished layout to sit for a day or two. You'll be surprised how much easier it is to spot flaws when you return to the layout with a fresh perspective.

**11.8** Once everything is in place, its time to *proofread and correct the finished pages*. Even though editing such as checking grammar, spelling, and proofreading took place in the content creation stages, much has changed. As text was placed, it is possible a few letters or words—or even an entire article—was overlooked or accidentally deleted.

If you wrote the article or laid out the page, this is one stage of the process you cannot do yourself. The person who made the mistakes typically has the hardest time recognizing them.

Enlist, instead, the talents of an expert copy editor—someone who possesses a talent for finding both the obvious problems and the near invisible over-sights. Have the copy editor read over the entire publication for text errors and

review the layout to spot errors such as a caption that doesn't match up with an illustration, an incorrect page number, or a missing photographer's credit and copyright notice.

**11.9** When the newsletter is complete, *save a copy of the document as a template* for future issues. To save space, remove illustrations that are specific to that particular issue and tag text that must be changed with double question marks (??). For example, in the nameplate, replace "December" with "Month??," and a Web address that changes periodically with "www.??.com." That way, when you produce the next issue, you can search the document for the double question marks to easily locate the recurring edit points.

**11.10** Finally, before you hand over your newsletter to a commercial printer to be reproduced, *have it reviewed by a mailing expert*. Take a copy of the document and a sample of the paper it will be printed on to your local post office or the mailing services provider that will distribute it to confirm that it follows the specifications you set and meets all the necessary postal regulations.

## Step 11: ASSEMBLY CHECKLIST

- **11.1** Select and purchase fonts
- **11.2** Establish the page size and grid
- **11.3** Place the foundation elements
- **11.4** Place the text
- **11.5** Place illustrations
- **11.6** Apply color
- **11.7** Adjust elements
- **11.8** Proofread and correct the finished pages
- **11.9** Save a template
- **11.10** Have it reviewed by a mailing expert

STEP 12

# Find a Printer

In printing, excellence is the minimum requirement. Skewed text, muddy photographs, or faded colors shout, "WE DON'T CARE."

No matter how well you plan and execute a smart, good-looking design, you must rely on the skills of a commercial printer to translate your computer files into a finished product. Finding a printer that's well-suited to the type of job you are printing, committed to producing a quality product, and willing to produce it for a reasonable price is a critical piece of the design-it-yourself puzzle.

SOURCE Illustration:
Photographs courtesy of
Printing Services, Inc.,
Richmond, Virginia

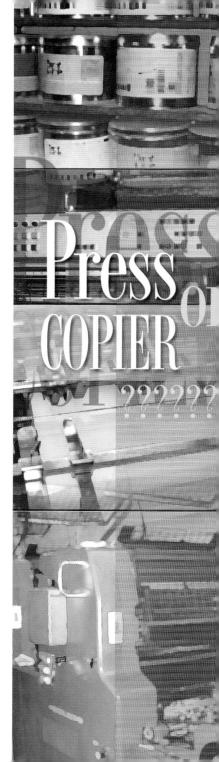

**12.1** The first stage is to *find a printer with the proper equipment.* Two of the most common systems used to reproduce newsletters are an offset lithographic press and a digital production printer (copier). There are other methods of printing equal to the task, but these typically offer the best mix of quality and price.

Offset lithography is, generally speaking, the best process for printing a one-color to four-color job at quantities of 500 or more. It can reproduce fine detail and big areas of color, and can print large enough sheet sizes to allow you to extend (bleed) images and areas of color off the edges of the sheet. It is possible to print less, but the difference between printing fifty and 500 impressions is insignificant—little more than the cost of the paper.

If you are printing 500 or fewer copies of a publication, a digital production printer (copier) such as Xerox's DocuTech (black and white) or DocuColor (four-color) systems produce acceptable quality for a reasonable price.

**12.2** When you first speak to the printer's representative, *explain the scope of the job* to determine if it fits within the printer's capabilities. In *Step 11.6: Apply Color,* page 188, you decided on the type and number of colors to use. Some printers specialize in printing one-color and two-color work and are ill-equipped to print four-color process, others aren't interested in anything but large runs of four-color, and so on. A rule of thumb is to avoid being the smallest job in a big shop or vice versa.

Be aware that it is not unusual for printers without the equipment to produce your job to accept it and broker it to a third party. Ask early on if the printer will be printing your project in-house. If they are sending it out, you may get a better price by going direct.

**12.3** *Verify that you and the printer are technically compatible.* Ask if the printer's prepress department supports the computer hardware and software you will use to produce the artwork, exactly how the files need to be set up, and how they charge for their services.

**12.4** Assuming all of the preliminary answers are to your liking, *ask to see and review some samples* of similar jobs the printer has produced. Look for good printing, not good design. The creative part of printing is normally in the client's hands, so a printer is more concerned with science than art. Check for bright, clean colors; for smooth, dense solid areas; for text and images that are focused and clear; and for images that are printed on the page squarely and in the correct position.

It also helps to show the printer an example of the quality you expect and the effects you are hoping to achieve. Take advantage of the expertise of veteran salespeople and their coworkers in the press room. They can provide a wealth of information and guidance.

**12.5** Before getting estimates, you will have to *choose paper.* Generally speaking, newsletters are printed on one of two types of paper or "stock"—coated or uncoated. Coated stock is the stock used for most magazines. It has a thin layer of clay-like substrate that creates a smooth, flat surface ideal for printing colored inks and superfine detail such as

photographs. Uncoated stock is the stock commonly used for stationery and is available in rough to smooth finishes. You can print four-color on uncoated stock, but the colors, because they are usually absorbed deeper into the surface of the sheet than on coated, produce a more subdued result. (For more about color, see *Step 11.6: Apply Color,* page 188.)

To see the alternatives, request paper samples from your printer or a local paper distributor. They can provide swatch books and printed samples of literally thousands of possible finishes, weights, and colors.

Paper is classified by weight and the weight you should choose depends on its use. A sixteen-page newsletter, for example, is printed on lighter stock than a four-page version. A typical eight-page newsletter might be printed on 70lb uncoated or 80lb coated stock.

The most obvious paper choice is the color. There is a seemingly endless rainbow of paper colors and a huge range of warm to cool whites. Ink colors are affected by the color of the paper. Yellow ink on white paper, for example, will look significantly different than yellow ink on a light shade of green.

Be sure to also consider opacity. Opacity is the property of paper that determines the degree to which a printed image shows through from one side of a sheet to the other. If the sheet is not opaque enough, you might see enough of the image from the opposite side for it to be distracting. Your printer representative

can help you gauge the amount of show-through likely from the paper you specify.

Finally, ask your printer for guidance. They may discourage you from using a certain sheet for a particular job because of past experience, incompatibility with their equipment, availability problems, and so on. As long as they have given you a wide range of finishes, weights, and color to choose from, it is best to follow their recommendations.

**12.6** Find at least two printers that can handle your job and request job estimates. Estimates can vary widely from printer to printer. Some base them on strict estimating formulas; others adjust for how busy they are and, therefore, how eager they are to have your business. Most are willing to bargain.

The cost of printing is based on the amount of time the job ties up the press and the size of the press needed to print the job. The more complex the job, the more complex the press needed to print it. You normally get the best price on the smallest press that can handle your job.

To prepare an estimate, the printer will need some preliminary information such as: the timetable, the number of colors, the overall size, the number of pages, the quantity, the paper you want it printed on, the form in which you will supply the artwork, the method for proofing, and how it will be the folded, bound, packaged, and delivered. See the *Printing Estimate Information Form* on the next page for more details. Also ask if you would be eligible for a discount if you were willing to commit to having it printed with them on a regular basis.

**12.7** Finally, review the printer's contract. Many printers include a detailed contract with their estimate. Printing is a complex combination of product and service that presents many opportunities for misunderstanding. Be certain you understand the intricacies of the legalese.

## Printing Estimate Information Form

### General

Job title

Release date                                    Delivery date

### Description

| | | | |
|---|---|---|---|
| Number of colors | Cover | Text | |
| Type of color | ☐ Spot  ☐ Process | ☐ Spot  ☐ Process | |
| Trim size | Folded (page) | Flat (spread) | |
| Number of pages | | Quantity | |

### Stock

| | | | |
|---|---|---|---|
| Cover stock | Type | Color | Weight |
| Text stock | Type | Color | Weight |

### Software

| | | |
|---|---|---|
| Application | | Version |
| Platform | ☐ Mac   ☐ Windows | |
| Resolution | | |
| Media | ☐ CD   ☐ DVD   ☐ Jaz   ☐ Zip   ☐ Other | |

### Proofing

| | |
|---|---|
| Type of proof | ☐ Blueline   ☐ Laser   ☐ Other |

### Finishing

| | | |
|---|---|---|
| Varnish/Laminate | Area | Type |
| Folds | | |
| Binding | ☐ Perfect bound   ☐ Saddle stitch | |
| Hole drilling | | |
| Packaging | | |
| Shipping | | |

### Instructions

---

### Step 12: PRINTER CHECKLIST

| 12.1 | Find a printer with the proper equipment |
|---|---|
| 12.2 | Explain the scope of the job |
| 12.3 | Verify technical compatibility |
| 12.4 | Review samples |
| 12.5 | Choose paper |
| 12.6 | Request two or more job estimates |
| 12.7 | Review the printer's contract |

STEP 13

# Prepare, Print, and Proof It

The printing process can produce 1,000 impressions of success as easily as it can produce 1,000 examples of failure. Whether you have your newsletter reproduced 100, 1,000, or 10,000 times, *you*—by the way you prepare the material for the press, oversee the printing, and review the results—control the outcome.

   Printing has three very distinct stages: preparation, execution, and follow-up. The first stage, commonly referred to as the "prepress" process, is the series of steps taken to prepare your project for printing. In prepress, the printer takes the files you created along with the fonts and images you linked to them, and translates them into a form their computer hardware and software understands.

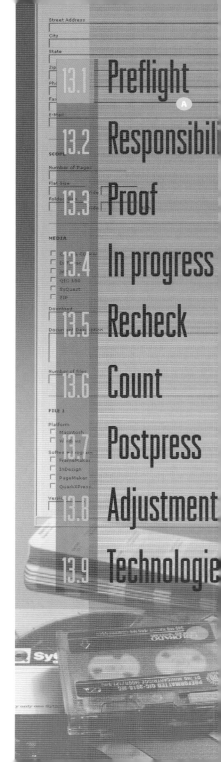

13.1 Preflight

13.2 Responsibili

13.3 Proof

13.4 In progress

13.5 Recheck

13.6 Count

13.7 Postpress

13.8 Adjustment

13.9 Technologie

The prepress process for a printing press, among other things, determines how each page is positioned on the sheet (imposition) to achieve the most economical use of space. It ensures the pages are perfectly aligned front to back. That screen values are applied to photographs and artwork. That a slight overlap, or "trap," is applied between colors that touch. And the colors are separated for making individual printing plates.

**13.1** In either case, your first responsibility of the prepress process is to *"preflight" your files*. Preflighting is the process of gathering together and reviewing all the elements necessary to translate what you create on your computer to the printer's computer. Most printers can provide you with a preflight checklist.

Some desktop publishing programs have a preflight feature that aids in the process. At minimum, the printer will require the names and descriptions of the document files and any other image files linked to them, the name and version number of the software program used to produce them, and copies of the fonts used (check your font license agreement for restrictions about sharing fonts).

**13.2** Before you hand over your files, be sure you and the printer *agree about who is responsible for what*. One printer might prefer to work with your actual desktop publishing program file, to open it in the program you used to produce it, and prepare it themselves. Another might assume you have prepared a file complete with such settings as screen frequency, screen angles, negative orientation, and others.

**13.3** Once your files are prepared for a printing press, you will be asked to *review and sign off on a proof* of your job before it is printed. A proof is a printout that should, as closely as possible, demonstrate the final printed piece.

There are many different types of proofs. Some printers still provide a blueline (named for its monochrome blue color) made by exposing a film negative on a sheet of light-sensitive paper. It shows a highly accurate representation of what to expect from the printing process minus actual color. If you specify more than one or two colors, a color proof is sometimes required to approximate the colors you should expect.

Today, in an ever-changing print marketplace, new and more accurate ways of proofing are available. Your printing representative can explain the differences, and show you examples of the systems they use.

Your responsibility, in any case, is the same: to check and recheck the proof thoroughly. Once you sign off on it, responsibility for everything shown on the proof is yours, even if it is the printer's mistake. This is an important distinction to understand. If something as simple as an errant line break eliminated an important phone number, and that mistake undermined your entire project, your approval may still be legally binding—leaving you and your organization to bear the entire cost of reprinting.

Use a red pen or pencil to circle errors and make notes. Are pages printed at the right size? Are the photographs, artwork, and text in the right places? Are the images and text clear and focused? Are the correct typefaces used? Did special characters such as fractions and copyright marks translate correctly? Circle scratches, dust, and broken characters that might be caused by impurities in the film used to

make the proof and that, in turn, will be used to make the printing plates. If there are significant changes, request a second proof so you are sure all the changes were made.

If printing will be done on a production copier, prepress primarily concerns translating the files to the printer's copier and reviewing sample copies before a complete run is produced.

**13.4** Good printing is the absence of mistakes. The proofs you sign off on gave you a good idea of what your finished job should look like. Now your responsibility shifts to seeing that the results are a fair representation of what you approved. There are two stages at which to intercept problems—during the printing process, and after it is complete.

Many printers are receptive to, and in fact encourage, clients to *check their jobs in progress* at the beginning of the press run. This is especially true if there is some part of the process that requires an aesthetic judgment—if, for example, you are using process colors (CMYK), the press operator can often fine-tune the result by increasing or decreasing the intensity of individual colors. But remember, press time is expensive. If you choose to approve your job on press, be prepared to give clear directions and to make quick decisions. Check with your printing representative to see what their policy is and requirements are for press checks.

Whether you are looking at a job in progress or postpress, the figures (page 196) show a few of the most obvious problems to look for. Though a small portion of just about every job will be spoiled by one or more of them, attentive press workers should spot and discard problem sheets. And, though quality varies from printer to printer, most would agree that problems this extreme are not considered deliverable.

Check your job in progress and, afterward, question anything that is distinctly different from the proof you approved. Watch for these potential printing problems (right).

**13.5** Repeat the process by *rechecking your job when it is delivered.* Look at a representative sample of pieces from the beginning, middle, and end of the run. If the middle third of the job is spoiled, you don't want to discover it through a phone call from a subscriber.

**13.6** Next, *do a rough count* to determine if you got the quantity of pieces you paid for. Count a stack of 100 pieces, measure the height of the stack, and roughly calculate if you are within ten percent of the quantity you ordered. Most printers consider ten percent over or under the amount you requested as acceptable. Therefore, if you need exactly 1000 copies, be sure to tell the printer beforehand that anything less is unacceptable. Some printers expect you to pay extra for overruns unless you agree otherwise in advance.

**13.7** Your final responsibility is to *oversee and approve postpress finishing*—how sheets are folded, bound, trimmed, drilled, and packaged. At a small press, these steps may be accomplished by a team of people using a series of individual devices. At the largest printer, the same steps may be completed on a single, computerized assembly line.

A traditional 8.5 by 11 inch, eight-page newsletter is printed front and back on two sheets slightly larger than 11 by 17 inches, which are then paired together, folded in half, and saddle-stitched—stapled on the fold. It is obvious if the pages were incorrectly paired: The pages will be out of order. If the margins are not uniform, the pages may not have been registered accurately front to back or trimmed accurately.

**Coverage**
Check the ink coverage—too little (A), normal (B), or too much (C).

**Mottle**
Check solid areas for mottle—uneven, spotty areas of ink.

**Registration and trapping**
All colors and shapes should be aligned, or registered, with great precision. Poor registration can result in a gap between ink colors (D).

**Pinholes and hickies**
A pinhole (E) is the result of a hole in the printing plate negative. Erratically shaped hickies (F) are caused by dirt or paper particles that adhere to the plate or rollers.

**Skew**
A crooked or skewed image (G) could be the result of a misaligned plate.

**Trimming**
Some of the most common problems occur after the job is printed. A page trimmed even slightly out of alignment can be drastically altered (H).

**Ghosting**
A doubled or blurred image, termed "ghosting," is typically caused by a misapplication of ink on the rollers.

**13.8** If the printer makes errors, it is reasonable to *negotiate an adjustment in the price*. If there are minor problems with your job, something even a meticulous reader would normally miss, you can request a reprint, but it may be more practical to ask for an adjustment of the price; most printers are amenable. If there are significant, obvious problems with your job, insist on a reprint. Though some readers might not notice a problem, it may cause others to judge your organization negatively.

**13.9** A final word about printing: there is no final word. The printing business, for some time, has been in and remains in fast forward. There are all types of developing technologies that solve the inherent problems of conventional prepress, printing, and postpress processes. Direct-to-press systems, for example, circumvent much of the time, practice, and cost necessary to prepare and produce printing plates. *Stay abreast of developing printing technologies*. Printing representatives can introduce you to new, less costly ways of doing things; you have only to judge whether they meet or exceed the standards of cost, accuracy, and quality set by conventional methods.

For a comprehensive look at the printing process, get a copy of the *Pocket Pal Graphic Arts Production Handbook* by International Paper from Signet Inc., 800-654-3889, 901-387-5560, www.pocketpalstore.com.

## Step 13: **PRINTING CHECKLIST**

**13.1** Preflight your files

**13.2** Determine who is responsible for what

**13.3** Review and sign off on a proof

**13.4** Check your job in progress

**13.5** Recheck your job after it is delivered

**13.6** Do a rough count

**13.7** Oversee and approve postpress finishing

**13.8** Negotiate a price adjustment for printing errors

**13.9** Stay abreast of developing printing technologies

STEP 14

# Mail It

In a complex marketplace, a superior product is the minimum requirement. The recipe for a successful newsletter includes measures of efficient distribution and vigilant promotion.

**14.1** If you did the research recommended in *Step 2: Do Some Research,* page 162, you discovered that mailing your newsletter is only complicated if you want it to be—and that complicated, in the case of newsletters, can be a good thing.

It may, for example, be complicated to understand and meet all of the postal regulations to qualify for a postage rate discount, but if you save ten cents per piece on the 750 pieces you mail once a month, you'd save roughly $900 the first year and $4,500 over a five-year period. This is a handsome return for a little complication and a few hours of research.

Now is the time to *review or gather the information* discussed in the research step. Does your newsletter qualify for a preferred rate? Do you understand what services a mailing services company has to offer?

To research rates and USPS postage rates, review the "Eligibility" section of the "Domestic Mail Manual (DMM)" at the USPS Postal Explorer at http://pe.usps.gov/ or visit your local post office.

**14.2** As you talk with the experts, you'll begin to appreciate the many variables that dictate which list management and mailing services are best suited to your situation. The quantity of newsletters you are distributing, the frequency at which you distribute them, the type of list you are using, the postage rates you qualify for, and so on, all play a role.

Before you can distribute a newsletter you must, obviously, *develop a mailing list* of those to whom it will be sent. You can develop and maintain your list using off-the-shelf database software or you can contract with a company that specializes in mailing list management.

Some of the advantages of a list management company include helping you define and standardize the information to be included in the list database; helping you acquire other lists and develop new sources of names; and managing the processes of converting and entering data, and purging names.

The answer to which to choose depends on what you're trying to accomplish and whether you prefer to pay the cost in time or money. If you are distributing your newsletter to an established list of 500 people, you clearly can do it yourself. Adding and removing names, and printing a set of labels for each issue shouldn't require massive

resources. If, on the other hand, you intend to build and maintain a list of 25,000 paid subscribers and will be actively marketing your letter to others, a dedicated internal or contract mailing list manager is a must.

**14.3** Next, *determine who will perform what mailing services*. Among the things a mailing services company can do is help you create a publication that qualifies for discounted postage rates. Apply postage by meter, indicia, or stamps. Print list addresses and other messages on the newsletter or apply conventional address labels. Fold your letter, inserting it into an envelope, or using other means to seal it. Presort, barcode, and/or comingle mailings to qualify for rate discounts. And transport materials from the printer to the post office.

**14.4** Finally, consider how you will *administer newsletter business*. There are many miscellaneous costs that are required of a publisher. Be sure to consider the time and money it costs to develop and maintain the run-of-the-mill systems that keep the mill running—phones, faxes, computer software and hardware, media, deliveries, and so on. Don't forget the practices of doing the accounting, managing the people, administrating the process, answering the phones, and so on.

No organization needs a newsletter. It needs a way to build relationships with its customers. Every organization needs a forum for spreading its ideas, demonstrating its products, and showing off its services. It needs ways of generating revenue, recruiting members, and building its credibility. An effective newsletter is not paperwork; it is a marketing tool. An organization does not need paperwork—it needs smart marketing tools with a real purpose.

# Newsletters

## SECTION 2, PART 2
# Design Recipes

PART 2: DESIGN RECIPES

# How to Use the Recipes

Now it's time to put the step-by-step process to work. The pages that follow present a cookbook of style recipes for a wide variety of newsletter designs.

The first two pages of each recipe show the nameplate and the overall style of the newsletter. The third and fourth show the basic elements—grid, type families, and illustrations used—and some distinguishing features that make a particular newsletter one-of-a-kind. Pages five through eight provide a detailed recipe and list of design ingredients.

Above all, remember this: These designs were created specifically for the Design-it-Yourself series—you are free to copy any recipe in whole or in part to produce your own materials. The only restriction is that you cannot claim any form of legal authorship of the copied design. Don't limit your thinking to using everything as-is. Combining ideas from several styles will produce the most unique newsletters.

**A: Definition**
The recipe begins with an explanation of the thinking behind its particular style.

**B: The nameplate**
The large version of the nameplate reveals the details you might miss at a smaller size.

**C: Page flow**
The page flow shows the imposition of pages—how the pages of the example shown would be printed front to back so the finished piece is in reading order. Measurements are expressed as width by height—17 by 11 inches means the sheet is 17 inches wide by 11 inches high.

**D: Software recommendations**
This caption lists the type of software required to create the artwork.

**E: Basic elements**
This page shows the grid—the invisible foundation of margins, columns, and guides to which all the elements on the page are aligned, the names of type families, and describes the mix of photographs and/or artwork.

**F: Distinguishing features**
Some of the design elements that make this newsletter one-of-a-kind.

**G: Newsletter recipe**
The rulers on each page show measurements in inches of where the final pages are trimmed, and the light gray guides show the grid used to position primary elements. Art and images that extend outside the bold gray outline mean the element bleeds off the edge of the page.

**H: The color palette**
All the projects are created using either four-color process, Solid PANTONE Colors, or simple black ink (see *Step 11.6: Apply color,* page 188). The palette identifies composition of CMYK mixes or the PANTONE Number and tint values of the solid colors.

**I: The ingredients**
The type used in each recipe is keyed, by number, to this list of ingredients—it includes the name of the typeface, the point size, line spacing (when there is more than one line of the same typeface), alignment, and the point size of lines. The listing of "12/13pt" means the text is 12 points and the line spacing is 13 points.

STYLE 1 (6 PAGES)

# Ad Banner

There are lots of reasons most publishers do not include advertising in their newsletters—dilution of the message, limited space, lack of resources to sell and coordinate placement, and so on.

Here's a simple solution that buys you the best of both worlds—editorial and design integrity plus a way to generate revenue.

At the bottom of each inside page is a 8 by 0.75 inch strip, perfect for a banner-like ad. Instead of having to design around odd-shaped ads, you can sell this space to non-competitive businesses that want to reach your audience. Allow them the freedom to sell—but maintain visual control—by restricting the ads to black-and-white.

## Fraction = Decimal Conversion

| Fraction | | Decimal |
|---|---|---|
| 1/16 | = | 0.0625 |
| 1/8 | = | 0.125 |
| 3/16 | = | 0.1875 |
| 1/4 | = | 0.25 |
| 5/16 | = | 0.3125 |
| 3/8 | = | 0.375 |
| 7/16 | = | 0.4375 |
| 1/2 | = | 0.5 |
| 9/16 | = | 0.5625 |
| 5/8 | = | 0.625 |
| 11/16 | = | 0.6875 |
| 3/4 | = | 0.75 |
| 13/16 | = | 0.8125 |
| 7/8 | = | 0.875 |
| 15/16 | = | 0.9375 |

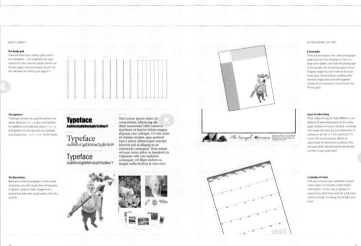

## J: The ingredient details

In this example, the number "13" points to the item; "Sidebar headline" is the type of item; "Impact" is the typeface; "36/32pt" means 36-point type on 32 points of leading (the space between the baselines of two rows of type); and "align center" is the alignment—aligned left or right, centered, or justified. Several examples employ customizable Adobe Multiple Master (MM) fonts such as Myriad MM (see page 225, item 1). Settings such as "700bd, 300cn" following the typeface name represent customized character weights and widths. See your Multiple Master documentation for details.

## K: Lorem Ipsum

Lorem ipsum is scrambled Latin text used by designers to demonstrate the approximate number of words it will take to fill an area of the layout before the actual text is specified.

### Pages 2 & 3

**12** Line 4pt; Headline Impact 18/16pt, align left; Text Minion 11/12pt, align left; Text subhead Minion 10pt, align left; Contact Franklin Gothic Book Condensed 7/8pt, align left; Page number Minion Italic 8pt, align left; **13** Sidebar headline Impact, 36/32pt, align center; Sidebar text Minion 16/18pt, align left; **14** Headline Frutiger Ultra Black 24pt, align left; Text Franklin Gothic Book Condensed 8/8pt, align left; Phone Frutiger Ultra Black 18pt, align left; **15** Headline Raleigh Gothic 39pt, align left; Text Franklin Gothic Book Condensed 8/8pt, align left; Phone Franklin Gothic Book Condensed 10pt, align left

Violet or PANTONE® 814

| | |
|---|---|
| 100% | |
| 35% | |
| 30% | |
| 10% | |

SOURCE Illustrations: Flowers (pg. 1) from *Seasons* from

STYLE 1 (6 PAGES)

# Ad Banner

There are lots of reasons most publishers do not include advertising in their newsletters—dilution of the message, limited space, lack of resources to sell and coordinate placement, and so on.

Here's a simple solution that buys you the best of both worlds—editorial and design integrity plus a way to generate revenue.

At the bottom of each inside page is an 8 by 0.75 inch strip, perfect for a banner-like ad. Instead of having to design around odd-shaped ads, you can sell this space to noncompetitive businesses that want to reach your audience. Allow them the freedom to sell—but maintain visual control—by restricting the ads to black-and-white.

**Page flow**
One 11 by 17 inch sheet with single-fold to 8.5 by 11, plus one 8.5 by 11 inch sheet inserted (loose).

**What you need**
General layout and design requires a desktop publishing program. Editing photographic images requires a digital imaging program. Dividing and reassembling the parts and pieces of vector clip art images and type requires a drawing program. (See *Step 7: Choose Your Tools*, page 176.)

# Sampler gardener

May 20??: News, opinion, how-to, events, gardener profiles, virtual tours, and more from the Sampler Garden Association

## INSPIRATION
### From the outside, in

Lorem ipsum dolor sit amet, consectetuer adipiscing elit, sed diam nonummy nibh euismod tincidunt ut laoreet dolore magna aliquam erat volutpat. Ut wisi enim ad minim veniam, quis nostrud exerci tation ullamcorper suscipit lobortis nisl ut aliquip ex ea commodo consequat.

Duis autem vel eum iriure dolor in hendrerit in vulputate velit esse molestie consequat, vel um dolore eu feugiat nulla facilisis at vero os et accumsan.

*From Jason B. Example,
The Gardener's Ring*

---

### DIRECTOR'S LETTER

# Don't!

*by Roger Example*

Vulputate velit esse molestie consequat, vel lorem ipsum dolor sit amet, consectetuer adipiscing elit, sed diam nonummy nibh euismod tincidunt ut laoreet dolore magna aliquam erat volutpat.

Minim veniam, quis nostrud exerci tation ullamcorper suscipit lobortis nisl ut aliquip ex ea commodo consequat. Duis autem vel eum iriure dolor in hendrerit in vulputate velit esse molestie consequat, vel illum dolore eu feugiat nulla facilisis at vero eros et accumsan et iusto odio dignissim qui blandit praesent luptatum zzril delenit augue duis dolore te feugait nulla facilisi.

autem vel eum iriure dolor in hendrerit in vulputate velit esse molestie consequat, vel illum dolore eu feugiat nulla facilisis at vero eros et accumsan et iusto odio dignissim qui blandit praesent luptatum

Lorem ipsum dolor sit amet, consectetuer adipiscing elit, sed diam nonummy nibh euismod tincidunt laoreet dolore magna aliquam erat

Lorem ipsum dolor sit amet, consectetuer adipiscing elit, nonummy nibh euismod laoreet dolore magna volutpat. Ut wisi enim ad quis nostrud exerci tation aliquip ex ea commodo consequat. Duis autem vel eum iriure dolor in hendrerit in autem vel eum iriure dolor in hendrerit in vulputate velit esse molestie consequat, vel illum dolore eu feugiat nulla facilisis at vero eros et accumsan et iusto odio dignissim qui blandit praesent luptatum

---

Lorem ipsum dolor sit amet, consectetuer adipiscing elit, sed diam nonummy nibh euismod tincidunt ut laoreet dolore magna aliquam erat volutpat. Ut wisi enim ad minim veniam, quis nostrud exerci tation aliquip ex ea commodo consequat. Duis autem vel eum iriure dolor in hendrerit in vulputate velit esse molestie adipiscing elit, sed diam nonummy nibh euismod tincidunt ut laoreet dolore magna aliquam erat volutpat. Ut wisi enim ad minim veniam, quis nostrud exerci tation aliquip ex ea commodo consequat.

Contact Morris Example: 987 654 3210 or name@emailaddressz.com;
More: http://www.yourwebaddressz.com/articles/recipe.htm

*Illustration caption lorem ipsum dolor sit consectetuer caption lorem amet, dolor adipiscing.*

## May

## The design grid

There are three basic column grids used in this newsletter—one small and two large columns for the cover, four equal columns for the text pages, and seven equal columns for the calendar. (See *Step 11.2: Establish the Page Size and Grid*, page 187.)

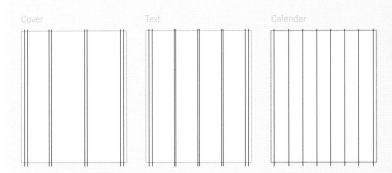

Cover

Text

Calendar

## The typefaces

Three type families are used throughout the layout. Big, bold **Impact**, a sans-serif typeface for headlines and eyebrows, classic **Minion**, a serif typeface for the text and text subhead, and unobtrusive **Franklin Gothic** for the details.

Impact

# Typeface
## AaBbEeGgKkMmQqRrSsWw!?

Minion

# Typeface
### AaBbEeGgKkMmQqRrSsW

Franklin Gothic Book Condensed

# Typeface
## AaBbEeGgKkMmQqRrSsWw!?

Minion

Text Lorem ipsum dolor sit amet, consectetuer adipiscing elit, sed diam nonummy nibh euismod tincidunt ut laoreet dolore magna aliquam erat volutpat. Ut wisi enim ad minim veniam, quis nostrud exerci tation ullamcorper suscipit lobortis nisl ut aliquip ex ea commodo consequat. Duis autem vel eum iriure dolor in hendrerit in vulputate velit esse molestie consequat, vel illum dolore eu feugiat nulla facilisis at vero eros.

## The illustrations

Black-and-white photographs of real people and places mix with royalty-free photographs of generic subjects. Insect images from a picture font add some visual variety and color accents.

DISTINGUISHING FEATURES

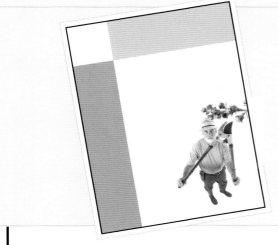

### A focal point

There are two reasons this cover photograph grabs your eye. First, because it is twice as large and a darker color than the photograph at the top left. And second, becuase it has an irregular shape. You don't need to illustrate every story. Concentrate on creating a few relevant images that work well together instead of just dropping in any pictures that fill the space.

### Space for advertising

What makes this layout really different is the addition of advertising space on the inside pages. Instead of trying to sell and coordinate odd shapes and sizes, ask your advertisers to prepare an ad that is, in this case, 8 by 0.75 inches. The resulting layout affords an opportunity for advertisers to present their message while maintaining the overall look and feel of your publication.

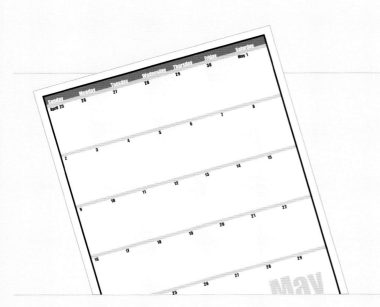

### A calendar of events

One way to ensure your newsletter remains within reach is to include current, helpful information—in this case, a calendar of events. If you don't have room for a full-size version, consider including a list of dates and times.

# Sampler
# gardener

May 20??: News, opinion, how-to, events, gardener profiles, virtual tours, and more from the Sampler Garden Association

## INSPIRATION
## From the outside, in

Lorem ipsum dolor sit amet, consectetuer adipiscing elit, sed diam nonummy nibh euismod tincidunt ut laoreet dolore magna aliquam erat volutpat. Ut wisi enim ad minim veniam, quis nostrud exerci tation ullamcorper suscipit lobortis nisl ut aliquip ex ea commodo consequat.

Duis autem vel eum iriure dolor in hendrerit in vulputate velit esse molestie consequat, vel illum dolore eu feugiat nulla facilisis at vero eros et accumsan.

*From Jason B. Example,*
*The Gardener's Ring*

## DIRECTOR'S LETTER
# Don't!

*by Roger Example*

Vulputate velit esse molestie consequat, vel lorem ipsum dolor sit amet, consectetuer adipiscing elit, sed diam nonummy nibh euismod tincidunt ut laoreet dolore magna aliquam erat volutpat.

Minim veniam, quis nostrud exerci tation ullamcorper suscipit lobortis nisl ut aliquip ex ea commodo consequat. Duis autem vel eum iriure dolor in hendrerit in vulputate velit esse molestie consequat, vel illum dolore eu feugiat nulla facilisis at vero eros et accumsan et iusto odio dignissim qui blandit praesent luptatum zzril delenit augue duis dolore te feugait nulla facilisi.
autem vel eum iriure dolor in hendrerit in vulputate velit esse molestie consequat, vel illum dolore eu feugiat nulla facilisis at vero eros et accumsan et iusto odio dignissim qui blandit praesent luptatum

Lorem ipsum dolor sit amet, consectetuer adipiscing elit, sed diam nonummy nibh euismod tincidunt laoreet dolore magna aliquam erat

Lorem ipsum dolor sit amet, consectetuer adipiscing elit, nonummy nibh euismod laoreet dolore magna volutpat. Ut wisi enim ad quis nostrud exerci tation aliquip ex ea commodo consequat. Duis autem vel eum iriure dolor in hendrerit in autem vel eum iriure dolor in hendrerit in vulputate velit esse molestie consequat, vel illum dolore eu feugiat nulla facilisis at vero eros et accumsan et iusto odio dignissim qui blandit praesent luptatum

Lorem ipsum dolor sit amet, consectetuer adipiscing elit, sed diam nonummy nibh euismod tincidunt ut laoreet dolore magna aliquam erat volutpat. Ut wisi enim ad minim veniam, quis nostrud exerci tation aliquip ex ea commodo consequat. Duis autem vel eum iriure dolor in hendrerit in vulputate velit esse molestie adipiscing elit, sed diam nonummy nibh euismod tincidunt ut laoreet dolore magna aliquam erat volutpat. Ut wisi enim ad minim veniam, quis nostrud exerci tation aliquip ex ea commodo consequat.

Contact Morris Example: 987 654 3210 or name@emailaddressz.com; More: http://www.your??addressz.com/articles/recipe.htm

*Illustration caption lorem ipsum dolor sit consectetuer caption lorem amet, dolor adipiscing.*

## May

## Cover (page 1)

**1** "Sampler" Impact, 48pt, align left; "gardener" Impact, 108pt, align left; **2** Subtitle Impact 12/12pt, align left; **3** Line 4pt; Eyebrow Impact 12pt, align left; Headline Impact 18/16pt, align left; Text Minion 11/12pt, align left; Signature Minion 10/11pt, align right **4** Eyebrow Impact 12pt, align left; Headline Impact 95pt, align left; Contributor Minion Italic 10pt, align left; Text Minion 11/12pt, align left; **5** Contact Franklin Gothic Book Condensed 7/8pt, align left; **6** Caption Minion Italic 9/10pt, align left; Month Impact 90pt, align left.

## Back Cover (page 6)

**7** Line 4pt; Eyebrow Impact 12pt, align left; Headline Impact 18/16pt, align left; Text Minion 11/12pt, align left; Contact Franklin Gothic Book Condensed 7/8pt, align left; Page number Minion Italic 8pt, align left; **8** Return address Franklin Gothic Book Condensed 8/8pt, align left; Teaser Impact 18/17pt, align left; **9** Mailing address Courier 9/9pt, align left; **10** Postage indicia Franklin Gothic Book Condensed 8/8pt, align center; **11** "Sampler" Impact, 18pt, align left; "gardener" Impact, 30pt, align left; Masthead text Franklin Gothic Book Condensed 9/10pt, align left; Text subhead Franklin Gothic Book Condensed 8pt, align left; Copyright Franklin Gothic Book Condensed 7pt, align left.

## Pages 2 & 3

**12** Line 4pt; Headline Impact 18/16pt, align left; Text Minion 11/12pt, align left; Text subhead Minion 10pt, align left; Contact Franklin Gothic Book Condensed 7/8pt, align left; Page number Minion Italic 8pt, align left; **13** Sidebar headline Impact, 36/32pt, align center; Sidebar text Minion 16/18pt, align left; **14** Headline Frutiger Ultra Black 24pt, align left; Text Franklin Gothic Book Condensed 8/8pt, align left; Phone Frutiger Ultra Black 18pt, align left; **15** Headline Raleigh Gothic 39pt, align left; Text Franklin Gothic Book Condensed 8/8pt, align left; Phone Franklin Gothic Book Condensed 10pt, align left

SOURCE Illustrations: Flowers (pg. 1) from *Seasons* from Eyewire, 800-661-9410, 403-262-8008, www.eyewire.com. © Eyewire, Inc., all rights reserved; Illustration Gardener with clippers (pg. 1), slides (pg. 6), flowers (pg. 2), spray, landscape (pg. 2) from *Photo-Objects 50,000, Vol II* from Hemera Technologies 819-772-8200, www.hemera.com, © Hemera Technologies Inc., all rights reserved; Woman (pg. 2) from *Faces 3* from RubberBall Productions 801-224-6886, www.rubberball.com, © RubberBall Productions, all rights reserved; Ship (pg. 3) from *Task Force Image Gallery* from NVTech, 800-387-0732, 613-727-8184, www.nvtech.com, © NVTech, all rights reserved.

SOURCE Type Families: Franklin Gothic, Frutiger, Impact, Minion, Adobe Systems, Inc. 800-682-3623, www.adobe.com/type; Raleigh Gothic, AGFA/Monotype, 888-988-2432, 978-658-0200, www.agfamonotype.com.

---

### By the book backyard garden

VIRTUAL 1998

Lorem ipsum dolor sit amet, consectetuer adipiscing elit, sed diam nonummy nibh euismod tincidunt ut laoreet dolore magna aliquam erat volutpat. Ut wisi enim ad minim veniam, quis nostrud exerci tation ullamcorper suscipit lobortis nisl ut aliquip ex ea commodo consequat.

Duis autem vel eum iriure dolor in hendrerit in vulputate velit esse molestie consequat, vel illum dolore eu feugiat nulla facilisis at vero eros et accumsan et iusto odio dignissim qui blandit praesent luptatum zzril delenit augue duis dolore te feugait nulla facilisi. Nam liber tempor cum soluta nobis eleifend option congue nihil imperdiet doming id quod mazim placerat facer possim assum. Lorem ipsum dolor sit amet, consectetuer adipiscing elit, sed diam nonummy nibh euismod tincidunt ut laoreet dolore

Lorem ipsum dolor sit amet, consectetuer adipiscing elit, sed diam nonummy nibh euismod tincidunt ut laoreet dolore magna aliquam erat volutpat. Ut wisi enim ad minim veniam, quis nostrud exerci tation ullamcorper suscipit lobortis nisl ut aliquip ex ea commodo consequat.

Duis autem vel eum iriure dolor in hendrerit in vulputate velit esse molestie consequat, vel illum dolore eu feugiat nulla facilisis at vero eros et accumsan et iusto odio dignissim qui blandit praesent luptatum zzril delenit augue duis dolore te feugait nulla facilisi. Nam liber tempor cum soluta nobis eleifend option congue nihil imperdiet doming id quod mazim placerat facer possim volutpat. Ut wisi enim ad minim veniam, quis nostrud exerci tation ullamcorper suscipit lobortis nisl ut

Lorem ipsum dolor sit amet, consectetuer adipiscing elit, sed diam nonummy nibh euismod tincidunt ut laoreet dolore magna aliquam erat volutpat. Ut wisi enim ad minim veniam, quis nostrud exerci tation ullamcorper suscipit lobortis nisl ut aliquip ex ea commodo consequat.

Duis autem vel eum iriure dolor in hendrerit in vulputate velit esse molestie consequat, vel illum dolore eu feugiat nulla facilisis at vero eros et accumsan et iusto odio dignissim qui blandit praesent luptatum zzril delenit augue duis dolore te feugait nulla facilisi. Nam liber tempor cum soluta nobis eleifend option congue nihil imperdiet doming id quod mazim placerat facer possim volutpat. Ut wisi enim ad minim veniam, quis nostrud exerci tation ullamcorper suscipit lobortis nisl ut

Contact Morris Example: 987 654 3210 or name@emailaddresssz.com; More: http://www.youwebaddress2.com/articles/recipe.htm

**Sampler gardener**

NEWSLETTER NAME (ISSN #1234-5678); May 20??, Volume One, Number Five, Published by Organization's Name, 3028 Example Road, Your City, ST 12345-6789. $12/yr. POSTMASTER: Send address changes to Publication Name, 3028 Example Road, Your City, ST 12345-6789. Copyright 20?? by Organization's Name. All rights reserved. Legal Disclaimer. Copyright Clearance Center.

ADVERTISING
For information about advertising in Publication Name, contact Name at 987 654 3210

3028 Example Road
P.O. Box 1245
Your City, ST 12345-6789
987 654 3210
987 654 3210 Fax
info@emailaddressz.com

EXECUTIVE DIRECTOR
Sarah Example
987 654 3210
name@emailaddressz.com

NEWSLETTER EDITOR
Dr. Fred Example
987 654 3210
name@emailaddressz.com

ART DIRECTOR
Milton Example

MEMBERSHIP
Duis autem vel eum iriure dolor in hendrerit in vulputate velit esse molestie consequat, vel illum dolore eu feugiat nulla facilisis at vero eros et accumsan et iusto odio dignissim qui blandit praesent luptatum zzril delenit augue duis dolore te feugait nulla facilisi.
© 20?? Your Company. All rights reserved.

page 6

3028 Example Road
P.O. Box 1245
Your City, ST 12345-6789

Non-Profit Organization
U.S. Postage Paid
Permit ???
Your City, ST 12345-6789

**Saturday, May 15th: Celebrate 25 years of great gardening with the Sampler Garden Association**

SANDRA EXAMPLE
SAMPLER CORPORATION
123 EXAMPLE BOULEVARD STE 200
YOUR CITY ST 12345 6789

---

### Mary Example: Queen of Weeds

*By Jayce Example* Lorem ipsum dolor sit amet, consectetuer adipiscing elit, sed diam nonummy nibh euismod tincidunt ut laoreet dolore magna aliquam erat volutpat. Ut wisi enim ad minim veniam, quis nostrud exerci tation ullamcorper suscipit lobortis nisl ut

**Flower-friendly**

987 654 3210

### The ultimate compost recipe

*By Morris Example*

Lorem ipsum dolor sit amet, consectetuer adipiscing elit, sed diam nonummy nibh euismod tincidunt ut laoreet dolore magna aliquam erat volutpat.

THE ULTIMATE COMPOST RECIPE
1 part Lorem ipsum
3 parts Dolor sit amet
1 part Consectetuer
3 parts Adipiscing elit
8-parts Sed diam

### How to garden like a farmer

*By Rocky Example*

Lorem ipsum dolor sit amet, consectetuer adipiscing elit, sed diam nonummy nibh euismod tincidunt ut laoreet dolore magna aliquam erat volutpat.

**Take a five-star restaurant to Italy**

## Page 4

**16** Headline Impact 36/32pt, align left; Text Minion 11/12pt, align left; Contributor Minion Italic 10pt, align left; Text Minion 11/12pt, align left; Page number Minion Italic 8pt, align left; Contact Franklin Gothic Book Condensed 7/8pt, align left; **17** Sidebar Headline Franklin Gothic Book Condensed 8/10pt, align left; Sidebar text Franklin Gothic Book Condensed 9/10pt, align left; **18** Subhead Franklin Gothic Book Condensed 8pt, align left; Headline Interstate Ultra Black 25pt, align center; Text Franklin Gothic Book Condensed 7/8pt, align left; Phone Interstate Ultra Black 12pt, align center

## Page 5

**19** "Sunday" Impact 14pt, align left; "April" Impact 12pt, align left; Time Minion 8pt, align left; Description Minion 10/10pt, align left; "SGA" Impact 12/12pt, align left; Month Impact 90pt, align left; Page number Minion Italic 8pt, align left; **20** Phone Frutiger Ultra Black 18pt, align left; Headline Bickham Script 40pt, align center; Subhead Copperplate Gothic 33BC 10pt, align center; Text 8/9pt, align left

## Color

To be printed in black and a solid PANTONE Color Ink as defined on the palette below (see Step 9.3). (Because this book is printed in process colors (CMYK), the illustration is only a simulation of the actual solid PANTONE Color).

SOURCE Illustrations: Insects (pg. 4) from Insecta picture font by Judith Sutcliffe; Cable (pg. 4) from *Task Force Image Gallery* from NVTech, 800-387-0732, 613-727-8184, www.nvtech.com, © NVTech, all rights reserved; Woman and dog from *Photo-Objects 50,000, Vol II* from Hemera Technologies 819-772-8200, www.hemera.com; © Hemera Technologies, all rights reserved

SOURCE Type Families: Bickham Script, Copperplate Gothic 33BC, Franklin Gothic, Impact, Minion, Adobe Systems, Inc. 800-682-3623, www.adobe.com/type; Interstate Ultra Black, Font Bureau, 617-423-8770, www.fontbureau.com.

# Friendly insects

*By Becky Example*

Lorem ipsum dolor sit amet, consectetuer adipiscing elit, sed diam nonummy nibh euismod tincidunt ut laoreet dolore magna aliquam erat volutpat. Ut wisi enim ad minim veniam, quis nostrud exerci tat ullamcorper suscipi lobortis nisl ut aliq ea commodo conseq

Duis autem vel eum iriure dolor in hendrerit in vulputate velit esse molestie consequat, vel illum dolore eu feugiat nulla facilisis at vero eros et accumsan et iusto odio dignissim qui blandit praesent luptatum zzril delenit augue duis dolore te feugait nulla facilisi.

Lorem ipsum dolor sit amet, consectetuer adipiscing elit, sed diam nonummy nibh euismod tincidunt ut laoreet dolore magna aliquam erat volutpat. Ut wisi enim ad minim veniam, quis

Iusto odio dignissim qui blandit praesent luptatum zzril delenit augue duis dolore te feugait nulla facilisi. Nam liber tempor cum soluta nobis eleifend option congue nihil imperdiet doming id quod mazim placerat facer possim assum.

Lorem ipsum dolor sit amet, consectetuer adipiscing elit, sed diam nonummy nibh euismod tincidunt ut laoreet dolore magna aliquam erat volutpat.

nostrud exerci tation ullamcorper suscipit lobortis nisl ut aliquip ex ea commodo consequat.

Iusto odio dignissim qui blandit praesent luptatum zzril delenit augue duis dolore te feugait nulla facilisi. Nam liber tempor cum soluta nobis eleifend option congue nihil imperdiet doming id quod mazim placerat facer possim assum.

Lorem ipsum dolor sit amet, consectetuer adipiscing elit, sed nonummy nibh eu tincidunt ut laoreet magna aliquam erat volutpat. Ut wisi enim ad minim veniam, quis nostrud exerci tation ullamcorper suscipit lobortis nisl ut aliquip ex ea commodo consequat.

A dipiscing elit, sed diam nonummy nibh euismod tincidunt ut laoreet dolore magna aliquam erat volutpat. Ut wisi enim ad minim veniam, quis nostrud exerci tation ullamcorper suscipit lobortis nisl ut aliquip ex ea commodo consequat. Duis autem vel eum iriure in hendrerit in velit esse molestie consequat, vel eu feugiat nulla vero eros et accumsan iusto odio dignissim magna aliquam erat qui volutpat. Ut wisi enim ad minim veniam, quis nostrud exerci tation ullamcorper suscipit lobortis nisl ut aliquip ex ea commodo consequat.

A dipiscing elit, sed diam nonummy nibh euismod tincidunt ut laoreet dolore magna

blandit praesent luptatum zzril delenit augue duis dolore te feugait nulla facilisi.

Lorem ipsum dolor sit amet, consectetuer adipiscing elit, sed diam nonummy nibh euismod tincidunt ut laoreet dolore magna aliquam erat volutpat. Ut wisi enim ad minim veniam, quis nostrud exerci tation ullamcorper suscipit lobortis nisl ut aliquip ex ea commodo consequat.

Lorem ipsum dolor sit amet, consectetuer adipiscing elit, sed diam nonummy nibh euismod tincidunt ut laoreet dolore magna aliquam erat volutpat. Ut wisi enim ad minim veniam, quis nostrud exerci tation ullamcorper suscipit lobortis nisl ut aliquip ex ea commodo consequat.

Duis autem vel eum iriure dolor in hendrerit in vulputate velit esse molestie consequat, vel illum dolore eu feugiat nulla facilisis at vero eros et accumsan et iusto odio dignissim qui blandit praesent luptatum zzril delenit augue duis dolore te feugait nulla facilisi.

Lorem ipsum dolor sit amet, consectetuer adipiscing elit, sed diam nonummy nibh euismod tincidunt ut laoreet dolore magna aliquam erat volutpat. Ut wisi enim ad minim veniam, quis nostrud exerci tation ullamcorper suscipit lobortis nisl ut aliquip ex ea commodo consequat.

nonummy nibh euismod tincidunt ut laoreet dolore magna aliquam erat volutpat. Ut wisi enim ad Lorem ipsum dolor sit amet, consectetuer adipiscing elit, sed diam nonummy nibh euismod tincidunt ut laoreet dolore magna aliquam erat volutpat. Ut wisi enim ad minim veniam, quis nostrud exerci tation ullamcorper suscipit lobortis nisl ut aliquip ex ea commodo consequat. Duis autem vel eum iriure dolor in hendrerit in vulputate velit.

Contact Morris Example: 987 654 3210 or name@emailaddressz.com; More: http:// www.yourwebaddress.com/articles/recipe.htm

**SAMPLER GARDENER BOARD OF DIRECTORS**

Tawana Example, President
name@youremailaddressz.com
Office: 987 654 3210

John Example, Secretary
name@youremailaddressz.com
Office: 987 654 3210

Shirley Example, Treasurer
name@youremailaddressz.com
Office: 987 654 3210

Nathan Example
name@youremailaddressz.com
Office: 987 654 3210

Lewis Example
name@youremailaddressz.com
Office: 987 654 3210

Meryl Example
name@youremailaddressz.com
Office: 987 654 3210

Ronda Example
name@youremailaddressz.com
Office: 987 654 3210

Lorem ipsum dolor sit amet, consectetuer

*page 4*

Lorem ipsum dolor sit amet, consectetuer adipiscing

**THROW IT AWAY!**

Lorem ipsum dolor sit amet, consectetuer adipiscing elit, sed diam nonummy nibh euismod tincidunt ut laoreet dolore magna

**987 654 3210**

Violet or
PANTONE® 814

| 100% |
| 35% |
| 30% |
| 10% |

| Sunday | Monday | Tuesday | Wednesday | Thursday | Friday | Saturday |
|---|---|---|---|---|---|---|
| **April 25** | **26** | **27** | **28** | **29** | **30** | **May 1** |
| | 9:45 A.M. Event Title Description lorem ipsum dolor sit amet, consectetuer adipiscing elit, sed diam nonummy nibh euismod tincidunt ut laoreet | 7:00 A.M. Reminder Title Description dolore magna aliquam erat volutpat. | 6:00 P.M. Event Title Description ut wisi enim ad minim veniam, quis nostrud exerci tation ullamcorper suscipit lobortis. | | | 11:00 A.M. Event Title Description ut wisi enim ad minim veniam, quis nostrud exerci tation ullamcorper suscipit. |
| **2** | **3** | **4** | **5** | **6** | **7** | **8** |
| | 7:00 A.M. Reminder Title Description dolore magna aliquam erat volutpat. More: http:// www.yourwebaddressz.com / calendar | 9:00 A.M. Reminder Title Description dolore magna aliquam erat volutpat. quis nostrud exerci tation ullamcorper suscipit lobortis nisl ut aliquip ex ea commodo. | | 6:00 P.M. Event Title Description ut wisi enim ad minim veniam, quis nostrud. | 8:00 & 9:00 P.M. Event Title Description ut wisi enim ad minim veniam, quis nostrud exerci tation ullamcorper suscipit. | |
| **9** | **10** | **11** | **12** | **13** | **14** | **15** |
| 4:30 P.M. Event Title Description lorem ipsum dolor sit amet, consectetuer adipiscing elit, sed diam nonummy euismod tincidunt ut laoreet | | | 6:00 P.M. Event Title Description ut wisi enim ad minim veniam, quis nostrud exerci tation ullamcorper suscipit lobortis nisl ut aliquip. | | 11:00 A.M. Event Title Description lorem ipsum dolor sit amet, consectetuer adipiscing elit, sed diam nonummy nibh euismod tincidunt ut laoreet. | **SGA 25th Annual Conference** 7:00 A.M. Event Title Description lorem ipsum dolor sit amet, consect. |
| **16** | **17** | **18** | **19** | **20** | **21** | **22** |
| | 6:00 P.M. Event Title Description ut wisi enim ad minim veniam, quis nostrud exerci tation ullamcorper. | 7:00 A.M. Reminder Title Description dolore magna aliquam erat volutpat. 6:00 P.M. Event Title Description ut wisi enim ad minim veniam. | | 5:00 P.M. Event Title Description ut wisi enim ad minim veniam, quis nostrud exerci tation ullamcorper suscipit lobortis nisl ut aliquip ex ea commodo. | | |
| **23** | **24** | **25** | **26** | **27** | **28** | **29** |
| 6:00 P.M. Event Title Description ut wisi enim ad minim | 7:00 A.M. Reminder Title Description. | | 5:00 P.M. Event Title Description ut wisi enim ad minim veniam, quis nostrud exerci | 6:00 P.M. Event Title Description ut wisi enim ad minim veniam, quis nostrud. | | 6:00 P.M. Event Title Description ut wisi |
| **30** 9:45 A.M. Reminder Title Description. | | | | | | |

May

*page 5*

*The Example Adventure*
AN UNUSUAL ADVENTURE BY TERRA SAMPLER

Lorem ipsum dolor sit amet, consectetuer adipiscing elit, sed diam nonummy nibh euismod tincidunt ut laoreet dolore magna aliquam erat volutpat.

8.5 W
11 H

STYLE 2 (4 PAGES)

# Bulletin

Bulletin means "for immediate broadcast," and this layout is designed to convey that same sense of urgency. But equally important is the fact that it is designed to be produced with bulletin-like speed.

It is a timesaver because all the headlines, text, and illustrations are framed within a single running column—instead of placing and arranging individual elements on individual pages, you simply decide on the order in which you want the articles to appear and insert them.

### And they lived happily ever after

Lorem ipsum dolor sit amet, consectetuer adipiscing elit, sed diam nonummy nibh euismod tincidunt ut lao reet dolore m aliquam erat volutpat. Ut wisi enim ad minim veniam, quis nostrud exerci tation ullamcorper suscipit lobortis nisl ut aliqu commodo consequat. Duis autem vel eum iriure dolor in hendrerit in vulputate velit esse molestie consequat, vel illum d feugiat nulla facilisis at vero eros et Nam liber tempor cum soluta nobis eleifend option congue nihil imperdiet doming ic mazim placerat facer possim assum. Ut wisi enim ad minim veniam, quis nostrud exerci tation ullam corper suscipit lobo ut aliquip ex ea commodo consequat.

Duis autem vel eum iriure dolor in hendrerit in vulputate velit esse molestie consequat, vel illum dolore eu feugiat nu facilisis at vero eros et accumsan et iusto odio dignissim qui blandit praesent luptatum zzril delenit augue duis dolore te nulla facilisi. Lorem ipsum dolor sit amet, consectetuer adipiscing elit, sed diam nonummy nibh euismod tincidunt ut lao dolore magna aliquam erat volutpat. Ut wisi enim ad minim veniam, suscipit lobortis nisl ut aliquip ex ea commodo conse Lorem ipsum dolor sit amet, consectetuer adipiscing elit, sed diam nonummy nibh euismod tincidunt ut lao reet dolore m aliquam erat volutpat. Ut wisi enim ad minim veniam, quis nostrud exerci tation ullamcorper suscipit lobortis nisl ut aliqu commodo consequat. Duis autem vel elit, sed diam nonummy nibh euismod tincidunt ut lao reet dolore magna.

Ut wisi enim ad minim veniam, quis nostrud exerci tation ullamcorper suscipit lobortis nisl ut aliquip ex ea commodo consequat. Duis autem vel eum iriure dolor in hendrerit in vulputate velit esseeum iriure dolor in hendrerit in vulputate ve molestie consequat, vel illum dolore eu feugiat nulla facilisis at vero eros et Nam liber tempor cum soluta nobis eleifend mazim placerat facer possim assum commodo consequat. A new customer, a new design, and a new way of thinking Lorem ipsum dolor sit amet, consectetuer adipiscing elit, sed diam nonummy nibh euismod tincidunt ut lao reet dolore m aliquam erat volutpat. Ut wisi enim ad minim veniam, quis nostrud exerci tation ullam corper suscipit lobortis nisl ut aliqu ea commodo consequat.

Duis autem vel eum iriure dolor in hendrerit in vulputate velit esse molestie consequat, vel illum dolore eu feugiat nu facilisis at vero eros et accumsan et iusto odio dignissim qui blandit praesent luptatum zzril delenit augue duis dolore te nulla facilisi. Lorem ipsum dolor sit amet, consectetuer adipiscing elit, sed diam nonummy nibh euismod tincidunt ut lao dolore magna aliquam erat volutpat. Ut wisi enim ad minim veniam, suscipit lobortis nisl ut aliquip ex ea commodo conse Lorem ipsum dolor sit amet, consectetuer adipiscing elit, sed diam nonummy nibh euismod tincidunt ut lao reet dolore m aliquam erat volutpat. Ut wisi enim ad minim veniam, quis nostrud exerci tation ullamcorper suscipit lobortis nisl ut aliqu commodo consequat. Duis autem vel elit, sed diam nonummy nibh euismod tincidunt ut lao reet dolore magna aliquam e volutpat.

Ut wisi enim ad minim veniam, quis nostrud exerci tation ullamcorper suscipit lobortis nisl ut aliquip ex ea commodo consequat. Duis autem vel eum iriure dolor in hendrerit in vulputate velit esseeum iriure dolor in hendrerit in vulputate ve molestie consequat, vel illum dolore eu feugiat nulla facilisis at vero eros et. *— Linda Example, Designer*

3028 Example Road, P.O. Box 1245, Your City, ST 12345-6789
Phone 987 654 3210  Fax  987 654 3210  E-mail  info@emailaddressz.com  Web  www.yourwebaddressz.com

### How can we help?

☐ Please call
   Best time? _____
☐ Send literature
   Regarding? _____
☐ Send customer package
   How many? _____
☐ Option four
   Best time? _____
☐ Option five
   How many? _____

Name
Title                                    Date
Company
Address
City                          State          Zip
Daytime Phone
E-mail address

#### May we ask?

Question 1
Question 2
Question 3

Please return you in the enclosed en envelope to:
J.R. Sampler & C
3028 Example R
P.O. Box 1245, Yo
12345-6789

### Page flow

Two 8.5 by 14 inch sheets (portrait) are folded into thirds to fit a standard 9.5 by 4.125 inch commercial envelope.

### What you need

General layout and design requires a desktop publishing program. Creating the collage of photographic images and type used in the nameplate requires a digital imaging program. (See *Step 7: Choose Your Tools*, page 176.)

# Broker Bulletin: SUMMER 20??

## Winning the Builder Association's annual award never crossed my mind...

Lorem ipsum dolor sit amet, consectetuer adipiscing elit, sed diam nonummy nibh euismod tincidunt ut laoreet dolore magna aliquam erat volutpat. Ut wisi enim ad minim veniam, quis nostrud exerci tation ullam corper suscipit lobortis nisl ut aliquip ex ea commodo consequat.

Duis autem vel eum iriure dolor in hendrerit in vulputate velit esse molestie consequat, vel illum dolore eu feugiat nulla facilisis at vero eros et accumsan et iusto odio dignissim qui blandit praesent luptatum zzril delenit augue duis dolore te feugait nulla facilisi. Lorem ipsum dolor sit amet, consectetuer adipiscing elit, sed diam nonummy nibh euismod tincidunt ut laoreet dolore magna aliquam erat volutpat. Lorem ipsum dolor sit amet, consectetuer adipiscing elit, sed diam nonummy nibh euismod tincidunt ut laoreet dolore magna aliquam erat volutpat. Ut wisi enim ad minim veniam, quis nostrud exerci tation ullamcorper suscipit lobortis nisl ut aliquip ex ea commodo consequat. Duis autem vel elit, sed diam nonummy.

Nibh euismod tincidunt ut laoreet dolore magna aliquam erat volutpat. Ut wisi enim ad minim veniam, quis nostrud exerci tation ullamcorper suscipit lobortis nisl ut aliquip ex ea commodo consequat. Duis autem vel eum iriure dolor in hendrerit in vulputate velit esseeum iriure dolor in hendrerit in vulputate velit esse molestie consequat, vel illum dolore eu feugiat nulla facilisis at vero eros et Nam liber tempor cum soluta nobis eleifend opquod mazim placerat facer possim assum commodo consequat. — *Jim Example, President*

## A morning sunshine, culinary masterpiece, everybody-sit-back-and-relax space

Lorem ipsum dolor sit amet, consectetuer adipiscing elit, sed diam nonummy nibh euismod tincidunt ut laoreet dolore magna aliquam erat volutpat. Ut wisi enim ad minim veniam, quis nostrud exerci tation ullamcorper suscipit lobortis nisl ut aliquip ex ea commodo consequat. Duis autem vel eum iriure dolor in hendrerit in vulputate velit esse molestie consequat, vel illum dolore eu feugiat nulla facilisis at vero eros et Nam liber tempor cum soluta nobis eleifend option congue nihil imperdiet doming id quod mazim placerat facer possim assum. Ut wisi enim ad minim veniam, quis nostrud exerci tation ullam corper suscipit lobortis nisl ut aliquip ex ea commodo consequat.

Duis autem vel eum iriure dolor in hendrerit in vulputate velit esse molestie consequat, vel illum dolore eu feugiat nulla facilisis at vero eros et accumsan et iusto odio dignissim qui blandit praesent luptatum zzril delenit augue duis dolore te feugait nulla facilisi. Lorem ipsum dolor sit amet, consectetuer adipiscing elit, sed diam nonummy nibh euismod tincidunt ut laoreet dolore magna aliquam erat volutpat. Lorem ipsum dolor sit amet, consectetuer adipiscing elit, sed diam nonummy nibh euismod tincidunt ut laoreet dolore magna aliquam erat volutpat. Duis autem vel elit, sed diam nonummy nibh euismod tincidunt ut laoreet dolore magna aliquam erat volutpat. Ut wisi enim ad minim veniam, quis nostrud exerci tation ullamcorper suscipit lobortis nisl ut aliquip ex ea commodo consequat. Duis autem vel eum iriure dolor in hendrerit in vulputate velit esse molestie consequat, vel illum dolore eu feugiat nulla facilisis at vero eros et Nam liber tempor cum soluta nobis eleifend opquod mazim placerat facer possim assum commodo consequat. — *Linda Example, Designer*

## Revealing the truth about closing costs

Lorem ipsum dolor sit amet, consectetuer adipiscing elit, sed diam nonummy nibh euismod tincidunt ut laoreet dolore magna aliquam erat volutpat. Ut wisi enim ad minim veniam, suscipit lobortis nisl ut aliquip ex ea commodo consequat. Lorem ipsum dolor sit amet, consectetuer adipiscing elit, sed diam nonummy nibh euismod tincidunt ut laoreet dolore magna aliquam erat volutpat. Ut wisi enim ad minim veniam, quis nostrud exerci tation ullamcorper suscipit lobortis nisl ut aliquip ex ea commodo consequat. Duis autem vel elit, sed diam nonummy nibh euismod tincidunt ut laoreet dolore magna aliquam erat Lorem ipsum dolor sit amet, consectetuer adipiscing elit, sed... Ut wisi enim ad minim ve...

### The design grid

A classic newsletter uses classic business letter form—a single column surrounded by a simple rectangular border. (See *Step 11.2: Establish the page size and grid,* page 187.)

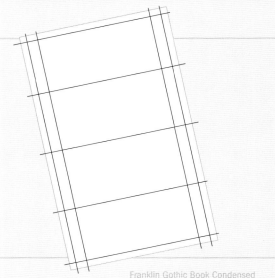

### The typefaces

The typefaces used are as simple and straightforward as the design. A classic serif—**Minion** for the headlines, subheads, and contact information, and easy-to-read sans serif **Franklin Gothic** for the text.

Minion

# Typeface
AaBbEeGgKkMmQqRrSsW

Franklin Gothic Book Condensed

# Typeface
AaBbEeGgKkMmQqRrSsWw!?

Franklin Gothic Book Condensed

Text Lorem ipsum dolor sit amet, consectetuer adipiscing elit, sed diam nonummy nibh euismod tincidunt ut laoreet dolore magna aliquam erat volutpat. Ut wisi enim ad minim veniam, quis nostrud exerci tation ullamcorper suscipit lobortis nisl ut aliquip ex ea commodo consequat. Duis autem vel eum iriure dolor in hendrerit in vulputate velit esse molestie consequat, vel illum dolore eu feugiat nulla facilisis at vero eros.

### The illustrations

The nameplate is a collage of the publisher's building projects plus a royalty-free photograph of roses, and a clip art symbol of the sun. It establishes the short, wide, panorama format uses throughout.

## DISTINGUISHING FEATURES

### Print it now, use it later

If you publish to a small list and want to produce your newsletter as needed, have the nameplate and border preprinted on a commercial printing press, then imprint individual sheets on your desktop printer. If the size of your list makes imprinting impractical and/or you opt for four- or two-color printing, you may still save money by preprinting a year's worth of sheets and having each issue copied onto the sheet using a production copier.

### Create a call to action

The coupon on the bottom of the last page asks, "How can we help?" It's an important question to ask. If you want your reader to take specific action, give them a way to take it—to return a coupon, fax back a form, visit a specific Web address, complete a phone survey, and so on. Every newsletter should leave no doubt of "where do we go from here?"

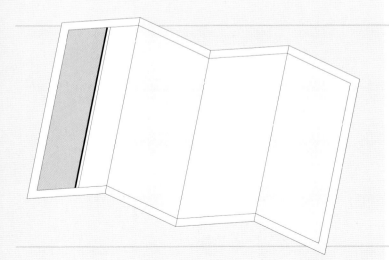

### Save on postage

Postage is often a significant part of a newsletter budget (see *Step 2.7: Gather Mailing Information and Expertise,* page 164). Designing to fit within the size and weight limitations of mailing regulations can save a significant amount of money over the life of a newsletter. These sheets are easily folded to fit a standard 9.5 x 4.125 inch commercial business envelope. It not only saves money—it keeps the contents of the letter confidential.

## Broker Bulletin: SUMMER 20??

### Winning the Builder Association's annual award never crossed my mind...

Lorem ipsum dolor sit amet, consectetuer adipiscing elit, sed diam nonummy nibh euismod tincidunt ut laoreet dolore magna aliquam erat volutpat. Ut wisi enim ad minim veniam, quis nostrud exerci tation ullam corper suscipit lobortis nisl ut aliquip ex ea commodo consequat.

Duis autem vel eum iriure dolor in hendrerit in vulputate velit esse molestie consequat, vel illum dolore eu feugiat nulla facilisis at vero eros et accumsan et iusto odio dignissim qui blandit praesent luptatum zzril delenit augue duis dolore te feugait nulla facilisi. Lorem ipsum dolor sit amet, consectetuer adipiscing elit, sed diam nonummy nibh euismod tincidunt ut laoreet dolore magna aliquam erat volutpat. Ut wisi enim ad minim veniam, suscipit lobortis nisl ut aliquip ex ea commodo consequat. Lorem ipsum dolor sit amet, consectetuer adipiscing elit, sed diam nonummy nibh euismod tincidunt ut laoreet dolore magna aliquam erat volutpat. Duis autem vel elit, sed diam nonummy.

Nibh euismod tincidunt ut laoreet dolore magna aliquam erat volutpat. Ut wisi enim ad minim veniam, quis nostrud exerci tation ullamcorper suscipit lobortis nisl ut aliquip ex ea commodo consequat. Duis autem vel eum iriure dolor in hendrerit in vulputate velit esseeum iriure dolor in hendrerit in vulputate velit esse molestie consequat, vel illum dolore eu feugiat nulla facilisis at vero eros et Nam liber tempor cum soluta nobis eleifend opquod mazim placerat facer possim assum commodo consequat. — *Jim Example, President*

### A morning sunshine, culinary masterpiece, everybody-sit-back-and-relax space

Lorem ipsum dolor sit amet, consectetuer adipiscing elit, sed diam nonummy nibh euismod tincidunt ut laoreet dolore magna aliquam erat volutpat. Ut wisi enim ad minim veniam, quis nostrud exerci tation ullamcorper suscipit lobortis nisl ut aliquip ex ea commodo consequat. Duis autem vel eum iriure dolor in hendrerit in vulputate velit esse molestie consequat, vel illum dolore eu feugiat nulla facilisis at vero eros et Nam liber tempor cum soluta nobis eleifend option congue nihil imperdiet doming id quod mazim placerat facer possim assum. Ut wisi enim ad minim veniam, quis nostrud exerci tation ullam corper suscipit lobortis nisl ut aliquip ex ea commodo consequat.

Duis autem vel eum iriure dolor in hendrerit in vulputate velit esse molestie consequat, vel illum dolore eu feugiat nulla facilisis at vero eros et accumsan et iusto odio dignissim qui blandit praesent luptatum zzril delenit augue duis dolore te feugait nulla facilisi. Lorem ipsum dolor sit amet, consectetuer adipiscing elit, sed diam nonummy nibh euismod tincidunt ut laoreet dolore magna aliquam erat volutpat. Ut wisi enim ad minim veniam, suscipit lobortis nisl ut aliquip ex ea commodo consequat. Lorem ipsum dolor sit amet, consectetuer adipiscing elit, sed diam nonummy nibh euismod tincidunt ut laoreet dolore magna aliquam erat volutpat. Duis autem vel elit, sed diam nonummy nibh euismod tincidunt ut laoreet dolore magna aliquam erat volutpat. Ut wisi enim ad minim veniam, quis nostrud exerci tation ullamcorper suscipit lobortis nisl ut aliquip ex ea commodo consequat. Duis autem vel eum iriure dolor in hendrerit in vulputate velit esseeum iriure dolor in hendrerit in vulputate velit esse molestie consequat, vel illum dolore eu feugiat nulla facilisis at vero eros et Nam liber tempor cum soluta nobis eleifend opquod mazim placerat facer possim assum commodo consequat. — *Linda Example, Designer*

### Revealing the truth about closing costs

Lorem ipsum dolor sit amet, consectetuer adipiscing elit, sed diam nonummy nibh euismod tincidunt ut laoreet dolore magna aliquam erat volutpat. Ut wisi enim ad minim veniam, suscipit lobortis nisl ut aliquip ex ea commodo consequat. Lorem ipsum dolor sit amet, consectetuer adipiscing elit, sed diam nonummy nibh euismod tincidunt ut laoreet dolore magna aliquam erat volutpat. Ut wisi enim ad minim veniam, quis nostrud exerci tation ullamcorper suscipit lobortis nisl ut aliquip ex ea commodo consequat. Duis autem vel elit, sed diam nonummy nibh euismod tincidunt ut laoreet dolore magna aliquam erat volutpat. Lorem ipsum dolor sit amet, consectetuer adipiscing elit, sed diam nonummy nibh euismod tincidunt.

Ut wisi enim ad minim veniam, quis nostrud exerci tation ullamcorper suscipit lobortis nisl ut aliquip ex ea commodo consequat. Duis autem vel eum iriure dolor in hendrerit in vulputate velit esseeum iriure dolor in hendrerit in vulputate velit esse molestie consequat, vel illum dolore eu feugiat nulla facilisis at vero eros et Nam liber tempor cum soluta nobis eleifend opquod mazim placerat facer possim assum commodo consequat. — *Melinda Example, Financing Specialist*

3028 Example Road, P.O. Box 1245, Your City, ST 12345-6789
Phone 987 654 3210 Fax 987 654 3210 E-mail info@emailaddressz.com Web www.yourwebaddressz.com

PAGE 1

## A strategy for absorbing interior design costs

Lorem ipsum dolor sit amet, consectetuer adipiscing elit, sed diam nonummy nibh euismod tincidunt ut laoreet dolore magna aliquam erat volutpat. Ut wisi enim ad minim veniam, quis nostrud exerci tation ullamcorper suscipit lobortis nisl ut aliquip ex ea commodo consequat. Duis autem vel eum iriure dolor in hendrerit in vulputate velit esse molestie consequat, vel illum dolore eu feugiat nulla facilisis at vero eros et Nam liber tempor cum soluta nobis eleifend option congue nihil imperdiet doming id quod mazim placerat facer possim assum. Lorem ipsum dolor sit amet, consectetuer adipiscing elit, sed diam nonummy nibh euismod tincidunt ut laoreet dolore magna aliquam erat volutpat. Ut wisi enim ad minim veniam, quis nostrud exerci tation ullam corper suscipit lobortis nisl ut aliquip ex ea commodo consequat.

Duis autem vel eum iriure dolor in hendrerit in vulputate velit esse molestie consequat, vel illum dolore eu feugiat nulla facilisis at vero eros et accumsan et iusto odio dignissim qui blandit praesent luptatum zzril delenit augue duis dolore te feugait nulla facilisi. Lorem ipsum dolor sit amet, consectetuer adipiscing elit, sed diam nonummy nibh euismod tincidunt ut laoreet dolore magna aliquam erat volutpat. Ut wisi enim ad minim veniam, quis nostrud exerci tation ullamcorper suscipit lobortis nisl ut aliquip ex ea commodo consequat. Lorem ipsum dolor sit amet, consectetuer adipiscing elit, sed diam nonummy nibh euismod tincidunt ut laoreet dolore magna aliquam erat volutpat. Ut wisi enim ad minim veniam, quis nostrud exerci tation ullamcorper suscipit lobortis nisl ut aliquip ex ea commodo consequat. Duis autem vel elit, sed diam nonummy nibh euismod tincidunt ut laoreet dolore magna aliquam erat volutpat.

Ut wisi enim ad minim veniam, quis nostrud exerci tation ullamcorper suscipit lobortis nisl ut aliquip ex ea commodo consequat. Duis autem vel eum iriure dolor in hendrerit in vulputate velit esseeum iriure dolor in hendrerit in vulputate velit esse molestie consequat, vel illum dolore eu feugiat nulla facilisis at vero eros et Nam liber tempor cum soluta nobis eleifend opquod mazim placerat facer possim assum commodo consequat. Ullamcorper suscipit lobortis nisl ut aliquip ex ea commodo consequat. Duis autem vel elit, sed diam nonummy nibh euismod tincidunt ut laoreet dolore magna aliquam erat volutpat. Ut wisi enim ad minim veniam, quis nostrud exerci tation ullamcorper suscipit lobortis nisl ut aliquip ex ea commodo consequat. Duis autem vel eum iriure dolor in hendrerit in vulputate velit esseeum iriure dolor in hendrerit in vulputate velit esse consequat, vel illum dolore eu feugiat nulla facilisis at vero eros et Nam liber tempor cum soluta nobis. — *Linda Example, Designer*

## A new customer, a new design, and a new way of thinking

Lorem ipsum dolor sit amet, consectetuer adipiscing elit, sed diam nonummy nibh euismod tincidunt ut laoreet dolore magna aliquam erat volutpat. Ut wisi enim ad minim veniam, quis nostrud exerci tation ullam corper suscipit lobortis nisl ut aliquip ex ea commodo consequat.

Duis autem vel eum iriure dolor in hendrerit in vulputate velit esse molestie consequat, vel illum dolore eu feugiat nulla facilisis at vero eros et accumsan et iusto odio dignissim qui blandit praesent luptatum zzril delenit augue duis dolore te feugait nulla facilisi. Lorem ipsum dolor sit amet, consectetuer adipiscing elit, sed diam nonummy nibh euismod tincidunt ut laoreet dolore magna aliquam erat volutpat. Ut wisi enim ad minim veniam, quis nostrud exerci tation ullamcorper suscipit lobortis nisl ut aliquip ex ea commodo consequat. Lorem ipsum dolor sit amet, consectetuer adipiscing elit, sed diam nonummy nibh euismod tincidunt ut laoreet dolore magna aliquam erat volutpat. Ut wisi enim ad minim veniam, quis nostrud exerci tation ullamcorper suscipit lobortis nisl ut aliquip ex ea commodo consequat. Duis autem vel elit, sed diam nonummy nibh euismod tincidunt ut laoreet dolore magna aliquam erat volutpat.

Ut wisi enim ad minim veniam, quis nostrud exerci tation ullamcorper suscipit lobortis nisl ut aliquip ex ea commodo consequat. Duis autem vel eum iriure dolor in hendrerit in vulputate velit esseeum iriure dolor in hendrerit in vulputate velit esse molestie consequat, vel illum dolore eu feugiat nulla facilisis at vero eros et Nam liber tempor cum soluta nobis eleifend opquod mazim placerat facer possim assum commodo consequat. Lorem ipsum dolor sit amet, consectetuer adipiscing elit, sed diam nonummy nibh euismod tincidunt ut laoreet dolore magna aliquam erat volutpat. Ut wisi enim ad minim veniam, quis nostrud exerci tation ullamcorper suscipit lobortis nisl ut aliquip ex ea commodo consequat. Lorem ipsum dolor sit amet, consectetuer adipiscing elit. — *Jim Example, President*

3028 Example Road, P.O. Box 1245, Your City, ST 12345-6789
Phone 987 654 3210 Fax 987 654 3210 E-mail info@emailaddressz.com Web www.yourwebaddressz.com

### Cover (page 1)

**1** "J.R. Sampler" Minion, 30pt, align center; "& COMPANY" Minion, 12pt, align center; **2** Title Minion, 24pt, align left; Date Minion, 24pt, align left; **3** Headline Minion, 14pt, align left; Text Franklin Gothic Book Condensed, 10/12pt, align left; **4** Contributor Minion Italic, 8pt, align left; **5** Contact Minion, 9/10pt, align left; **6** Page number Franklin Gothic Book Condensed, 9pt, align right; **7** Copyright Franklin Gothic Book Condensed, 6pt, align right; **8** Line .5pt

### Page 2

**9** Headline Minion, 14pt, align left; Text Franklin Gothic Book Condensed, 10/12pt, align left; **10** Contributor Minion, 8pt, align left; **11** Contact Minion, 9/10pt, align left; Page number Franklin Gothic Book Condensed, 9pt, align right; **12** Line .5pt

217

**Page 3**

**13** Headline Minion, 14pt, align left; Text Franklin Gothic Book Condensed, 10/12pt, align left; **14** Contributor Minion, 8pt, align left; **15** Text chart Franklin Gothic Book Condensed, 7/16pt, align left; Line .5pt; **16** Contact Minion, 9/10pt, align left; Page number Franklin Gothic Book Condensed, 9pt, align right; **17** Line .5pt

**Page 4**

**18** Headline Minion, 14pt, align left; Text Franklin Gothic Book Condensed, 10/12pt, align left; **19** Contributor Minion, 8pt, align left; **20** Contact Minion, 9/10pt, align left; Page number Franklin Gothic Book Condensed, 9pt, align right; Line .5pt; **21** Coupon headline Minion, 24/21pt, align left; **22** Checkbox text Franklin Gothic Book Condensed, 9pt, align right; Checkbox fill-in Franklin Gothic Book Condensed, 7pt, align right, Line .5pt; **23** Checkbox fill-in Franklin Gothic Book Condensed, 7pt, align right, Line .5pt; **24** Fill-in subhead Minion, 12pt, align left; **25** Return address Franklin Gothic Book Condensed, 7/9pt, align right

3

## Sampler City real estate news

Sed diam nonummy nibh euismod tincidunt ut laoreet dolore magna aliquam erat volutpat. Ut wisi enim ad minim veniam, quis nostrud exerci tation ullam corper suscipit lobortis nisl ut aliquip ex ea commodo consequat. Source: Reporter, Publication

Duis autem vel eum iriure dolor in hendrerit in vulputate velit esse molestie consequat, vel illum dolore eu feugiat nulla facilisis at vero eros et accumsan et iusto odio dignissim qui blandit praesent luptatum zzril delenit augue duis dolore te feugait nulla facilisi. Lorem ipsum dolor sit amet, consectetuer adipiscing elit, sed diam nonummy nibh euismod tincidunt ut laoreet dolore magna aliquam erat volutpat. Ut wisi enim ad minim veniam, suscipit lobortis nisl ut aliquip. Source: Reporter, Publication

Lorem ipsum dolor sit amet, consectetuer adipiscing elit, sed diam nonummy nibh euismod tincidunt ut laoreet dolore magna aliquam erat volutpat. Ut wisi enim ad minim veniam, laoreet dolore magna aliquam quis nostrud exerci tation ullamcorper suscipit lobortis nisl ut aliquip ex ea commodo consequat. Duis autem vel eum, sed diam nonummy nibh euismod tincidunt ut laoreet dolore magna aliquam erat volutpat. — Source: Reporter, Publication

## The blueprint as a sales tool

Lorem ipsum dolor sit amet, consectetuer adipiscing elit, sed diam nonummy nibh euismod tincidunt ut laoreet dolore magna aliquam erat volutpat. Ut wisi enim ad minim veniam, quis nostrud exerci tation ullamcorper suscipit lobortis nisl ut aliquip ex ea commodo consequat. Duis autem vel eum iriure dolor in hendrerit in vulputate velit esse molestie consequat, vel illum dolore eu feugiat nulla facilisis at vero eros et Nam liber tempor cum soluta nobis eleifend option congue nihil imperdiet doming id quod mazim placerat facer possim assum. Ut wisi enim ad minim veniam, quis nostrud exerci tation ullam corper suscipit lobortis nisl ut aliquip ex ea commodo consequat.

Duis autem vel eum iriure dolor in hendrerit in vulputate velit esse molestie consequat, vel illum dolore eu feugiat nulla facilisis at vero eros et accumsan et iusto odio dignissim qui blandit praesent luptatum zzril delenit augue duis dolore te feugait nulla facilisi. Lorem ipsum dolor sit amet, consectetuer adipiscing elit, sed diam nonummy nibh euismod tincidunt ut laoreet dolore magna aliquam erat volutpat. Ut wisi enim ad minim veniam, quis nostrud exerci tation. — Linda Example, Designer

## Under construction

Duis autem vel eum iriure dolor in hendrerit in vulputate velit esse molestie consequat, vel illum dolore eu feugiat nulla facilisis at vero eros et accumsan et iusto odio dignissim qui blandit praesent luptatum zzril delenit augue duis dolore te feugait nulla facilisi. Lorem ipsum dolor sit amet, consectetuer adipiscing elit, sed diam nonummy nibh euismod tincidunt ut laoreet dolore magna aliquam erat volutpat. Ut wisi enim ad minim veniam, quis nostrud exerci tation ullamcorper suscipit lobortis nisl ut aliquip ex ea commodo consequat.

| DEVELOPMENT | ZONE | ADDRESS | ZIP | DATE | TYPE | PRICE | SUPERVISOR | DESIGNER |
|---|---|---|---|---|---|---|---|---|
| Example Hills | 23 | 123 Example Hills Road | 12345-6789 | 00/00 | French Country | 350 | Davis | Tanner |
| Example Springs | 44 | 456 Example Springs Road | 12345-6789 | 00/00 | Transitional | 350 | Meade | Witton |
| Example Glen | 31 | 789 Example Glen Street | 12345-6789 | 00/00 | Transitional | 350 | Davis | Walker |
| Example Glen | 31 | 123 Example Glen Street | 12345-6789 | 00/00 | Transitional | 350 | Davis | Witton |
| Example River Branch | 22 | 456 Example Branch Street | 12345-6789 | 00/00 | Colonial | 350 | Davis | Walker |
| Example Springs | 44 | 789 Example Springs Road | 12345-6789 | 00/00 | French Country | 350 | Sampson | Mase |
| Example Estates | 45 | 123 Example Estates Road | 12345-6789 | 00/00 | Transitional | 350 | Davis | Tripp |
| Example Run | 43 | 456 Example Run | 12345-6789 | 00/00 | Colonial | 350 | Reed | Smith |
| Example Estates | 45 | 789 Example Estates Road | 12345-6789 | 00/00 | French Country | 350 | Reed | Smith |

Lorem ipsum dolor sit amet, consectetuer adipiscing elit, sed diam nonummy nibh euismod tincidunt ut laoreet dolore magna aliquam erat volutpat. Ut wisi enim ad minim veniam, quis nostrud exerci tation ullamcorper suscipit lobortis nisl ut aliquip ex ea commodo consequat. Duis autem vel eum iriure dolor in vulputate velit esse molesti.

3028 Example Road, P.O. Box 1245, Your City, ST 12345-6789
Phone 987 654 3210 Fax 987 654 3210 E-mail info@emailaddressz.com Web www.yourwebaddressz.com

PAGE 3

8.5 W
14 H

## And they lived happily ever after

Lorem ipsum dolor sit amet, consectetuer adipiscing elit, sed diam nonummy nibh euismod tincidunt ut laoreet dolore magna aliquam erat volutpat. Ut wisi enim ad minim veniam, quis nostrud exerci tation ullamcorper suscipit lobortis nisl ut aliquip ex ea commodo consequat. Duis autem vel eum iriure dolor in hendrerit in vulputate velit esse molestie consequat, vel illum dolore eu feugiat nulla facilisis at vero eros et Nam liber tempor cum soluta nobis eleifend option congue nihil imperdiet doming id quod mazim placerat facer possim assum. Ut wisi enim ad minim veniam, quis nostrud exerci tation ullam corper suscipit lobortis nisl ut aliquip ex ea commodo consequat.

Duis autem vel eum iriure dolor in hendrerit in vulputate velit esse molestie consequat, vel illum dolore eu feugiat nulla facilisis at vero eros et accumsan et iusto odio dignissim qui blandit praesent luptatum zzril delenit augue duis dolore te feugait nulla facilisi. Lorem ipsum dolor sit amet, consectetuer adipiscing elit, sed diam nonummy nibh euismod tincidunt ut laoreet dolore magna aliquam erat volutpat. Ut wisi enim ad minim veniam, suscipit lobortis nisl ut aliquip ex ea commodo consequat. Lorem ipsum dolor sit amet, consectetuer adipiscing elit, sed diam nonummy nibh euismod tincidunt ut laoreet dolore magna aliquam erat volutpat. Ut wisi enim ad minim veniam, quis nostrud exerci tation ullamcorper suscipit lobortis nisl ut aliquip ex ea commodo consequat. Duis autem vel elit, sed diam nonummy nibh euismod tincidunt ut laoreet dolore magna.

Ut wisi enim ad minim veniam, quis nostrud exerci tation ullamcorper suscipit lobortis nisl ut aliquip ex ea commodo consequat. Duis autem vel eum iriure dolor in hendrerit in vulputate velit esseeum iriure dolor in hendrerit in vulputate velit esse molestie consequat, vel illum dolore eu feugiat nulla facilisis at vero eros et Nam liber tempor cum soluta nobis eleifend opquod mazim placerat facer possim assum commodo consequat. A new customer, a new design, and a new way of thinking Lorem ipsum dolor sit amet, consectetuer adipiscing elit, sed diam nonummy nibh euismod tincidunt ut laoreet dolore magna aliquam erat volutpat. Ut wisi enim ad minim veniam, quis nostrud exerci tation ullam corper suscipit lobortis nisl ut aliquip ex ea commodo consequat.

Duis autem vel eum iriure dolor in hendrerit in vulputate velit esse molestie consequat, vel illum dolore eu feugiat nulla facilisis at vero eros et accumsan et iusto odio dignissim qui blandit praesent luptatum zzril delenit augue duis dolore te feugait nulla facilisi. Lorem ipsum dolor sit amet, consectetuer adipiscing elit, sed diam nonummy nibh euismod tincidunt ut laoreet dolore magna aliquam erat volutpat. Ut wisi enim ad minim veniam, suscipit lobortis nisl ut aliquip ex ea commodo consequat. Lorem ipsum dolor sit amet, consectetuer adipiscing elit, sed diam nonummy nibh euismod tincidunt ut laoreet dolore magna aliquam erat volutpat. Ut wisi enim ad minim veniam, quis nostrud exerci tation ullamcorper suscipit lobortis nisl ut aliquip ex ea commodo consequat. Duis autem vel elit, sed diam nonummy nibh euismod tincidunt ut laoreet dolore magna aliquam erat volutpat.

Ut wisi enim ad minim veniam, quis nostrud exerci tation ullamcorper suscipit lobortis nisl ut aliquip ex ea commodo consequat. Duis autem vel eum iriure dolor in hendrerit in vulputate velit esseeum iriure dolor in hendrerit in vulputate velit esse molestie consequat, vel illum dolore eu feugiat nulla facilisis at vero eros et. — *Linda Example, Designer*

3028 Example Road, P.O. Box 1245, Your City, ST 12345-6789
Phone  987 654 3210  Fax  987 654 3210  E-mail  info@emailaddressz.com  Web  www.yourwebaddressz.com

PAGE 4

## How can we help?

☐ Please call
Best time? _____

☐ Send literature
Regarding? _____

☐ Send customer package
How many? _____

☐ Option four
Best time? _____

☐ Option five
How many? _____

Name _____

Title _____  Date _____

Company _____

Address _____

City _____  State _____  Zip _____

Daytime Phone _____

E-mail address _____

### May we ask?

Question 1 _____

Question 2 _____

Question 3 _____

Please return your response in the enclosed postage-paid envelope to:
J.R. Sampler & Company
3028 Example Road
P.O. Box 1245, Your City, ST
12345-6789

STYLE 3 (16 PAGES)

# Elements

Every design is made up of component parts—elements. In this case the elements are the same basic shape—squares. Using such repeatable, easily defined shapes has two big advantages. First, it simplifies the design process—when you know ahead of time that everything must fit a defined space and proportion, there are fewer decisions to be made. Second, it's memorable—design with repeated shapes has a distinct look and feel that people will remember.

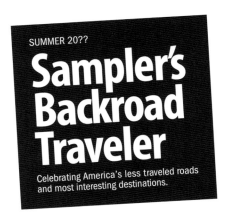

SUMMER 20??

## Sampler's Backroad Traveler

Celebrating America's less traveled roads and most interesting destinations.

**The best new GPS accessories**

Duis autem vel eum iriure dolor in hendrerit in vulputate velit esse molestie consequat, vel illum dolore eu feugiat nulla facilisis at vero eros et accumsan et iusto odio dignissim qui blandit praesent luptatum zzril delenit augue duis.

Contact Name Example: 987 654 3210 or name@email addressz.com; More: http://www.yourwebaddressz.com/articles/articlename.htm

### Lunch at Maine's favorite fish place

By MARLOW EXAMPLE - Lorem ipsum dolor sit amet, onsectetuer adipiscing elit, sed diam nonummy nibh euismod tincidunt ut laoreet dolore magna aliquam erat volutpat. Ut wisi enim ad minim veniam, quis nostrud exerci tation ullamcorper suscipit lobortis nisl ut aliquip ex ea commodo consequat. Lorem ipsum dolor sit amet, onsectetuer adipiscing elit, sed diam nonummy nibh euismod tincidunt ut laoreet dolore magna aliquam erat volutpat. Ut wisi enim ad minim veniam, quis nostrud exerci tation ullamcorper suscipit lobortis nisl ut aliquip ex ea commodo consequat lorem ipsum dolor sit amet, onsectetuer.

SUBHEAD TEXT

Ut wisi enim ad minim veniam, quis nostrud exerci tation ullamcorper suscipit lobortis nisl ut aliquip ex ea commodo consequat. Duis autem vel eum iriure dolor in hendrerit in vulputate velit esse molestie consequat, velillum dolore eu feugiat nulla facilisis at vero eros et accumsan et iusto odio dignissim qui blandit praesent luptatum zzril delenit augue duis dolore te feugait nulla facilisi. Nam liber tempor cum soluta nobis eleifend option congue nihil imperdiet ut laoreet dolore magna aliquam erat augue Ut wisi enim ad minim veniam, quis.

Contact Name Example: 987 654 3210 or name@email addressz.com; More: http://www.yourwebaddressz.com/articles/articlename.htm

### Utah, Route 601

# Two hundred southeast of n

By TINA EXAMPLE - Lorem ipsum dolor sit amet, onsectetuer adipiscing elit, sed diam nonummy nibh euismod tincidunt ut laoreet dolore magna aliquam erat volutpat. Ut wisi enim ad minim veniam, quis nostrud exerci tation ullamcorper suscipit lobortis nisl ut aliquip ex ea commodo consequat.

Duis autem vel eum iriure dolor in hendrerit in vulputate velit esse molestie consequat, vel illum dolore eu feugiat nulla facilisis at vero eros et accumsan et iusto odio dignissim qui blandit praesent luptatum zzril delenit augue duis dolore te feugait nulla facilisi.

SUBHEAD TEXT

Ut wisi enim ad minim veniam, quis nostrud exerci tation ullamcorper suscipit lobortis nisl ut aliquip ex ea commodo consequat. Duis autem vel eum iriure dolor in hendrerit in vulputate velit esse molestie consequat, velillum dolore eu feugiat nulla facilisis at vero eros et accumsan et iusto odio dignissim qui blandit praesent luptatum zzril delenit augue duis dolore te feugait nulla facilisi. Nam liber tempor cum soluta nobis eleifend option congue nihil imperdiet doming id quod mazim placerat facer possim assum. Lorem ipsum dolor sit amet, consectetuer adipiscing elit, sed diam nonummy nibh euismod tincidunt ut laoreet dolore magna aliquam erat augue

Ut wisi nostru loborti conseq dolor in

molest feugiat accums blandit augue c SUBHE Lorem i adipisc euismo magna ipsum ir

10 7
12 5
14 3
16 1

### Page flow

Four 17 by 11 inch sheets (landscape) with a single-fold to 8.5 by 11 inches and saddle-stitched.

 **What you need**

General layout and design requires a desktop publishing program. Editing photographic images requires a digital imaging program. Editing vector artwork such as the maps requires a drawing program. (See *Step 7: Choose Your Tools*, page 176.)

www.yourwebaddressz.com

**Small Towns of the Big City**
Page 12

SUMMER 20??

# Sampler's Backroad Traveler

Celebrating America's less traveled roads and most interesting destinations.

**CONTENTS**

### The design grid

This layout doesn't just rely on an grid—it is a grid. One or more uniformly sized squares, to be exact, 2.584 inches wide by 2.5 inches high. A full page is three blocks wide by four blocks tall. (See *Step 11.2: Establish the Page Size and Grid*, page 187.)

### The typefaces

Simple typefaces allow illustrations and colors to play a more important visual role. In this case the **Myriad** family is used for the headlines and **Franklin Gothic** for the text.

Myriad MM 700bd 300cn

# Typeface
**AaBbEeGgKkMmQqRrSsWw!?**

Franklin Gothic Book Condensed

# Typeface
AaBbEeGgKkMmQqRrSsWw!?

Franklin Gothic Book Condensed

Text Lorem ipsum dolor sit amet, consectetuer adipiscing elit, sed diam nonummy nibh euismod tincidunt ut laoreet dolore magna aliquam erat volutpat. Ut wisi enim ad minim veniam, quis nostrud exerci tation ullamcorper suscipit lobortis nisl ut aliquip ex ea commodo consequat. Duis autem vel eum iriure dolor in hendrerit in vulputate velit esse molestie consequat, vel illum dolore eu feugiat nulla facilisis at vero eros.

### The illustrations

There are thousands of photographers worldwide who maintain files of literally millions of photographs. They take pictures of the regions in which they live and the places they visit, or specialize in specific subject areas such as sea life or aviation. If you are looking for a specific photograph of a specific person, place, or thing, it can be worth your while to search the Web for one of these artists and to arrange to buy the rights to use a certain image. Two examples of sites that present the work of hundreds of photographers at a time are www.agpix.com and www.phototakeuse.com.

### Build with blocks

The building block concept makes producing illustrations easy—everything must fit within a block, be one-quarter the size, twice the size, or a multiple thereof.

### Show where to find it

Maps are a good way to add practical information to your newsletter. These maps from www.mapresources.com are drawing files that can be edited to add or remove many levels of detail. One layer, for example, includes county boundaries, another, medium-size city names, still another, rivers, and so on. Simplifying a map allows you to focus on just the necessary details.

### Pay attention to the details

There are many subtleties to good design— a combination of details in the creation and arrangement of illustrations and type the reader may not be even notice but nonetheless plays a big part in the overall look and feel of the finished piece. For example, using a digital imaging program to add ghosted images to the cover quietly contributes to its design.

2 · www.yourwebaddressz.com

# Word from the road

Lorem ipsum dolor sit amet, onsectetuer adipiscing elit, sed diam nonummy nibh euismod tincidunt ut laoreet dolore magna aliquam erat volutpat. Ut wisi enim ad minim veniam, quis nostrud exerci tation ullamcorper suscipit lobortis nisl ut aliquip ex ea commodo consequat. Lorem ipsum dolor sit amet, onsectetuer adipiscing elit, sed diam nonummy nibh euismod tincidunt ut laoreet dolore magna aliquam erat volutpat. Ut wisi enim ad minim veniam, quis nostrud exerci tation ullamcorper suscipit lobortis nisl ut aliquip ex ea commodo consequat lorem ipsum dolor sit amet, onsectetuer.

Ut wisi enim ad minim veniam, quis dolor in hendrerit in vulputate velit esse molestie consequat, velillum dolore eu feugiat nulla facilisis at vero eros et accumsan et iusto odio dignissim qui blandit praesent luptatum zzril delenit augue duis dolore te feugait nulla facilisi.

Nam liber tempor cum soluta nobis eleifend option congue nihil imperdiet doming id quod mazim placerat facer possim assum vero eros et accumsan et iusto odio dignissim qui blandit praesent luptatum zzril delenit.

*Terry Example*
Terri Example, *Editor*

# And I thought: This is where I belong—among the ponds and fire fish

By TERRY EXAMPLE - Lorem ipsum dolor sit amet, onsectetuer adipiscing elit, sed diam nonummy nibh euismod tincidunt ut laoreet dolore magna aliquam erat volutpat. Ut wisi enim ad minim veniam, quis nostrud exerci tation ullamcorper suscipit lobortis nisl ut aliquip ex ea commodo consequat. Lorem ipsum dolor sit amet, onsectetuer adipiscing elit, sed diam nonummy nibh euismod tincidunt ut laoreet dolore magna aliquam erat.

Lorem ipsum dolor sit amet, onsectetuer adipiscing elit, sed diam nonummy nibh veniam, quis nostrud exerci tation ullamcorper suscipit lobortis nisl ut aliquip ex ea commodo consequat. Ut wisi enim ad minim veniam, quis nostrud exerci tation ullamcorper.

Contact Name Example: 987 654 3210 or name@email addressz.com; More: http://www.yourwebaddressz.com/articles/articlename.htm

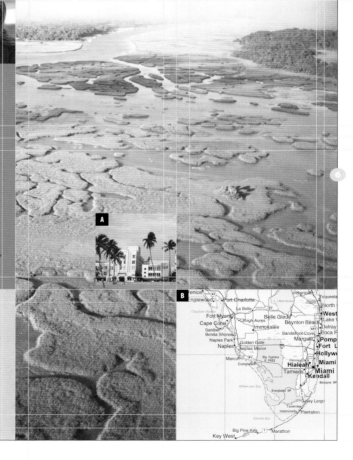

A

B

# The best new GPS accessories

Duis autem vel eum iriure dolor in hendrerit in vulputate velit esse molestie consequat, vel illum dolore eu feugiat nulla facilisis at vero eros et accumsan et iusto odio dignissim qui blandit praesent luptatum zzril delenit augue duis.

Contact Name Example: 987 654-3210 or name@email address; More: http://www.yourwebaddressz.com/articles/articlename.html

## Lunch at Tanya's favorite fish place

By MARLOW EXAMPLE - Lorem ipsum dolor sit amet, onsectetuer adipiscing elit, sed diam nonummy nibh euismod tincidunt ut laoreet dolore magna aliquam erat volutpat. Ut wisi enim ad minim veniam, quis nostrud exerci tation ullamcorper suscipit lobortis nisl ut aliquip ex ea commodo consequat. Lorem ipsum dolor sit amet, onsectetuer adipiscing elit, sed diam nonumy nibh euismod tincidunt ut laoreet dolore magna aliquam erat volutpat. Ut wisi enim ad minim veniam, quis nostrud exerci tation ullamcorper suscipit lobortis nisl ut aliquip ex ea commodo consequat lorem ipsum dolor sit amet, onsectetuer.

SUBHEAD TEXT

Ut wisi enim ad minim veniam, quis nostrud exerci tation ullamcorper suscipit lobortis nisl ut aliquip ex ea commodo consequat. Duis autem vel eum iriure dolor in hendrerit in vulputate velit esse molestie consequat, velillum dolore eu feugiat nulla facilisi. Lorem ipsum dolor sit amet, onsectetuer adipiscing elit, sed diam nonumy nibh euismod tincidunt ut laoreet dolore magna aliquam erat volutpat. Ut wisi enim ad minim veniam, quis.

Nam liber tempor cum soluta nobis eleifend option congue nihil imperdiet ut laoreet dolore magna aliquam erat augue Ut wisi enim ad minim veniam, quis.

Contact Name Example: 987 654-3210 or name@email address; More: http://www.yourwebaddressz.com/articles/articlename.htm

## Utah, Route 601
# Two hundred miles southeast of nowhere

By TINA EXAMPLE - Lorem ipsum dolor sit amet, onsectetuer adipiscing elit, sed diam nonummy nibh euismod tincidunt ut laoreet dolore magna aliquam erat volutpat. Ut wisi enim ad minim veniam, quis nostrud exerci tation ullamcorper suscipit lobortis nisl ut aliquip ex ea commodo consequat.

Duis autem vel eum iriure dolor in hendrerit in vulputate velit esse molestie consequat, vel illum dolore eu feugiat nulla facilisis at vero eros et accumsan et iusto odio dignissim qui blandit praesent luptatum zzril delenit augue duis dolore te feugait nulla facilisi.

SUBHEAD TEXT

Ut wisi enim ad minim veniam, quis nostrud exerci tation ullamcorper suscipit lobortis nisl ut aliquip ex ea commodo consequat. Duis autem vel eum iriure dolor in hendrerit in vulputate velit esse molestie consequat, vel illum dolore eu feugiat nulla facilisis at vero eros et accumsan et iusto odio dignissim qui blandit praesent luptatum zzril delenit augue duis dolore te feugait nulla facilisi. Nam liber tempor cum soluta nobis eleifend option congue nihil imperdiet doming id quod mazim placerat facer possim assum. Lorem ipsum dolor sit amet, consectetuer adipiscing elit, sed diam nonummy nibh euismod tincidunt ut laoreet dolore magna aliquam erat augue

Ut wisi enim ad minim veniam, quis nostrud exerci tation ullamcorper suscipit loboriis nisl ut aliquip ex ea commodo consequat. Duis autem vel eum iriure dolor in hendrerit in vulputate velit esse

Caption ut wisi enim ad minim veniam nostrud exerci tation ullamcorper suscipit

molestie consequat, vel illum dolore eu feugiat nulla facilisis at vero eros et accumsan et iusto odio dignissim qui blandit praesent luptatum zzril delenit augue duis dolore te feugait nulla facilisi.

SUBHEAD TEXT

Lorem ipsum dolor sit amet, consectetuer adipiscing elit, sed diam nonummy nibh euismod tincidunt ut laoreet dolore magna aliquam erat volutpat. Lorem ipsum dolor sit amet, consectetuer

continued on page 4

Sampler's Backroad Traveler · Summer 20?? · 3

---

# The wave waterfall

By PILLSBURY EXAMPLE - Lorem ipsum dolor sit amet, onsectetuer adipiscing elit, sed diam nonummy nibh euismod tincidunt ut laoreet dolore magna aliquam erat volutpat. Ut wisi enim ad minim veniam, quis nostrud exerci tation ullamcorper suscipit lobortis nisl ut aliquip ex ea commodo consequat.

SUBHEAD TEXT

Ut wisi enim ad minim veniam, quis nostrud exerci tation ullamcorper suscipit lobortis nisl ut aliquip ex ea commodo consequat.

Sampler's Backroad Traveler · 123 Example Road · Your City, ST 12345-6789

## How to find an honest-to goodness outdoor outfitter

SANDRA EXAMPLE
SAMPLER CORPORATION
123 EXAMPLE BOULEVARD STE 200
YOUR CITY ST 12345 6789

## Small Towns of the Big City

# Sampler's Backroad Traveler

www.yourwebaddressz.com

---

## Page 2 & 3

**1** Running head Franklin Gothic Book Condensed, 9pt, align left or right; **Eyebrow** Franklin Gothic Book Condensed, 10pt, align left; **Headline, medium** Myriad MM, 700bd, 300cn, 42/34pt, align left; **Text** Franklin Gothic Book Condensed, 10/12pt, align left; **2** Signature Emmascript MVB 15pt, align right; **Title** Franklin Gothic Book Condensed, 7pt, align center; **3** Masthead Franklin Gothic Book Condensed, 10/12pt, align left; **4** Headline, small Myriad MM, 700bd, 300cn, 25/22pt, align left; **Text** Franklin Gothic Book Condensed, 10/12pt, align left; **5** Contact link Franklin Gothic Book Condensed, 7/8pt, align left; **6** Line .5pt; **7** Caption Franklin Gothic Book Condensed, 9/10pt, align left; **8** Illustration label Myriad MM, 700bd, 300cn, 9pt, align center; **9** "continued" Franklin Gothic Book Condensed, 7pt, align left

## Cover & Back Cover (page 1 & 16)

**10** Issue date Franklin Gothic Book Condensed, 10pt, align left; **Title** Myriad MM, 700bd, 300cn, 48/38pt, align left; **Defining phrase** Franklin Gothic Book Condensed, 10/10pt, align left; **11** Headline, small Myriad MM, 700bd, 300cn, 25/22pt, align left; **Page number** Franklin Gothic Book Condensed, 10pt, align left; **12** Running head Franklin Gothic Book Condensed, 9pt, align right; **13** Contents title Franklin Gothic Book Condensed, 9pt, align left; **Contents text** Franklin Gothic Book Condensed, 8/10.5pt, align left **14** Headline, large Myriad MM, 700bd, 300cn, 48/38pt, align left; **Text** Franklin Gothic Book Condensed, 10/12pt, align left; **Subhead** Gothic Book Condensed, 10/12pt, align left; **Contact link** Franklin Gothic Book Condensed, 7/8pt, align left; **15** Illustration label Myriad MM, 700bd, 300cn, 9pt, align center; **16** Return address Franklin Gothic Book Condensed, 9/11pt, align left; **Headline** Myriad MM, 700bd, 300cn, 25/22pt, align left; **Page number** Franklin Gothic Book Condensed, 10pt, align left; **17** "Attention Mailroom" Franklin Gothic Book Condensed, 7/8pt, align left; **Address label** Arial 10/10pt, align left; **18** Postage indicia Franklin Gothic Book Condensed, 8/8pt, align center

SOURCE Illustrations: Location photographs (pg. 1, 2, 3, 16) from *US Landmarks and Travel* from PhotoDisc, 800-979-4413, 206-441-9355, www.photodisc.com, © PhotoDisc, all rights reserved; Maps from Map Resources, 800-334-4291, 609-397-1611, www.mapresources.com, © Map Resources, all rights reserved; Woman (pg. 2) from *Faces 3* from RubberBall Productions 801-224-6886, www.rubberball.com, © RubberBall Productions, all rights reserved.

SOURCE Type Families: Emmascript, Franklin Gothic, Myriad, Adobe Systems, Inc. 800-682-3623, www.adobe.com/type.

**Page 4**

**19** Running head Franklin Gothic Book Condensed, 9pt, align left or right; "continued" Franklin Gothic Book Condensed, 7pt, align left; Headline, small Myriad MM, 700bd, 300cn, 25/22pt, align left; Text Franklin Gothic Book Condensed, 10/12pt, align left; Subhead Gothic Book Condensed, 10/12pt, align left; Contact link Franklin Gothic Book Condensed, 7/8pt, align left

**Page 5**

**20** Headline, medium Myriad MM, 700bd, 300cn, 42/34pt, align left; Text Franklin Gothic Book Condensed, 10/12pt, align left; Contact link Franklin Gothic Book Condensed, 7/8pt, align left; **21** Running head Franklin Gothic Book Condensed, 9pt, align left or right; **22** Headline, very small Myriad MM, 700bd, 300cn, 15/14pt, align left; **23** Illustration label Myriad MM, 700bd, 300cn, 9pt, align center;

**Color**

Printed in four-color process (Step 11.6) using values of cyan, magenta, yellow, and black (CMYK) as defined on the color palette below. Actual color will vary.

SOURCE Illustrations: Location photographs (pg. 4, 5) from *US Landmarks and Travel* from PhotoDisc, 800-979-4413, 206-441-9355, www.photodisc.com, © PhotoDisc, all rights reserved; Maps from Map Resources, 800-334-4291, 609-397-1611, www.mapresources.com, © Map Resources, all rights reserved.

SOURCE Type Families: Franklin Gothic, Myriad, Adobe Systems, Inc. 800-682-3623, www.adobe.com/type.

4 · www.yourwebaddressz.com

continued from page 1

## Two hundred miles southeast of nowhere

Lorem ipsum dolor sit amet, onsectetuer adipiscing elit, sed diam nonummy nibh euismod tincidunt ut laoreet dolore magna aliquam erat volutpat. Ut wisi enim ad minim veniam, quis nostrud exerci tation ullamcorper suscipit lobortis nisl ut feugiat nulla facilisi.

SUBHEAD TEXT

Ut wisi enim ad minim veniam, quis hendrerit in vulputate velit esse molestie consequat, vel illum dolore eu feugiat nulla facilisis at vero eros et accumsan et iusto odio dignissim qui blandit praesent luptatum zzril delenit augue duis dolore te feugait nulla facilisi. Lorem ipsum dolor sit amet, consectetuer adipiscing elit, sed diam nonummy nibh euismod tincidunt ut laoreet dolore magna aliquam erat volutpat. Ut wisi enim ad minim veniam, quis nostrud exerci tation ullamcorper suscipit lobortis nisl ut aliquip ex ea commodo consequat.

Duis autem vel eum iriure dolor in hendrerit in vulputate velit esse molestie consequat, vel illum dolore eu feugiat nulla facilisis at vero eros et accumsan et iusto odio dignissim qui blandit praesent luptatum zzril delenit augue duis dolore te feugait nulla facilisi.

SUBHEAD TEXT

Ut wisi enim ad minim veniam, quis nostrud exerci tation ullamcorper suscipit lobortis nisl ut aliquip ex ea commodo consequat. Duis autem vel eum iriure dolor in hendrerit in vulputate velit esse molestie consequat, velillum dolore eu feugiat nulla facilisis at vero eros et accumsan et iusto odio dignissim qui blandit praesent luptatum zzril delenit augue duis dolore te feugait nulla facilisi. Nam liber tempor cum soluta nobis eleifend option congue nihil imperdiet doming id quod mazim placerat facer possim assum. Lorem ipsum dolor sit

amet, consectetuer adipiscing elit, sed diam nonummy nibh euismod tincidunt ut laoreet dolore magna aliquam erat augue Ut wisi enim ad minim veniam, quis nostrud exerci tation ullamcorper suscipit lobortis nisl ut aliquip ex ea commodo consequat. Duis autem vel eum iriure dolor in hendrerit in vulputate velit esse molestie consequat, vel illum dolore eu feugiat nulla facilisis at vero eros et accumsan et iusto odio dignissim qui blandit praesent luptatum zzril delenit praesent luptatum zzril delenit augue duis dolore te feugait nulla facilisi vel eum iriure dolor in hendrerit

in vulputate. Lorem ipsum dolor sit amet, consectetuer adipiscing elit, sed diam nonummy nibh euismod tincidunt ut laoreet dolore magna aliquam erat volutpat. Lorem ipsum dolor sit amet, consectetuer autem vel eum iriure dolor in hendrerit in vulputate velit esse molestie consequat, vel illum dolore eu feugiat nulla facilisis at vero eros et accumsan et iusto odio dignissim qui blandit praesent luptatum zzril delenit augue duis dolore te feugait nulla facilisi. Duis autem vel eum iriure dolor in hendrerit in vulputate velit esse molestie consequat, vel illum dolore eu feugiat nulla facilisis at vero eros et accumsan et iusto odio dignissim qui blandit praesent luptatum zzril delenit augue duis dolore te feugait nulla facilisi.

SUBHEAD TEXT

Ut wisi enim ad minim veniam, quis nostrud exerci tation ullamcorper suscipit lobortis nisl ut aliquip ex ea commodo consequat. Duis autem vel eum iriure dolor in hendrerit in vulputate velit esse molestie consequat, vel

## In the dream area of Wyoming

Duis autem vel eum iriure dolor in hendrerit in vulputate velit esse molestie consequat, vel illum dolore eu feugiat nulla facilisis at vero eros et accumsan et iusto odio dignissim qui blandit praesent luptatum zzril delenit augue duis.

Contact Name Example: 987 654 3210 or name@email addressz.com; More: http://www.yourwebaddressz.com/articles/articlename.htm

illum dolore eu feugiat nulla facilisis at vero eros et accumsan et iusto odio dignissim qui blandit praesent luptatum zzril delenit augue duis dolore te feugait nulla facilisi. Lorem ipsum dolor sit amet, consectetuer adipiscing elit, sed diam nonummy nibh euismod tincidunt ut laoreet dolore magna aliquam erat volutpat.Lorem ipsum dolor sit amet, consectetuer adipiscing elit, sed diam nonummy nibh euismod tincidunt ut laoreet dolore magna aliquam erat volutpat

luptatum zzril delenit augue duis dolore te feugait nulla facilisi. Ut wisi enim ad minim veniam, quis nostrud exerci tation ullamcorper suscipit lobortis nisl ut aliquip ex ea commodo consequat. Duis autem vel eum iriure dolor in hendrerit in vulputate velit esse molestie consequat, vel illum dolore eu feugiat nulla facilisis at vero eros et accumsan et iusto odio dignissim qui blandit praesent luptatum zzril delenit augue duis dolore te feugait nulla facilisi. Nam liber tempor cum soluta nobis eleifend option congue nihil imperdiet doming id quod mazim placerat facer lobortis nisl ut aliquip ex ea commodo consequat. Duis autem vel eum iriure dolor in hendrerit in vulputate velit esse molestie consequat, vel illum dolore eu feugiat nulla facilisis at vero eros et accumsan et iusto odio dignissim qui blandit praesent luptatum zzril delenit augueduis dolore te feugait nulla praesent

Contact Name Example: 987 654 3210 or name@email addressz.com; More: http://www.yourwebaddressz.com/articles/articlename.htm

### Process Colors

| C90 | M0 | Y90 | K0 |
|-----|-----|-----|-----|
| C0 | M60 | Y10 | K0 |
| C0 | M3 | Y50 | K0 |

## Roadside discovery: The amazing art of neon

A well designed space is comfortable, it helps the people within it to be more productive, and it reflects your organization's style.

Place your text in this position. To achieve the same look, choose a similar font and duplicate the size, spacing and alignment settings.

To match the overall page design, duplicate the positioning of each element and its proportion to the other elements on the page. Place your text in this position.

To achieve the same look, choose a similar font and duplicate the size, spacing and alignment settings. Place your text in this position. To achieve the same look, choose a similar font and duplicate the size, spacing and alignment settings.

Contact Name Example: 987 654 3210 or name@email addressz.com; More: http://www.yourwebaddressz.com/articles/articlename.htm

# High tech and the simple life

By GARY EXAMPLE - Ut wisi enim ad minim veniam, quis hendrerit in vulputate velit esse molestie consequat, vel illum dolore eu feugiat nulla facilisis at vero eros et

enim ad minim veniam, quis nostrud Duis autem vel eum iriure dolor in hendrerit in vulputate velit esse molestie consequat, vel illum dolore eu feugiat nulla facilisis at vero eros et accumsan et iusto odio dignissim qui blandit praesent luptatum zzril delenit augue duis dolore te feugait nulla facilisi nibh euismod tincidunt ut laoreet dolore magna aliquam erat augue Ut wisi enim ad minim veniam, quis nostrud exerci tation.

Contact Name Example: 987 654 3210 or name@email addressz.com; More: http://www.yourwebaddressz.com/articles/articlename.htm

accumsan et iusto odio dignissim qui blandit praesent luptatum zzril delenit augue duis dolore te feugait nulla facilisi. Lorem ipsum dolor sit amet, consectetuer adipiscing elit, sed diam. nonummy nibh euismod tincidunt ut laoreet dolore magna aliquam erat volutpat.Lorem ipsum dolor sit amet, onsectetuer adipiscing elit, sed diam nonummy nibh euismod tincidunt ut laoreet dolore magna aliquam erat volutpat. Ut wisi enim ad minim veniam, quis nostrud exerci tation ullamcorper suscipit lobortis nisl ut aliquip ex ea commodo consequat. Ut wisi

STYLE 4 (12 PAGES)

# Icons

Icons, symbols, signs, and other simple, bold graphic images are the hub around which all elements of this newsletter turn. Big and bold, they anchor the page and make a distinct impression.

The trick to sustaining such a design is to find enough of them to illustrate your newsletter, issue after issue. Fortunately there are many sources— collections of symbols from companies such as www.ultimatesymbol.com, individual images culled from clip art collections, parts of individual clip art images, and symbols in font form— picture fonts.

AUGUST 20??:
News, events, and resources for car fanatics
from The Sampler Automobile Club

## A new concept in concept cars

BY ROBIN EXAMPLE

Lorem ipsum dolor sit amet, consectetuer adipiscing elit, sed diam nonummy nibh euismod tincidunt ut laoreet dolore magna aliquam erat volutpat. Ut wisi enim ad minim veniam, quis nostrud exerci tation ullam corper suscipit lobortis nisl ut aliquip ex ea commodo consequat. Duis autem vel eum iriure dolor in hendrerit in vulputate velit esse molestie consequat, vel illum dolore eu feugiat nulla facilisis at vero eros et accumsan et iusto odio dignissim qui blandit praesent luptatum zzril delenit augue duis dolore te feugait nulla facilisi.

Lorem ipsum dolor sit amet, consectetuer adipiscing elit, sed diam nonummy nibh euismod tincidunt ut laoreet dolore magna aliquam erat volutpat. Ut wisi enim ad minim veniam, quis nostrud exerci tation ullamcorper suscipit lobortis nisl ut aliquip ex ea commodo consequat. Duis autem vel eum iriure dolor in hendrerit in vulputate velit esse molestie consequat, vel illum dolore eu feugiat nulla facilisis at vero eros et Nam liber tempor cum soluta nobis eleifend option congue nihil imperdiet doming id quod mazim placerat facer possim assum.

Lorem ipsum dolor sit amet, consectetuer adipiscing elit, sed diam nonummy nibh euismod tincidunt ut laoreet dolore magna aliquam erat volutpat. Ut wisi enim ad minim veniam, quis nostrud exerci tation ullamcorper suscipit lobortis nisl ut aliquip ex ea commodo consequat. Lorem ipsum dolor sit amet, consectetuer adipiscing elit, sed diam nonummy nibh euismod tincidunt ut laoreet dolore erat volutpat.

Contact Robin Example: 987 654 3210 or name@emailaddressz.com; More: http://www.yourwebbaddressz.com/articles/storyname.htm

## How to ada technologie classic auto

BY LINDA EXAMPLE

Lorem ipsum dolor sit amet consectetuer adipiscing elit, sed diam nonummy nibh euismod tincidunt ut laoreet dolore magna aliquam erat volutpat. Ut wisi enim ad minim veniam, quis nostrud exerci tation aliquip ex ea commodo consequat.

Duis autem vel eum iriure dolor in hendrerit in vulputate velit esse molestie consequat, vel illum dolore eu feugiat nulla facilisis at vero eros et accumsan et iusto odio dignissim qui blandit praesent luptatum zzril delenit augue duis dolore te feugait nulla facilisi. Ut wisi enim ad minim veniam, quis nostrud exerci tation aliquip ex ea commodo consequat. Autem vel eum iriure dolor in hendrerit in vulputate velit esse molestie consequat, vel illum dolore eu feugiat nulla facilisis at vero eros et accumsan et iusto odio dignissim qui blandit praesent luptatum zzril delenit augue duis dolore te feugait nulla facilisi. Lorem ipsum dolor sit amet, consectetuer adipiscing elit, sed diam nonum my nibh euismod tincidunt ut laoreet dolore magna aliquam erat volutpat. Ut wisi enim ad minim veniam, quis nostrud exerci tation ullamcorper suscipit lobortis nisl ut aliquip ex ea commodo consequat.

Duis autem vel eum iriure dolor in hendrerit in vulputate velit esse molestie consequat, vel illum dolore eu feugiat nulla facilisis at vero eros et Nam liber tempor cum soluta nobis eleifend option congue nihil imperdiet doming id quod mazim placerat facer possim assum quis nostrud exerci tation ullamcorper suscipit lobortis nisl ut aliquip ex ea commodo consequat. Duis autem vel eum iriure dolor in hendrerit in vulputate velit esse

molest
vulputa
nulla fa
cum so
imperdi
facer p
vero. Le
adipisc
euismo
aliquar
veniam
suscipi
consec
hendre
consec
facilisis
dignissi
delenit
facilisi.

6

## Page flow

Three 17 by 11 inch sheets (landscape) are folded once to 8.5 by 11 inches and saddle-stitched.

## What you need

General layout and design requires a desktop publishing program. Editing photographic images requires a digital imaging program. Dividing and reassembling the parts and pieces of vector clip art images and type requires a drawing program. (See *Step 7: Choose Your Tools*, page 176.)

AUGUST 20??:
News, events, and resources for car fanatics
from The Sampler Automobile Club

## TOP STORY

# Nation's largest foreign automotive exposition coming to Sampler

| INSIDE | Page |
|---|---|
| Article title one ipsum dolor sit amet | Cover |
| Article title two dolor sit amet | 2 |
| Article title three sit amet | 2 |
| Article title four ipsum dolor sit amet | 3 |
| Article title five ipsum | 3 |
| Article title six ipsum dolor | 4 |
| Article title seven ipsum dolor sit amet | 4 |
| Article title eight dolor sit amet | 5 |
| Article title nine ipsum sit amet | 5 |
| Article title ten ipsum dolor sit amet | 6 |
| Article title eleven ipsum dolor sit | 6 |
| Article title twelve dolor sit amet | 6 |
| Article title thirteen ipsum sit amet | 7 |
| Article title fourteen ipsum dolor | 8 |

BY ROGER EXAMPLE

Lorem ipsum dolor sit amet, consectetuer adipiscing elit, sed diam nonummy nibh euismod tincidunt ut laoreet dolore magna aliquam erat volutpat. Ut wisi enim ad minim veniam, quis nostrud exerci tation ullam corper suscipit lobortis nisl ut aliquip ex ea commodo consequat. Duis autem vel eum iriure dolor in hendrerit in vulputate velit esse molestie consequat, vel illum dolore eu feugiat nulla facilisis at vero eros et accumsan et iusto odio dignissim qui blandit praesent luptatum zzril delenit augue duis dolore te feugait nulla facilisi.

Lorem ipsum dolor sit amet, consectetuer adipiscing elit, sed diam nonummy nibh euismod tincidunt ut laoreet dolore magna aliquam erat volutpat. Ut wisi enim ad minim veniam, quis nostrud exerci tation ullamcorper suscipit lobortis nisl ut aliquip ex ea commodo consequat. Duis autem vel eum iriure dolor in hendrerit in vulputate velit esse molestie

continued on page 3

## The design grid

This design is built on a three-column grid. Note how the cover differs from the pages that follow—the headline and article text span two of the three columns. (See *Step 11.2: Establish the Page Size and Grid, page 187.*)

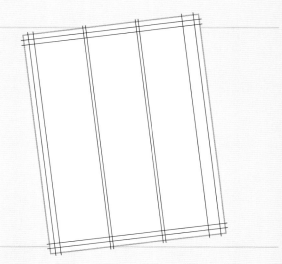

## The typefaces

The big, bold sans serif face used for the nameplate is **Interstate Ultra Black**—everything else is **Franklin Gothic**. Does it look like more than two typefaces? Using different typeface weights and sizes for headlines, subheads, and text is a good way to add interest *and* maintain a particular style.

Interstate Ultra Black

# Typeface
## AaBbEeGgKkMmQqRr

Franklin Gothic Condensed

# Typeface
### AaBbEeGgKkMmQqRrSsWw!?

Franklin Gothic Book Condensed

# Typeface
AaBbEeGgKkMmQqRrSsWw!?

Franklin Gothic Book Condensed

Text Lorem ipsum dolor sit amet, consectetuer adipiscing elit, sed diam nonummy nibh euismod tincidunt ut laoreet dolore magna aliquam erat volutpat. Ut wisi enim ad minim veniam, quis nostrud exerci tation ullamcorper suscipit lobortis nisl ut aliquip ex ea commodo consequat. Duis autem vel eum iriure dolor in hendrerit in vulputate velit esse molestie consequat, vel illum dolore eu feugiat nulla facilisis at vero eros.

## The illustrations

The icons are not without meaning. On pages 6 and 7, for example, two images of cars are sliced in half and combined to represent the contrast between new and old. If they were solid black and white, the icons might overwhelm the design. Making them a second color or shades of that color helps to blend them into the page, and the accompanying photographs of people add a sense of the real to the abstract.

## DISTINGUISHING FEATURES

### Establish a focus

The front pages of most newsletters follow the newspaper model—multiple stories are presented in the hope that one will attract the reader's attention. This layout takes a different tack, one more akin to a magazine—it features a top story and lists what's to come via a table of contents labeled "INSIDE." This tactic promotes the idea of leading your reader through your message step-by-step, rather than encouraging the kind of wandering around made so pervasive by the World Wide Web. You are the best judge of which method best suits your audience.

### Get the most from a second color

Desktop publishing programs allow you to define and apply tints of a color to different elements of the layout. In this case, the second color is applied full strength and in shades of 50 percent, 30 percent, and 15 percent to artwork, shapes, lines, and text. That variety makes the layout look and feel as if more than just black and one other color are being used.

### Make your newsletter profitable

Recall the mention of advertising? (See *Step 3.3: Develop a Marketing Plan,* page 167.) In this case the publisher's costs are defrayed through a classified advertising section. What type of advertising can you offer to readers and sponsors that would lessen your costs or perhaps even make you a profit? Is there someone trying to reach the same audience? Can you enlist advertisers or sponsors? Can you sell someone else's product or a service?

SAMPLER
**AUTO
NEWS**

AUGUST 20??:
News, events, and resources for car fanatics
from The Sampler Automobile Club

TOP STORY

# Nation's largest foreign automotive exposition coming to Sampler

BY ROGER EXAMPLE

Lorem ipsum dolor sit amet, consectetuer adipiscing elit, sed diam nonummy nibh euismod tincidunt ut laoreet dolore magna aliquam erat volutpat. Ut wisi enim ad minim veniam, quis nostrud exerci tation ullam corper suscipit lobortis nisl ut aliquip ex ea commodo consequat. Duis autem vel eum iriure dolor in hendrerit in vulputate velit esse molestie consequat, vel illum dolore eu feugiat nulla facilisis at vero eros et accumsan et iusto odio dignissim qui blandit praesent luptatum zzril delenit augue duis dolore te feugait nulla facilisi.

Lorem ipsum dolor sit amet, consectetuer adipiscing elit, sed diam nonummy nibh euismod tincidunt ut laoreet dolore magna aliquam erat volutpat. Ut wisi enim ad minim veniam, quis nostrud exerci tation ullamcorper suscipit lobortis nisl ut aliquip ex ea commodo consequat. Duis autem vel eum iriure dolor in hendrerit in vulputate velit esse molestie

continued on page 3

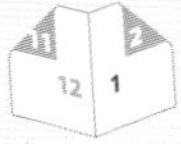

**AUGUST 20??:**
News, events, and resources for car fanatics.
from The Sampler Automobile Club

SAMPLER
AUTO
NEWS

# A parking drama

BY FRANKLIN EXAMPLE

Lorem ipsum dolor sit amet, consectetuer adipiscing elit, sed diam nonummy nibh euismod tincidunt ut laoreet dolore magna aliquam erat volutpat. Ut wisi enim ad minim veniam, quis nostrud exerci tation ullam corper suscipit lobortis nisl ut aliquip ex ea commodo consequat.

Duis autem vel eum iriure dolor in hendrerit in vulputate velit esse molestie consequat, vel illum dolore eu feugiat nulla facilisis at vero eros et accumsan et iusto odio dignissim qui blandit praesent luptatum zzril delenit augue duis dolore te feugait nulla facilisi. Ut wisi enim ad minim veniam, quis nostrud exerci tation ullamcorper suscipit lobortis nisl ut aliquip ex ea commodo consequat. Autem vel eum iriure dolor in hendrerit in vulputate velit esse molestie consequat, vel illum dolore eu feugiat nulla facilisis at vero eros et accumsan et iusto odio dignissim qui blandit praesent luptatum zzril delenit augue duis dolore te feugait nulla facilisi.

Lorem ipsum dolor sit amet, consectetuer adipiscing elit, sed diam nonum

Lorem ipsum dolor sit amet, consectetuer adipiscing elit, sed diam nonummy nibh euismod tincidunt ut laoreet dolore

magna aliquam erat volutpat. Ut wisi enim ad minim veniam, quis nostrud exerci tation ullam corper suscipit lobortis nisl ut aliquip ex ea commodo consequat. Duis autem vel eum iriure dolor in hendrerit in vulputate velit esse molestie consequat, vel illum dolore eu feugiat nulla facilisis at vero eros et accumsan et iusto odio dignissim qui blandit praesent luptatum zzril delenit augue duis dolore te feugait nulla facilisi. Lorem ipsum dolor sit amet, consectetuer adipiscing elit, sed diam nonummy nibh euismod tincidunt ut laoreet dolore magna aliquam erat volutpat. Ut wisi enim ad minim veniam, quis nostrud exerci tation ullamcorper suscipit lobortis nisl ut aliquip ex ea commodo consequat. Duis autem vel eum iriure dolor in hendrerit in vulputate velit esse molestie consequat, vel illum dolore eu feugiat nulla facilisis at vero eros et accumsan et iusto odio dignissim qui blandit praesent luptatum zzril delenit augue duis dolore te feugait nulla facilisi.

Contact Franklin Example: 987 654 3210 or name@email addressz.com; More: http://www.yourwebaddressz.com/articles/storyname.htm

## A 90 year-old man, his 75 year-old car, and 17 miles of road

BY DILLON EXAMPLE

Lorem ipsum dolor sit amet, consectetuer adipiscing elit, sed diam nonummy nibh euismod tincidunt ut laoreet dolore magna aliquam erat volutpat. Ut wisi enim ad minim veniam, quis nostrud exerci tation ullam corper suscipit lobortis nisl ut aliquip ex ea commodo consequat. Duis autem vel eum iriure dolor in hendrerit in vulputate velit esse molestie consequat, vel illum dolore eu feugiat nulla facilisis at vero eros et accumsan et iusto odio dignissim qui blandit praesent luptatum zzril delenit augue duis dolore te feugait nulla facilisi.

Lorem ipsum dolor sit amet, consectetuer adipiscing elit, sed diam nonummy nibh euismod tincidunt ut laoreet dolore magna aliquam erat volutpat. Ut wisi enim ad minim veniam, quis nostrud exerci tation ullamcorper suscipit lobortis nisl ut aliquip ex ea commodo consequat. Duis autem vel eum iriure dolor in hendrerit in vulputate velit esse molestie consequat, vel illum dolore eu feugiat nulla facilisis at vero eros et Nam liber tempor cum soluta nobis eleifend option congue nihil imperdiet doming id quod mazim placerat facer possim assum.

Contact Dillon Example: 987 654 3210 or name@emailaddressz.com; More: www.yourwebaddressz.com/articles/storyname.htm

The Sampler Automobile Club
P.O. Box 1245
Your City, ST 12345-6789

Non-Profit Organization
U.S. Postage Paid
Permit ???
Your City, ST 12345-6789

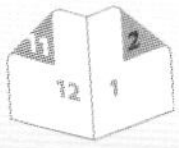

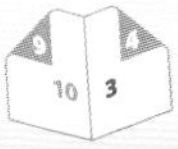

## Inside: 8 ways to finance your next vehicle with little or no interest

SANDRA EXAMPLE
SAMPLER CORPORATION
123 EXAMPLE BOULEVARD STE 200
YOUR CITY ST 12345 6789

---

### Which car models are the classics of the future?
BY FRANK EXAMPLE

Lorem ipsum dolor sit amet, consectetuer adipiscing elit, sed diam nonummy nibh euismod tincidunt ut laoreet dolore magna aliquam erat volutpat. Ut wisi enim ad minim veniam, quis nostrud exerci tation ullam corper suscipit lobortis nisl ut aliquip ex ea commodo consequat. Duis autem vel eum iriure dolor in hendrerit in vulputate velit esse molestie consequat, vel illum dolore eu feugiat nulla facilisis at vero eros et accumsan et iusto odio dignissim qui blandit praesent luptatum zzril delenit augue duis dolore te feugait nulla facilisi. Lorem ipsum dolor sit amet, consectetuer adipiscing elit, sed diam nonummy nibh euismod tincidunt ut laoreet dolore magna aliquam erat volutpat. Ut wisi enim ad minim veniam, quis nostrud exerci tation ullamcorper suscipit lobortis nisl ut

aliquip ex ea commodo consequat. Lorem ipsum dolor sit amet, consectetuer adipiscing elit, sed diam nonummy nibh euismod tincidunt ut laoreet dolore magna aliquam erat volutpat. Ut wisi enim ad minim veniam, quis nostrud exerci tation ullam corper suscipit lobortis nisl ut aliquip ex ea commodo consequat. Duis autem vel eum iriure dolor in hendrerit in vulputate velit esse molestie consequat, vel illum dolore eu feugiat nulla facilisis at vero eros et accumsan et iusto odio dignissim qui blandit praesent luptatum zzril delenit augue duis dolore te feugait nulla facilisi. Lorem ipsum dolor sit amet, consectetuer adipiscing elit, sed diam nonummy nibh euismod tincidunt ut laoreet dolore magna aliquam erat volutpat. Ut wisi enim ad minim veniam, quis nostrud exerci tation ullamcorper suscipit lobortis nisl ut

SAMPLER AUTO NEWS
3329 Example Road, P.O. Box 1245
987 654 3210
987 654 3210
987 654 3210 Fax
info@emailaddressz.com

EXECUTIVE DIRECTOR
Sarah Example
987 654 3210
name@emailaddressz.com

NEWSLETTER EDITOR
Charles Example
987 654 3210
name@emailaddressz.com

ART DIRECTOR
Mitton Example

MEMBERSHIP
Duis autem vel eum iriure dolor in hendrerit in vulputate velit esse molestie consequat, vel illum dolore eu feugiat nulla facilisis at vero eros et accumsan et iusto odio dignissim qui blandit praesent luptatum zzril delenit augue duis dolore te feugait nulla facilisi. Lorem ipsum dolor sit amet, consectetuer adipiscing elit, sed diam nonummy nibh euismod tincidunt ut laoreet dolore magna aliquam erat volutpat. Ut wisi enim ad minim veniam, quis nostrud exerci tation ullamcorper suscipit lobortis nisl ut aliquip ex ea commodo consequat.

NEWSLETTER NAME 2008 #123+34570, August 20??, Issue One, Number Two. Published by Organization's Name. 3329 Example Road, Your City, ST 12345-6789. Copyright 20?? POSTMASTER: Send address changes to Publication Name. 3329 Example Road, Your City, ST 12345-6789. Copyright 20?? by Organization's Name. All rights reserved. Legal Disclaimer Copyright Clearance
© 20?? Org Company. All rights reserved.

### Sampler Foreign Automotive Expo

Lorem ipsum dolor sit amet, consectetuer adipiscing elit, sed diam nonummy nibh euismod tincidunt ut laoreet dolore magna aliquam erat volutpat. Ut wisi enim ad minim veniam, quis nostrud exerci tation ullam corper suscipit lobortis nisl ut aliquip ex ea commodo consequat. Duis autem vel eum iriure dolor in hendrerit in vulputate velit esse molestie consequat, vel illum dolore eu feugiat nulla facilisis at vero eros et accumsan et iusto odio dignissim qui blandit praesent luptatum zzril delenit augue duis dolore te feugait nulla facilisi.

SUBHEAD TEXT
Lorem ipsum dolor sit amet, consectetuer adipiscing elit, sed diam nonummy nibh euismod tincidunt ut laoreet dolore magna aliquam erat volutpat. Ut wisi enim ad minim veniam, quis nostrud exerci tation ullamcorper suscipit lobortis nisl ut aliquip ex ea commodo consequat. Duis autem vel eum iriure dolor in hendrerit in vulputate velit esse molestie consequat, vel illum dolore eu feugiat nulla facilisis at vero eros et

Contact Roger Example: 987 654 3210 or name@emailaddressz.com; More: http://www.yourwebaddressz.com/articles/storyname.htm

nonummy nibh euismod tincidunt ut laoreet dolore magna aliquam erat volutpat. Ut wisi enim ad minim veniam, quis nostrud exerci tation ullamcorper suscipit lobortis nisl ut aliquip ex ea commodo consequat. Lorem ipsum dolor sit amet, consectetuer adipiscing

### New Products: The ultimate paints and premium coatings
BY RICHARDSON EXAMPLE

Lorem ipsum dolor sit amet, consectetuer adipiscing elit, sed diam nonummy nibh euismod tincidunt ut laoreet dolore magna aliquam erat volutpat. Ut wisi enim ad minim veniam, quis nostrud exerci tation ullamcorper suscipit lobortis nisl ut aliquip ex ea commodo consequat. Duis autem vel eum iriure dolor in hendrerit in vulputate velit esse molestie consequat, vel illum dolore eu feugiat nulla facilisis at vero eros et accumsan et iusto odio dignissim qui blandit praesent luptatum zzril delenit augue duis dolore te feugait nulla facilisi. Lorem ipsum dolor sit amet, consectetuer adipiscing elit, sed diam nonummy nibh euismod tincidunt ut laoreet dolore magna aliquam erat volutpat. Ut wisi enim ad minim veniam, quis nostrud exerci tation ullamcorper suscipit lobortis nisl ut aliquip ex ea commodo consequat. Lorem ipsum dolor sit amet, consectetuer adipiscing elit, sed diam nonummy nibh euismod tincidunt ut laoreet dolore magna aliquam erat volutpat. Ut wisi enim ad minim veniam, quis nostrud exerci tation ullamcorper suscipit lobortis nisl ut

Contact Richardson Example: 987 654 3210 or name@emailaddressz.com

SAMPLER
AUTO
NEWS

---

## Cover (page 1)

**1** Eyebrow Franklin Gothic Book Condensed, 12pt, align left; Headline, large Franklin Gothic Book Condensed, 48/40pt, align left; Contributor Franklin Gothic Book Condensed, 8pt, align left; Text Franklin Gothic Book Condensed, 12/14pt, align left; "continued" Franklin Gothic Book Condensed Italic, 8pt, align left; **2** "SAMPLER" Interstate Ultra Black, 24pt, justified; "AUTO" Interstate Ultra Black, 45pt, justified; "NEWS" Interstate Ultra Black, 42pt, justified; **3** Date/defining phrase Franklin Gothic Book Condensed, 8/9pt, align left; **4** Contents Franklin Gothic Book Condensed, 7/16pt, align left; Lines .5pt; **5** Line .5pt

## Back Cover (page 12)

**6** Headline, large Franklin Gothic Condensed, 48/40pt, align left; Contributor Franklin Gothic Book Condensed, 8pt, align left; Text Franklin Gothic Book Condensed, 10/12pt, align left; "continued" Franklin Gothic Book Condensed, 8pt, align left; **7** "SAMPLER" Interstate Ultra Black, 15pt, justified; "AUTO" Interstate Ultra Black, 29pt, justified; "NEWS" Interstate Ultra Black, 28pt, justified; **8** Headline, small Franklin Gothic Condensed, 20/20pt, align left; **9** Contact link Franklin Gothic Book Condensed, 7/8pt, align left; **10** Return address Franklin Gothic Book Condensed, 8/8pt, align left; Teaser headline Franklin Gothic Condensed, 25/23pt, align left; **11** Label address Arial, 9/9pt, align left; **10** Postage indicia Franklin Gothic Book Condensed, 8/8pt, align center; Line .5pt

## Pages 2 & 3

**12** Date/defining phrase Franklin Gothic Book Condensed, 8/9pt, align left; Headline, small Franklin Gothic Condensed, 20/20pt, align left; Contributor Franklin Gothic Book Condensed, 8pt, align left; Text Franklin Gothic Book Condensed, 10/12pt, align left; Contact link Franklin Gothic Book Condensed, 7/8pt, align left; **13** Masthead subhead Franklin Gothic Book Condensed, 8pt, align left; Masthead text Franklin Gothic Book Condensed, 9/10pt, align left; Copyright Franklin Gothic Book Condensed, 7pt, align left; Line .5pt; **14** Light headline, large Franklin Gothic Book Condensed, 36/30pt, align left; "continued" Franklin Gothic Book Condensed, 8pt, align left; **15** Caption Franklin Gothic Book Condensed, 7/8pt, align left; **16** "SAMPLER" Interstate Ultra Black, 15pt, justified; "AUTO" Interstate Ultra Black, 29pt, justified; "NEWS" Interstate Ultra Black, 28pt, justified; **17** Page numbers Franklin Gothic Book Condensed, 8pt, align left or right

SOURCE Illustrations: Gas gauge (pg. 1), cars (pg. 1, 2, 12), cones (pg. 3), parking meter (pg. 12) from Image Club ArtRoom Transportation from Eyewire, 800-661-9410, 403-262-8008, www.eyewire.com. © Eyewire, Inc., all rights reserved; Woman (pg. 3) from Faces 1 from RubberBall Productions 801-224-6886, www.rubberball.com. © RubberBall Productions, all rights reserved.

SOURCE Type Families: Franklin Gothic, Arial, Adobe Systems, Inc. 800-682-3623, www.adobe.com/type; Interstate, Font Bureau, 617-423-8770, www.fontbureau.com.

AUGUST 20??
News, events, and resources for car fanatics
from The Sampler Automobile Club

18

# Extreme fluids

BY MARTY EXAMPLE, MASTER MECHANIC

Lorem ipsum dolor sit amet, consectetuer adipiscing elit, sed diam nonummy nibh euismod tincidunt ut laoreet dolore magna aliquam erat volutpat. Ut wisi enim ad minim veniam, quis nostrud exerci tation ullam corper suscipit lobortis nisl ut aliquip ex ea commodo consequat. Duis autem vel eum iriure dolor in hendrerit in vulputate velit esse molestie consequat, vel illum dolore eu feugiat nulla facilisis at vero eros et accumsan et iusto odio dignissim qui blandit praesent luptatum zzril delenit augue duis dolore te feugait nulla facilisi.

Lorem ipsum dolor sit amet, consectetuer adipiscing elit, sed diam nonummy nibh euismod tincidunt ut laoreet dolore magna aliquam erat volutpat. Ut wisi enim ad minim veniam, quis nostrud tation ullamcorper suscipit lobortis nisl ut aliquip ex ea commodo consequat. Duis autem vel eum iriure dolor in hendrerit in vulputate velit esse molestie consequat, vel illum dolore eu feugiat nulla facilisis at vero eros et Nam liber tempor cum soluta nobis eleifend option congue nihil imperdiet doming id quod mazim placerat facer possim assum.

Lorem ipsum dolor sit amet, consectetuer adipiscing elit, sed diam nonummy nibh euismod tincidunt ut laoreet dolore magna aliquam erat volutpat. Ut wisi enim ad minim

Lorem ipsum dolor sit amet, consectetuer adipiscing elit, sed diam nonummy nibh aliquam erat volutpat. Ut wisi enim ad minim veniam, quis nostrud exerci tation ea commodo consequat. Lorem ipsum dolor sit amet, consectetuer adipiscing elit, sed diam nonummy nibh euismod tincidunt ut laoreet corper suscipit lobortis nisl ut aliquip ex ea commodo consequat. Duis autem vel eum iriure dolor in hendrerit in vulputate velit esse molestie consequat, vel illum dolore eu praesent luptatum zzril delenit augue duis dolore te feugait nulla facilisi.

## SUBHEAD TEXT

Lorem ipsum dolor sit amet, consectetuer adipiscing elit, sed diam nonummy nibh euismod tincidunt ut laoreet dolore magna

aliquam erat volutpat. Ut wisi enim ad minim veniam, quis nostrud tation ullamcorper suscipit lobortis nisl ut aliquip ex ea commodo consequat. Duis autem vel eum iriure dolor in hendrerit in vulputate velit esseeum iriure dolor in hendrerit in vulputate velit esse molestie consequat, vel illum dolore eu feugiat nulla facilisis at vero eros et Nam liber tempor cum soluta nobis eleifend opquod mazim placerat facer possim assum commodo consequat. Lorem ipsum dolor sit amet, consectetuer adipiscing elit, sed diam nonummy nibh euismod tincidunt ut laoreet dolore magna aliquam erat volutpat. Ut wisi enim ad minim veniam, quis nostrud exerci tation aliquip ex ea commodo consequat.

Duis autem vel eum iriure dolor in hendrerit in vulputate velit esse molestie

Contact Marty Example: 987 654 3210 or name@emailaddress.com. More: http://www.yourwebaddress.com/articles/storyname.htm

19

# Member's Market

Lorem ipsum dolor sit amet, consectetuer adipiscing elit, sed diam nonummy nibh euismod tincidunt ut laoreet dolore magna aliquam erat volutpat. Ut wisi enim ad minim veniam, quis nostrud tation ullam corper suscipit lobortis nisl ut aliquip ex ea commodo consequat. Duis autem vel eum iriure dolor in hendrerit in vulputate velit esse molestie consequat, vel illum dolore eu feugiat nulla facilisis at vero eros et accumsan et iusto odio dignissim qui blandit praesent luptatum zzril delenit augue duis dolore te feugait nulla facilisi.

Lorem ipsum dolor sit amet, consectetuer adipiscing elit, sed diam nonummy nibh euismod tincidunt ut laoreet dolore magna aliquam erat volutpat. Ut wisi enim ad minim veniam, quis nostrud tation ullamcorper suscipit lobortis nisl ut aliquip ex ea commodo consequat. Lorem ipsum dolor sit amet, consectetuer

Lorem ipsum dolor sit amet, consectetuer adipiscing elit, sed diam nonummy nibh euismod tincidunt ut laoreet dolore magna aliquam erat volutpat. Ut wisi enim ad minim veniam, quis nostrud exerci tation ullamcorper suscipit lobortis nisl ut aliquip ex ea commodo consequat. Lorem ipsum dolor sit amet,

Contact Member's Market: 987 654 3210 or name@emailaddress.com. More: http://www.yourwebaddress.com/articles/storyname.htm

20

SAMPLER AUTO NEWS 21

VEHICLE NAME > Description lorem ipsum dolor sit amet, consectetuer adipiscing elit, sed diam nonummy nibh euismod tincidunt ut laoreet dolore magna aliquam erat volutpat. Ut wisi enim ad minim veniam, quis nostrud exerci tation ullamcorper suscipit lobortis nisl ut aliquip ex ea commodo consequat. Lorem ipsum dolor sit amet, consectetuer adipiscing elit, sed diam nonummy nibh euismod

$0000 > Seller Name > 987 654 3210 > name@e-mail.com

VEHICLE NAME > Description lorem ipsum dolor sit amet, consectetuer adipiscing elit, sed diam nonummy nibh euismod tincidunt ut laoreet dolore magna aliquam erat volutpat. Ut wisi enim ad minim veniam, quis nostrud exerci tation aliquip ex ea commodo consequat. Lorem ipsum dolor sit amet, consectetuer adipiscing elit, sed diam nonummy nibh euismod

$0000 > Seller Name > 987 654 3210 > name@e-mail.com

VEHICLE NAME > Description lorem ipsum dolor sit amet, consectetuer adipiscing elit, sed diam nonummy nibh euismod tincidunt ut laoreet dolore magna aliquam erat volutpat. Ut wisi enim ad minim veniam, quis nostrud exerci tation aliquip ex ea commodo consequat. Lorem ipsum dolor sit amet, consectetuer adipiscing elit, sed diam nonummy nibh euismod

$0000 > Seller Name > 987 654 3210 > name@e-mail.com

VEHICLE NAME > Description lorem ipsum dolor sit amet, consectetuer adipiscing elit, sed diam nonummy nibh euismod tincidunt ut laoreet dolore magna aliquam erat volutpat. Ut wisi enim ad minim veniam, quis nostrud exerci tation aliquip ex ea commodo consequat. Lorem ipsum dolor sit amet, consectetuer adipiscing elit, sed diam nonummy nibh euismod

$0000 > Seller Name > 987 654 3210 > name@e-mail.com

VEHICLE NAME > Description lorem ipsum dolor sit amet, consectetuer adipiscing elit, sed diam nonummy nibh euismod tincidunt ut laoreet dolore magna aliquam erat volutpat. Ut wisi enim ad minim veniam, quis nostrud exerci tation aliquip ex ea commodo consequat. Lorem ipsum dolor sit amet, consectetuer adipiscing elit, sed diam nonummy nibh euismod

$0000 > Seller Name > 987 654 3210 > name@e-mail.com

VEHICLE NAME > Description lorem ipsum dolor sit amet, consectetuer adipiscing elit, sed diam nonummy nibh euismod tincidunt ut laoreet dolore magna aliquam erat volutpat. Ut wisi enim ad minim veniam, quis nostrud exerci tation aliquip ex ea commodo consequat. Lorem ipsum dolor sit amet, consectetuer adipiscing elit, sed diam nonummy nibh euismod

$0000 > Seller Name > 987 654 3210 > name@e-mail.com

VEHICLE NAME > Description lorem ipsum dolor sit amet, consectetuer adipiscing elit, sed diam nonummy nibh euismod tincidunt ut laoreet dolore magna aliquam erat volutpat. Ut wisi enim ad minim veniam, quis nostrud exerci tation aliquip ex ea commodo consequat. Lorem ipsum dolor sit amet, consectetuer adipiscing elit, sed diam nonummy nibh euismod

$0000 > Seller Name > 987 654 3210 > name@e-mail.com

---

## Pages 4 & 5

**18** Date/defining phrase Franklin Gothic Book Condensed, 8/9pt, align left; Headline, large Franklin Gothic Condensed, 42/38pt, align left; Contributor Franklin Gothic Book Condensed, 8pt, align left; Text Franklin Gothic Book Condensed, 10/12pt, align left; Contact link Franklin Gothic Book Condensed, 7/8pt, align left; **19** Headline, small Franklin Gothic Condensed, 20/20pt, align left; **20** Classified listings Franklin Gothic Book Condensed, 8/8.3pt, align left; Line .5pt; **21** Page numbers Franklin Gothic Book Condensed, 8pt, align left or right; **21** "SAMPLER" Interstate Ultra Black, 15pt, justified; "AUTO" Interstate Ultra Black, 29pt, justified; "NEWS" Interstate Ultra Black, 28pt, justified; Line .5pt

### Color

To be printed in black and a solid PANTONE Color Ink as defined on the palette below (see Step 9.3). (Because this book is printed in process colors (CMYK), the illustration is only a simulation of the actual solid PANTONE Color).

Teal or
PANTONE® 3278

| | |
|---|---|
| 100% | |
| 50% | |
| 30% | |
| 15% | |

AUGUST 20??
News, events, and resources for car fanatics
from The Sampler Automobile Club

SAMPLER AUTO NEWS

## A new concept in concept cars
BY ROBIN EXAMPLE

Lorem ipsum dolor sit amet, consectetuer adipiscing elit, sed diam nonummy nibh euismod tincidunt ut laoreet dolore magna aliquam erat volutpat. Ut wisi enim ad minim veniam, quis nostrud exerci tation ullam corper suscipit lobortis nisl ut aliquip ex ea commodo consequat. Duis autem vel eum iriure dolor in hendrerit in vulputate velit esse molestie consequat, vel illum dolore eu feugiat nulla facilisis at vero eros et accumsan et iusto odio dignissim qui blandit praesent luptatum zzril delenit augue duis dolore te feugait nulla facilisi.

Lorem ipsum dolor sit amet, consectetuer adipiscing elit, sed diam nonummy nibh euismod tincidunt ut laoreet dolore magna aliquam erat volutpat. Ut wisi enim ad minim veniam, quis nostrud exerci tation ullamcorper suscipit lobortis nisl ut aliquip ex ea commodo consequat. Lorem ipsum dolor sit amet, consectetuer adipiscing elit, sed diam nonummy nibh euismod tincidunt ut laoreet dolore magna aliquam erat volutpat. Ut wisi enim ad minim veniam, quis nostrud exerci tation suscipit lobortis nisl ut aliquip ex ea commodo consequat. Lorem ipsum dolor sit amet, consectetuer adipiscing elit, sed diam nonummy nibh euismod tincidunt ut laoreet dolore magna aliquam erat volutpat.

Contact Robin Example: 987 654 3210 or
name@emailaddressz.com. More: http://
www.yourwebaddressz.com/articles/storyname.htm

## How to adapt new technologies to classic automobiles
BY LINDA EXAMPLE

Lorem ipsum dolor sit amet consectetuer adipiscing elit, sed diam nonummy tincidunt ut laoreet dolore magna aliquam erat volutpat. Ut wisi enim ad minim veniam, quis nostrud exerci tation aliquip ex ea commodo consequat.

Duis autem vel eum iriure dolor in hendrerit in vulputate velit esse molestie consequat, vel illum dolore eu feugiat nulla facilisis at vero eros et accumsan et iusto odio dignissim qui blandit praesent luptatum zzril delenit augue duis dolore te feugait nulla facilisi. Lorem ipsum dolor sit amet, consectetuer adipiscing elit, sed diam nonummy nibh euismod tincidunt ut laoreet dolore magna aliquam erat volutpat. Ut wisi enim ad minim veniam, quis nostrud exerci tation ullamcorper suscipit lobortis nisl ut aliquip ex ea commodo consequat. Duis autem vel eum iriure dolor in hendrerit in vulputate velit esse molestie consequat, vel illum dolore eu feugiat nulla facilisis at vero eros et accumsan et iusto odio dignissim qui blandit praesent luptatum zzril delenit augue duis dolore te feugait nulla facilisi. Lorem ipsum dolor sit amet, consectetuer adipiscing elit, sed diam nonummy nibh euismod tincidunt ut laoreet dolore magna aliquam erat volutpat. Ut wisi enim ad minim veniam, quis nostrud exerci tation ullamcorper suscipit lobortis nisl ut aliquip ex ea commodo consequat. Duis autem vel eum iriure dolor in hendrerit in vulputate velit esse

molestie consequat, iriure dolor in hendrerit in vulputate velit esse vel illum dolore eu feugiat nulla facilisis at vero eros et Nam liber tempor cum soluta nobis eleifend option congue nihil imperdiet doming id quod mazim placerat facer possim assum. Vulputate nulla facilisis at vero. Lorem ipsum dolor sit amet, consectetuer adipiscing elit, sed diam nonummy nibh euismod tincidunt ut laoreet dolore magna aliquam erat volutpat. Ut wisi enim ad minim veniam, quis nostrud exerci tation ullam corper suscipit lobortis nisl ut aliquip ex ea commodo consequat. Duis autem vel eum iriure dolor in hendrerit in vulputate velit esse molestie consequat, vel illum dolore eu feugiat nulla facilisis at vero eros et accumsan et iusto odio dignissim qui blandit praesent luptatum zzril delenit augue duis dolore te feugait nulla facilisi. Lorem ipsum.

Lorem ipsum dolor sit amet, consectetuer adipiscing elit, sed diam nonummy nibh euismod tincidunt ut laoreet dolore magna aliquam erat volutpat. Ut wisi enim ad minim veniam, quis nostrud exerci tation ullamcorper suscipit lobortis nisl ut aliquip ex ea commodo consequat. Lorem ipsum dolor sit amet, consectetuer adipiscing elit, sed diam nonummy nibh euismod tincidunt ut laoreet dolore magna aliquam erat volutpat.

### SUBHEAD TEXT

Lorem ipsum dolor sit amet, consectetuer adipiscing elit, sed diam nonummy nibh euismod tincidunt ut laoreet dolore magna aliquam erat volutpat. Ut wisi enim ad minim veniam, quis nostrud exerci tation ullamcorper suscipit lobortis nisl ut aliquip ex ea commodo consequat. Duis autem vel eum iriure dolor in hendrerit in vulputate velit esse molestie consequat, vel illum dolore eu feugiat nulla facilisis at vero eros et Nam liber tempor cum

Contact Linda Example: 987 654 3210 or
name@emailaddressz.com. More: http://
www.yourwebaddressz.com/articles/storyname.htm

---

## Pages 6 & 7

**22** Date/defining phrase Franklin Gothic Book Condensed, 8/9pt, align left; Light headline, small Franklin Gothic Book Condensed, 24/22pt, align left; Contributor Franklin Gothic Book Condensed, 8pt, align left; Text Franklin Gothic Book Condensed, 10/12pt, align left; Contact link Franklin Gothic Book Condensed, 7/8pt, align left; **23** Headline, large Franklin Gothic Condensed, 48/40pt, align left; **24** Page numbers Franklin Gothic Book Condensed, 8pt, align left or right; **25** "SAMPLER" Interstate Ultra Black, 15pt, justified; "AUTO" Interstate Ultra Black, 29pt, justified; "NEWS" Interstate Ultra Black, 28pt, justified; Line .5pt

SOURCE Illustrations: Gas gauge (pg. 5, 7), motorcycles (pg. 4, 5), cars (pg. 6, 7) from *Image Club ArtRoom Transportation* from Eyewire, 800-661-9410, 403-262-8008, www.eyewire.com. © Eyewire, Inc., all rights reserved; Man (pg. 4), woman (pg. 6) from *Faces 1* from RubberBall Productions 801-224-6886, www.rubberball.com. © RubberBall Productions, all rights reserved; Vehicle photographs from *ClickArt 200,000* from Broderbund, available from software retailers worldwide, © T/Maker, all rights reserved.

SOURCE Type Families: Franklin Gothic, Adobe Systems, Inc. 800-682-3623, www.adobe.com/type; Interstate, Font Bureau, 617-423-8770, www.fontbureau.com.

STYLE 5 (16 PAGES)

# Jacket

Remember jolt thinking? (See page 167.) This is a jolt thinking jacket—the best of both worlds—a newsletter with both the flash of four-color and the frugality of black and white.

The idea is to print a year's worth of slick, four-color jackets to wrap around your regular black-and-white newsletter. The jacket's 9.5 inch height allows a 1.5 inch slice of the newsletter inside to peek out the top of the jacket to reveal the issue date and an illustration designed to entice the reader inside.

In this case, the jacket is printed with recurring information and the organization's logo in bold, bright colors. Your version could just as easily incorporate a photograph or some other appropriate artwork.

September

September Feature

## Research chaos— Lynn Example's harrowing trip into science-fiction writing

BY THOMAS EXAMPLE

Lorem ipsum dolor sit amet, consectetuer adipiscing elit, sed diam nonummy nibh euismod tincidunt ut laoreet dolore magna aliquam erat volutpat. Ut wisi enim ad minim veniam, quis nostrud exerci tation aliquip ex ea commodo consequat. Lorem ipsum dolor sit amet, consectetuer adipiscing elit, sed diam nonummy nibh euismod tincidunt ut laoreet dolore magna aliquam erat volutpat. Ut wisi enim ad minim veniam, quis nostrud exerci tation aliquip ex ea commodo consequat.

Autem vel eum iriure dolor in hendrerit in vulputate velit esse molestie consequat, vel illum dolore eu feugiat nulla facilisis at vero eros et accumsan et iusto odio dignissim qui blandit praesent luptatum zzril delenit augue duis dolore te feugait nulla facilisi. Lorem ipsum dolor sit amet, consectetuer adipiscing elit, sed diam nonum. Autem vel eum iriure dolor in hendrerit in vulputate velit esse molestie consequat, vel illum dolore eu feugiat nulla facilisis at vero eros et accumsan et iusto odio dignissim qui blandit praesent luptatum zzril delenit augue duis dolore te feugait nulla facilisi.

Lorem ipsum dolor sit amet. Autem vel eum iriure dolor in hendrerit in vulputate velit esse molestie consequat, vel illum dolore eu feugiat nulla facilisis at vero eros et accumsan et iusto odio dignissim qui blandit praesent luptatum zzril delenit augue duis dolore te feugait nulla facilisi. Autem vel eum iriure dolor in hendrerit in vulputate velit esse molestie consequat, vel illum dolore eu feugiat nulla

facilisis at vero eros. Set accumsan et iusto odio dignissim qui blandit praesent luptatum zzril delenit augue duis dolore te feugait nulla facilisi. Lorem ipsum dolor sit amet, consectetuer adipiscing elit, sed diam nonum.

Autem vel eum iriure dolor in hendrerit in vulputate velit esse molestie consequat, vel illum dolore eu feugiat nulla facilisis at vero eros et accumsan et iusto odio dignissim qui blandit praesent luptatum zzril delenit augue duis dolore te feugait nulla facilisi. Lorem ipsum dolor sit amet, consectetuer adipiscing elit, sed diam nonum. Lorem ipsum dolor sit amet, consectetuer adipiscing elit, sed diam nonummy nibh euismod tincidunt ut laoreet dolore magna aliquam erat volutpat.

Lorem ipsum dolor sit amet, consectetuer adipiscing elit, sed diam nonum. Autem vel eum iriure dolor in sed diam nonum. Lorem ipsum dolor sit amet, consectetuer adipiscing elit, sed diam nonummy hendrerit in vulputate velit esse molestie consequat, vel illum dolore eu feugiat nulla facilisis at vero eros et accumsan et iusto odio dignissim qui blandit praesent luptatum zzril delenit augue duis dolore te feugait nulla facilisi. Lorem ipsum dolor sit amet, consectetuer adipiscing elit, sed diam nonum. Lorem ipsum dolor sit amet, consectetuer adipiscing elit, sed diam nonummy nibh euismod tincidunt ut laoreet dolore magna aliquam erat volutpat. Lorem ipsum dolor sit amet, consectetuer.

*continued on page 8*

Mark

## Five fea circ nev

BY GRA

Lorem adipisc euismo aliquar veniam commo

1 / Au vulputa illum d eros et blandit duis do ipsum elit, sed

2 / Au vulputa illum d eros et blandit duis do ipsum amet, c nonum hendre conseq facilisis dignissi delenit facilisi. consec

3 / Au vulputa illum d eros et blandit duis do

### Page flow

One 9.5 by 11 inch sheet (landscape) and three 17 by 11 inch sheets (landscape) are stacked, folded to 8.5 by 11 inches and saddle-stitched.

### What you need

General layout and design requires a desktop publishing program. Editing photographic images requires a digital imaging program. Dividing and reassembling the parts and pieces of vector clip art images and type requires a drawing program. (See *Step 7: Choose Your Tools*, page 176.)

September 20??

Sampler
# PREFIX
News, events, and resources
for writers from
The Sampler Writer's Society

ling
e-

sectetuer
my nibh
ore magna
im ad minim
an aliquip ex ea

n hendrerit in
nsequat, vel
lisis at vero
dignissim qui
delenit augue
si. Lorem
uer adipiscing

n hendrerit in
nsequat, vel
lisis at vero
dignissim qui
delenit augue
si. Lorem
m dolor sit
t, sed diam
olor in
molestie
eugiat nulla
e et iusto odio
uptatum zzril
gait nulla
net,

n hendrerit in
nsequat, vel
lisis at vero
dignissim qui
delenit augue
si.

ntinued on page 12

3

## The design grid

Both the jacket and the inserts are built on a three-column grid. (See *Step 11.2: Establish the Page Size and Grid*, page 187.)

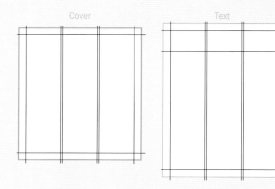

## The typefaces

This newsletter employs a Adobe Multiple Master Typeface—Myriad. A multiple master is a typeface you can customize by changing attributes such as weight: thin to heavy; width: condensed to extended; and its style and optical size. This is an example of the thousands of versions you can create of a single multiple master and testament to the adaptability of a well-designed face.

Myriad MM 700bd 300cn

**Typeface**
**AaBbEeGgKkMmQqRrSsWw!?**

Myriad MM 830bl 700se

**Typeface**
**AaBbEeGgKkMmQqRrS**

Myriad MM 215lt 700se

Typeface
AaBbEeGgKkMmQqRrSsW

Myriad MM 250wt 500wd

Text Lorem ipsum dolor sit amet, consectetuer adipiscing elit, sed diam nonummy nibh euismod tincidunt ut laoreet dolore magna aliquam erat volutpat. Ut wisi enim ad minim veniam, quis nostrud exerci tation ullamcorper suscipit lobortis nisl ut aliquip ex ea commodo consequat. Duis autem vel eum iriure dolor in hendrerit in vulputate velit esse molestie consequat, vel illum dolore eu feugiat nulla facilisis at vero eros.

## The illustrations

The jacket for your newsletter might feature photographs, artwork, or, as in this example, a simple, brightly colored version of the organization's logo. The image on the inside is designed to represent the subject matter of the page on which it appears—in this case, science fiction.

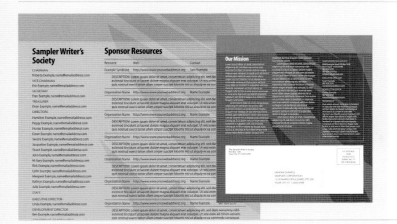

### Use the jacket to your advantage

Print the four-color jacket with information that repeats issue to issue—the nameplate, masthead, mailing area, and other useful information such as a mission statement and a list of resources. The example also includes a full page of advertising sold to a sponsor to defray the cost of printing or for profit. The 12-page black-and-white portion of the newsletter is reproduced, collated with the jacket, then folded and saddle-stitched.

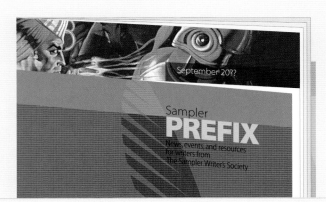

### Standardize the size and shape of illustrations

The jacket's 9.5 inch height allows a 1.5 inch slice of the newsletter inside to peek out the top of the jacket to reveal the issue date and an illustration designed to entice the reader inside. Standardizing the size and shape of images simplifies production—you know exactly how many images you need and their exact size.

### Use a piece of an illustration

Sometimes the best illustrations are those that first appear as part of a larger image. Looking for something simple and bold? Look for a small part of the complex whole. The quill used as the predominant element of the newsletter jacket was culled from a clip art image.

**16** 1

## Our Mission

Lorem ipsum dolor sit amet, consectetuer adipiscing elit, sed diam nonummy nibh euismod tincidunt ut laoreet dolore magna aliquam erat volutpat. Ut wisid enim ad minim veniam, quis nostrud exerci tation ullam corper suscipit lobortis nisl ut aliquip ex ea commodo consequat. Duis autem vel eum iriure dolor in hendrerit in vulputate velit esse molestie consequat, vel illum dolore eu feugiat nulla facilisis at vero eros et accumsan et iusto odio dignissim qui blandit praesent luptatum zzril delenit augue duis dolore te feugait nulla facilisi.

Lorem ipsum dolor sit amet, consectetuer adipiscing elit, sed diam nonummy nibh euismod tincidunt ut laoreet dolore magna aliquam erat volutpat. Ut wisi enim ad minim veniam, quis nostrud exerci tation ullamcorper suscipit lobortis nisl ut aliquip ex ea commodo consequat. Duis autem vel eum iriure dolor in hendrerit in vulputate velit esse molestie consequat, vel illum dolore eu feugiat nulla facilisis at vero eros et Nam liber tempor cum soluta nobis eleifend option congue nihil

imperdiet doming id quod mazim placerat facer possim assum.

Lorem ipsum dolor sit amet, consectetuer adipiscing elit, sed diam nonummy nibh euismod tincidunt ut laoreet dolore magna aliquam erat volutpat. Ut wisi enim ad minim veniam, quis nostrud exerci tation ullamcorper suscipit lobortis nisl ut ipsum dolor sit amet, consectetuer adipiscing elit, sed diam nonummy nibh euismod tincidunt ut laoreet dolore magna aliquam erat volutpat. Ut wisi enim ad minim veniam, quis nostrud exerci tation ullam corper suscipit lobortis nisl ut aliquip ex ea commodo consequat. Duis autem vel eum iriure dolor in hendrerit in vulputate velit esse molestie consequat, vel illum dolore eu feugiat nulla facilisis at vero eros et accumsan et iusto odio dignissim qui blandit praesent luptatum zzril delenit augue duis dolore te feugait nulla facilisi.

Lorem ipsum dolor sit amet, consectetuer adipiscing elit, sed diam nonummy nibh euismod tincidunt ut laoreet dolore magna aliquam erat volutpat.

SAMPLER WRITER'S SOCIETY
3028 Example Road, P.O. Box 1245
Your City, ST 12345-6789
987 654 3210
987 654 3210 Fax
info@emailaddressz.com

EXECUTIVE DIRECTOR
Sarah Example
987 654 3210
name@emailaddressz.com

NEWSLETTER EDITOR
Charles Example
987 654 3210
name@emailaddressz.com

MEMBERSHIP
Duis autem vel eum iriure dolor in hendrerit in vulputate velit esse molestie consequat, vel illum dolore eu feugiat nulla facilisis at vero eros et accumsan et iusto odio dignissim qui blandit praesent luptatum zzril delenit augue duis dolore te feugait nulla facilisi. Duis autem vel eum iriure dolor in hendrerit in vulputate velit esse molestie consequat, vel illum dolore eu feugiat nulla facilisis at vero eros et Nam liber tempor cum soluta nobis eleifend option congue nihil imperdiet doming id quod mazim placerat facer possim assum quis nostrud exerci tation ullamcorper suscipi.

The Sampler Writer's Society
P.O. Box 1245
Your City, ST 12345-6789

U.S. POSTAGE
PAID
YOUR CITY, ST
PERMIT NO. ???
ZIP CODE 98765

SANDRA EXAMPLE
SAMPLER CORPORATION
123 EXAMPLE BOULEVARD STE 200
YOUR CITY ST  12345 6789

8.5 W
9.5 H

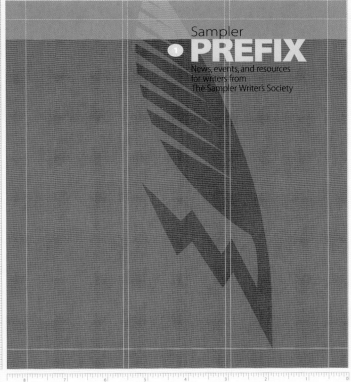

Sampler
# PREFIX
News, events, and resources
for writers from
The Sampler Writer's Society

## Cover (page 1)
**1** "Sampler" Myriad MM, 215lt, 700se, 28pt, align left;
"PREFIX" Myriad MM, 830bl, 700se, 62pt, align left;
Defining phrase Myriad MM, 250wt, 500wd, 18pt,
align left;

## Back Cover (page 16)
**2** Headline, small Myriad MM, 700bd, 300cn, 24pt,
align left; Text Myriad MM, 250wt, 500wd, 10/12pt,
align left; **3** Masthead subhead Myriad MM, 215lt,
700se, 8pt, align left; Masthead text Myriad MM,
250wt, 500wd, 9/10pt, align left; Line .5pt; **4** Return
address Myriad MM, 215lt, 700se, 8/9pt, align left;
**5** Label address Arial, 10/10pt, align left; Postage
indicia Myriad MM, 215lt, 700se, 8/8pt, align center;
Line .5pt

## Pages 2 & 15
**6** Ad headline Mona Lisa Solid, 24/36pt, align left;
Line .5pt; Ad text Garamond Light Condensed, 10/
16pt, align left; "SAMPLER SCHOOL" Myriad MM,
700bd, 300cn, 8pt, align left; Ad address Garamond
Light Condensed Italic, 8/10pt, align left; **7** Line .5pt;
**8** Headline, small Myriad MM, 700bd, 300cn, 24/
24pt, align left; Subhead Myriad MM, 215lt, 700se,
8pt, align left; Text Myriad MM, 250wt, 500wd, 9/
10pt, align left; **9** Headline, small Myriad MM, 700bd,
300cn, 24/24pt, align left; Text chart Myriad MM,
250wt, 500wd, 9/10pt, align left; Line .5pt

## Color
Printed in four-color process (Step 11.6) using
values of cyan, magenta, yellow, and black (CMYK)
as defined on the color palette below. Actual color
will vary.

### Process Colors

| | | | | | | |
|---|---|---|---|---|---|---|
| C35 | M50 | Y0 | K0 | C25 | M0 | Y70 | K0 |
| C40 | M45 | Y0 | K0 | C20 | M0 | Y60 | K0 |
| C0 | M90 | Y85 | K0 | C0 | M40 | Y75 | K0 |
| C0 | M80 | Y90 | K0 | C0 | M30 | Y80 | K0 |

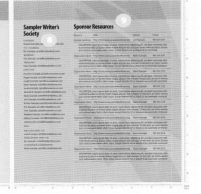

Sampler Writer's Society

Sponsor Resources

Twenty miles south
of Memphis there
is a place every
writer should know

SOURCE Illustrations: Quill from *Image Club ArtRoom*
*Schoolsville* from Eyewire, 800-661-9410, 403-262-8008,
www.eyewire.com. © Eyewire, Inc., all rights reserved;
Roadway (pg. 2) from *US Landmarks and Travel* from
PhotoDisc, 800-979-4413, 206-441-9355,
www.photodisc.com, © PhotoDisc, all rights reserved.

SOURCE Type Families: Arial, Garamond, Mona Lisa, Myriad,
Adobe Systems, Inc. 800-682-3623, www.adobe.com/
type.

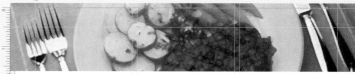

Illustration

## Working with a food stylist

BY DOUGLAS EXAMPLE

Lorem ipsum dolor sit amet, consectetuer adipiscing elit, sed diam nonummy nibh euismod tincidunt ut laoreet dolore magna aliquam erat volutpat. Ut wisi enim ad minim veniam, quis nostrud exerci tation aliquip ex ea commodo consequat.

Lorem ipsum dolor sit amet, consectetuer adipiscing elit, sed diam nonum. Autem vel eum iriure dolor in hendrerit in vulputate velit esse molestie consequat, vel illum dolore eu feugiat nulla facilisis at vero eros et accumsan et iusto odio dignissim qui blandit praesent luptatum zzril delenit augue duis dolore te feugiat nulla facilisi. Autem vel eum iriure dolor in hendrerit in vulputate velit esse molestie consequat, vel illum dolore eu feugiat nulla facilisis at vero eros.

Set accumsan et iusto odio dignissim qui blandit praesent luptatum zzril delenit augue duis dolore te feugiat nulla facilisi. Lorem ipsum dolor sit amet, consectetuer adipiscing elit, sed diam nonum. Autem vel eum iriure dolor in hendrerit in vulputate velit esse molestie consequat, vel illum dolore eu feugiat nulla facilisis at vero eros et accumsan et iusto odio dignissim qui blandit praesent luptatum zzril delenit augue duis dolore te feugiat nulla facilisi. Lorem ipsum dolor sit amet, consectetuer adipiscing elit, sed diam nonummy nibh euismod tincidunt ut laoreet dolore magna aliquam erat volutpat.

Contact Douglas Example 987 654 3210 or name@email addressz.com, More: http://www.yourwebaddressz.com/articles/storyname.htm

14

Writing skills

## Use quotations to establish and build credibility

BY JUDY EXAMPLE

Lorem ipsum dolor sit amet, consectetuer adipiscing elit, sed diam nonummy nibh euismod tincidunt ut laoreet dolore magna aliquam erat volutpat. Ut wisi enim ad minim veniam, quis nostrud exerci tation aliquip ex ea commodo consequat. Autem vel eum iriure dolor in hendrerit in vulputate velit esse molestie consequat, vel illum dolore eu feugiat nulla facilisis at vero eros et accumsan et iusto odio dignissim qui blandit praesent luptatum zzril delenit augue duis dolore te feugiat nulla facilisi.

Lorem ipsum dolor sit amet, consectetuer adipiscing elit, sed diam nonum. Autem vel eum iriure dolor in hendrerit in vulputate velit esse molestie consequat, vel illum dolore eu feugiat nulla facilisis at vero eros et accumsan et iusto odio dignissim qui blandit praesent luptatum zzril delenit augue duis dolore te feugiat nulla facilisi. Lorem ipsum dolor sit amet. Autem vel eum iriure dolor in hendrerit in vulputate velit esse molestie consequat, vel illum dolore eu feugiat nulla facilisis at vero eros.

Set accumsan et iusto odio dignissim qui blandit praesent luptatum zzril delenit augue duis dolore te feugiat nulla facilisi. Lorem ipsum dolor sit amet, consectetuer adipiscing elit, sed diam nonum. Autem vel eum iriure dolor in hendrerit in vulputate velit esse molestie consequat, vel illum dolore eu feugiat nulla facilisis at vero eros et accumsan et iusto odio dignissim qui blandit praesent luptatum zzril delenit augue duis dolore te feugiat nulla facilisi. Lorem ipsum dolor sit amet, consectetuer adipiscing elit, sed diam nonum. Lorem ipsum dolor sit amet, consectetuer

adipiscing elit, sed diam nonummy nibh euismod tincidunt ut laoreet dolore magna aliquam erat volutpat.

Ut wisi enim ad minim veniam, quis nostrud exerci tation ullam corper suscipit lobortis nisl ut aliquip ex ea commodo consequat. Duis autem vel eum iriure. Set accumsan et iusto odio dignissim qui blandit praesent luptatum zzril delenit augue duis dolore te feugiat nulla facilisi. Lorem ipsum dolor sit amet, consectetuer adipiscing elit, sed diam nonum. Autem vel eum iriure dolor in hendrerit in vulputate velit esse.

Contact Judy Example 987 654 3210 or name@email addressz.com, More: http://www.yourwebaddressz.com/articles/storyname.htm

Business of writing

## How to gauge the quality of a technical translation

BY KATHY EXAMPLE

Lorem ipsum dolor sit amet, consectetuer adipiscing elit, sed diam nonummy nibh euismod tincidunt ut laoreet dolore magna aliquam erat volutpat. Ut wisi enim ad minim veniam, quis nostrud exerci tation aliquip ex ea commodo consequat. Autem vel eum iriure dolor in hendrerit in vulputate velit esse molestie consequat, vel illum dolore eu feugiat nulla facilisis at vero eros et accumsan et iusto odio dignissim qui blandit praesent luptatum zzril delenit augue duis dolore te feugiat nulla facilisi. Lorem ipsum dolor sit amet, consectetuer adipiscing elit, sed diam nonum. Autem vel eum iriure dolor in hendrerit in vulputate velit esse molestie consequat, vel illum dolore eu feugiat nulla facilisis at vero eros et accumsan et iusto odio dignissim qui blandit praesent luptatum zzril delenit augue duis dolore te feugiat nulla facilisi. Lorem ipsum dolor sit amet. Autem vel eum iriure dolor in hendrerit in.

Contact Kathy Example: 987 654 3210 or name@email addressz.com, More: http://www.yourwebaddressz.com/articles/storyname.htm

SOURCE Illustrations: Magician from *Sci-Fi Pulps* from Time Tunnel, 888-650-6050, 480-354-3000, www.timetunnel.com. © Time Tunnel, Inc., all rights reserved; Place setting, (covered wagons, pg. 88), from *ClickArt 200,000* from Broderbund, available from software retailers worldwide, © T/Maker, all rights reserved.

SOURCE Type Families: Myriad, Adobe Systems, Inc. 800-682-3623, www.adobe.com/type.

September 20??

## September Feature

# Research chaos— Lynn Example's harrowing trip into science-fiction writing

BY THOMAS EXAMPLE

Lorem ipsum dolor sit amet, consectetuer adipiscing elit, sed diam nonummy nibh euismod tincidunt ut laoreet dolore magna aliquam erat volutpat. Ut wisi enim ad minim veniam, quis nostrud exerci tation aliquip ex ea commodo consequat. Lorem ipsum dolor sit amet, consectetuer adipiscing elit, sed diam nonummy nibh euismod tincidunt ut laoreet dolore magna aliquam erat volutpat. Ut wisi enim ad minim veniam, quis nostrud exerci tation aliquip ex ea commodo consequat.

Autem vel eum iriure dolor in hendrerit in vulputate velit esse molestie consequat, vel illum dolore eu feugiat nulla facilisis at vero eros et accumsan et iusto odio dignissim qui blandit praesent luptatum zzril delenit augue duis dolore te feugait nulla facilisi. Lorem ipsum dolor sit amet, consectetuer adipiscing elit, sed diam nonum. Autem vel eum iriure dolor in hendrerit in vulputate velit esse molestie consequat, vel illum dolore eu feugiat nulla facilisis at vero eros et accumsan et iusto odio dignissim qui blandit praesent luptatum zzril delenit augue duis dolore te feugait nulla facilisi.

Lorem ipsum dolor sit amet. Autem vel eum iriure dolor in hendrerit in vulputate velit esse molestie consequat, vel illum dolore eu feugiat nulla facilisis at vero eros et accumsan et iusto odio dignissim qui blandit praesent luptatum zzril delenit augue duis dolore te feugait nulla facilisi. Autem vel eum iriure dolor in hendrerit in vulputate velit esse molestie consequat, vel illum dolore eu feugiat nulla

facilisis at vero eros. Set accumsan et iusto odio dignissim qui blandit praesent luptatum zzril delenit augue duis dolore te feugait nulla facilisi. Lorem ipsum dolor sit amet, consectetuer adipiscing elit, sed diam nonum.

Autem vel eum iriure dolor in hendrerit in vulputate velit esse molestie consequat, vel illum dolore eu feugiat nulla facilisis at vero eros et accumsan et iusto odio dignissim qui blandit praesent luptatum zzril delenit augue duis dolore te feugait nulla facilisi. Lorem ipsum dolor sit amet, consectetuer adipiscing elit, sed diam nonum. Lorem ipsum dolor sit amet, consectetuer adipiscing elit, sed diam nonummy nibh euismod tincidunt ut laoreet dolore magna aliquam erat volutpat.

Lorem ipsum dolor sit amet, consectetuer adipiscing elit, sed diam nonum. Autem vel eum iriure dolor in sed diam nonum. Lorem ipsum dolor sit amet, consectetuer adipiscing elit, sed diam nonummyhendrerit in vulputate velit esse molestie consequat, vel illum dolore eu feugiat nulla facilisis at vero eros et accumsan et iusto odio dignissim qui blandit praesent luptatum zzril delenit augue duis dolore te feugait nulla facilisi. Lorem ipsum dolor sit amet, consectetuer adipiscing elit, sed diam nonum. Lorem ipsum dolor sit amet, consectetuer adipiscing elit, sed diam nonummy nibh euismod tincidunt ut laoreet dolore magna aliquam erat volutpat. Lorem ipsum dolor sit amet, consectetuer.

continued on page 8

## Marketing

## Five tips for selling features to large-circulation newspapers

BY GRACE EXAMPLE

Lorem ipsum dolor sit amet, consectetuer adipiscing elit, sed diam nonummy nibh euismod tincidunt ut laoreet dolore magna aliquam erat volutpat. Ut wisi enim ad minim veniam, quis nostrud exerci tation aliquip ex ea commodo consequat.

1 / Autem vel eum iriure dolor in hendrerit in vulputate velit esse molestie consequat, vel illum dolore eu feugiat nulla facilisis at vero eros et accumsan et iusto odio dignissim qui blandit praesent luptatum zzril delenit augue duis dolore te feugait nulla facilisi. Lorem ipsum dolor sit amet, consectetuer adipiscing elit, sed diam nonum.

2 / Autem vel eum iriure dolor in hendrerit in vulputate velit esse molestie consequat, vel illum dolore eu feugiat nulla facilisis at vero eros et accumsan et iusto odio dignissim qui blandit praesent luptatum zzril delenit augue duis dolore te feugait nulla facilisi. Lorem ipsum dolor sit amet, consectetuer adipiscing elit, sed diam nonum. Autem vel eum iriure dolor in hendrerit in vulputate velit esse molestie consequat, vel illum dolore eu feugiat nulla facilisis at vero eros et accumsan et iusto odio dignissim qui blandit praesent luptatum zzril delenit augue duis dolore te feugait nulla facilisi. Lorem ipsum dolor sit amet, consectetuer adipiscing elit,

3 / Autem vel eum iriure dolor in hendrerit in vulputate velit esse molestie consequat, vel illum dolore eu feugiat nulla facilisis at vero eros et accumsan et iusto odio dignissim qui blandit praesent luptatum zzril delenit augue duis dolore te feugait nulla facilisi.

continued on page 12

8.5 W 11 H

## STYLE 6 (12 PAGES)

# Lines

In architecture, a building's inward structure is often used as an integral part of its outward design. The same is true with this newsletter—the lines of the underlying grid are used as a primary design element. And, like a well-designed building, a well-designed newsletter is suited to its purpose and a pleasure to see.

A strong design is also a strong communicator—key information is highlighted, images tell a story, and everything is easy to find and read. Design may include some decoration, but decoration is not design.

**MUSIC MINISTRY**

## New type of music for a new type of service

BY DAN EXAMPLE

Lorem ipsum dolor sit amet, consectetuer adipiscing elit, sed diam nonummy nibh euismod tincidunt ut laoreet dolore magna aliquam erat volutpat. Ut wisi enim ad minim veniam, quis nostrud exerci tation ullam corper suscipit lobortis nisl ut aliquip ex ea commodo consequat.

Duis autem vel eum iriure dolor in hendrerit in vulputate velit esse molestie consequat, vel illum dolore eu feugiat nulla facilisis at vero eros et accumsan et iusto odio dignissim qui blandit praesent luptatum zzril delenit augue duis dolore te feugait nulla facilisi. Lorem ipsum dolor sit amet, consectetuer adipiscing elit, sed diam nonummy nibh euismodLorem ipsum dolor sit amet, consectetuer adipiscing elit, sed diam nonummy nibh euismod tincidunt ut laoreet dolore magna

aliquam erat volutpat. Ut wisi enim ad minim veniam, quis nostrud exerci tation aliquip ex ea commodo consequat.

Duis autem vel eum iriure dolor in hendrerit in vulputate velit esse molestie consequat, vel illum lorem ipsum dolor sit amet, consectetuer adipiscing elit, sed diam nonummy nibh euismod tincidunt ut laoreet dolore magna aliquam erat volutpat. Ut wisi enim ad minim veniam, quis nostrud exerci tation ullam corper suscipit lobortis nisl ut aliquip ex ea commodo consequat. Duis autem vel eum iriure dolor in hendrerit in vulputate.

Velit esse molestie consequat, vel illum dolore eu feugiat nulla facilisis at vero eros et accumsan et iusto odio dignissim qui blandit praesent luptatum zzril delenit augue duis dolore te feugait nulla facilisi. Lorem ipsum dolor sit amet, consectetuer adipiscing elit, sed diam nonummy nibh euismo lorem ipsum dolor sit amet, consectetuer adipiscing elit, sed diam nonummy nibh euismod tincidunt ut laoreet dolore magna.

Aliquam erat volutpat. Ut wisi enim ad minim veniam, quis nostrud exerci tation aliquip ex ea commodo consequat. Lorem ipsum dolor sit amet, consectetuer

adipiscing elit, sed diam nonum nibh euismod tincidunt ut laoree dolore magna aliquam erat volutpat.consectetuer adipiscing elit, sed diam nonummy nibh euismod tincidunt ut laoreet dolore magna aliquam erat volutpat.

☐ Contact Timothy Example: 987 654 3210 name@emailaddressz.com; More: http://www.yourwebaddressz.com/storyname.htm

**PRAYER LIFE**

## One if by land two if by air

BY TIMOTHY EXAMPLE

Ut wisi enim ad minim veniam, quis nostrud exerci tation ullam corper suscipit lobortis nisl ut aliquip ex ea commodo consequat. Lorem ipsum dolor sit amet, consectetuer adipiscing elit, sed diam nonummy nibh euismod tincidunt ut laoreet dolore magna aliquam erat volutpat. Ut wisi enim ad minim veniam, quis nostrud exerci tation ullam corper suscipit lobortis nisl ut aliquip ex ea commodo consequat. ullamcorper suscipit lobortis nisl ut aliquip ex ea commodo consequat.

Duis autem vel eum iriure dolor in hendrerit in vul putate velit esse molestie conse quat, vel illum dolore

The Sampler Church
P.O. Box 1245
Your City, ST 12345-6789

May Bible Study: Do I confine my love to friends and family?

SANDRA EXAMPLE
SAMPLER CORPORATION
123 EXAMPLE BOULEVARD STE 200
YOUR CITY ST 12345 6789

12

**Page flow**
Three 17 by 11 inch sheets (landscape) are folded to 8.5 by 11 inches and saddle-stitched.

**What you need**
General layout and design requires a desktop publishing program. Dividing and reassembling the parts and pieces of vector clip art images and type requires a drawing program. (See *Step 7: Choose Your Tools,* page 176.)

# Good News

from The Sampler Church

MAY 20??:
Events, local history, and the good news of God for the community of Sampler and beyond from the Sampler Church

## OUR PURPOSE

Lorem ipsum dolor sit amet, consectetuer adipiscing elit, sed diam nonummy nibh euismod tincidunt ut laoreet dolore magna aliquam erat volutpat. Ut wisi enim ad minim veniam, quis nostrud exerci tation ullam corper suscipit lobortis nisl dignissim qui blandit praesent ut aliquip ex ea commodo consequat. Duis autem vel eum iriure dolor in hendrerit in vulputate velit esse molestie consequat, vel illum dolore eu.

### MAY HIGHLIGHTS

| | | |
|---|---|---|
| Sun 2nd | 6:00 PM | Fellowship Dinner |
| Wed 5th | 7:00 AM | Event two |
| Thu 6th | 8:00 PM | Event three |
| n 9th | 8:00 PM | Event four |
| 9th | 10:00 PM | Event five |
| 12th | 11:00 PM | Event six |
| 13th | 12:00 PM | Event seven |
| 3th | 1:00 PM | Event eight |
| 5th | 2:00 PM | Event nine |
| 9th | 3:00 PM | Event ten |
| th | 4:00 PM | Event eleven |
| d | 5:00 PM | Event twelve |
| h | 6:00 PM | Event thirteen |
| | 7:00 PM | Event fourteen |

## FOREIGN MISSIONS

## The spaceman, the reindeer, and the congregation

BY KAREN EXAMPLE

Lorem ipsum dolor sit amet, consectetuer adipiscing elit, sed diam nonummy nibh euismod tincidunt ut laoreet dolore magna aliquam erat volutpat. Ut wisi enim ad minim veniam, quis nostrud exerci tation ullam corper suscipit lobortis nisl ut aliquip ex ea commodo consequat.

Duis autem vel eum iriure dolor in hendrerit in vulputate velit esse molestie consequat, vel illum dolore eu feugiat nulla facilisis at vero eros et accumsan et iusto odio dignissim qui blandit praesent luptatum zzril delenit augue duis dolore te feugait nulla facilisi. Lorem ipsum dolor sit amet, consectetuer adipiscing elit, sed diam nonummy nibh euismodLorem ipsum dolor sit amet, consectetuer adipiscing elit, sed diam nonummy nibh euismod tincidunt ut laoreet dolore magna aliquam erat volut pat. Ut wisi

ullamcorper suscipit lobortis nisl ut aliquip ex ea commodo consequat. Duis autem vel eum iriure dolor in hendrerit in vulputate velit esse molestie consequat, vel illum dolore eu feugiat nulla facilisis at vero eros et Nam liber tempor cum soluta nobis eleifend option congue nihil imperdiet doming id quod mazim placerat facer possim assum. Lorem ipsum dolor sit amet,

consectetuer adipiscing elit, sed diam nonummy nibh euismod tincidunt ut laoreet dolore magna aliquam erat volutpat. Ut wisi enim ad minim veniam, quis nostrud exerci tation ullamcorper suscipit lobortis nisl ut aliquip ex ea commodo consequat ut laoreet dolore magna aliquam erat.

Contact Karen Example: 987 654 3210 or name@emailaddressz.com; More: http://www.yourwebaddressz.com/storyname.htm

## FROM THE PASTOR

## Lay leaders thrust into an unexpected, hands-on mission experience– 30 years in the making

BY RALPH EXAMPLE

Lorem ipsum dolor sit amet, consectetuer adipiscing elit, sed diam nonummy nibh euismod tincidunt ut laoreet dolore magna aliquam erat volutpat. Ut wisi enim ad minim veniam, quis nostrud exerci tation ullam corper suscipit lobortis nisl ut aliquip ex ea commodo consequat. Duis autem vel eum iriure dolor in hendrerit in vulputate.

Velit esse molestie consequat, vel illum dolore eu feugiat nulla facilisis at vero eros et accumsan et iusto odio

dignissim qui blandit praesent luptatum zzril delenit augue duis dolore te feugait nulla facilisi. Lorem ipsum dolor sit amet, consectetuer adipiscing elit, sed diam nonummy nibh euismodLorem ipsum dolor sit amet, consectetuer.

Dipiscing elit, sed diam nonummy nibh euismod tincidunt ut laoreet dolore magna aliquam erat volutpat. Ut wisi enim ad minim veniam, quis nostrud exerci tation aliquip ex ea commodo consequat. Lorem ipsum dolor sit amet, consectetuer adipiscing elit, sed diam nonummy dolore magna aliquam erat dolore magna volutpat. Ut wisi enim ad minim veniam, quis nostrud exerci tation ullam corper suscipit lobortis nisl ut aliquip ex ea commodo consequat. Lorem ipsum dolor sit amet, consectetuer adipiscing elit, sed.

Contact Ralph Example: 987 654 3210 or name@emailaddressz.com; More: http://www.yourwebaddressz.com/storyname.htm

## The design grid

In this case, what you see above the surface—the lines and boxes—is the four-column grid below the surface. (See *Step 11.2: Establish the Page Size and Grid*, page 187.)

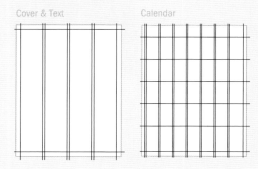

Cover & Text          Calendar

## The typefaces

This newsletter employs an Adobe Multiple Master Typeface—Myriad. A multiple master is a typeface you can customize by changing attributes such as weight: thin to heavy; width: condensed to extended; and its style and optical size. This is an example of the thousands of versions you can create of a single multiple master.

Myriad MM 700bd 300cn

## Typeface
### AaBbEeGgKkMmQqRrSsWw!?

Myriad MM 215lt 700se

## Typeface
AaBbEeGgKkMmQqRrSsW

Myriad MM 250wt 500wd

Text Lorem ipsum dolor sit amet, consectetuer adipiscing elit, sed diam nonummy nibh euismod tincidunt ut laoreet dolore magna aliquam erat volutpat. Ut wisi enim ad minim veniam, quis nostrud exerci tation ullamcorper suscipit lobortis nisl ut aliquip ex ea commodo consequat. Duis autem vel eum iriure dolor in hendrerit in vulputate velit esse molestie consequat, vel illum dolore eu feugiat nulla facilisis at vero eros.

## The illustrations

Normally you would not employ such a wide variety of drawing styles—symbols, a realistic silhouette, dreamlike wood-cuts, and a cartoon. Too many styles weaken visual continuity. All that changes when you apply the same color to all the images—a common color makes them look as though they belong together.

## DISTINGUISHING FEATURES

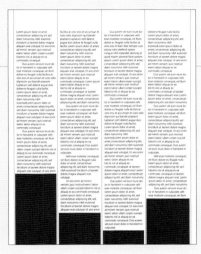

> Contact Bernadine Example: 987 654 3210 or name@emailaddressz.com; More: http://www.yourwebaddressz.com/storyname.htm

### Continue the conversation

Newsletters are all about building relationships with readers. Including a contact link at the bottom of each article invites readers to communicate with the people whose reporting and opinions they read. What kind of information to provide is, of course, up to you. The standard used here and throughout *Design It Yourself: Newsletters* demonstrates how you might provide the name of the person who wrote the article, their phone number, e-mail address, and a Web address. That link might provide an extension of or update to the article, access to online information about the subject, and/or the writer's bio or resume.

### Vary the length of text

All of the text may begin at the same place at the top of the page but the length of that text varies significantly from column to column and page to page. Making the text in one column shorter than the next is a little design trick with two big advantages—it allows writers to write a rough versus a very specific number of words and it allows designers more latitude with placing and sizing artwork.

### Set the rules, break the rules

The vertical grid lines establish a very uniform look and feel to this layout. Consequently, an element that breaks the uniformity draws attention to itself and adds visual interest. Overlapping lines with artwork and artwork with lines keeps the design interesting, as do boxes of text and illustrations that span two or more columns.

# Good News

from
The Sampler
Church

MAY 20??:
Events, local history, and the good news of
God for the community of Sampler and
beyond from the Sampler Church

## OUR PURPOSE

Lorem ipsum dolor sit amet, consectetuer adipiscing elit, sed diam nonummy nibh euismod tincidunt ut laoreet dolore magna aliquam erat volutpat. Ut wisi enim ad minim veniam, quis nostrud exerci tation ullam corper suscipit lobortis nisl dignissim qui blandit praesent ut aliquip ex ea commodo consequat. Duis autem vel eum iriure dolor in hendrerit in vulputate velit esse molestie consequat, vel illum dolore eu.

### MAY HIGHLIGHTS

| | | |
|---|---|---|
| Sun 2nd | 6:00 PM | Fellowship Dinner |
| Wed 5th | 7:00 AM | Event two |
| Thu 6th | 8:00 PM | Event three |
| Sun 9th | 8:00 PM | Event four |
| Sun 9th | 10:00 PM | Event five |
| Wed 12th | 11:00 PM | Event six |
| Thu 13th | 12:00 PM | Event seven |
| Thu 13th | 1:00 PM | Event eight |
| Sun 16th | 2:00 PM | Event nine |
| Wed 19th | 3:00 PM | Event ten |
| Wed 20th | 4:00 PM | Event eleven |
| Sun 23rd | 5:00 PM | Event twelve |
| Wed 26th | 6:00 PM | Event thirteen |
| Sun 30th | 7:00 PM | Event fourteen |

## FOREIGN MISSIONS

# The spaceman, the reindeer, and the congregation

BY KAREN EXAMPLE

Lorem ipsum dolor sit amet, consectetuer adipiscing elit, sed diam nonummy nibh euismod tincidunt ut laoreet dolore magna aliquam erat volutpat. Ut wisi enim ad minim veniam, quis nostrud exerci tation ullam corper suscipit lobortis nisl ut aliquip ex ea commodo consequat.

Duis autem vel eum iriure dolor in hendrerit in vulputate velit esse molestie consequat, vel illum dolore eu feugiat nulla facilisis at vero eros et accumsan et iusto odio dignissim qui blandit praesent luptatum zzril delenit augue duis dolore te feugait nulla facilisi. Lorem ipsum dolor sit amet, consectetuer adipiscing elit, sed diam nonummy nibh euismodLorem ipsum dolor sit amet, consectetuer adipiscing elit, sed diam nonummy nibh euismod tincidunt ut laoreet dolore magna aliquam erat volut pat. Ut wisi

ullamcorper suscipit lobortis nisl ut aliquip ex ea commodo consequat. Duis autem vel eum iriure dolor in hendrerit in vulputate velit esse molestie consequat, vel illum dolore eu feugiat nulla facilisis at vero eros et Nam liber tempor cum soluta nobis eleifend option congue nihil imperdiet doming id quod mazim placerat facer possim assum. Lorem ipsum dolor sit amet, consectetuer adipiscing elit, sed diam nonummy nibh euismod tincidunt ut laoreet dolore magna aliquam erat volutpat. Ut wisi enim ad minim veniam, quis nostrud exerci tation ullamcorper suscipit lobortis nisl ut aliquip ex ea commodo consequat ut laoreet dolore magna aliquam erat.

Contact Karen Example: 987 654 3210 or name@emailaddressz.com; More: http://www.yourwebaddressz.com/storyname.htm

## FROM THE PASTOR

# Lay leaders thrust into an unexpected, hands-on mission experience– 30 years in the making

BY RALPH EXAMPLE

Lorem ipsum dolor sit amet, consectetuer adipiscing elit, sed diam nonummy nibh euismod tincidunt ut laoreet dolore magna aliquam erat volutpat. Ut wisi enim ad minim veniam, quis nostrud exerci tation ullam corper suscipit lobortis nisl ut aliquip ex ea commodo consequat. Duis autem vel eum iriure dolor in hendrerit in vulputate.

Velit esse molestie consequat, vel illum dolore eu feugiat nulla facilisis at vero eros et accumsan et iusto odio

dignissim qui blandit praesent luptatum zzril delenit augue duis dolore te feugait nulla facilisi. Lorem ipsum dolor sit amet, consectetuer adipiscing elit, sed diam nonummy nibh euismodLorem ipsum dolor sit amet, consectetuer.

Dipiscing elit, sed diam nonummy nibh euismod tincidunt ut laoreet dolore magna aliquam erat volutpat. Ut wisi enim ad minim veniam, quis nostrud exerci tation aliquip ex ea commodo consequat. Lorem ipsum dolor sit amet, consectetuer adipiscing elit, sed diam nonummy nibh euismod tincidunt ut laoreet dolore magna aliquam erat dolore magna volutpat. Ut wisi enim ad minim veniam, quis nostrud exerci tation ullam corper suscipit lobortis nisl ut aliquip ex ea commodo consequat. Lorem ipsum dolor sit amet, consectetuer adipiscing elit, sed.

Contact Ralph Example: 987 654 3210 or name@emailaddressz.com; More: http://www.yourwebaddressz.com/storyname.htm

8.5 W
11 H

## Cover (page 1)

**1** "Good" Myriad MM, 215lt, 700se, 48/38pt, justified; "from" Myriad MM, 215lt, 700se, 16/16pt, align left; **2** Defining phrase Myriad MM, 250wt, 500wd, 8/9pt, align left; **3** Eyebrow Myriad MM, 250wt, 500wd, 7pt, align left; Text Myriad MM, 250wt, 500wd, 10/12pt, align left; Text chart Myriad MM, 250wt, 500wd, 7/16pt, align left; **4** Headline, small Myriad MM, 215lt, 700se, 20/18pt, align left; Contributor Myriad MM, 250wt, 500wd, 7pt, align left; **5** Headline, large Myriad MM, 215lt, 700se, 24/23pt, align left; **6** Line .5pt; **7** Contact link 250wt, 500wd, 7/8pt, align left

## Back Cover (page 16)

**8** "Good" Myriad MM, 215lt, 700se, 24/18pt, align left; "from" Myriad MM, 215lt, 700se, 10/10pt, align left; **9** Eyebrow Myriad MM, 250wt, 500wd, 7pt, align left; Headline, small Myriad MM, 215lt, 700se, 20/18pt, align left; Contributor Myriad MM, 250wt, 500wd, 7pt, align left; Text Myriad MM, 250wt, 500wd, 10/12pt, align left; Contact link 250wt, 500wd, 7/8pt, align left; **10** Return address Myriad MM, 250wt, 500wd, 8/10pt, align left; Teaser headline Myriad MM, 215lt, 700se, 20/20pt, align left; **11** Label address Arial, 10/10pt, align left; Postage indicia Myriad MM, 250wt, 500wd, 8/10pt, align center; Line .5pt **12** Line .5pt **13** Page number Myriad MM, 250wt, 500wd, 8pt, align left or right

## Pages 2 & 3

**14** "Good" Myriad MM, 215lt, 700se, 24/18pt, align left; "from" Myriad MM, 215lt, 700se, 10/10pt, align left; **15** Eyebrow Myriad MM, 250wt, 500wd, 7pt, align left; Headline, small Myriad MM, 215lt, 700se, 20/18pt, align left; Contributor Myriad MM, 250wt, 500wd, 7pt, align left; Text Myriad MM, 250wt, 500wd, 10/12pt, align left; Contact link 250wt, 500wd, 7/8pt, align left; 16 Line .5pt **17** "Purpose" Myriad MM, 215lt, 700se, 80pt, align left; Box text Myriad MM, 215lt, 700se, 17/19pt, align left; **18** Page number Myriad MM, 250wt, 500wd, 8pt, align left or right

## Color

To be printed in black and a solid PANTONE Color Ink as defined on the palette below (see Step 9.3). (Because this book is printed in process colors (CMYK), the illustration is only a simulation of the actual solid PANTONE Color).

---

MUSIC MINISTRY

### New type of music for a new type of service

BY DAN EXAMPLE

Lorem ipsum dolor sit amet, consectetuer adipiscing elit, sed diam nonummy nibh euismod tincidunt ut laoreet dolore magna aliquam erat volutpat. Ut wisi enim ad minim veniam, quis nostrud exerci tation ullam corper suscipit lobortis nisl ut aliquip ex ea commodo consequat.

Duis autem vel eum iriure dolor in hendrerit in vulputate velit esse molestie consequat, vel illum dolore eu feugiat nulla facilisis at vero eros et accumsan et iusto odio dignissim qui blandit praesent luptatum zzril delenit augue duis dolore te feugait nulla facilisi. Lorem ipsum dolor sit amet, consectetuer adipiscing elit, sed diam nonummy nibh euismodLorem ipsum dolor sit amet, consectetuer adipiscing elit, sed diam nonummy nibh euismod tincidunt ut laoreet dolore magna

Good News from The Sampler Church

The Sampler Church
P.O. Box 1245
Your City, ST 12345-6789

### May Bible Study: Do I confine my love to friends and family?

U.S. POSTAGE PAID
YOUR CITY, ST
PERMIT NO. ???
ZIP CODE 98765

SANDRA EXAMPLE
SAMPLER CORPORATION
123 EXAMPLE BOULEVARD STE 200
YOUR CITY ST 12345 6789

PRAYER LIFE

### One if by land, two if by air

BY TIMOTHY EXAMPLE

**Page 8**

**19** Eyebrow Myriad MM, 250wt, 500wd, 7pt, align left; **Headline, small** Myriad MM, 215lt, 700se, 20/18pt, align left; **Contributor** Myriad MM, 250wt, 500wd, 7pt, align left; **Text** Myriad MM, 250wt, 500wd, 10/12pt, align left; **Contact link** 250wt, 500wd, 7/8pt, align left; **20** "Good" Myriad MM, 215lt, 700se, 24/18pt, align left; "from" Myriad MM, 215lt, 700se, 10/10pt, align left; **21** Box text Myriad MM, 215lt, 700se, 16/16.5pt, align left; **22** Line .5pt **23** Page number Myriad MM, 250wt, 500wd, 8pt, align left or right

**Page 9**

**24** Day Myriad MM, 215lt, 700se, 13pt, align left; **25** Date Myriad MM, 215lt, 700se, 13pt, align left; Description Myriad MM, 250wt, 500wd, 9/10pt, align left; **26** Month Myriad MM, 215lt, 700se, 60pt, align right; Line .5pt

SOURCE Illustrations: Mother/daughter (pg. 8), daughter/ bike from *Electronic Clipper* from Dynamic Graphics, 800-255-8800, 309-688-8800, www.dgusa.com, © Dynamic Graphics, all rights reserved.

SOURCE Type Families: Arial, Myriad, Adobe Systems, Inc. 800-682-3623, www.adobe.com/type.

FAMILY 19

## The spiritual connection between mother and daughter

BY BERNADINE EXAMPLE

Lorem ipsum dolor sit amet, consectetuer adipiscing elit, sed diam nonummy nibh euismod tincidunt ut laoreet dolore magna aliquam erat volutpat. Ut wisi enim ad minim veniam, quis nostrud exerci tation ullam corper suscipit lobortis nisl ut aliquip ex ea commodo consequat.

Duis autem vel eum iriure dolor in hendrerit in vulputate velit esse molestie consequat, vel illum dolore eu feugiat nulla facilisis at vero eros et accumsan et iusto odio dignissim qui blandit praesent luptatum zzril delenit augue duis dolore te feugait nulla facilisi. Lorem ipsum dolor sit amet, consectetuer adipiscing elit, sed diam nonummy nibh euismodLorem ipsum dolor sit amet, consectetuer adipiscing elit, sed diam nonummy nibh euismod tincidunt ut laoreet dolore magna aliquam erat volutpat. Ut wisi enim ad minim veniam, quis nostrud exerci tation aliquip ex ea commodo consequat.

Duis autem vel eum iriure dolor in hendrerit in vulputate velit esse molestie consequat, vel illum dolore eu feugiat nulla facilisis at vero eros et accumsan et iusto odio dignissim qui blandit praesent luptatum zzril delenit augue duis dolore te feugait nulla facilisi. Lorem ipsum dolor sit amet, consectetuer adipiscing elit, sed diam nonummy nibh euismodLorem ipsum dolor sit amet, consectetuer adipiscing elit, sed diam nonummy nibh euismod tincidunt ut laoreet dolore magna aliquam erat volutpat. Ut wisi enim ad minim veniam, quis nostrud exerci tation ullam corper suscipit lobortis nisl ut aliquip ex ea commodo consequat. Duis autem vel eum iriure dolor in hendrerit in vulputate.

Velit esse molestie consequat, vel illum dolore eu feugiat nulla

8

facilisis at vero eros et accumsan et iusto odio dignissim qui blandit praesent luptatum zzril delenit augue duis dolore te feugait nulla facilisi. Lorem ipsum dolor sit amet, consectetuer adipiscing elit, sed diam nonummy nibh euismod lorem ipsum dolor sit amet, consectetuer adipiscing elit, sed diam nonummy nibh euismod tincidunt ut laoreet dolore magna aliquam erat volutpat. Ut wisi enim ad minim veniam, quis nostrud exerci tation aliquip ex ea commodo consequat. Lorem ipsum

dolor sit amet, consectetuer adipiscing elit, sed diam nonummy nibh euismod tincidunt ut laoreet dolore magna aliquam erat volutpat.

Ut wisi enim ad minim veniam, quis nostrud exerci tation ullam corper suscipit lobortis nisl ut aliquip ex ea commodo consequat. Lorem ipsum dolor sit amet, consectetuer adipiscing elit, sed diam nonummy nibh euismod tincidunt ut laoreet dolore magna aliquam erat volutpat. Ut wisi enim ad minim veniam, quis nostrud exerci tation ullam corper suscipit lobortis nisl ut aliquip ex ea commodo consequat. ullamcorper suscipit lobortis nisl ut aliquip ex ea commodo consequat.

Duis autem vel eum iriure dolor in hendrerit in vulputate velit esse molestie consequat, vel illum dolore eu feugiat nulla facilisis at vero eros et Nam liber tempor cum soluta nobis eleifend option congue nihil imperdiet doming id quod mazim placerat facer possim assum. Lorem ipsum dolor sit amet, consectetuer adipiscing elit, sed diam nonummy nibh euismod tincidunt ut laoreet dolore magna aliquam erat volutpat. Ut wisi enim ad minim veniam, quis nostrud exerci tation ullamcorper suscipit

lobortis nisl ut aliquip ex ea commodo consequat ut laoreet dolore magna aliquam erat. Lorem ipsum dolor sit amet, consectetuer adipiscing elit, sed diam nonummy nibh euismod tincidunt ut laoreet dolore magna aliquam erat volutpat. Ut wisi enim ad minim veniam, quis nostrud exerci tation ullam corper suscipit lobortis nisl ut aliquip ex ea commodo consequat.

Duis autem vel eum iriure dolor in hendrerit in vulputate velit esse molestie consequat, vel illum dolore eu feugiat nulla facilisis at vero eros et accumsan et iusto odio dignissim qui blandit praesent luptatum zzril delenit augue duis

### Good News
from The Sampler Church 20

Duis autem vel eum iriure dolor in hendrerit in vulputate velit esse molestie consequat, vel illum dolore eu feugiat nulla facilisis at vero eros et accumsan et iusto odio dignissim qui blandit praesent luptatum zzril delenit augue duis dolore te feugait nulla facilisi. Lorem ipsum dolor sit amet, consectetuer adipiscing elit, sed diam nonummy nibh euismodLorem ipsum dolor sit amet, consectetuer adipiscing elit, sed diam nonummy nibh euismod tincidunt ut laoreet dolore magna aliquam erat volutpat. Ut wisi enim ad minim veniam, quis nostrud exerci tation ullam corper suscipit lobortis nisl ut aliquip ex ea commodo consequat. Duis autem vel eum iriure dolor in hendrerit in vulputate velit esse molestie consequat, vel illum

> "When Dory was two lorem ipsum dolor sit amet, consectetuer adipiscing elit, sed diam nonummy nibh euismod tincidunt ut laoreet dolore magna aliquam erat volutpat. Ut wisi enim ad minim veniam." 21

22

lorem ipsum dolor sit amet, consectetuer adipiscing elit, sed.

Contact Bernadine Example 987 654 3210 or name@emailaddressz.com; More http:// www.yourwebaddressz.com/storyname.htm

## Blue or PANTONE® 300 Colors

| | |
|---|---|
| 100% | |
| 70% | |
| 40% | |
| 35% | |
| 30% | |
| 20% | |
| 15% | |
| 10% | |

| Sunday | Monday 24 | Tuesday | Wednesday | Thursday | Friday | Saturday |
|---|---|---|---|---|---|---|
| 3<br>9:45 AM<br>Sunday School<br><br>11:00 AM<br>Parent/Child<br>Dedication<br>Worship Service<br><br>4:30 PM<br>Youth Program | 4<br>7:30 PM<br>Explorer Scouts | 5<br>7:00 AM<br>Prayer Breakfast | 6<br>9:45 AM 25<br>Pre-kindergarten<br>Committee<br><br>6:00 PM<br>Fellowship Dinner<br><br>7:00 PM<br>Bible Study | 7<br>7:30 AM<br>Mom's Group<br>Meeting | 8 | 9<br>1:00 PM<br>Example Wedding |
| 10<br>0:00 AM<br>Event Name<br><br>0:00 AM<br>Event Name<br><br>0:00 AM<br>Event Name | 11<br>0:00 AM<br>Event Name<br><br>0:00 AM<br>Event Name | 12<br>0:00 AM<br>Event Name | 13<br>0:00 AM<br>Event Name<br><br>0:00 AM<br>Event Name<br><br>0:00 AM<br>Event Name | 14<br>0:00 AM<br>Event Name<br><br>0:00 AM<br>Event Name | 15<br>0:00 AM<br>Event Name | 16<br>0:00 AM<br>Event Name<br><br>0:00 AM<br>Event Name |
| 17<br>0:00 AM<br>Event Name<br><br>0:00 AM<br>Event Name<br><br>0:00 AM<br>Event Name | 18<br>0:00 AM<br>Event Name<br><br>0:00 AM<br>Event Name | 19<br>0:00 AM<br>Event Name | 20<br>0:00 AM<br>Event Name<br><br>0:00 AM<br>Event Name<br><br>0:00 AM<br>Event Name | 21<br>0:00 AM<br>Event Name<br><br>0:00 AM<br>Event Name | 22<br>0:00 AM<br>Event Name | 23<br>0:00 AM<br>Event Name<br><br>0:00 AM<br>Event Name |
| 24<br>0:00 AM<br>Event Name<br><br>0:00 AM<br>Event Name<br><br>0:00 AM<br>Event Name | 25<br>0:00 AM<br>Event Name<br><br>0:00 AM<br>Event Name | 26<br>0:00 AM<br>Event Name | 27<br>0:00 AM<br>Event Name<br><br>0:00 AM<br>Event Name<br><br>0:00 AM<br>Event Name | 28<br>0:00 AM<br>Event Name<br><br>0:00 AM<br>Event Name | 29<br>0:00 AM<br>Event Name | 30<br>0:00 AM<br>Event Name<br><br>0:00 AM<br>Event Name |
| 31<br>0:00 AM<br>Event Name<br><br>0:00 AM<br>Event Name<br><br>0:00 AM<br>Event Name | JUNE 1<br>0:00 AM<br>Event Name<br><br>0:00 AM<br>Event Name | 2<br>0:00 AM<br>Event Name | 3<br>0:00 AM<br>Event Name<br><br>0:00 AM<br>Event Name<br><br>0:00 AM<br>Event Name | 4<br>0:00 AM<br>Event Name<br><br>0:00 AM<br>Event Name | 5<br>0:00 AM<br>Event Name | 5<br>0:00 AM<br>Event Name<br><br>0:00 AM<br>Event Name |

May 26

8.5 W
11 H

STYLE 7 (2 PAGES)

# Newspaper

There are at least two fundamental differences between a newspaper and a newsletter. First, a newspaper typically covers a specific geographic area—a town or a city—while a newsletter covers an area of interest. Second, a newspaper generally covers a broad area of interest and a newsletter covers a specific area of interest—instead of sports, a specific sport such as rodeo riding.

Their commonality, of course, is they both are media for presenting news. Publishing a newsletter in newspaper form on a 17 by 11 inch page offers a unique opportunity to present newsletter content with the urgency a newspaper format conveys.

### Page flow

One 17 by 11 inch sheet (portrait) is folded to 11 by 8.5 inches.

### What you need

General layout and design requires a desktop publishing program. Editing photographic images requires a digital imaging program. Dividing and reassembling the parts and pieces of vector clip art images and type requires a drawing program. (See *Step 7: Choose Your Tools*, page 176.)

STORY ONE TEASE Lorem ipsum dolor sit amet, consectetuer adipiscing elit, sed diam nonummy nibh euismod tincidunt ut laoreet dolore. Lorem ipsum dolor sit amet, consectetuer adipiscing elit, sed diam nonummy nibh euismod tincidunt ut laoreet dolore.

STORY TWO TEASE Lorem ipsum dolor sit amet, consectetuer adipiscing elit, sed diam nonummy nibh euismod tincidunt ut laoreet dolore.

WOW NOW!

# SAMPLER MONEY

SINCE 1979: News, opinion, information, how-to, events, people profiles, and more from Sampler Financial Services. Lorem ipsum dolor sit amet, consectetuer adipiscing.

.com
tor
ddressz.com
210

VOL. 7 NO. 2

FINANCIAL EDITORIALS, OPINION, & INFORMATION

# rement Fiasco
# ds To Planner-
# ent Tensions

### analysis reveals unexpected results

by Roger Example
LER MONEY STAFF WRITER

ipsum dolor sit amet, tetuer adipiscing elit, sed nonummy nibh euismod unt ut laoreet dolore ma- aliquam erat volutpat. Ut enim ad minim veniam, nostrud exerci tation mcorper suscipit lobortis ut aliquip ex ea commodo sequat. Duis autem vel eum ure dolor in hendrerit in lputate velit esse molestie nsequat, vel illum dolore eu ugiat nulla facilisis at vero eros

diam nonummy nibh euismod tincidunt ut laoreet dolore magna aliquam erat volutpat. Ut wisi enim ad minim veniam, quis nostrud exerci tation ullamcorper suscipit lobortis nisl ut aliquip ex ea commodo consequat. Lorem ipsum dolor sit amet, consectetuer adipiscing elit, sed diam nonummy nibh euismod tincidunt ut laoreet dolore magna aliquam erat volutpat. Ut wisi enim ad minim veniam, quis nostrud exerci tation ullamcorper suscipit lobortis nisl ut aliquip ex ea commodo consequat. Duis

Lorem ipsum dolor sit amet, consectetuer adipiscing elit, sed diam nonummy nibh euismod tincidunt ut laoreet dolore magna aliquam erat volutpat. Ut wisi enim ad minim veniam, quis nostrud exerci tation ullamcorper suscipit lobortis nisl ut aliquip e ea commodo consequat. Duis autem vel eum iriure dolor in hendrerit in vulputate velit esse molestie.

## The design grid

Of all the contemporary print media, newspapers best demonstrate the value of a grid. They show how using a series of horizontal and vertical lines to divide pages makes for a more structured, easier to follow flow of information. The large page size makes it easy to see. This grid is five columns wide; many are six. For a comprehensive guide to grids see *The Grid: A modular system for the design production of newspapers, magazines, and books,* by Allen Hurlburt (John Wiley & Sons, Inc., 1978).

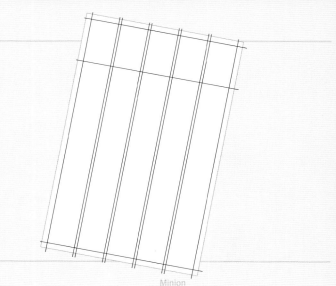

## The typefaces

This newsletter employs an Adobe Multiple Master Typeface—**Myriad**. A multiple master is a typeface you can customize by changing attributes such as weight: thin to heavy; width: condensed to extended; and its style and optical size. This is an example of the thousands of versions you can create of a single multiple master and testament to the adaptability of a well-designed face.

Racer

# Typeface
AaBbEeGgKkMmQqRrSsWw!?

Interstate Compressed Black

# Typeface
AaBbEeGgKkMmQqRrSsWw!?

Franklin Gothic Book Condensed

# Typeface
AaBbEeGgKkMmQqRrSsWw!?

Minion

# Typeface
AaBbEeGgKkMmQqRrSsWw!

Minion

Text Lorem ipsum dolor sit amet, consectetuer adipiscing elit, sed diam nonummy nibh euismod tincidunt ut laoreet dolore magna aliquam erat volutpat. Ut wisi enim ad minim veniam, quis nostrud exerci tation ullamcorper suscipit lobortis.

## The illustrations

Newspapers are a design standard. Most readers have a clear expectation of what they look like and what they contain. They are easy to illustrate because the reader's expectation is, recognized or not, that a different style of illustration is often used with every article— in many cases an orchestrated patchwork of photographs and artwork. On just two pages this example incorporates four different illustration styles—photographs, charts, and two different drawing styles.

### Tease your topics

The dictionary defines a "teaser" as a device used to arouse interest in what is to follow. The idea, of course, is to use the area at the very top of the cover to present highlights that will draw readers into the publication. You can employ the technique in your version of this layout or incorporate it into your own design.

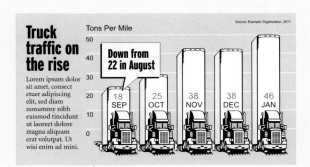

### Show what you mean

When someone asks, "Who is your favorite person?" you don't think about the spelling of their name, "T-a-n-y-a" or "M-e-l-v-i-n," you picture his or her face—a reminder that we think in pictures, not words. That's why incorporating well-conceived and -executed artwork improves communication. Information graphics meld visual signals with data to make a point with the speed of sight. You know, without reading a single word, this chart deals with transportation and that the trend is up.

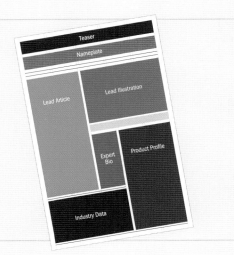

### Deconstruct designs you admire

One way to become a better designer is to deconstruct designs you admire. This design, for example, evolved from the study of many different newspaper designs—not an exact copy of any particular design, but an interpretation incorporating some of the best ideas: the relative size of the headlines to the text; the sequence of headline, subhead, contributor, and title; the idea of placing teasers at the top of the page; and so on.

www.yourwebaddressz.com
David R. Example, Editor
E-mail name@emailaddressz.com
Telephone 987 654 3210
Fax 987 654 3210

# SAMPLER MONEY

*SINCE 1979: News, opinion, information, how-to, events, people profiles, and more from Sampler Financial Services. Lorem ipsum dolor sit amet, consectetuer adipiscing.*

FEBRUARY 20?? — FINANCIAL EDITORIALS, OPINION, & INFORMATION — VOL. 7 NO. 2

# Retirement Fiasco Leads To Planner-Client Tensions

*New analysis reveals unexpected results*

By Roger Example
SAMPLER MONEY STAFF WRITER

Lorem ipsum dolor sit amet, consectetuer adipiscing elit, sed diam nonummy nibh euismod tincidunt ut laoreet dolore magna aliquam erat volutpat. Ut wisi enim ad minim veniam, quis nostrud exerci tation ullamcorper suscipit lobortis nisl ut aliquip ex ea commodo consequat. Duis autem vel eum iriure dolor in hendrerit in vulputate velit esse molestie consequat, vel illum dolore eu feugiat nulla facilisis at vero eros et accumsan et iusto odio dignissim qui blandit praesent luptatum zzril delenit augue duis dolore te feugait nulla facilisi.

Lorem ipsum dolor sit amet, consectetuer adipiscing elit, sed diam nonummy nibh euismod tincidunt ut laoreet dolore magna aliquam erat volutpat. Ut wisi enim ad minim veniam, quis nostrud exerci tation ullamcorper suscipit lobortis nisl ut aliquip ex ea commodo consequat. Duis autem vel eum iriure dolor in vulputate velit esse molestie consequat, vel illum dolore eu feugiat nulla facilisis at vero eros et Nam liber tempor cum soluta nobis eleifend option congue nihil imperdiet doming id quod mazim placerat facer possim assum.

Lorem ipsum dolor sit amet, consectetuer adipiscing elit, sed

diam nonummy nibh euismod tincidunt ut laoreet dolore magna aliquam erat volutpat. Ut wisi enim ad minim veniam, quis nostrud exerci tation ullamcorper suscipit lobortis nisl ut aliquip ex ea commodo consequat. Lorem ipsum dolor sit amet, consectetuer adipiscing elit, sed diam nonummy nibh euismod tincidunt ut laoreet dolore magna aliquam erat volutpat. Ut wisi enim ad minim veniam, quis nostrud exerci tation ullamcorper suscipit lobortis nisl ut aliquip ex ea commodo consequat. Duis autem vel eum iriure dolor in hendrerit in vulputate velit esse molestie consequat, vel illum dolore eu feugiat nulla facilisis at vero eros et Nam liber tempor cum soluta nobis eleifend option congue nihil imperdiet doming id quod mazim placerat facer possim assum.

*Lorem ipsum dolor sit amet, consectetuer adipiscing elit, sed diam nonummy nibh euismod tincidunt ut laoreet dolore magna aliquam erat volutpat. Ut wisi enim ad minim veniam, quis nostrud exerci tation ullamcorper suscipit lobortis nisl ut aliquip ex ea commodo consequat. Duis autem vel eum iriure dolor in hendrerit in vulputate velit esse molestie.*

## Battle begins to force Example to pay for future acquisitions

By Martin Example
SAMPLER MONEY LEGAL WRITER

Lorem ipsum dolor sit amet, consectetuer adipiscing elit, sed diam nonummy nibh euismod tincidunt ut laoreet dolore magna aliquam erat volutpat. Ut wisi enim ad minim veniam, quis nostrud exerci tation ullamcorper suscipit lobortis nisl ut aliquip ex ea commodo consequat.

Lorem ipsum dolor sit amet, consectetuer adipiscing elit, sed diam nonummy nibh euismod tincidunt ut laoreet dolore magna aliquam erat.

Lorem ipsum dolor sit amet, consectetuer adipiscing elit, sed diam nonummy nibh euismod tincidunt ut laoreet dolore magna aliquam erat volutpat. Ut wisi enim ad minim veniam, quis nostrud exerci tation aliquip ex ea commodo consequat. Duis autem vel eum iriure dolor in hendrerit in vulputate velit esse molestie consequat, vel illum dolore eu feugiat nulla facilisis at vero eros et accumsan.

Contact Martin Example: 987 654 3210 or name@emailaddressz.com; More: http://www.yourwebaddressz.com/articles/recipe.htm

# New Commissioner named by SMT

*Henry Example to step down in February*

By Jason K. Example
CONTRIBUTING EDITOR

Lorem ipsum dolor sit amet, consectetuer adipiscing elit, sed diam nonummy nibh euismod tincidunt ut laoreet dolore magna aliquam erat volutpat. Ut wisi enim ad minim veniam, quis nostrud exerci tation ullamcorper suscipit lobortis nisl ut aliquip ex ea commodo consequat. Duis autem vel eum iriure dolor in hendrerit in vulputate velit esse molestie consequat, vel illum dolore eu feugiat nulla facilisis at vero eros et accumsan et iusto odio dignissim qui blandit praesent luptatum zzril delenit augue duis dolore te feugait nulla facilisi.

Lorem ipsum dolor sit amet, consectetuer adipiscing elit, sed diam nonummy nibh euismod tincidunt ut laoreet dolore magna aliquam erat volutpat. Ut wisi enim ad minim veniam, quis nostrud exerci tation ullamcorper suscipit lobortis nisl ut aliquip ex ea commodo consequat. Duis autem vel eum iriure dolor in hendrerit in vulputate velit esse molestie consequat, vel illum dolore eu feugiat nulla facilisis at vero eros et Nam liber tempor cum soluta nobis eleifend option congue ni-

hil imperdiet doming id quod mazim placerat facer possim assum.

Lorem ipsum dolor sit amet, consectetuer adipiscing elit, sed diam nonummy nibh euismod tincidunt ut laoreet dolore magna aliquam erat volutpat. Ut wisi enim ad minim veniam, quis nostrud exerci tation ullamcorper suscipit lobortis nisl ut aliquip ex ea commodo consequat. Lorem ipsum dolor sit amet, consectetuer adipiscing elit, sed diam nonummy nibh euismod tincidunt ut laoreet dolore magna aliquam erat volutpat. Ut wisi enim ad minim veniam, quis nostrud exerci tation ullamcorper suscipit lobortis nisl ut aliquip ex ea commodo consequat. Duis autem vel eum iriure dolor in hendrerit in vulputate velit esse molestie consequat, vel illum dolore eu feugiat nulla facilisis at vero eros et Nam liber tempor cum soluta nobis eleifend option congue nihil imperdiet doming id quod mazim placerat facer possim assum.

Lorem ipsum dolor sit amet, consectetuer adipiscing elit, sed diam nonummy nibh congue nihil imperdiet doming.

Contact Jason Example: 987 654 3210 or name@emailaddressz.com; More: http://www.yourwebaddressz.com/articles/recipe.htm

## Truck traffic on the rise

Lorem ipsum dolor sit amet, consect etuer adipiscing elit, sed diam nonummy nibh euismod tincidunt ut laoreet dolore magna aliquam erat volutpat. Ut wisi enim ad mini.

Tons Per Mile

Source: Example Organization, 20??

**Down from 22 in August**

| | | | | |
|---|---|---|---|---|
| 18 SEP | 25 OCT | 38 NOV | 38 DEC | 46 JAN |

Contact Roger Example: 987 654 3210 or name@emailaddressz.com; More: http://www.yourwebaddressz.com/articles/recipe.htm

*(column continues)* Lorem ipsum dolor sit amet, consectetuer adipiscing elit, sed diam nonummy nibh euismod tincidunt ut laoreet dolore magna aliquam erat volutpat. Ut wisi enim ad minim veniam, quis nostrud exerci tation ullamcorper suscipit lobortis nisl ut aliquip ex ea commodo consequat. Duis autem vel eum iriure dolor in hendrerit in vulputate velit esse molestie consequat, vel illum dolore eu feugiat nulla facilisis at vero eros et Nam liber tempor cum soluta nobis eleifend option congue ni-

**Front (page 1)**

**1** *"Sampler"* Racer, 132pt, align center; Nameplate text box Minion, 8/12pt, align left; Line .5pt; **2** Tease text box Minion, 12/12pt, align left; *"WOW"* Interstate Compressed Black, 30/20pt, align center; Line .5pt; **3** Dateline Minion, 9pt, align left, right, center; Lines .5pt; **4** Headline, large Interstate Compressed Black, 48/44pt, align left; Subhead Minion, 18pt, align left; Contributor Minion, 10pt, align center; Title Minion, 9pt, align center; Line .5pt; Text Minion, 11/12pt, justified; Contact link Franklin Gothic Book Condensed, 7/8pt, align center; **5** Headline, small Minion, 20/19pt, align left; **6** Caption Minion, 9/11pt, align left; Double line .5pt; **7** Info graphic headline Interstate Compressed Black, 30/26pt, align center; Info graphic text Minion, 11/12pt, align left; *"Tons"* Arial, 12pt, align left; *"50"* Arial, 10pt, align left; *"Down"* Interstate Compressed Black, 30/26pt, align center; *"Source"* Arial, 5pt, align right; Bottom line 4pt

**Color**

Printed in black and white.

**Back (page 2)**
**8** Double line .5pt; Headline, large Interstate Compressed Black, 48/44pt, align left; Subhead Minion, 18pt, align left; Contributor Minion, 10pt, align center; Title Minion, 9pt, align center; Line .5pt; Text Minion, 11/12pt, justified; Contact link Franklin Book Condensed, 7/8pt, align center; **9** Caption Minion, 9/11pt, align left; **10** Headline, small Minion, 20/19pt, align left; **11** Chart title Arial 7pt, align left; "TSE" Arial 6pt, align left; "9100" Arial 6pt, align left; "A" Arial 7pt, align left; **12** Headline, Medium Minion, 36/34pt, align left; Line, bottom 4pt

SOURCE Illustrations: Presenter (pg. 2) from *Corporate Motion* from RubberBall Productions 801-224-6886, www.rubberball.com. © RubberBall Productions, all rights reserved; Moneybag, House (pg. 2) from *Task Force Image Gallery* from NVTech, 800-387-0732, 613-727-8184, www.nvtech.com, © NVTech, all rights reserved.

SOURCE Type Families: Franklin Gothic, Minion, Racer, Adobe Systems, Inc. 800-682-3623, www.adobe.com/type; Interstate, Font Bureau, 617-423-8770, www.fontbureau.com.

# New anthem for credit card sellers: WOW NOW!

## Marketing takes primary focus

By Tanya Example
SAMPLER MONEY STAFF WRITER

Lorem ipsum dolor sit amet, consectetuer adipiscing elit, sed diam nonummy nibh euismod tincidunt ut laoreet dolore magna aliquam erat volutpat. Ut wisi enim ad minim veniam, quis nostrud exerci tation ullamcorper suscipit lobortis nisl ut aliquip ex ea commodo consequat. Duis autem vel eum iriure dolor in hendrerit in vulputate velit esse molestie consequat, vel illum dolore eu feugiat nulla facilisis at vero eros et accumsan et iusto odio dignissim qui blandit praesent luptatum zzril delenit augue duis dolore te feugait nulla facilisi.

Lorem ipsum dolor sit amet, consectetuer adipiscing elit, sed diam nonummy nibh euismod tincidunt ut laoreet dolore magna aliquam erat volutpat. Ut wisi enim ad minim veniam, quis nostrud exerci tation ullamcorper suscipit lobortis nisl ut aliquip ex ea commodo consequat. Duis autem vel eum iriure dolor in hendrerit in vulputate velit esse molestie consequat,

eu feugiat nulla facilisis at vero eros et Nam liber tempor cum soluta nobis eleifend option congue nihil imperdiet doming id quod mazim placerat facer possim assum.

Lorem ipsum dolor sit amet, consectetuer adipiscing elit, sed diam nonummy nibh euismod tincidunt ut laoreet dolore magna aliquam erat volutpat. Ut wisi enim ad minim veniam, quis nostrud exerci tation ullamcorper suscipit lobortis nisl ut aliquip ex ea commodo consequat. Lorem ipsum dolor sit amet, consectetuer adipiscing elit, sed diam nonummy nibh euismod tincidunt ut laoreet dolore magna aliquam erat volutpat. Ut wisi enim ad minim veniam, quis nostrud exerci tation ullamcorper suscipit lobortis nisl ut aliquip ex ea commodo consequat. Duis autem vel eum iriure dolor in r sit amet, consectetuer adipiscing ut aliquip ex ea consequat.

Contact Tanya Example: 987 654 3210 or name@emailaddressz.com; More: http:// www.yourwebaddressz.com/articles/recipe.htm

Lorem ipsum dolor si ..met, consectetuer adipiscing elit, sed diam nonummy nibh euismod tincidunt ut laoreet dolore magna aliquam erat volutpat. Ut wisi enim ad minim veniam, quis nostrud exerci tation ullamcorper.

# Meadows is king of the dollar wizards

By Wilton Example
SAMPLER MONEY STAFF WRITER

Lorem ipsum dolor sit amet, consectetuer adipiscing elit, sed diam nonummy nibh euismod tincidunt ut laoreet dolore magna aliquam erat volutpat. Ut wisi enim ad minim veniam, quis nostrud exerci tation ullamcorper suscipit lobortis nisl ut aliquip ex ea commodo consequat. Duis autem vel eum iriure dolor in hendrerit in vulputate velit esse molestie consequat, vel illum dolore eu feugiat nulla facilisis at vero eros et accumsan et iusto odio dignissim qui blandit praesent luptatum zzril delenit augue

duis dolore te feugait nulla facilisi dolor sit amet, consectetuer adipiscing elit, sed diam nonummy nibh euismod.

Lorem ipsum dolor sit amet, consectetuer adipiscing elit, sed diam nonummy nibh euismod tincidunt ut laoreet dolore magna aliquam erat volutpat. Ut wisi enim ad minim veniam, quis nostrud exerci tation ullamcorper dolor sit amet, consectetuer adipiscing elit, sed diam nonummy nibh euismod suscipit lobortis nisl ut aliquip ex ea commodo consequat. Duis autem vel eum iriure dolor in hendrerit in.

Contact Wilton Example: 987 654 3210 or name@emailaddressz.com; More: http:// www.yourwebaddressz.com/articles/recipe.htm

# Controversial new legislation limits lender liability

## Realtors inherit more responsibility

By Marshall Example
CONTRIBUTING EDITOR

Lorem ipsum dolor sit amet, consectetuer adipiscing elit, sed diam nonummy nibh euismod tincidunt ut laoreet dolore magna aliquam erat volutpat. Ut wisi enim ad minim veniam, quis nostrud exerci tation ullamcorper suscipit lobortis nisl ut aliquip ex ea commodo consequat. Duis autem vel eum iriure dolor in hendrerit in vulputate velit esse molestie consequat, vel illum dolore eu

feugiat nulla facilisis at vero eros et accumsan et iusto odio dignissim qui blandit praesent luptatum zzril delenit augue duis dolore te feugait nulla facilisi.

Lorem ipsum dolor sit amet, consectetuer adipiscing elit, sed diam nonummy nibh euismod tincidunt ut laoreet dolore magna aliquam erat volutpat. Ut wisi enim ad minim veniam, quis nostrud exerci tation ullamcorper suscipit lobortis nisl ut aliquip ex ea commodo consequat. Duis autem vel eum

iriure dolor in hendrerit in vulputate velit esse molestie consequat, vel illum dolore eu feugiat nulla facilisis at vero eros et Nam liber tempor cum soluta nobis eleifend option congue nihil imperdiet doming id quod mazim placerat facer possim assum.

Lorem ipsum dolor sit amet, consectetuer adipiscing elit, sed diam nonummy nibh euismod tincidunt ut laoreet dolore magna aliquam erat volutpat. Ut wisi enim ad minim veniam, quis nostrud exerci tation ullamcorper suscipit lobortis nisl ut aliquip ex ea commodo consequat. Lorem ipsum dolor sit amet, consectetuer adipiscing elit, sed diam nonummy nibh euismod tincidunt ut laoreet dolore magna aliquam erat volutpat. Lorem ipsum dolor sit amet, consectetuer.

Contact Marshall Example: 987 654 3210 or name@emailaddressz.com; More: http:// www.yourwebaddressz.com/articles/recipe.htm

# Early talk about countdown on year end losses

By Helen Example
SAMPLER MONEY STAFF WRITER

Lorem ipsum dolor sit amet, consectetuer adipiscing elit, sed diam nonummy nibh euismod tincidunt ut laoreet dolore magna aliquam erat volutpat. Ut wisi enim ad minim veniam, quis nostrud exerci tation aliquip ex ea commodo consequat. Duis autem vel eum iriure dolor in hendrerit in

**Technology Stocks > TSE 300 close**

vulputate velit esse molestie consequat, vel illum dolore eu feugiat nulla facilisis at vero eros et accumsan.

Lorem ipsum dolor sit amet, consectetuer adipiscing elit, sed diam nonummy nibh euismod tincidunt ut laoreet dolore magna aliquam erat volutpat. Ut wisi enim ad minim veniam, quis nostrud exerci tation ullamcorper suscipit lobortis nisl ut aliquip ex ea commodo consequat. Lorem ipsum dolor sit amet, consectetuer adipiscing elit, sed diam nonummy nibh euismod tincidunt ut laoreet dolore magna aliquam erat volutpat. Ut wisi enim ad minim veniam, quis nostrud exerci tation ullamcorper suscipit lobortis nisl ut aliquip ex ea commodo consequat. Duis autem vel eum iriure dolor in r sit amet, consectetuer adipiscing ut aliquip ex ea consequat.

Lorem ipsum dolor sit amet, consectetuer adipiscing elit, sed diam nonummy nibh euismod tincidunt ut laoreet dolore magna aliquam erat volutpat. Lorem ipsum dolor sit amet, consectetuer adipiscing elit, sed diam nonummy nibh.

Contact Helen Example: 987 654 3210 or name@emailaddressz.com; More: http:// www.yourwebaddressz.com/articles/recipe.htm

STYLE 8 (16 PAGES)

# Objects

Can you see what makes this recipe unique? Yes, objects—specifically objects on a white background. What makes the technique so appealing is the ease with which it can be produced. With digital imaging software programs such as Adobe Photoshop and Jasc Software's Paint Shop Pro, it is easy to remove the background from an existing photograph and place it on a white background.

The same programs also allow you to create a simple shadow behind the image to make it look as if it is floating slightly above the surface of the page. The same technique can also be applied to type.

There are also many photographic image collections intentionally shot against white backgrounds to be used for just this purpose or to superimpose over some other background.

**Sampler density**

---

2   JUNE 2077: News, opinion, events, resources, and more from The Manufacturer's Association of Sampler

### Industry Watch: Slate of nominees for ABCD named; Miller to head Example Products; More

by Robin Example

Lorem ipsum dolor sit amet, consectetuer adipiscing elit, sed diam nonummy nibh euismod tincidunt ut laoreet dolore magna aliquam erat volutpat. Ut wisi enim ad minim veniam, quis nostrud exerci tation ullam corper suscipit lobortis nisl ut aliquip ex ea commodo consequat. Duis autem vel eum iriure dolor in hendrerit in vulputate velit esse molestie consequat, vel illum dolore eu feugiat nulla facilisis at vero eros et accumsan et iusto odio dignissim qui blandit praesent luptatum zzril delenit augue duis dolore te feugait nulla facilisi.

Lorem ipsum dolor sit amet, consectetuer adipiscing elit, sed diam nonummy nibh euismod tincidunt ut laoreet dolore magna aliquam erat volutpat. Ut wisi enim ad minim veniam, quis nostrud exerci tation ullamcorper suscipit lobortis nisl ut aliquip ex ea commodo consequat. Duis autem vel eum iriure dolor in hendrerit in vulputate velit esse molestie consequat, vel illum dolore eu feugiat nulla facilisis at vero eros et Nam liber tempor cum soluta nobis eleifend option congue nihil imperdiet doming id quod mazim placerat facer possim assum.

Lorem ipsum dolor sit amet, consectetuer adipiscing elit, sed diam nonummy nibh euismod tincidunt ut laoreet dolore magna aliquam erat volutpat. Ut wisi enim ad minim veniam, quis nostrud exerci tation ullamcorper suscipit lobortis nisl ut aliquip ex ea commodo consequat. Lorem ipsum dolor sit amet, consectetuer adipiscing elit, sed diam nonummy nibh euismod tincidunt ut laoreet dolore erat volutpat.

 Contact Robin Example: 987 654 3210 or name@emailaddressz.com; More: http://www.yourwebaddressz.com/articles/storyname.htm

### The game electroch engineeri

By Linda Example

Worem ipsum dolor sit amet, consectetuer adipiscing elit, sed diam nonummy nibh euismod tincidunt ut laoreet dolore magna aliquam erat volutpat. Ut wisi enim ad minim veniam, quis nostrud exerci tation aliquip ex ea commodo consequat.

Duis autem vel eum iriure dolor in hendrerit in vulputate velit esse molestie consequat, vel illum dolore eu feugiat nulla facilisis at vero eros et accumsan et iusto odio dignissim qui blandit praesent luptatum zzril delenit augue duis dolore te feugait nulla facilisi. Ut wisi enim ad minim veniam, quis nostrud exerci tation aliquip ex ea commodo consequat. Autem vel eum iriure dolor in hendrerit in vulputate velit esse molestie consequat, vel illum dolore eu feugiat nulla facilisis at vero eros et accumsan et iusto odio dignissim qui blandit praesent luptatum zzril delenit augue duis dolore te feugait nulla facilisi. Lorem ipsum dolor sit amet,

consec my nibl magna minim ullamce ea com hendre conseq facilisi soluta imperd facer p ullamce ea com iriure d molesti vulputa nulla cum so imperdi facer p at vero

---

**Page flow**

Four 17 by 11 inch sheets (landscape) are folded to 8.5 by 11 inches and saddle-stitched.

**What you need**

General layout and design requires a desktop publishing program. Editing photographic images requires a digital imaging program. (See *Step 7: Choose Your Tools*, page 176.)

www.yourwebaddressz.org

Sampler

# density

JUNE 20??:
News, opinion, events,
resources, and more
from The Manufacturer's
Association of Sampler

## Density Exclusive:
## How budget tightening snuffed out the industry's bright light

**by Roger Example**

Lorem ipsum dolor sit amet, consectetuer adipiscing elit, sed diam nonummy nibh euismod tincidunt ut laoreet dolore magna aliquam erat volutpat. Ut wisi enim ad minim veniam, quis nostrud exerci tation ullam corper suscipit lobortis nisl ut aliquip ex ea commodo consequat. Duis autem vel eum iriure dolor in vulputate velit esse molestie consequat, vel illum dolore eu feugiat nulla facilisis at vero eros et accumsan et iusto odio dignissim qui blandit praesent luptatum zzril delenit augue duis dolore te feugait nulla facilisi.

Lorem ipsum dolor sit amet, consectetuer adipiscing elit, sed diam nonummy nibh euismod tincidunt ut laoreet dolore magna aliquam erat volutpat. Ut wisi enim ad minim veniam, quis nostrud exerci tation ullamcorper suscipit lobortis nisl ut aliquip ex ea commodo consequat. Duis autem vel eum iriure dolor in hendrerit in vulputate velit esse molestie consequat, vel illum dolore eu feugiat nulla facilisis at vero eros et Nam liber tempor cum soluta nobis eleifend option congue nihil imperdiet doming id quod mazim placerat facer possim assum.

Lorem ipsum dolor sit amet, consectetuer adipiscing elit, sed diam nonummy nibh euismod tincidunt ut laoreet dolore magna aliquam erat volutpat. Ut wisi enim ad minim veniam, quis nostrud exerci tation ullamcorper suscipit lobortis nisl ut aliquip ex ea commodo consequat. Lorem ipsum dolor sit amet, consectetuer adipiscing elit, sed diam nonummy nibh euismod

Ut wisi enim ad minim veniam, quis nostrud exerci tation ullamcorper suscipit lobortis nisl ut aliquip ex ea commodo consequat. Duis autem vel eum iriure dolor in hendrerit in vulputate velit esseeum iriure dolor in hendrerit in vulputate velit esse molestie consequat, vel illum dolore eu feugiat nulla facilisis at vero eros et Nam liber tempor cum soluta nobis eleifend opquod mazim placerat facer possim assum commodo consequat.

▷ Contact Roger Example: 987 654 3210 or name@emailaddressz.com; More: http://www.yourwebaddressz.com/articles/storyname.htm

## How-to:
## A return to marketing fundamentals

**By Linda Example**

Lorem ipsum dolor sit amet, consectetuer adipiscing elit, sed diam nonummy nibh euismod tincidunt ut laoreet dolore magna aliquam erat volutpat. Ut wisi enim ad minim veniam, quis nostrud exerci tation aliquip ex ea commodo consequat.

Duis autem vel eum iriure dolor in hendrerit in vulputate velit esse molestie consequat, vel illum dolore eu feugiat nulla facilisis at vero eros et accumsan et iusto odio dignissim qui blandit praesent luptatum zzril delenit augue duis dolore te feugait nulla facilisi. Ut wisi enim ad minim veniam, quis nostrud exerci tation aliquip ex ea commodo consequat. Autem vel eum iriure dolor in hendrerit in vulputate velit esse molestie consequat, vel illum dolore eu feugiat nulla facilisis at vero eros et accumsan et iusto odio dignissim qui blandit praesent luptatum zzril delenit augue duis dolore te feugait nulla facilisi. Lorem ipsum dolor sit amet, consectetuer adipiscing elit, sed diam nonum my nibh euismod tincidunt ut laoreet dolore magna aliquam erat volutpat. Ut wisi enim ad minim veniam, quis nostrud exerci tation ullamcorper suscipit lobortis nisl ut aliquip ex ea commodo consequat.

Duis autem vel eum iriure dolor in hendrerit in vulputate velit esse molestie consequat, vel illum dolore eu feugiat nulla

facilisis at vero eros et Nam liber tempor cum soluta nobis eleifend option congue nihil imperdiet doming id quod mazim placerat facer possim assum quis nostrud exerci tation ullamcorper suscipit lobortis nisl ut aliquip ex ea commodo consequat. Duis autem vel eum iriure dolor in hendrerit in vulputate velit esse molestie consequat, iriure dolor in hendrerit in vulputate velit esse vel illum dolore eu feugiat nulla facilisis at vero eros et Nam liber tempor cum soluta nobis eleifend option congue nihil imperdiet doming id quod mazim placerat facer possim assum. Vulputate nulla facilisis at vero.

Lorem ipsum dolor sit amet, consectetuer adipiscing elit, sed diam nonummy nibh euismod tincidunt ut laoreet dolore magna aliquam erat volutpat. Ut wisi enim ad minim veniam, quis nostrud exerci tation ullamcorper suscipit lobortis nisl. Lorem ipsum dolor sit amet, consectetuer adipiscing elit, sed diam nonummy nibh euismod. Lorem ipsum dolor sit amet, consectetuer adipiscing elit, sed diam nonummy nibh euismod tincidunt ut laoreet dolore magna aliquam erat volutpat. Ut wisi enim ad minim veniam, quis nostrud exerci tation ullamcorper suscipit lobortis nisl. Lorem ipsum dolor sit amet, consectetuer adipiscing elit, sed diam nonummy nibh euismod tincidunt ut laoreet dolore magna aliquam erat volutpat. Ut wisi enim ad minim veniam, quis nostrud exerci tation aliquip ex ea commodo consequat facilisis at vero eros et accumsan et iusto odio dignissim qui blandit praesent luptatum.

▷ Contact Linda Example: 987 654 3210 or name@emailaddressz.com; More: http://www.yourwebaddressz.com/articles/storyname.htm

DESIGN RECIPES: OBJECTS

I've been anodized

### The design grid

This recipe employs another simple, versatile, three-column grid. (See *Step 11.2: Establish the Page Size and Grid*, page 187.)

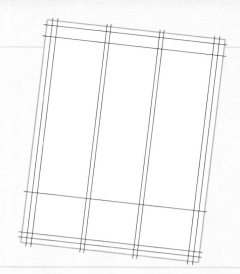

### The typefaces

The American Type Founders Company Specimen Book and Catalogue describes Franklin Gothic as "always in style." That catalogue was published in 1923. These variations of Franklin Gothic prove the point—the best typefaces work as well today as they did when they were first conceived.

Franklin Gothic Heavy

# Typeface
## AaBbEeGgKkMmQqRrSsW

Franklin Gothic Book Condensed

# Typeface
AaBbEeGgKkMmQqRrSsWw!?

Franklin Gothic Book Condensed

Text Lorem ipsum dolor sit amet, consectetuer adipiscing elit, sed diam nonummy nibh euismod tincidunt ut laoreet dolore magna aliquam erat volutpat. Ut wisi enim ad minim veniam, quis nostrud exerci tation ullamcorper suscipit lobortis nisl ut aliquip ex ea commodo consequat. Duis autem vel eum iriure dolor in hendrerit in vulputate velit esse molestie consequat, vel illum dolore eu feugiat nulla facilisis at vero eros.

### The illustrations

All of the photographs shown here, minus one, are from royalty-free collections (the "I've been anodized" part on page 1 was shot for this specific client). By matching the look and feel of custom photographs to existing collections of images, you multiply design possibilities and keep a lid on your budget.

## DISTINGUISHING FEATURES

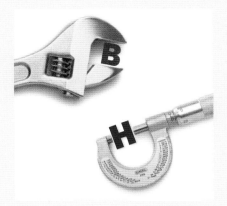

### Mix type with images

Adding a word or, in this case, a letter to a stock or royalty-free photograph makes it one-of-a-kind. The letters here stand for the subjects of the articles—B for Budget and H for Hot. Like a conventional drop cap, they add an element of interest and a spot of color.

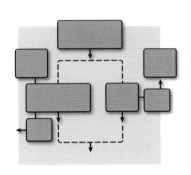

### Get technical

Don't shy away from flowcharts, diagrams, and other technical illustrations. They may not be the most attractive visual elements of a design, but, first and foremost, a newsletter is a tool of communication. Rather than avoid the complex, take the time to break it into its simplest form and to match the design of the material to its surroundings. In this case, adding color to a flowchart and a shadow similar to the objects on other pages makes it fit right in.

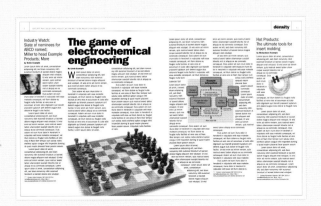

### Choose one emphasis per spread

Most newsletters have at least two levels of design: first, the overall design; then the design of each individual spread of pages (two facing pages). At the spread level, one way to direct a reader's attention is to make one article more visually important than the others. In this example, that is accomplished by making the headline bolder, by adding a drop cap to the beginning of the text, and by using a large illustration to anchor the article to the bottom of the page.

www.yourwebaddressz.org

## Sampler
# density

JUNE 20??:
News, opinion, events,
resources, and more
from The Manufacturer's
Association of Sampler

## Density Exclusive: How budget tightening snuffed out the industry's bright light

**by Roger Example**

Lorem ipsum dolor sit amet, consectetuer adipiscing elit, sed diam nonummy nibh euismod tincidunt ut laoreet dolore magna aliquam erat volutpat. Ut wisi enim ad minim veniam, quis nostrud exerci tation ullam corper suscipit lobortis nisl ut aliquip ex ea commodo consequat. Duis

autem vel eum iriure dolor in vulputate velit esse molestie consequat, vel illum dolore eu feugiat nulla facilisis at vero eros et accumsan et iusto odio dignissim qui blandit praesent luptatum zzril delenit augue duis dolore te feugait nulla facilisi.

Lorem ipsum dolor sit amet, consectetuer adipiscing elit, sed diam nonummy nibh euismod tincidunt ut laoreet dolore magna aliquam erat volutpat. Ut wisi enim ad minim veniam, quis nostrud exerci tation ullamcorper suscipit lobortis nisl ut aliquip ex ea commodo consequat. Duis autem vel eum iriure dolor in vulputate velit esse molestie consequat, vel illum dolore eu feugiat nulla facilisis at vero eros et Nam liber tempor cum soluta nobis eleifend option congue nihil imperdiet doming id quod mazim placerat facer possim assum.

Lorem ipsum dolor sit amet, consectetuer adipiscing elit, sed diam nonummy nibh euismod tincidunt ut laoreet dolore magna aliquam erat volutpat. Ut wisi enim ad minim veniam, quis nostrud exerci tation ullamcorper suscipit lobortis nisl ut aliquip ex ea commodo consequat. Lorem ipsum dolor sit amet, consectetuer adipiscing elit, sed diam nonummy nibh euismod

---

Ut wisi enim ad minim veniam, quis nostrud exerci tation ullamcorper suscipit lobortis nisl ut aliquip ex ea commodo consequat. Duis autem vel eum iriure dolor in hendrerit in vulputate velit esseeum iriure do-lor in hendrerit in vulputate velit esse molestie consequat, vel illum dolore eu feugiat nulla facilisis at vero eros et Nam liber tempor cum soluta nobis eleifend opquod mazim placerat facer possim assum commodo consequat.

> Contact Roger Example: 987 654 3210 or name@emailaddressz.com; More: http://www.yourwebaddressz.com/articles/storyname.htm

## How-to: A return to marketing fundamentals

**By Linda Example**

Lorem ipsum dolor sit amet, consectetuer adipiscing elit, sed diam nonummy nibh euismod tincidunt ut laoreet dolore magna aliquam erat volutpat. Ut wisi enim ad minim veniam, quis nostrud exerci tation aliquip ex ea commodo consequat.

Duis autem vel eum iriure dolor in hendrerit in vulputate velit esse molestie consequat, vel illum dolore eu feugiat nulla facilisis at vero eros et accumsan et iusto odio dignissim qui blandit praesent luptatum zzril delenit augue duis dolore te feugait nulla facilisi. Ut wisi enim ad minim veniam, quis nostrud exerci tation aliquip ex ea commodo consequat. Autem vel eum iriure dolor in hendrerit in vulputate velit esse molestie consequat, vel illum dolore eu feugiat nulla facilisis at vero eros et accumsan et iusto odio dignissim qui blandit praesent luptatum zzril delenit augue duis dolore te feugait nulla facilisi. Lorem ipsum dolor sit amet, consectetuer adipiscing elit, sed diam nonum my nibh euismod tincidunt ut laoreet dolore magna aliquam erat volutpat. Ut wisi enim ad minim veniam, quis nostrud exerci tation ullamcorper suscipit lobortis nisl ut aliquip ex ea commodo consequat.

Duis autem vel eum iriure dolor in hendrerit in vulputate velit esse molestie consequat, vel illum dolore eu feugiat nulla

---

facilisis at vero eros et Nam liber tempor cum soluta nobis eleifend option congue nihil imperdiet doming id quod mazim placerat facer possim assum quis nostrud exerci tation ullamcorper suscipit lobortis nisl ut aliquip ex ea commodo consequat. Duis autem vel eum iriure dolor in hendrerit in vulputate velit esse molestie consequat, iriure dolor in hendrerit in vulputate velit esse vel illum dolore eu feugiat nulla facilisis at vero eros et Nam liber tempor cum soluta nobis eleifend option congue nihil imperdiet doming id quod mazim placerat facer possim assum. Vulputate nulla facilisis at vero.

Lorem ipsum dolor sit amet, consectetuer adipiscing elit, sed diam nonummy nibh euismod tincidunt ut laoreet dolore magna aliquam erat volutpat. Ut wisi enim ad minim veniam, quis nostrud exerci tation ullamcorper suscipit lobortis nisl. Lorem ipsum dolor sit amet, consectetuer adipiscing elit, sed diam nonummy nibh euismod. Lorem ipsum dolor sit amet, consectetuer adipiscing elit, sed diam nonummy nibh euismod tincidunt ut laoreet dolore magna aliquam erat volutpat. Ut wisi enim ad minim veniam, quis nostrud exerci tation ullamcorper suscipit lobortis nisl. Lorem ipsum dolor sit amet, consectetuer adipiscing elit, sed diam nonummy nibh euismod tincidunt ut laoreet dolore magna aliquam erat volutpat. Ut wisi enim ad minim veniam, quis nostrud exerci tation aliquip ex ea commodo consequat facilisis at vero eros et accumsan et iusto odio dignissim qui blandit praesent luptatum.

> Contact Linda Example: 987 654 3210 or name@emailaddressz.com; More: http://www.yourwebaddressz.com/articles/storyname.htm

I've been anodized

**density** 16

# Static build up—
# by the book

By Franklin Example

Lorem ipsum dolor sit amet, consectetuer adipiscing elit, sed diam nonummy nibh euismod tincidunt ut laoreet dolore magna aliquam erat volutpat. Ut wisi enim ad minim veniam, quis nostrud exerci tation aliquip ex ea commodo consequat.

Duis autem vel eum iriure dolor in hendrerit in vulputate velit esse molestie consequat, vel illum dolore eu feugiat nulla facilisis at vero eros et iusto odio dignissim qui blandit praesent luptatum zzril delenit augue duis dolore te feugait nulla facilisi. Ut wisi enim ad minim veniam, quis nostrud exerci tation aliquip ex ea commodo consequat. Autem vel eum ad iriure dolor in hendrerit in vulputate velit esse molestie consequat, vel illum dolore eu feugiat nulla facilisis at vero eros et accumsan et iusto odio dignissim qui blandit praesent luptatum zzril delenit augue duis dolore te feugait nulla facilisi. Lorem ipsum dolor sit amet, consectetuer adipiscing elit, sed diam nonum

Lorem ipsum dolor sit amet, consectetuer adipiscing elit, sed diam nonummy nibh euismod tincidunt ut laoreet dolore magna aliquam erat volutpat. Ut wisi enim ad minim veniam, quis nostrud exerci tation ullam corper suscipit lobortis nisl ut aliquip ex ea commodo consequat. Duis autem vel eum iriure dolor in hendrerit in vulputate velit esse molestie consequat, vel illum dolore eu feugiat nulla facilisis at vero eros et accumsan et iusto

dignissim qui blandit praesent luptatum zzril delenit augue duis dolore te feugait nulla facilisi. Lorem ipsum dolor sit amet, consectetuer adipiscing elit, sed diam nonummy nibh euismod tincidunt ut laoreet dolore magna aliquam erat volutpat. Ut wisi enim ad minim veniam, quis nostrud exerci tation ullamcorper suscipit lobortis nisl ut aliquip ex ea commodo consequat. Duis autem vel eum iriure dolor in hendrerit in vulputate velit esse molestie consequat, vel illum dolore eu feugiat nulla facilisis at vero.

Contact Franklin Example: 987 654 3210 or name@emailaddressz.com; More: http://www.yourwebaddressz.com/articles/storyname.htm

## Salary Survey:
## 200 companies tell a surprising story
by Dillon Example

Lorem ipsum dolor sit amet, consectetuer adipiscing elit, sed diam nonummy nibh euismod tincidunt ut laoreet dolore magna aliquam erat volutpat. Ut wisi enim ad minim veniam, quis nostrud exerci tation ullam corper suscipit lobortis nisl ut aliquip ex ea commodo consequat. Duis autem vel eum molestie consequat, vel illum dolore eu et iusto odio dignissim qui blandit praesent luptatum zzril delenit augue duis dolore te feugait nulla facilisi.

Lorem ipsum dolor sit amet, consectetuer adipiscing elit, sed diam nonummy nibh euismod tincidunt ut laoreet dolore magna aliquam erat volutpat. Ut wisi enim ad minim veniam, quis nostrud exerci tation ullamcorper suscipit lobortis nisl ut aliquip ex ea commodo consequat. Duis autem vel eum iriure dolor in hendrerit in vulputate velit esse molestie consequat, vel illum dolore eu feugiat nulla facilisis at vero eros et Nam liber tempor cum soluta nobis eleifend option congue nihil imperdiet doming id quod mazim placerat facer possim assum.

Lorem ipsum dolor sit amet, consectetuer adipiscing elit, sed diam nonummy nibh euismod tincidunt ut laoreet dolore magna

Contact Dillon Example: 987 654 3210 or name@emailaddressz.com; More: http://www.yourwebaddressz.com/articles/storyname.htm

The Manufacturer's Association of Sampler
3028 Example Road
P.O. Box 1245
Your City, ST 12345-6789

**Join us for the MAS Gala Dinner on September 30 in Houston**

SANDRA EXAMPLE
SAMPLER CORPORATION
123 EXAMPLE BOULEVARD STE 200
YOUR CITY ST 12345 6789

U.S. POSTAGE
PAID
YOUR CITY, ST
PERMIT NO. ???
ZIP CODE 98765

---

## Cover (page 1)

**1** "Sampler" Franklin Gothic Book Condensed, 20pt, align left; "density" Franklin Gothic Heavy, 100pt, align center; Date/defining phrase Franklin Gothic Book Condensed, 8/9pt, align left; **2** Web address Franklin Gothic Book Condensed, 9pt, align center; **3** Headline, small Franklin Gothic Condensed, 20/20pt, align left; Contributor Franklin Gothic Heavy, 8pt, align left; Text Franklin Gothic Book Condensed, 10/12pt, align left; Contact link Franklin Gothic Book Condensed, 7/8pt, align left; **4** Line .5pt; **5** "I've" Franklin Gothic Book Condensed, 15pt, align center

## Back Cover (page 16)

**6** "Sampler" Franklin Gothic Book Condensed, 8pt, align left; "density" Franklin Gothic Heavy, 20pt, align center; **7** Headline, large Franklin Gothic Heavy, 48/40pt, align left; Contributor Franklin Gothic Heavy, 8pt, align left; Text Franklin Gothic Book Condensed, 10/12pt, align left; Contact link Franklin Gothic Book Condensed, 7/8pt, align left; **8** Headline, small Franklin Gothic Condensed, 20/20pt, align left; **9** Line .5pt; **10** Return address Franklin Gothic Book Condensed, 8/9pt, align left; Headline, large Franklin Gothic Heavy, 18/17pt, align left; **11** Label address Arial, 10/10pt, align left; **10** Postage indicia Franklin Gothic Book Condensed, 8/8pt, align center; Line .5pt

## Color

Printed in four-color process (Step 11.6) using values of cyan, magenta, yellow, and black (CMYK) as defined on the color palette below. Actual color will vary.

---

SOURCE Illustrations: Clouds (pg. 1) from *Image Club* from Eyewire, 800-661-9410, 403-262-8008, www.eyewire.com. © Eyewire, Inc., all rights reserved; Wrench (pg. 1), CMCD *Just Tools*, Hand/booklet from CMCD *Just Hands*, from PhotoDisc, 800-979-4413, 206-441-9355, www.photodisc.com, © CMCD, all rights reserved; Anodized part (pg. 1) courtesy of APC, Inc.

SOURCE Type Families: Arial, Franklin Gothic, Adobe Systems, Inc. 800-682-3623, www.adobe.com/type.

## Pages 2 & 3

**12** Page number/running head Franklin Gothic Book Condensed, 8pt, align left; **13** Headline, small Franklin Gothic Condensed, 20/20pt, align left; Contributor Franklin Gothic Heavy, 8pt, align left; Text Franklin Gothic Book Condensed, 10/12pt, align left; Contact link Franklin Gothic Book Condensed, 7/8pt, align left; **14** Headline, large Franklin Gothic Heavy, 48/40pt, align left; Drop cap Franklin Gothic Book Condensed, 44pt, align left; **15** "Sampler" Franklin Gothic Book Condensed, 8pt, align left; "density" Franklin Gothic Heavy, 20pt, align center; **16** Line .5pt

## Pages 4 & 5

**17** Page number/running head Franklin Gothic Book Condensed, 8pt, align left; **18** Headline, small Franklin Gothic Condensed, 20/20pt, align left; Contributor Franklin Gothic Heavy, 8pt, align left; Text Franklin Gothic Book Condensed, 10/12pt, align left; Contact link Franklin Gothic Book Condensed, 7/8pt, align left; **19** "Air" Franklin Gothic Book Condensed, 200pt, align left; Headline, small Franklin Gothic Condensed, 20/20pt, align left; **20** Drop cap Franklin Gothic Heavy, 48pt, align left; **21** Subhead Franklin Gothic Condensed, 9pt, align left; **22** Masthead Franklin Gothic Condensed, 9/10pt, align left; Masthead subhead Franklin Gothic Condensed, 8pt, align left; **24** Copyright Franklin Gothic Condensed, 7pt, align left

SOURCE Illustrations: Woman (pg. 2) from Faces 1, Pilot (pg. 4) from Faces 2 from RubberBall Productions 801-224-6886, www.rubberball.com. © RubberBall Productions, all rights reserved; Chess (pg. 2), CMCD Everyday Objects 1, Caliper (pg. 3) CMCD Just Tools from PhotoDisc, 800-979-4413, 206-441-9355, www.photodisc.com, © CMCD, all rights reserved.

SOURCE Type Families: Franklin Gothic, Adobe Systems, Inc. 800-682-3623, www.adobe.com/type.

## density

Lorem ipsum dolor sit amet, consectetuer adipiscing elit, sed diam nonummy nibh euismod tincidunt ut laoreet dolore magna aliquam erat volutpat. Ut wisi enim ad minim veniam, quis nostrud exerci tation ullam corper suscipit lobortis nisl ut aliquip ex ea commodo consequat. Duis autem vel eum iriure dolor in hendrerit in vulputate velit esse molestie consequat, vel illum dolore eu feugiat nulla facilisis at vero eros et accumsan et iusto odio dignissim qui blandit praesent luptatum zzril delenit augue duis dolore te feugait nulla facilisi n vulputate velit esse molestie consequat, vel illum dolore eu feugiat nulla facili.

SUBHEAD TEXT

Lorem ipsum dolor sit amet, consect etuer adipiscing elit, sed diam nonummy nibh euismod tincidunt ut laoreet dolore magna aliquam erat volutpat. Ut wisi enim ad minim veniam, quis nos rud exerci tation ullamcorper suscipit lobortis nisl ut aliquip ex ea commodo consequat. Duis autem vel eum iriure dolor in hendrerit in vulputate velit esse molestie consequat, vel illum dolore eu feugiat nulla facilisis at vero eros et Nam liber tempor cum soluta nobis eleifend option congue nihil imperdiet doming id quod mazim placerat facer possim assum.

Lorem ipsum dolor sit amet, consectetuer adipiscing elit, sed diam nonummy nibh euismod tincidunt ut laoreet dolore magna aliquam erat volutpat. Ut wisi enim ad minim veniam, quis nostrud exerci tation ullamcorper suscipit lobortis nisl ut aliquip ex ea commodo consequat. Lorem ipsum dolor sit amet, consectetuer adipiscing elit, sed diam nonummy nibh euismod tincidunt ut laoreet dolore magna aliquam erat volutpat. Ut wisi

Example
Information

Example
Information

Lorem ipsum dolor sit amet, consectetuer adipiscing elit, sed diam nonummy

Example
Information

Example flow chart Information

Flow chart info

Flow

Chart

Ldolore magna aliquam erat volutpat. Ut wisi enim ad minim veniam, quis nos rud exerci tation ullamcorper.

Source: Example Organization, 20??

Flow chart info

enim ad minim veniam, quis nostrud exerci tation ullamcorper suscipit lobortis nisl ut aliquip ex ea commodo consequat. Duis autem vel elit, sed diam nonummy nibh euismod tincidunt ut laoreet dolore magna aliquam erat volutpat.

Ut wisi enim ad minim veniam, quis nostrud exerci tation ullamcorper suscipit lobortis nisl ut aliquip ex ea commodo consequat. Duis autem vel eum iriure dolor in hendrerit in vulputate velit esseeum iriure do-lor in hendrerit in vulputate velit esse molestie consequat, vel illum dolore eu feugiat nulla facilisis at vero eros et Nam liber tempor cum soluta nobis eleifend opquod mazim placerat facer possim assum commodo consequat. Lorem ipsum dolor sit amet, consectetuer adipiscing elit, sed diam nonummy nibh euismod tincidunt ut laoreet dolore ma-gna aliquam erat volutpat. Ut wisi enim ad minim veniam, quis nostrud exerci tation aliquip ex ea commodo consequat.

Duis autem vel eum iriure dolor in hendrerit in vulputate velit esse molestie consequat, vel illum dolore eu feugiat nulla facilisis at vero eros et accumsan et iusto odio dignissim qui blandit praesent luptatum zzril delenit augue duis dolore te feugait nulla facilisi. Ut wisi enim ad minim veniam, quis nostrud exerci tation aliquip ex ea commodo consequat. Autem vel eum iriure dolor in hendrerit in vulputate velit esse molestie.

Duis autem vel eum iriure dolor in hendrerit in vulputate velit esse molestie consequat, iriure dolor in hendrerit in vulputate velit esse vel illum dolore eu.

Contact Linda Example: 987 654 3210 or name@emailaddressz.com; More: http://www.yourwebaddressz.com/articles/storyname.htm

commodo consequat. Duis autem vel eum iriure dolor in hendrerit in vulputate velit esse molestie consequat, vel illum dolore eu feugiat nulla facilisis at vero eros et Nam liber tempor cum soluta nobis eleifend option congue nihil imperdiet doming id quod mazim placerat possim assum.

Lorem ipsum dolor sit amet, consectetuer adipiscing elit, sed diam nonummy nibh euismod tincidunt ut laoreet dolore magna aliquam erat volutpat. Ut wisi enim ad minim veniam, quis nostrud exerci tation ullamcorper suscipit lobortis nisl ut aliquip ex ea commodo consequat. Lorem ipsum dolor sit amet, consectetuer adipiscing elit, sed diam nonummy nibh euismod tincidunt ut laoreet dolore magna aliquam erat volutpat. Ut wisi

## Hot Products:
# The ultimate tools for insert molding

**by Richardson Example**

Lorem ipsum dolor sit amet, consectetuer adipiscing elit, sed diam nonummy nibh euismod tincidunt ut laoreet dolore magna aliquam erat volutpat. Ut wisi enim ad minim veniam, quis nostrud exerci tation ullam corper suscipit lobortis nisl ut aliquip ex ea commodo consequat. Duis autem vel eum iriure dolor in hendrerit in vulputate velit esse molestie consequat, vel illum dolore eu feugiat nulla facilisis at vero eros et accumsan et iusto odio dignissim qui blandit praesent luptatum zzril delenit augue duis dolore te feugait nulla facilisi.

Lorem ipsum dolor sit amet, consectetuer adipiscing elit, sed diam nonummy nibh euismod tincidunt ut laoreet dolore magna aliquam erat volutpat. Ut wisi enim ad minim veniam, quis nostrud exerci tation ullamcorper suscipit lobortis nisl ut aliquip ex ea commodo consequat. Duis autem vel eum iriure dolor in vulputate velit esse molestie consequat, vel illum dolore eu feugiat nulla facilisis at vero eros et Nam liber tempor cum soluta nobis eleifend option congue nihil imperdiet doming id quod mazim placerat facer possim assum.

Lorem ipsum dolor sit amet, consectetuer adipiscing elit, sed diam nonummy nibh euismod tincidunt ut laoreet dolore magna aliquam erat volutpat. Ut wisi enim ad minim veniam, quis nostrud exerci tation ullamcorper suscipit lobortis nisl ut aliquip ex ea commodo consequat. Lorem ipsum dolor sit amet, consectetuer adipiscing elit, sed diam nonummy nibh euismod tincidunt ut laoreet dolore erat volutpat.

Contact Richardson Example: 987 654 3210 or name@emailaddressz.com; More: http://www.yourwebaddressz.com/articles/storyname.htm

STYLE 9 (2 PAGES)

# Postcard

Could a newsletter in postcard form achieve some or most of the things you envision your conventional newsletter achieving? It would certainly hook you up with readers on a regular basis and provide a venue for promoting products, services, and your way of thinking. But the real value of creating a postcard newsletter is for what it doesn't do— it doesn't take as long to write and design, it doesn't cost as much to produce, and, in many cases, it doesn't cost as much to mail.

Plus, if your audience has only a passing interest in your subject matter, a postcard newsletter doesn't require the kind of time and effort it takes to explore a sixteen-page newsletter.

**SAMPLER Play! NEWSLETTER**

**News, Views, and Resources for Audio Engineers**

MISSION:Lorem ipsum dolor sit amet, consectetuer adipiscing elit, sed diam nonummy nibh euismod tincidunt ut laoreet dolore magna aliquam erat volutpat. Ut wisi enim ad minim veniam, quis nostrud exerci tation ullamcorper suscipit lobortis nisl ut aliquip ex ea commodo.

DECEMBER 20??, Volume

## What you n to know ab new Digita audio stan

*by Christine Example*

Lorem ipsum dolor sit am adipiscing elit, sed diam r euismod tincidunt ut lao aliquam erat volutpat. Ut minim veniam, quis nostr ullam corper suscipit lobc ex ea commodo consequ eum iriure dolor in hendr velit esse molestie conseo dolore eu feugiat nulla fao et accumsan et iusto odic blandit praesent luptatun augue duis dolore te feug Lorem ipsum dolor sit am adipiscing elit, sed diam r euismod tincidunt ut laor aliquam erat volutpat. Ut minim veniam, quis nostr ullamcorper suscipit lobo ex ea commodo consequa

Duis autem vel eum hendrerit in vulputate veli consequat, vel illum dolore facilisis at vero eros et Nan cum soluta nobis eleifend hil imperdiet doming id qu

**Page flow**
One landscape 6 by 9 inch card.

**What you need**
General layout and design requires a desktop publishing program. Editing photographic images requires a digital imaging program. Dividing and reassembling the parts and pieces of vector clip art images and type requires a drawing program. (See *Step 7: Choose Your Tools*, page 176.)

, Published by Organization's Name

placerat facer possim assum. Lorem ipsum dolor sit amet, consectetuer adipiscing elit, sed diam nonummy nibh euismod tincidunt ut laoreet dolore magna aliquam erat volutpat. Ut wisi enim ad minim veniam, suscipit lobortis nisl ut aliquip ex ea commodo consequat.

Lorem ipsum dolor sit amet, consectetuer adipiscing elit, sed diam nonummy nibh euismod tincidunt ut laoreet dolore magna aliquam erat volutpat. Ut wisi enim ad minim veniam, quis nostrud exerci tation ullamcorper suscipit lobortis nisl ut aliquip ex ea commodo consequat. Duis autem vel elit, sed diam nonummy nibh euismod tincidunt ut laoreet dolore magna aliquam erat volutpat.

Ut wisi enim ad minim veniam, quis nostrud exerci tation ullamcorper suscipit lobortis nisl ut aliquip ex ea commodo

consequat. Duis autem vel eum iriure dolor in hendrerit in vulputate velit esseeum iriure dolor in hendrerit in vulputate velit esse molestie consequat, vel illum dolore eu feugiat nulla facilisis at vero eros et Nam liber tempor cum soluta nobis eleifend opquod mazim placerat facer possim assum commodo consequat. Ut wisi enim ad minim veniam, quis nostrud exerci tation.

Contact Christine Example: 987 654 3210 or name@emailaddressz.com

### SAMPLER PLAY!
*3028 Example Road*
*P.O. Box 1245, Your City, ST 12345-6789*
*Phone      987 654 3210*
*Fax        987 654 3210*
*E-mail     info@emailaddressz.com*
*Web        www.yourwebaddressz.com*

SAMPLER PLAY!
3028 Example Road
P.O. Box 1245
Your City, ST 12345-6789

U.S. POSTAGE
PAID
YOUR CITY, S

SANDRA EXAMPLE
SAMPLE

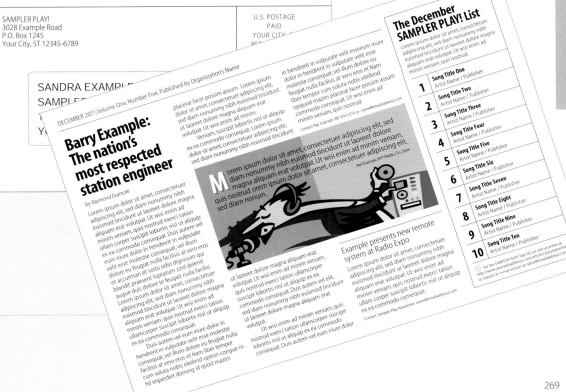

### The design grid

Both cards are based on the same four-column grid. (See *Step 11.2: Establish the Page Size and Grid*, page 187.)

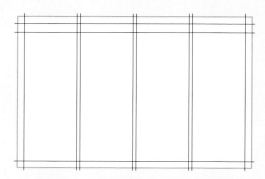

### The typefaces

On the first card, the word "Play!" matches the playful attitude of the jukebox illustration. The smooth, simple lines of the accompanying sans serif typefaces allow the illustrations to take the lead. The typefaces on the second card represent the businesslike end of the spectrum—an elegant script and a chiseled serif.

Myriad MM 700bd 300cn

**Typeface**
**AaBbEeGgKkMmQqRrSsWw!?**

Space Toaster

**TYPEFACE**
AaBbEEGgKkMmQqRRSsWw!?

Bickham Script

*Typeface*
*AaBbEeGgKkMm2qRrS*

Copperplate 33BC

**TYPEFACE**
**AABBEEGGKKMMQQR**

Minion Condensed

Typeface
AaBbEeGgKkMmQqRrSsWw!?

Franklin Gothic Book Condensed

Typeface
AaBbEeGgKkMmQqRrSsWw!?

### The illustrations

Like the typefaces, the illustrations represent two very different approaches. Bold, distinct shapes and bright colors give the jukebox and engineer illustrations a sense of humor. The unique, complex collages of technology and money do justice to the formal nature of The Sampler Fund card.

## DISTINGUISHING FEATURES

### Invite the reader back

A sensitive business person doesn't call a client or prospect on the phone and expect them to drop everything that moment to talk. They ask, "Do you have a minute?" A sensitive designer does the same thing. Instead of assuming a reader will drop everything the moment your newsletter arrives, include some at-a-glance elements that will convince them to return—a headline that promises a significant benefit, the results of a survey, a diagram, or, as in this case, a checklist.

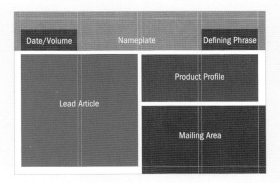

### Make it look and feel like a newsletter

Remember, when you create a postcard newsletter, you will be presenting information in a way readers are used to seeing in another form—8.5 by 11 inches with multiple pages. For that reason, it pays to make your postcard look something like a conventional newsletter. Label it as a "NEWSLETTER," include a conventional nameplate with a defining phrase, and be sure to include a date and volume/issue numbers. Write your copy in news form—who, what, where, when, and why. And save the hard selling for other materials—make your newsletter equally as interesting to someone who does not plan to buy your product, service, or idea.

### Follow mailing guidelines and regulations

Before you print anything intended to be mailed without an envelope, show a mockup of what you plan to print to the mailing experts at your local post office. Mailing regulations change, instructions are misinterpreted, something is left out, the size is half an inch too large to qualify for a preferred rate. Confirming your newsletter meets postal regulations can save you lots of time and money.

DECEMBER 20??, Volume One, Number Five, Published by Organization's Name

# What you need to know about the new Digital QRD audio standard

*by Christine Example*

Lorem ipsum dolor sit amet, consectetuer adipiscing elit, sed diam nonummy nibh euismod tincidunt ut laoreet dolore magna aliquam erat volutpat. Ut wisi enim ad minim veniam, quis nostrud exerci tation ullam corper suscipit lobortis nisl ut aliquip ex ea commodo consequat. Duis autem vel eum iriure dolor in hendrerit in vulputate velit esse molestie consequat, vel illum dolore eu feugiat nulla facilisis at vero eros et accumsan et iusto odio dignissim qui blandit praesent luptatum zzril delenit augue duis dolore te feugait nulla facilisi. Lorem ipsum dolor sit amet, consectetuer adipiscing elit, sed diam nonummy nibh euismod tincidunt ut laoreet dolore magna aliquam erat volutpat. Ut wisi enim ad minim veniam, quis nostrud exerci tation ullamcorper suscipit lobortis nisl ut aliquip ex ea commodo consequat.

Duis autem vel eum iriure dolor in hendrerit in vulputate velit esse molestie consequat, vel illum dolore eu feugiat nulla facilisis at vero eros et Nam liber tempor cum soluta nobis eleifend option congue nihil imperdiet doming id quod mazim

placerat facer possim assum. Lorem ipsum dolor sit amet, consectetuer adipiscing elit, sed diam nonummy nibh euismod tincidunt ut laoreet dolore magna aliquam erat volutpat. Ut wisi enim ad minim veniam, suscipit lobortis nisl ut aliquip ex ea commodo consequat.

Lorem ipsum dolor sit amet, consectetuer adipiscing elit, sed diam nonummy nibh euismod tincidunt ut laoreet dolore magna aliquam erat volutpat. Ut wisi enim ad minim veniam, quis nostrud exerci tation ullamcorper suscipit lobortis nisl ut aliquip ex ea commodo consequat. Duis autem vel elit, sed diam nonummy nibh euismod tincidunt ut laoreet dolore magna aliquam erat volutpat.

Ut wisi enim ad minim veniam, quis nostrud exerci tation ullamcorper suscipit lobortis nisl ut aliquip ex ea commodo

consequat. Duis autem vel eum iriure dolor in hendrerit in vulputate velit esseeum iriure dolor in hendrerit in vulputate velit esse molestie consequat, vel illum dolore eu feugiat nulla facilisis at vero eros et Nam liber tempor cum soluta nobis eleifend opquod mazim placerat facer possim assum commodo consequat. Ut wisi enim ad minim veniam, quis nostrud exerci tation.

Contact Christine Example 987 654 3210 or name@emailaddressz.com

**SAMPLER PLAY!**
*3028 Example Road*
*P.O. Box 1245, Your City, ST 12345-6789*
*Phone*     987 654 3210
*Fax*        987 654 3210
*E-mail*    info@emailaddressz.com
*Web*       www.yourwebaddressz.com

**SAMPLER PLAY!**

N E W S L E T T E R

**News, Views, and Resources for Audio Engineers**

MISSION: Lorem ipsum dolor sit amet, consectetuer adipiscing elit, sed diam nonummy nibh euismod tincidunt ut laoreet dolore magna aliquam erat volutpat. Ut wisi enim ad minim veniam, quis nostrud exerci tation ullamcorper suscipit lobortis nisl ut aliquip ex ea commodo.

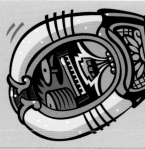

SAMPLER PLAY!
3028 Example Road
P.O. Box 1245
Your City, ST 12345-6789

U.S. POSTAGE
PAID
YOUR CITY, ST
PERMIT NO. ???
ZIP CODE 98765

SANDRA EXAMPLE
SAMPLER CORPORATION
123 EXAMPLE BOULEVARD STE 200
YOUR CITY ST  12345 6789

## The December SAMPLER PLAY! List

Lorem ipsum dolor sit amet, consectetuer adipiscing elit, sed diam nonummy nibh euismod tincidunt ut laoreet dolore magna aliquam erat volutpat. Ut wisi enim ad minim veniam, quis nostrud.

| | |
|---|---|
| 1 | **Song Title One** <br> Artist Name / Publisher |
| 2 | **Song Title Two** <br> Artist Name / Publisher |
| 3 | **Song Title Three** <br> Artist Name / Publisher |
| 4 | **Song Title Four** <br> Artist Name / Publisher |
| 5 | **Song Title Five** <br> Artist Name / Publisher |
| 6 | **Song Title Six** <br> Artist Name / Publisher |
| 7 | **Song Title Seven** <br> Artist Name / Publisher |
| 8 | **Song Title Eight** <br> Artist Name / Publisher |
| 9 | **Song Title Nine** <br> Artist Name / Publisher |
| 10 | **Song Title Ten** <br> Artist Name / Publisher |

DECEMBER 2077, Volume One, Number Five, Published by Organization's Name

## Barry Example: The nation's most respected station engineer

by Raymond Example

Lorem ipsum dolor sit amet, consectetuer adipiscing elit, sed diam nonummy nibh euismod tincidunt ut laoreet dolore magna aliquam erat volutpat. Ut wisi enim ad minim veniam, quis nostrud exerci tation ullam corper suscipit lobortis nisl ut aliquip ex ea commodo consequat. Duis autem vel eum iriure dolor in hendrerit in vulputate velit esse molestie consequat, vel illum dolore eu feugiat nulla facilisi at vero eros et accumsan et iusto odio dignissim qui blandit praesent luptatum zzril delenit augue duis dolore te feugait nulla facilisi. Lorem ipsum dolor sit amet, consectetuer adipiscing elit, sed diam nonummy nibh euismod tincidunt ut laoreet dolore magna aliquam erat volutpat. Ut wisi enim ad minim veniam, quis nostrud exerci tation ullamcorper suscipit lobortis nisl ut aliquip ex ea commodo consequat.

Duis autem vel eum iriure dolor in hendrerit in vulputate velit esse molestie consequat, vel illum dolore eu feugiat nulla facilisis at vero eros et Nam liber tempor cum soluta nobis eleifend option congue nihil imperdiet doming id quod mazim

placerat facer possim assum. Lorem ipsum dolor sit amet, consectetuer adipiscing elit, sed diam nonummy nibh euismod tincidunt ut laoreet dolore magna aliquam erat volutpat. Ut wisi enim ad minim.

Veniam, suscipit lobortis nisl ut aliquip ex ea commodo consequat. Lorem ipsum dolor sit amet, consectetuer adipiscing elit, sed diam nonummy nibh euismod tincidunt

in hendrerit in vulputate velit esseeum iriure dolor in hendrerit in vulputate velit esse molestie consequat, vel illum dolore eu feugiat nulla facilisis at vero eros et Nam liber tempor cum soluta nobis eleifend oopquod mazim placerat facer possim assum commodo consequat. Ut wisi enim ad minim veniam, quis nostrud.

**M**orem ipsum dolor sit amet, consectetuer adipiscing elit, sed diam nonummy nibh euismod tincidunt ut laoreet dolore magna aliquam erat volutpat. Ut wisi enim ad minim veniam, quis nostrud. orem ipsum dolor sit amet, consectetuer adipiscing elit, sed diam nonum.

Red Example: WTP/Radio, City, State

Contact Ray Example: 987-654-3210 or name@emailaddresss.com

Example presents new remote system at Radio Expo

Lorem ipsum dolor sit amet, consectetuer adipiscing elit, sed diam nonummy nibh euismod tincidunt ut laoreet dolore magna aliquam erat volutpat. Ut wisi enim ad minim veniam, quis nostrud exerci tation ullam corper suscipit lobortis nisl ut aliquip ex ea commodo consequat.

ut laoreet dolore magna aliquam erat volutpat. Ut wisi enim ad minim veniam, quis nostrud exerci tation ullamcorper suscipit lobortis nisl ut aliquip ex ea commodo consequat. Duis autem vel elit, sed diam nonummy nibh euismod tincidunt ut laoreet dolore magna volutpat.

Ut wisi enim ad minim veniam, quis nostrud exerci tation ullamcorper suscipit lobortis nisl ut aliquip ex ea commodo consequat. Duis autem vel eum iriure dolor

Contact Sampler Play, Newsletter name@emailaddresss.com

---

### Front (page 1)

**1** "Sampler" Myriad MM, 700bd, 300cn, 24pt, align center; "play!" Space Toaster, 80pt, align center; "NEWSLETTER" Franklin Gothic Book Condensed, 8/9pt, align center; Defining phrase Myriad MM, 700bd, 300cn, 11/12pt, align center; Text Myriad MM, 250wt, 500wd, 9/10pt, align left; **2** Date Myriad MM, 250wt, 500wd, 9pt, align left; Line .5pt;

**3** Headline, large Myriad MM, 700bd, 300cn, 24/22pt, align left; Contributor Myriad MM Italic, 250wt, 500wd, 8pt, align left; Text Myriad MM, 250wt, 500wd, 9/10pt, align left; **4** Line .5pt; Contact link headline Myriad MM, 700bd, 300cn, 9pt, align left; Contact link text Myriad MM Italic, 250wt, 500wd, 9/10pt, align left; Copyright Myriad MM, 250wt, 500wd, 6pt, align left; **5** Line .5pt; Return address Myriad MM, 250wt, 500wd, 8/8pt, align left; **6** Label address Arial, 10/10pt, align left; Postage indicia Myriad MM, 250wt, 500wd, 7/6pt, align center; Line .5pt

### Back (page 2)

**7** Date Myriad MM, 250wt, 500wd, 9pt, align left; Line .5pt; **8** Headline, large Myriad MM, 700bd, 300cn, 24/22pt, align left; Contributor Myriad MM Italic, 250wt, 500wd, 8pt, align left; Text Myriad MM, 250wt, 500wd, 9/10pt, align left; Contact link Myriad MM, 250wt, 500wd, 6pt, align left; **9** Drop cap Myriad MM, 700bd, 300cn, 40pt, align left; Illustration text Myriad MM, 250wt, 500wd, 11/11pt, align left; Credit Myriad MM, 250wt, 500wd, 6pt, align right; **10** Headline, small Myriad MM, 250wt, 500wd, 12/12pt, align left; Text Myriad MM, 250wt, 500wd, 9/10pt, align left; **11** Line .5pt; Checklist headline Myriad MM, 700bd, 300cn, 18/16pt, align left; Checklist text Myriad MM, 250wt, 500wd, 8/9pt, align left; Number Myriad MM, 700bd, 300cn, 18pt, align center; Checklist title Myriad MM, 700bd, 300cn, 9pt, align left; Checklist Author Myriad MM, 250wt, 500wd, 9pt, align left; Contact link text Myriad MM, 250wt, 500wd, 6/6pt, align left;

### Color

Printed in four-color process (Step 11.6) using values of cyan, magenta, yellow, and black (CMYK) as defined on the color palette below. Actual color will vary.

### Front (page 3)

**12** "THE" Copperplate Gothic 33BC, 14pt, align left; "Sampler" Bickham Script, 65pt, align center; "FUND" Copperplate Gothic 33BC, 60pt, align center; "NEWSLETTER" Franklin Gothic Book Condensed, 8pt, align center; **13** Date/defining phrase Myriad MM, 250wt, 500wd, 8/9pt, align left; **14** Contact link Myriad MM Italic, 250wt, 500wd, 8/9pt, align left; **15** Line .5pt; Headline Minion, 18/17pt, align left; Contributor Minion Condensed Italic, 8pt, align left; Text Minion Condensed, 9/10pt, align left; **16** Line .5pt; Contact link Myriad MM, 250wt, 500wd, 6/7pt, align left; **17** Return address Myriad MM, 250wt, 500wd, 7/8pt, align left; **18** Label address Arial, 10/10pt, align left; Postage indicia Myriad MM, 250wt, 500wd, 7/6pt, align center; Line .5pt

### Back (page 4)

**19** Line .5pt; Headline Minion, 18/17pt, align left; Contributor Minion Condensed, 8pt, align left; Text Minion Condensed, 9/10pt, align left; Contact link Myriad MM, 250wt, 500wd, 6/7pt, align left; **20** Copyright Myriad MM, 250wt, 500wd, 6pt, align left; **21** Line .5pt

### Color

Printed in four-color process (Step 11.6) using values of cyan, magenta, yellow, and black (CMYK) as defined on the color palette below. Actual color will vary.

SOURCE Illustrations: Technology collage (pg. 3), Money collage (pg. 4) from Encore Images Ltd., +44 (0) 1372 220 390, www.en-core.net. © Encore Images Ltd., all rights reserved. Supreme Court (pg. 4) from *Destinations: Washington D.C.* from Digital Stock/Corbis, 800-260-0444, www.corbisimages.com. © Corbis, all rights reserved.

SOURCE Type Families: Arial, Copperplate, Minion, Myriad, Adobe Systems, Inc. 800-682-3623, www.adobe.com/type.

## High court to rule on critical investment issue

*by Martin Example*

Lorem ipsum dolor sit amet, consectetuer adipiscing elit, sed diam nonummy nibh euismod tincidunt ut laoreet dolore magna aliquam erat volutpat. Ut wisi enim ad minim veniam, quis nostrud exerci tation ullam corper suscipit lobortis nisl ut aliquip ex ea commodo consequat. Duis autem vel eum iriure dolor in hendrerit in vulputate velit esse molestie consequat, vel illum dolore eu feugiat nulla facilisis at vero eros et accumsan et iusto odio dignissim qui blandit praesent luptatum zzril delenit augue duis dolore te feugait nulla.

Contact Martin Example: 987 654 3210 or name@emailaddress2.com

## Home products–oriented prospectus to debut in 20?:

*by Daniel Example*

Ut wisi enim ad minim veniam, quis nostrud exerci tation ullam corper suscipit lobortis nisl ut aliquip ex ea commodo consequat. Duis autem vel eum iriure dolor in hendrerit in vulputate velit esse molestie consequat, vel illum dolore eu feugiat nulla facilisis at vero eros et accumsan et iusto odio dignissim qui blandit praesent luptatum zzril delenit augue duis dolore te feugait nulla facilisi. Lorem ipsum dolor sit amet, consectetuer adipiscing elit, sed diam nonummy nibh euismod tincidunt ut laoreet dolore magna aliquam erat volutpat.

Contact Daniel Example: 987 654 3210 or name@emailaddress2.com

## Minimize new year portfolio surprises

*by Daniel Example*

Ut wisi enim ad minim veniam, quis nostrud exerci tation ullam corper suscipit lobortis nisl ut aliquip ex ea commodo consequat. Duis autem vel eum iriure dolor in hendrerit in vulputate velit esse molestie consequat, vel illum dolore eu feugiat nulla facilisis at vero eros et accumsan et iusto odio dignissim qui blandit praesent luptatum zzril delenit augue

Contact Tom Example: 987 654 3210 or name@emailaddress2.com

## The best international funds are often managed domestically

*by Toni Example*

Lorem ipsum dolor sit amet, consectetuer adipiscing elit, sed diam nonummy nibh euismod tincidunt ut laoreet dolore magna aliquam erat volutpat. Ut wisi enim ad minim veniam, quis nostrud exerci tation ullamcorper suscipit lobortis nisl ut aliquip ex ea commodo consequat. Duis autem vel eum iriure dolor in hendrerit in vulputate velit esse molestie consequat, vel illum dolore eu feugiat nulla

facilisis at vero eros et Nam liber tempor cum soluta nobis eleifend option congue nihil imperdiet doming id quod mazim placerat facer possim assum. Lorem ipsum dolor sit amet, consectetuer adipiscing elit, sed diam nonummy nibh euismod tincidunt ut laoreet dolore magna aliquam erat volutpat. Ut wisi enim ad minim veniam, suscipit lobortis nisl ut aliquip ex ea commodo consequat.

Ut wisi enim ad minim veniam, quis nostrud exerci tation ullamcorper suscipit lobortis nisl ut aliquip ex ea commodo consequat. Lorem ipsum dolor sit amet, consectetuer adipiscing elit, sed diam nonummy nibh euismod tincidunt ut laoreet dolore magna aliquam erat volutpat. Ut wisi enim ad minim veniam, quis nostru.

duis dolore te feugait nulla facilisi. Lorem ipsum dolor sit amet, consectetuer adipiscing elit, sed diam nonummy nibh euismod tincidunt ut laoreet dolore magna aliquam erat volutpat. Ut wisi enim ad minim veniam, quis nostrud exerci tation ullamcorper suscipit lobortis nisl ut aliquip ex ea commodo consequat.

Fourth Quarter, Volume Two
The thinking behind the action

# THE *Sampler*

# FUND
### N E W S L E T T E R

## How to read between the lines of an annual report

*by Christine Example*

Lorem ipsum dolor sit amet, consectetuer adipiscing elit, sed diam nonummy nibh euismod tincidunt ut laoreet dolore magna aliquam erat volutpat. Ut wisi enim ad minim veniam, quis nostrud exerci tation ullam corper suscipit lobortis nisl ut aliquip ex ea commodo consequat. Duis autem vel eum iriure dolor in hendrerit in vulputate velit esse molestie consequat, vel illum dolore eu feugiat nulla facilisis at vero eros et accumsan et iusto odio dignissim qui blandit praesent luptatum zzril delenit augue duis dolore te feugait nulla facilisi. Lorem ipsum dolor sit amet, consectetuer adipiscing elit, sed diam nonummy nibh euismod tincidunt ut laoreet dolore magna aliquam erat volutpat. Ut wisi enim ad minim veniam, quis nostrud exerci tation ullamcorper suscipit lobortis nisl ut aliquip ex ea commodo consequat.

Duis autem vel eum iriure dolor in hendrerit in vulputate velit esse molestie consequat, vel illum dolore eu feugiat nulla

facilisis at vero eros et Nam liber tempor cum soluta nobis eleifend option congue nihil imperdiet doming id quod mazim placerat facer possim assum. Lorem ipsum dolor sit amet, consectetuer adipiscing elit, sed diam nonummy nibh euismod tincidunt ut laoreet dolore magna aliquam erat volutpat. Ut wisi enim ad minim veniam, suscipit lobortis nisl ut aliquip ex ea commodo consequat.

Ut wisi enim ad minim veniam, quis nostrud exerci tation ullamcorper suscipit lobortis nisl ut aliquip ex ea commodo consequat.

1. Duis autem vel eum iriure dolor in hendrerit in vulputate velit dolor.

2. Hendrerit in vulputate velit esse molestie consequat, vel illum dolore eu feugiat.

3. Facilisis at vero eros et nam liber tempor soluta nobis eleifend opquod mazim.

Lorem ipsum dolor sit amet, consectetuer adipiscing elit, sed diam nonummy nibh euismod tincidunt ut laoreet dolore magna aliquam erat volutpat. Ut wisi enim ad minim veniam, quis nostrud exerci tation ullam corper suscipit lobortis nisl ut.

## Guide to year-end tax statements

*by James Example*

Ut wisi enim ad minim veniam, quis nostrud exerci tation ullam corper suscipit lobortis nisl ut aliquip ex ea commodo consequat. Duis autem vel eum iriure dolor in hendrerit in vulputate velit esse molestie consequat, vel illum dolore eu feugiat nulla facilisis at vero eros et accumsan et iusto odio dignissim qui blandit praesent luptatum zzril delenit augue

duis dolore te feugait nulla facilisi. Lorem ipsum dolor sit amet, consectetuer adipiscing elit, sed diam nonummy nibh euismod tincidunt ut laoreet dolore magna aliquam erat volutpat. Ut wisi enim ad minim veniam, quis nostrud exerci tation ullamcorper suscipit lobortis nisl ut aliquip ex ea commodo consequat.

Duis autem vel eum iriure dolor in hendrerit in vulputate velit esse molestie consequat, vel illum dolore eu feugiat nulla.

Contact Christine Example 987 654 3210 or
name@emailaddressz.com

Phone    987 654 3210
Fax       987 654 3210
E-mail    info@emailaddressz.com
Web       www.yourwebaddressz.com

Contact James Example 987 654 3210 or
name@emailaddressz.com

THE SAMPLER FUND
3028 Example Road
P.O. Box 1245
Your City, ST 12345-6789

U.S. POSTAGE
PAID
YOUR CITY, ST
PERMIT NO. ???
ZIP CODE 98765

SANDRA EXAMPLE
SAMPLER CORPORATION
123 EXAMPLE BOULEVARD STE 200
YOUR CITY ST  12345 6789

STYLE 10 (8 PAGES)

# Squared

Grids establish boundaries. You can view that as confining or liberating. Liberating because boundaries free you from having to remake basic design decisions, page after page, that a grid establishes. Instead, a grid such as this allows you to devote your energy to improving the quality of the elements placed within it—the ideas, the writing, and how each is illustrated.

The repeated square shape used in the nameplate, text boxes, and many of the photographs becomes the second primary design element. You can increase or decrease the size of the squares, or place squares beside or on top of each other, but the square remains the theme.

SAMPLER **GOV. NEWSLINE**

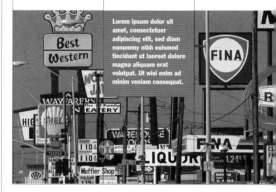

6     NOVEMBER 20??     **GOV. NEWSLINE**

CITY/STATE

## Taking the next generation of business underground

By Jeffrey Example

Lorem ipsum dolor sit amet, consectetuer adipiscing elit, sed diam nonummy nibh euismod tincidunt ut laoreet dolore magna aliquam erat volutpat. Ut wisi enim ad minim veniam, quis nostrud exerci tation ullam corper suscipit lobortis nisl ut aliquip ex ea commodo consequat.

Duis autem vel eum iriure dolor in hendrerit in vulputate velit esse molestie consequat, vel illum dolore eu feugiat nulla facilisis at vero eros et accumsan et iusto odio dignissim qui blandit praesent luptatum zzril delenit augue

duis dolore te feugait nulla facilisi.

Lorem ipsum dolor sit amet, consectetuer adipiscing elit, sed diam nonummy nibh euismod tincidunt ut laoreet dolore magna aliquam erat volutpat. Ut wisi enim ad minim veniam, quis nostrud exerci tation ullamcorper suscipit lobortis nisl ut aliquip ex ea commodo consequat. Duis autem vel eum iriure dolor in hendrerit in vulputate velit esse molestie consequat, vel illum dolore eu feugiat nulla facilisis at vero eros et Nam liber tempor cum soluta nobis eleifend option congue nihil imperdiet doming id quod mazim placerat facer possim assum.

Lorem ipsum dolor sit amet, consectetuer adipiscing elit, sed diam nonummy nibh euismod tincidunt ut laoreet dolore magna aliquam erat volutpat. Ut wisi enim ad

minim veniam, quis nostrud exerci tation ullamcorper suscipit lobortis nisl ut aliquip ex ea commodo consequat. Lore ipsum dolor sit amet, consectetuer adipiscing elit, sed diam nonummy nibh euismo tincidunt ut laoreet dolore

**Questions or comments about Sampler GOV. Newsline? Contact Rache Example, our community and Public Affairs Coordinator. Call 987 654 3210 or e-mail name@ emailaddressz.com**

magna aliquam erat volutpat Ut wisi enim ad minim veniam, quis nostrud exerci tation ullamcorper suscipit lobortis nisl ut aliquip ex ea commodo consequat. Duis

Lorem ipsum dolor sit amet, consectetuer adipiscing elit, sed diam nonummy nibh euismod tincidunt ut laoreet dolore magna aliquam erat volutpat. Ut wisi enim ad minim veniam consequat.

Best Western

FINA

**Page flow**
Two 17 by 11 inch sheets (landscape) are folded to 8.5 by 11 inches and are saddle-stitched.

## What you need

General layout and design requires a desktop publishing program. Editing photographic images requires a digital imaging program. Dividing and reassembling the parts and pieces of vector clip art images and type requires a drawing program. (See *Step 7: Choose Your Tools*, page 176.)

SAMPLER

# GOV. NEWSLINE

The latest news and information from Sampler GOV. Newsline— a nationwide network of people, places, and resources

CITY/STATE

## A most unusual day for a very uncommon man

By Martin Example

Lorem ipsum dolor sit amet, consectetuer adipiscing elit, sed diam nonummy nibh euismod tincidunt ut laoreet dolore magna aliquam erat volutpat. Ut wisi enim ad minim veniam, quis nostrud exerci tation ullam corper suscipit lobortis nisl ut aliquip ex ea commodo consequat. Duis autem vel eum iriure dolor in hendrerit in vulputate velit esse molestie consequat, vel illum dolore eu feugiat nulla facilisis at vero eros et accumsan et iusto odio dignissim qui blandit praesent luptatum zzril delenit augue duis dolore te feugait nulla facilisi.

Lorem ipsum dolor sit amet, consectetuer adipiscing elit, sed diam nonummy nibh euismod tincidunt ut laoreet dolore magna aliquam erat volutpat. Ut wisi enim ad minim veniam, quis nostrud exerci tation ullamcorper suscipit lobortis nisl ut aliquip ex

**Robert Example and four-year-old Charles work side by side.**

ea commodo consequat. Duis autem vel eum iriure dolor in hendrerit in vulputate velit esse molestie consequat, vel illum dolore eu feugiat nulla facilisis at vero eros et Nam liber tempor cum soluta nobis eleifend option congue nihil imperdiet doming id quod mazim placerat facer possim assum.

Lorem ipsum dolor sit amet, consectetuer adipiscing elit, sed diam nonummy nibh euismod tincidunt ut laoreet dolore magna aliquam erat volutpat. Ut wisi enim ad

minim veniam, quis nostrud exerci tation ullamcorper suscipit lobortis nisl ut aliquip ex ea commodo consequat. Lorem ipsum dolor sit amet, consectetuer adipiscing elit, sed diam nonummy nibh euismod tincidunt ut laoreet dolore magna aliquam erat volutpat. Ut wisi enim ad minim veniam, quis nostrud exerci tation ullamcorper suscipit lobortis nisl ut aliquip ex ea commodo consequat. Vel illum dolore eu feugiat nullas.

Contact Martin Example: 987 654 3210 or name@emailaddressz.com; More: http://www.yourwebaddressz.com/articles/storyname.htm

**November proPle:** When Mike Example told his wife Jenny he thought they should ride cross-country on an antique motorcycle, she thought he must have been kidding. He wasn't.

Lorem ipsum dolor sit amet, consectetuer adipiscing elit, sed diam nonummy nibh euismod tincidunt ut laoreet dolore magna aliquam erat volutpat. Ut wisi enim ad minim veniam, quis nostrud exerci tation ullam corper suscipit lobortis nisl ut aliquip ex ea commodo consequat. Duis autem vel eum iriure dolor in hendrerit in vulputate velit esse molestie consequat, vel illum dolore eu feugiat.

continued on page 4

### The design grid

This grid is different than some of the others in that the space below the area that holds the page numbers and nameplate are also divided into five square vertical columns. The result allows you to stack five illustrations and/or text boxes, as shown on page 5 of the example. (See *Step 11.2: Establish the Page Size and Grid,* page 187.)

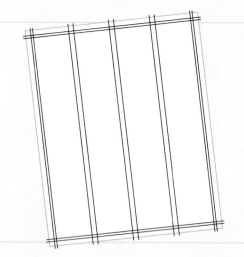

### The typefaces

**Giza** is a typeface with a big personality, so it grabs lots of attention. The smooth, simple sans serif **Franklin Gothic** headlines allow the nameplate and the photographs to take center stage. The serif text face, **Minion,** adds an air of elegance.

Giza Seven Seven

# **Typeface**
**AaBbEeGgKkMmQq**

Minion

# Typeface
AaBbEeGgKkMmQqRrSsWw!?

Franklin Gothic Condensed

# **Typeface**
**AaBbEeGgKkMmQqRrSsWw!**

Franklin Gothic Book Condensed

# Typeface
AaBbEeGgKkMmQqRrSsWw!?

Minion

Text Lorem ipsum dolor sit amet, consectetuer adipiscing elit, sed diam nonummy nibh euismod tincidunt ut laoreet dolore magna aliquam erat volutpat. Ut wisi enim ad minim veniam, quis nostrud exerci tation ullamcorper suscipit lobortis nisl ut aliquip ex ea.

### The illustrations

This recipe contrasts photographs, which by nature are visually complex, with the simplicity of bold symbols.

## DISTINGUISHING FEATURES

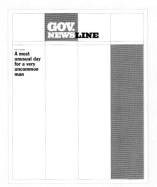

### Add a color to your style

Choosing and repeating a distinctive color can contribute to establishing a style for your organization. Supporting a well-conceived message with the consistent use of colors, typefaces, and style of illustration helps readers to recognize you amid the din of everyday dealings.

### Focus on the essence of your illustration

Cropping, the act of eliminating certain parts of an illustration, helps you get to the heart of it. Instead of the typical high-school-yearbook head and shoulders pose, move closer to the subject and eliminate distracting background information.

### Keep information confidential

The back cover of this newsletter does not include a mailing area. Some publications include information you don't want to share with anyone but the subscriber. Some are distributed within an organization by other means. Plus, enclosing your newsletter in an envelope allows you to include other material such as a cover letter, a product flyer, a coupon, a return envelope for a survey, and so on.

NOVEMBER 20??  SAMPLER

# GOV. NEWSLINE

The latest news and information from Sampler GOV. Newsline—a nationwide network of people, places, and resources

**Robert Example and four-year-old Charles work side by side.**

## CITY/STATE

# A most unusual day for a very uncommon man

By Martin Example

Lorem ipsum dolor sit amet, consectetuer adipiscing elit, sed diam nonummy nibh euismod tincidunt ut laoreet dolore magna aliquam erat volutpat. Ut wisi enim ad minim veniam, quis nostrud exerci tation ullam corper suscipit lobortis nisl ut aliquip ex ea commodo consequat. Duis autem vel eum iriure dolor in hendrerit in vulputate velit esse molestie consequat, vel illum dolore eu feugiat nulla facilisis at vero eros et accumsan et iusto odio dignissim qui blandit praesent luptatum zzril delenit augue duis dolore te feugait nulla facilisi.

Lorem ipsum dolor sit amet, consectetuer adipiscing elit, sed diam nonummy nibh euismod tincidunt ut laoreet dolore magna aliquam erat volutpat. Ut wisi enim ad minim veniam, quis nostrud exerci tation ullamcorper suscipit lobortis nisl ut aliquip ex

ea commodo consequat. Duis autem vel eum iriure dolor in hendrerit in vulputate velit esse molestie consequat, vel illum dolore eu feugiat nulla facilisis at vero eros et Nam liber tempor cum soluta nobis eleifend option congue nihil imperdiet doming id quod mazim placerat facer possim assum.

Lorem ipsum dolor sit amet, consectetuer adipiscing elit, sed diam nonummy nibh euismod tincidunt ut laoreet dolore magna aliquam erat volutpat. Ut wisi enim ad

minim veniam, quis nostrud exerci tation ullamcorper suscipit lobortis nisl ut aliquip ex ea commodo consequat. Lorem ipsum dolor sit amet, consectetuer adipiscing elit, sed diam nonummy nibh euismod tincidunt ut laoreet dolore magna aliquam erat volutpat. Ut wisi enim ad minim veniam, quis nostrud exerci tation ullamcorper suscipit lobortis nisl ut aliquip ex ea commodo consequat. Vel illum dolore eu feugiat nullas.

Contact Martin Example: 987 654 3210 or name@emailaddressz.com; More: http://www.yourwebaddressz.com/articles/storyname.htm

**November proPle: When Mike Example told his wife Jenny he thought they should ride cross-country on an antique motorcycle, she thought he must have been kidding. He wasn't.**

Lorem ipsum dolor sit amet, consectetuer adipiscing elit, sed diam nonummy nibh euismod tincidunt ut laoreet dolore magna aliquam erat volutpat. Ut wisi enim ad minim veniam, quis nostrud exerci tation ullam corper suscipit lobortis nisl ut aliquip ex ea commodo consequat. Duis autem vel eum iriure dolor in hendrerit in vulputate velit esse molestie consequat, vel illum dolore eu feugiat.

continued on page 4

Within the mockup:

6   NOVEMBER 20??   **GOV. NEWSLINE**

The latest news and information from Sampler GOV. Newsline

CITY/STATE

**Taking the next generation of business underground**

By Jeffrey Example

Lorem ipsum dolor sit amet, consectetuer adipiscing elit, sed diam nonummy nibh euismod tincidunt ut laoreet dolore magna aliquam erat volutpat. Ut wisi enim ad minim veniam, quis nostrud exerci tation ullam corper suscipit lobortis nisl ut aliquip ex ea commodo consequat.

Duis autem vel eum iriure dolor in hendrerit in vulputate velit esse molestie consequat, vel illum dolore eu feugiat nulla facilisis at vero eros et accumsan et iusto odio dignissim qui blandit praesent luptatum zzril delenit augue

duis dolore te feugait nulla facilisi.

Lorem ipsum dolor sit amet, consectetuer adipiscing elit, sed diam nonummy nibh euismod tincidunt ut laoreet dolore magna aliquam erat volutpat. Ut wisi enim ad minim veniam, quis nostrud exerci tation ullamcorper suscipit lobortis nisl ut aliquip ex ea commodo consequat. Duis autem vel eum iriure dolor in hendrerit in vulputate velit esse molestie consequat, vel illum dolore eu feugiat nulla facilisis at vero eros et Nam liber tempor cum soluta nobis eleifend option congue nihil imperdiet doming id quod mazim placerat facer possim assum.

Lorem ipsum dolor sit amet, consectetuer adipiscing elit, sed diam nonummy nibh euismod tincidunt ut laoreet dolore magna aliquam erat volutpat. Ut wisi enim ad

**Questions or comments about Sampler GOV. Newsline? Contact Rachel Example, our community and Public Affairs Coordinator. Call 987 654 3210 or e-mail name@emailaddressz.com**

minim veniam, quis nostrud exerci tation ullamcorper suscipit lobortis nisl ut aliquip ex ea commodo consequat. Lorem ipsum dolor sit amet, consectetuer adipiscing elit, sed diam nonummy nibh euismod tincidunt ut laoreet dolore

magna aliquam erat volutpat. Ut wisi enim ad minim veniam, quis nostrud exerci tation ullamcorper suscipit lobortis nisl ut aliquip ex ea commodo consequat. Duis

autem vel elit, sed diam nonummy nibh euismod tincidunt ut laoreet dolore magna aliquam erat volutpat.

Ut wisi enim ad minim veniam, quis nostrud exerci tation ullamcorper suscipit lobortis nisl ut aliquip ex ea commodo consequat. Duis autem vel eum iriure dolor in hendrerit in vulputate velit esseeum iriure dolor in hendrerit in vulputate velit esse molestie consequat, vel illum dolore eu feugiat nulla facilisis at vero eros et Nam liber tempor cum soluta nobis eleifend opquod mazim placerat facer possim assum commodo consequat. Lorem ipsum dolor sit amet, consectetuer adipiscing elit, sed diam nonummy nibh euismod tincidunt ut laoreet dolore magna aliquam erat volutpat.

Contact Jeffrey Example: 987 654 3210 or name@emailaddressz.com; More: http://www.yourwebaddressz.com/articles/storyname.htm

**Lorem ipsum dolor sit amet, consectetuer adipiscing elit, sed diam nonummy nibh euismod tincidunt ut laoreet dolore magna aliquam erat volutpat. Ut wisi enim ad minim veniam consequat.**

8.5 W
11 H

---

---

## Cover (page 1)

**1** Date Franklin Gothic Book Condensed, 8/9pt, align right; Eyebrow Franklin Gothic Book Condensed, 9pt, align left; "GOV." Giza Seven Seven, 58pt, align center; "NEWSLINE" Giza Seven Seven, 38pt, align left; **2** Defining phrase Franklin Gothic Book Condensed, 9/12pt, align left; **3** Eyebrow Franklin Gothic Book Condensed, 9pt, align left; Headline, large Franklin Gothic Condensed, 24/23pt, align left; Contributor Franklin Gothic Book Condensed, 10pt, align left; Serif text Minion, 10/14pt, align left, Contact link Franklin Gothic Book Condensed, 8/9pt, align left; **4** Caption, large Franklin Gothic Condensed, 11/14pt, align left; **5** Headline, medium Franklin Gothic Condensed, 20/20pt, align left; Sans serif text Franklin Gothic Book Condensed, 10/14pt, align left; "continued" Franklin Gothic Book Condensed, 8pt, align left; **6** Lines .5pt

## Back Cover (page 8)

**7** Date Franklin Gothic Book Condensed, 9pt, align right; "GOV." Giza Seven Seven, 20pt, align center; "NEWSLINE" Giza Seven Seven, 13pt, align left; **8** Defining phrase Franklin Gothic Book Condensed, 9/12pt, align left; Page numbers Franklin Gothic Book Condensed, 9pt, align left or right; **9** Eyebrow Franklin Gothic Book Condensed, 9pt, align left; Headline, small Franklin Gothic Condensed, 18/18pt, align left; Contributor Franklin Gothic Book Condensed, 10pt, align left; Serif text Minion, 10/14pt, align left, Contact link Franklin Gothic Book Condensed, 8/9pt, align left; **10** Caption, large Franklin Gothic Condensed, 11/14pt, align left; **11** Caption, large Franklin Gothic Condensed, 11/14pt, align left; **12** Lines .5pt

## Color

To be printed in black and a solid PANTONE Color Ink as defined on the palette below (see *Step 9.3*). (Because this book is printed in process colors (CMYK), the illustration is only a simulation of the actual solid PANTONE Color).

## Pages 2 & 3

**13 Date** Franklin Gothic Book Condensed, 9pt, align right; **"GOV."** Giza Seven Seven, 20pt, align center; **"NEWSLINE"** Giza Seven Seven, 13pt, align left; **14 Page numbers** Franklin Gothic Book Condensed, 9pt, align left or right; **15 Eyebrow** Franklin Gothic Book Condensed, 9pt, align left; **Headline, small** Franklin Gothic Condensed, 18/18pt, align left; **Contributor** Franklin Gothic Book Condensed, 10pt, align left; **Serif text** Minion, 10/14pt, align left; **Contact link** Franklin Gothic Book Condensed, 8/9pt, align left; **16 Box eyebrow** Franklin Gothic Book Condensed, 9pt, align left; **Box text, large** Franklin Gothic Condensed, 18/26pt, align left; **Box, contributor** Franklin Gothic Book Condensed, 8pt, align right; **17 Box text, small** Franklin Gothic Condensed, 11/14pt, align left; **Box, contributor** Franklin Gothic Book Condensed, 8/9pt, align left; **18 Defining phrase** Franklin Gothic Book Condensed, 9/12pt, align left; **19 Caption, small** Franklin Gothic Condensed, 9/12pt, align left; **20 Lines** .5pt

## Pages 4 & 5

**21 Date** Franklin Gothic Book Condensed, 9pt, align right; **"GOV."** Giza Seven Seven, 20pt, align center; **"NEWSLINE"** Giza Seven Seven, 13pt, align left; **22 Page numbers** Franklin Gothic Book Condensed, 9pt, align left or right; **23 Eyebrow** Franklin Gothic Book Condensed, 9pt, align left; **Headline, small** Franklin Gothic Condensed, 18/18pt, align left; **Contributor** Franklin Gothic Book Condensed, 10pt, align left; **Serif text** Minion, 10/14pt, align left, **Contact link** Franklin Gothic Book Condensed, 8/9pt, align left; **24 Box eyebrow** Franklin Gothic Book Condensed, 9pt, align left; **Box text, large** Franklin Gothic Condensed, 18/18pt, align left; **25 Box text, small** Franklin Gothic Condensed, 9/12pt, align left; **26 Box text, small** Franklin Gothic Condensed, 11/14pt, align left; **Box, contributor** Franklin Gothic Book Condensed, 8/9pt, align left; **27 Caption, small** Franklin Gothic Condensed, 9/12pt, align left; **28 Box eyebrow** Franklin Gothic Book Condensed, 9pt, align left; **Box text, large** Franklin Gothic Condensed, 18/24pt, align left; **Box, contributor** Franklin Gothic Book Condensed, 8pt, align right; **29 Lines** .5pt

The latest news and information from Sampler GOV. Newsline

5

CITY/STATE
### How do we know it's right?
From yourwebaddressz.com

Lorem ipsum dolor sit amet, consectetuer adipiscing elit, sed diam nonummy nibh euismod tincidunt ut laoreet dolore magna aliquam erat volutpat. Ut wisi enim ad minim veniam, quis nostrud exerci tation ullam corper suscipit lobortis nisl ut aliquip ex ea commodo conseq. Duis autem vel eum iriure dolor in hendrerit in vulputate velit esse molestie consequat, vel illum dolore eu feugiat nulla facilisis at vero eros et accumsan et iusto odio dignissim qui blandit praesent luptatum zzril delenit augue duis dolore te feugait nulla facilisi.

Lorem ipsum dolor sit amet, consectetuer adipiscing elit, sed diam nonummy nibh euismod tincidunt ut laoreet dolore magna aliquam erat volutpat. Ut wisi enim ad minim veniam, quis nostrud exerci tation ullamcorper suscipit lobortis nisl ut aliquip ex ea commodo consequat. Duis autem vel eum iriure dolor in hendrerit in vulputate velit esse

Lorem ipsum dolor sit amet, consectetuer adipiscing elit, sed diam nonummy ut laoreet dolore.

molestie consequat, vel illum dolore eu feugiat nulla facilisis at vero eros et Nam liber tempor cum soluta nobis eleifend option congue nihil imperdiet doming id quod mazim placerat facer possim assum.

Lorem ipsum dolor sit amet, consectetuer adipiscing elit, sed diam nonummy nibh euismod tincidunt ut laoreet dolore magna aliquam erat volutpat. Ut wisi enim ad minim veniam, quis nostrud exerci tation ullamcorper suscipit lobortis nisl ut aliquip ex ea commodo consequat.

Lorem ipsum dolor sit amet, consectetuer adipiscing elit, sed diam nonummy nibh euismod tincidunt ut laoreet dolore magna aliquam erat volutpat. Nulla facilisis at vero eros et Nam liber tempor cum soluta nobis eleifend opquod mazim placerat facer possim assum commodo consequat Nulla facilisis at vero.

CITY/STATE
### John Example organizes the ultimate benePt tournament
By Greta Example

Lorem ipsum dolor sit amet, consectetuer adipiscing elit, sed diam nonummy nibh euismod tincidunt ut laoreet dolore magna aliquam erat volutpat. Ut wisi enim ad minim veniam, quis nostrud exerci tation ullam corper suscipit lobortis nisl ut aliquip ex ea commodo consequat.

Duis autem vel eum iriure

dolor in hendrerit in vulputate velit esse molestie consequat, vel illum dolore eu feugiat nulla facilisis at vero eros et nissim qui blandit praesent luptatum zzril delenit augue duis dolore te feugait nulla facilisi.

Lorem ipsum dolor sit amet, consectetuer adipiscing elit, sed diam nonummy nibh euismod tincidunt ut laoreet dolore magna aliquam erat volutpat.

Contact Greta Example: 987 654 3210 or name@emailaddressz.com; More; http://www.yourwebaddressz.com/articles/storyname.htm

WELL SAID
**"Research is an organized method of Pnding out what you are going to do when you can't keep on doing what you are doing now."**

Charles F. Kettering

---

GOV NEWSLINE
NOVEMBER 20??

CITY/STATE
### Taking the next generation of business underground
By James Example

Lorem ipsum dolor sit amet, consectetuer adipiscing elit, sed diam nonummy nibh euismod tincidunt ut laoreet dolore magna aliquam erat volutpat.

**"Ut wisi enim ad minim veniam, quis nostrud exerci tation ullam corper suscipit lobortis nisl ut aliquip ex ea commodo consequat, vel illum dolore eu feugiat nulla facilisis at vero eros et accumsan et iusto odio dignissim qui blandit praesent."**

Duis autem vel eum iriure dolor in hendrerit in vulputate velit esse molestie consequat.

CITY/STATE
### Taking the next generation of business underground
By Mark Example

Lorem ipsum dolor sit amet, consectetuer adipiscing elit, sed diam nonummy nibh euismod tincidunt ut laoreet dolore magna aliquam erat volutpat.

CITY/STATE
### Lisa Example organizes the ultimate benePt tournament
By Cindy Example

Lorem ipsum dolor sit amet, consectetuer adipiscing elit, sed diam nonummy nibh euismod tincidunt ut laoreet dolore magna aliquam erat volutpat.

**GOV. NEWSLINE**

CITY/STATE

# Celebrate a 75-year history of food, music, and great theatre

By Amanda Example

Lorem ipsum dolor sit amet, consectetuer adipiscing elit, sed diam nonummy nibh euismod tincidunt ut laoreet dolore magna aliquam erat volutpat. Ut wisi enim ad minim veniam, quis nostrud exerci tation ullam corper suscipit lobortis nisl ut aliquip ex ea commodo consequat.

Duis autem vel eum iriure dolor in hendrerit in vulputate velit esse molestie consequat, vel illum dolore eu feugiat nulla facilisis at vero eros et accumsan et iusto odio dignissim qui blandit praesent luptatum zzril delenit augue duis dolore te feugait nulla delenit facilisi.

Lorem ipsum dolor sit amet, consectetuer adipiscing elit, sed diam nonummy nibh euismod tincidunt ut laoreet dolore magna aliquam erat volutpat. Ut wisi enim ad minim veniam, quis nostrud exerci tation ullamcorper suscipit lobortis nisl ut aliquip ex ea commodo consequat.

Contact Amanda Example: 987 654 3210 or name@emailaddressz.com; More: http://www.yourwebaddressz.com/articles/storyname.htm

CITY/STATE

# Example joins Sampler State as Division Sales Manager

By R. M. Example

Lorem ipsum dolor sit amet, consectetuer adipiscing elit, sed diam nonummy nibh euismod tincidunt ut laoreet dolore magna aliquam erat volutpat. Ut wisi enim ad minim veniam, quis nostrud exerci tation ullam corper suscipit lobortis nisl ut aliquip ex ea commodo consequat.

Duis autem vel eum iriure dolor in hendrerit in vulputate velit esse molestie consequat, vel illum dolore eu feugiat nulla facilisis at vero eros et accumsan et iusto odio dignissim qui blandit praesent luptatum zzril delenit augue duis dolore te feugait nulla delenit facilisi.

Lorem ipsum dolor sit amet, consectetuer adipiscing elit, sed diam nonummy nibh euismod tincidunt ut laoreet dolore magna aliquam erat volutpat.

Contact R. M. Example: 987 654 3210 or name@emailaddressz.com; More: http://www.yourwebaddressz.com/articles/storyname.htm

NATIONWIDE

# Thank you for your ongoing commitment and years service to Sampler City

**November marks the Pfth year Jeremy Example has served our Atlanta Sales OfPce—three of those as the ofPce's top producer. Well done Jeremy!**

Jeremy Example is the Atlanta Sales Manager. Contact 987 654 3210 or name@emailaddressz.com

**Lorem ipsum dolor sit amet, consectetuer adipiscing elit, sed diam nonummy nibh euismod tincidunt ut laoreet dolore magna aliquam erat.**

Name Example is the Job Title. Contact 987 654 3210 or name@emailaddressz.com

Lorem ipsum dolor sit amet, consectetuer adipiscing elit, sed diam nonummy nibh euismod tincidunt ut laoreet dolore magna aliquam erat volutpat. Ut wisi enim ad minim veniam, quis nostrud exerci tation ullam corper suscipit lobortis nisl ut aliquip ex ea commodo consequat. Ut wisi enim ad minim veniam.

**Lorem ipsum dolor sit amet, consectetuer adipiscing elit, sed diam nonummy nibh euismod tincidunt ut laoreet dolore magna aliquam erat.**

Name Example is the Job Title. Contact 987 654 3210 or name@emailaddressz.com

**Lorem ipsum dolor sit amet, consectetuer adipiscing elit, sed diam nonummy nibh euismod tincidunt ut laoreet dolore magna aliquam erat.**

Name Example is the Job Title. Contact 987 654 3210 or name@emailaddressz.com

STYLE 11 (12 PAGES)

# Tabs

Part newsletter, part Web site—this is another recipe that employs jolt thinking (see page 167), the act of reexamining the reasons behind a design to invent better alternatives.

The layout employs some of the same ideas as a Web site—it divides the publication into discrete areas of interest, it uses folder tabs at the top of each page to remind you where you are, and provides links to an online site that offers expanded coverage of topics, updates of articles, and links to associated resources.

### Page flow

Three 17 by 11 inch sheets (landscape) are folded to 8.5 by 11 inches and saddle-stitched.

### What you need

General layout and design requires a desktop publishing program. Creating and editing the tabs artwork require a digital imaging program. Dividing and reassembling the parts and pieces of vector clip art images and type requires a drawing program. (See *Step 7: Choose Your Tools*, page 176.)

# SAMPLER
# Grocery
## BUSINESS

| Welcome | Finance | Legal | Wholesalers | Resources |

Everything you need to know about running a small grocery business in a big world     JUNE 20?? / Vol 5 / No 7

# Foodservice academic programs tackle food safety

## University of Example increases enrollment

**by Raymond Example**

Lorem ipsum dolor sit amet, consectetuer adipiscing elit, sed diam nonummy nibh euismod tincidunt ut laoreet dolore magna aliquam erat volutpat. Ut wisi enim ad minim veniam, quis nostrud exerci tation ullam corper suscipit lobortis nisl ut aliquip ex ea commodo consequat. Duis autem vel eum iriure dolor in hendrerit in vulputate velit esse molestie consequat, vel illum dolore eu feugiat nulla facilisis at vero eros et accumsan et iusto odio dignissim qui blandit praesent luptatum zzril delenit augue duis dolore te feugait nulla facilisi.

SUBHEAD TEXT

Lorem ipsum dolor sit amet, consectetuer adipiscing elit, sed diam nonummy nibh euismod tincidunt ut laoreet dolore magna aliquam erat volutpat. Ut wisi enim ad minim veniam, quis nostrud exerci tation ullamcorper suscipit lobortis nisl ut aliquip ex ea commodo consequat. Duis autem vel eum iriure dolor in hendrerit in vulputate velit esse molestie consequat, vel illum dolore eu feugiat nulla facilisis at vero eros et Nam liber tempor cum soluta nobis eleifend option congue nihil imperdiet doming id quod mazim placerat facer possim assum.

Lorem ipsum dolor sit amet, consectetuer adipiscing elit, sed diam nonummy nibh euismod tincidunt ut laoreet dolore magna aliquam erat volutpat. Ut wisi enim ad minim veniam,

suscipit lobortis nisl ut aliquip ex ea commodo consequat. Lorem ipsum dolor sit amet, consectetuer adipiscing elit, sed diam nonummy nibh euismod tincidunt ut laoreet dolore magna aliquam erat volutpat. Ut wisi enim ad minim veniam, quis nostrud exerci tation ullamcorper suscipit lobortis nisl ut aliquip ex ea commodo consequat. Duis autem vel elit, sed diam nonummy nibh euismod tincidunt ut laoreet dolore magna aliquam erat volutpat.

Ut wisi enim ad minim veniam, quis nos trud exerci tation ullamcorper suscipit lobortis nisl ut aliquip ex ea commodo consequat. Duis autem vel eum iriure dolor in hendrerit in vulputate velit esseeum iriure dolor in hendrerit in vulputate velit esse molestie consequat, vel illum dolore eu feugiat nulla facilisis at vero eros et Nam liber tempor cum soluta nobis eleifend opquod mazim placerat facer possim assum commodo consequat. Lorem ipsum dolor sit amet, consectetuer adipiscing elit, sed diam nonummy nibh euismod tincidunt ut laoreet dolore magna aliquam erat volutpat. Ut wisi enim ad minim veniam, quis nostrud exerci tation ullamcorper suscipit lobortis nisl ut aliquip.

Contact Raymond Example: 987 654 3210 or name@emailaddressz.com; More: http://www.yourwebaddressz.com/articles/storyname.htm

## Research reveals revised shopping patterns among city dwellers

**By Maryanne Example**

Lorem ipsum dolor sit amet, consectetuer adipiscing elit, sed diam nonummy nibh euismod tincidunt ut laoreet dolore magna aliquam erat volutpat. Ut wisi enim ad minim veniam, quis nostrud exerci tation aliquip ex ea commodo consequat. Duis autem vel eum iriure dolor in hendrerit in vulputate velit esse molestie consequat, vel illum dolore eu feugiat nulla facilisis at vero eros et accumsan et iusto odio dignissim qui blandit praesent luptatum zzril delenit augue duis dolore te feugait nulla facilisi. Ut wisi enim ad minim veniam, quis nostrud exerci tation aliquip ex ea commodo consequat. Autem vel eum iriure dolor in hendrerit in vulputate velit esse molestie consequat, vel illum dolore eu feugiat nulla facilisis at vero eros et accumsan et iusto odio dignissim qui blandit praesent luptatum zzril delenit augue duis dolore te feugait nulla facilisi. Lorem ipsum dolor sit amet, consectetuer adipiscing elit, sed diam nonum my nibh gna aliquam erat volutpat. Ut wisi enim ta tion ullamcorper suscipit lobortis nisl.

Contact Maryanne Example: 987 654 3210 or name@emailaddressz.com; More: http://www.yourwebaddressz.com/articles/storyname.htm

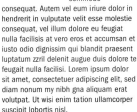

DESIGN RECIPES: TABS

### The design grid

This grid consists of three columns positioned on the page to accommodate the tab artwork. (See *Step 11.2: Establish the Page Size and Grid, page 187.*)

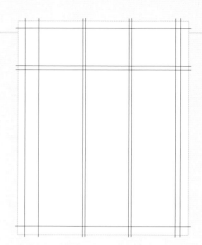

### The typefaces

Three sans-serif type families in one layout? Yes—the distinctions are subtle but serve the purpose of distinguishing two areas—the Web page and the newsletter. **Cosmos** for the nameplate and **Verdana** for the tab labels. And **Franklin Gothic** for the newsletter headlines and text.

Cosmos Extra Bold

**Typeface**
**AaBbEeGgKkMmQqRrS**

Franklin Gothic Condensed

**Typeface**
**AaBbEeGgKkMmQqRrSs**

Verdana

Typeface
AaBbEeGgKkMmQqRrS

Franklin Gothic Book Condensed

Typeface
AaBbEeGgKkMmQqRrSsWw!?

Franklin Gothic Book Condensed

Text Lorem ipsum dolor sit amet, consectetuer adipiscing elit, sed diam nonummy nibh euismod tincidunt ut laoreet dolore magna aliquam erat volutpat. Ut wisi enim ad minim veniam, quis nostrud exerci tation ullamcorper suscipit lobortis nisl ut aliquip laoreet dolore magna.

### The illustrations

The Web page backgrounds, of all the illustrations included in this book, were the most difficult to produce. Creating illustrations from scratch, incorporating clip art (the food basket), and applying shadows takes a clear understanding of how to use a digital imaging program.

DISTINGUISHING FEATURES

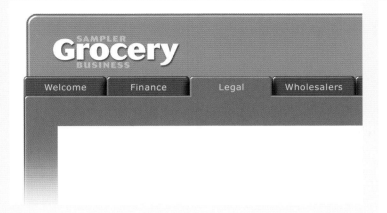

### Create the illusion of depth

The advent of digital imaging programs such as Adobe Photoshop added a new dimension to the design of conventional page design—depth. In this case, there are two things that contribute to the illusion of depth. The first is the shadows behind each of the folder tabs, the word "Grocery," and the food basket. Second is the subtle lightening of the color of the highlighted tab.

### Use a single style of illustration

Notice that there is one illustration style used throughout the newsletter—a bold, colorful, whimsical style. With a large enough, subject-specific collection of clip art, it is possible to use a single illustration style for a period of time—one style per issue, one per year, or until you have exhausted the possibilities. Limiting the number of styles adds a visual consistency *and* saves product time. The trick is to be vigilant about illustrating your message. When you choose artwork that is more decoration than illustration, you risk losing the reason for being.

### Use a familiar metaphor

This Weblike layout brings Web thinking to a newsletter—tabs divide the publication into areas of interest, they keep the reader oriented, and the contact links offer expanded coverage. What other design metaphors might work well for a newsletter? How about a big-city newspaper (see page 106), a slick magazine, a racy tabloid, a television guide, and so on.

# Grocery
**SAMPLER**
**BUSINESS**

Welcome | Finance | Legal | Wholesalers | Resources

Everything you need to know about running a small grocery business in a big world | JUNE 20?? / Vol 5 / No 7

# Foodservice academic programs tackle food safety

## University of Example increases enrollment

**by Raymond Example**

Lorem ipsum dolor sit amet, consectetuer adipiscing elit, sed diam nonummy nibh euismod tincidunt ut laoreet dolore magna aliquam erat volutpat. Ut wisi enim ad minim veniam, quis nostrud exerci tation ullam corper suscipit lobortis nisl ut aliquip ex ea commodo consequat. Duis autem vel eum iriure dolor in hendrerit in vulputate velit esse molestie consequat, vel illum dolore eu feugiat nulla facilisis at vero eros et accumsan et iusto odio dignissim qui blandit praesent luptatum zzril delenit augue duis dolore te feugait nulla facilisi.

SUBHEAD TEXT

Lorem ipsum dolor sit amet, consectetuer adipiscing elit, sed diam nonummy nibh euismod tincidunt ut laoreet dolore magna aliquam erat volutpat. Ut wisi enim ad minim veniam, quis nostrud exerci tation ullamcorper suscipit lobortis nisl ut aliquip ex ea commodo consequat. Duis autem vel eum iriure dolor in hendrerit in vulputate velit esse molestie consequat, vel illum dolore eu feugiat nulla facilisis at vero eros et Nam liber tempor cum soluta nobis eleifend option congue nihil imperdiet doming id quod mazim placerat facer possim assum.

Lorem ipsum dolor sit amet, consectetuer adipiscing elit, sed diam nonummy nibh euismod tincidunt ut laoreet dolore magna aliquam erat volutpat. Ut wisi enim ad minim veniam,

suscipit lobortis nisl ut aliquip ex ea commodo consequat. Lorem ipsum dolor sit amet, consectetuer adipiscing elit, sed diam nonummy nibh euismod tincidunt ut laoreet dolore magna aliquam erat volutpat. Ut wisi enim ad minim veniam, quis nostrud exerci tation ullamcorper suscipit lobortis nisl ut aliquip ex ea commodo consequat. Duis autem vel elit, sed diam nonummy nibh euismod tincidunt ut laoreet dolore magna aliquam erat volutpat.

Ut wisi enim ad minim veniam, quis nos trud exerci tation ullamcorper suscipit lobortis nisl ut aliquip ex ea commodo consequat. Duis autem vel eum iriure dolor in hendrerit in vulputate velit esseeum iriure dolor in hendrerit in vulputate velit esse molestie consequat, vel illum dolore eu feugiat nulla facilisis at vero eros et Nam liber tempor cum soluta nobis eleifend opquod mazim placerat facer possim assum commodo consequat. Lorem ipsum dolor sit amet, consectetuer adipiscing elit, sed diam nonummy nibh euismod tincidunt ut laoreet dolore magna aliquam erat volutpat. Ut wisi enim ad minim veniam, quis nostrud exerci tation ullamcorper suscipit lobortis nisl ut aliquip.

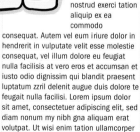

Contact Raymond Example: 987 654 3210 or name@emailaddressz.com; More: http://www.yourwebaddressz.com/articles/storyname.htm

## Research reveals revised shopping patterns among city dwellers

**By Maryanne Example**

Lorem ipsum dolor sit amet, consectetuer adipiscing elit, sed diam nonummy nibh euismod tincidunt ut laoreet dolore magna aliquam erat volutpat. Ut wisi enim ad minim veniam, quis nostrud exerci tation aliquip ex ea commodo consequat. Duis autem vel eum iriure dolor in hendrerit in vulputate velit esse molestie consequat, vel illum dolore eu feugiat nulla facilisis at vero eros et accumsan et iusto odio dignissim qui blandit praesent luptatum zzril delenit augue duis dolore te feugait nulla facilisi. Ut wisi enim ad minim veniam, quis nostrud exerci tation aliquip ex ea commodo consequat. Autem vel eum iriure dolor in hendrerit in vulputate velit esse molestie consequat, vel illum dolore eu feugiat nulla facilisis at vero eros et accumsan et iusto odio dignissim qui blandit praesent luptatum zzril delenit augue duis dolore te feugait nulla facilisi. Lorem ipsum dolor sit amet, consectetuer adipiscing elit, sed diam nonum my nibh gna aliquam erat volutpat. Ut wisi enim tation ullamcorper suscipit lobortis nisl.

Contact Maryanne Example: 987 654 3210 or name@emailaddressz.com; More: http://www.yourwebaddressz.com/articles/storyname.htm

8.5 W
11 H

## Grocery
### SAMPLER / BUSINESS

### Opinion
# A new breed of jobber

by Daniel Example

Lorem ipsum dolor sit amet, consectetuer adipiscing elit, sed diam nonummy nibh euismod tincidunt ut laoreet dolore magna aliquam erat volutpat. Ut wisi enim ad minim veniam, quis nostrud exerci tation ullam corper suscipit lobortis nisl ut aliquip ex ea commodo consequat. Duis autem vel eum iriure dolor in hendrerit in vulputate velit esse molestie consequat, vel illum dolore eu feugiat nulla facilisis at vero eros et accumsan et iusto odio dignissim qui blandit praesent luptatum zzril delenit augue duis dolore te feugait nulla facilisi.

Lorem ipsum dolor sit amet, consectetuer adipiscing elit, sed diam nonummy nibh euismod tincidunt ut laoreet dolore magna aliquam erat volutpat. Ut wisi enim ad minim veniam, quis nostrud exerci tation ullamcorper suscipit lobortis nisl ut aliquip ex ea

commodo consequat. Duis autem vel eum iriure dolor in hendrerit in vulputate velit esse molestie consequat, vel illum dolore eu feugiat nulla facilisis at vero eros et Nam liber tempor cum soluta nobis eleifend option congue nihil imperdiet doming id quod mazim placerat facer possim assum.

Lorem ipsum dolor sit amet, consectetuer adipiscing elit, sed diam nonummy nibh euismod tincidunt ut laoreet dolore magna aliquam. Lorem ipsum dolor sit amet, consectetuer adipiscing elit, sed diam nonummy nibh euismod tincidunt ut laoreet dolore magna aliquam erat volutpat.

SUBHEAD TEXT

Ut wisi enim ad minim veniam, quis nostrud exerci tation ullamcorper suscipit lobortis nisl ut aliquip ex ea commodo consequat. Duis autem vel eum iriure do-lor in hendrerit in vulputate velit esse molestie consequat, vel illum dolore eu feugiat nulla facilisis at vero eros et Nam liber tempor cum soluta nobis eleifend option congue nihil imperdiet doming id quod mazim placerat facer possim assum.

Lorem ipsum dolor sit amet, consectetuer adipiscing elit, sed diam nonummy nibh euismod tincidunt ut laoreet dolore magna aliquam. Lorem ipsum dolor sit amet, consectetuer adipiscing elit, sed diam nonummy nibh euismod tincidunt ut laoreet dolore magna aliquam erat volutpat. Ut wisi enim ad minim veniam, quis nostrud exerci tation ullamcorper suscipit lobortis nisl ut aliquip ex ea

ex ea commodo consequat. Duis autem vel eum iriure dolor in hendrerit in vulputate velit esse molestie consequat, vel illum dolore eu feugiat nulla facilisis at vero eros et Nam liber tempor cum soluta nobis eleifend option congue nihil imperdiet doming id quod mazim placerat facer possim assum.

Lorem ipsum dolor sit amet, consectetuer adipiscing elit, sed diam nonummy nibh euismod tincidunt ut laoreet dolore magna aliquam. Lorem ipsum dolor sit amet, consectetuer adipiscing elit, sed diam nonummy nibh euismod tincidunt ut laoreet dolore magna aliquam. Lorem ipsum dolor sit amet, consectetuer adipiscing elit, sed diam nonummy nibh euismod tincidunt ut laoreet dolore magna aliquam erat volutpat. Ut wisi enim ad minim veniam, quis nostrud exerci tation ullamcorper suscipit lobortis nisl ut aliquip ex ea commodo consequat. Lorem ipsum dolor sit amet, consectetuer adipiscing elit, sed diam nonummy nibh euismod tincidunt ut laoreet dolore magna aliquam erat volutpat.

Contact Daniel Example: 987 654 3210 or name@emailaddressz.com; More: http://www.yourwebaddressz.com/articles/storyname.htm

SAMPLER GROCERY BUSINESS
3028 Example Road
P.O. Box 1245
Your City, ST 12345-6789

SANDRA EXAMPLE
SAMPLER CORPORATION
123 EXAMPLE BOULEVARD STE 200
YOUR CITY ST 12345 6789

U.S. POSTAGE
PAID
YOUR CITY, ST
PERMIT NO. ???
ZIP CODE 98765

## Cover (page 1)

**1** "SAMPLER" Cosmos Extra Bold, 11pt, align center; "Grocery" Cosmos Extra Bold, 38pt, align center; "Welcome" Verdana, 8pt, align center; **2** Tab subtitle/date Franklin Gothic Book Condensed, 10pt, align left; **3** Line .5pt; Headline, large Franklin Gothic Heavy, 35/28pt, align left; Subhead Franklin Gothic Book Condensed, 16/16pt, align left; Contributor Franklin Gothic Heavy, 8pt, align left; Text Franklin Gothic Book Condensed, 10/12pt, align left; Text subhead Franklin Gothic Book Condensed, 9pt, align left; Contact link Franklin Gothic Book Condensed, 7/8pt, align left; **4** Headline, small Franklin Gothic Book Condensed, 20/20pt, align left; **5** Page number Franklin Gothic Book Condensed, 8pt, align left

## Back cover (page 8)

**6** "SAMPLER" Cosmos Extra Bold, 8pt, align center; "Grocery" Cosmos Extra Bold, 28pt, align center; "Welcome" Verdana, 8pt, align center; **7** Line .5pt; Tab subtitle Franklin Gothic Book Condensed, 10pt, align left; Headline, large Franklin Gothic Heavy, 35/28pt, align left; Contributor Franklin Gothic Heavy, 8pt, align left; Text Franklin Gothic Book Condensed, 10/12pt, align left; Text subhead Franklin Gothic Book Condensed, 9pt, align left; Contact link Franklin Gothic Book Condensed, 7/8pt, align left; **8** Line .5pt; Return address Franklin Gothic Book Condensed, 8/8pt, align left; **9** Label address Arial, 10/10pt, align left; Postage indicia Franklin Gothic Book Condensed, 8/8pt, align center; Line .5pt; **10** Page number Franklin Gothic Book Condensed, 8pt, align left

## Color

Printed in four-color process (Step 11.6) using values of cyan, magenta, yellow, and black (CMYK) as defined on the color palette below. Actual color will vary.

SOURCE Illustrations: Refrigerator, Bread/bottle/basket (pg. 1) from *Task Force Image Gallery* from NVTech, 800-387-0732, 613-727-8184, www.nvtech.com, © NVTech, all rights reserved. Man (pg. 12) from *Faces 3* from RubberBall Productions 801-224-6886, www.rubberball.com. © RubberBall Productions, all rights reserved.

SOURCE Type Families: Arial, Cosmos, Franklin Gothic, Adobe Systems, Inc. 800-682-3623, www.adobe.com/type; Verdana, Microsoft Corporation, www.microsoft.com/type.

## Pages 2 & 3

**11** "SAMPLER" Cosmos Extra Bold, 8pt, align center; "Grocery" Cosmos Extra Bold, 28pt, align center; "Welcome" Verdana, 8pt, align center; **12** Tab subtitle Franklin Gothic Book Condensed, 10pt, align left; **13** Line .5pt; Headline, large Franklin Gothic Heavy, 35/28pt, align left; Subhead Franklin Gothic Book Condensed, 16/16pt, align left; Contributor Franklin Gothic Heavy, 8pt, align left; Text Franklin Gothic Book Condensed, 10/12pt, align left; **14** Text subhead Franklin Gothic Book Condensed, 9pt, align left; Contact link Franklin Gothic Book Condensed, 7/8pt, align left; **15** Masthead text Franklin Gothic Book Condensed, 8/9pt, align left; Copyright Franklin Gothic Book Condensed, 6pt, align left; **16** Line .5pt; Headline, small Franklin Gothic Book Condensed, 20/20pt, align left; **17** Page number Franklin Gothic Book Condensed, 8pt, align left

## Page 8

**18** "SAMPLER" Cosmos Extra Bold, 8pt, align center; "Grocery" Cosmos Extra Bold, 28pt, align center; "Welcome" Verdana, 8pt, align center; **19** Tab subtitle Franklin Gothic Book Condensed, 10pt, align left; **20** Line .5pt; Headline, large Franklin Gothic Heavy, 35/28pt, align left; Subhead Franklin Gothic Book Condensed, 16/16pt, align left; Contributor Franklin Gothic Heavy, 8pt, align left; Text Franklin Gothic Book Condensed, 10/12pt, align left; Text subhead Franklin Gothic Book Condensed, 9pt, align left; Contact link Franklin Gothic Book Condensed, 7/8pt, align left; **21** Page number Franklin Gothic Book Condensed, 8pt, align left

## Page 12

**22** "SAMPLER" Cosmos Extra Bold, 8pt, align center; "Grocery" Cosmos Extra Bold, 28pt, align center; "Welcome" Verdana, 8pt, align center; **23** Tab subtitle Franklin Gothic Book Condensed, 10pt, align left; **24** Line .5pt; Headline, large Franklin Gothic Heavy, 35/28pt, align left; Subhead Franklin Gothic Book Condensed, 16/16pt, align left; Contributor Franklin Gothic Heavy, 8pt, align left; Text Franklin Gothic Book Condensed, 10/12pt, align left; Text subhead Franklin Gothic Book Condensed, 9pt, align left; Contact link Franklin Gothic Book Condensed, 7/8pt, align left; **25** Page number Franklin Gothic Book Condensed, 8pt, align left

SOURCE Illustrations: Bread/bottle/basket (pg. 2, 4, 8), Moneybag (pg. 3), Apple (pg. 8) from *Task Force Image Gallery* from NVTech, 800-387-0732, 613-727-8184, www.nvtech.com, © NVTech, all rights reserved. Man from *Faces 3* from RubberBall Productions 801-224-6886, www.rubberball.com. © RubberBall Productions, all rights reserved.

SOURCE Type Families: Cosmos, Franklin Gothic, Adobe Systems, Inc. 800-682-3623, www.adobe.com/type; Verdana, Microsoft Corporation, www.microsoft.com/type.

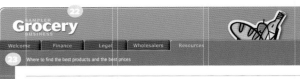

## Grocery

### What is the the world's most popular fruit?

The answer is sure to surprise you

by Trevor Example

Lorem ipsum dolor sit amet, consect etuer adipiscing elit, sed diam nonummy nibh euismod tincidunt ut laoreet dolore magna aliquam erat volutpat. Ut wisi enim ad minim veniam, quis nostrud exerci tation ullam corper suscipit lobortis nisl ut aliquip ex ea commodo consequat. Duis autem vel eum iriure dolor in hendrerit in vulputate velit esse consequat, vel illum dolore eu feugiat nulla facilisis at vero eros et iusto odio dignissim qui blandit praesent luptatum zzril delenit augue duis dolore te feugait nulla facilisi.

Lorem ipsum dolor sit amet, consectetuer adipiscing elit, sed diam nonummy nibh euismod tincidunt ut laoreet dolore magna aliquam erat volutpat. Ut wisi enim ad minim veniam, quis nostrud exerci tation ullamcorper suscipit lobortis nisl ut aliquip ex ea commodo consequat. Duis autem vel eum iriure dolor in hendrerit in vulputate velit esse molestie consequat, vel illum dolore eu feugiat nulla facilisis at vero eros et Nam liber tempor cum soluta nobis eleifend option congue nihil imperdiet doming id quod mazim placerat facer possim assum.

Lorem ipsum dolor sit amet, consectetuer adipiscing elit, sed diam nonummy nibh euismod tincidunt ut laoreet dolore magna aliquam erat volutpat. Ut wisi enim ad minim veniam,

suscipit lobortis nisl ut aliquip ex ea commodo consequat. Lorem ipsum dolor sit amet, consectetuer adipiscing elit, sed laoreet dolore magna aliquam erat volutpat. Ut wisi enim ad minim veniam, quis nostrud exerci tation ullamcorper suscipit lobortis nisl ut aliquip ex ea commodo consequat. Duis autem vel eum iriure dolor in hendrerit in vulputate velit esse molestie consequat, vel illum dolore eu feugiat nulla facilisis at vero eros et Nam liber tempor cum soluta nobis eleifend option congue nihil imperdiet doming id quod mazim placerat facer possim assum.

**SUBHEAD TEXT**

Ut wisi enim ad minim veniam, quis nostrud exerci tation ullamcorper suscipit lobortis nisl ut aliquip ex ea commodo consequat. Duis autem vel eum iriure dolor in hendrerit in vulputate velit esseeum iriure dolor in hendrerit in vulputate velit esse molestie consequat, vel illum dolore eu feugiat nulla facilisis at vero eros et Nam liber tempor cum soluta nobis eleifend ooquod mazim placerat facer possim assum. Lorem ipsum dolor sit amet, nonummy nibh euismod tincidunt ut laoreet dolore magna aliquam erat volutpat. Ut wisi enim ad minim veniam, quis nostrud exerci tation ullam corper

suscipit lobortis nisl ut aliquip ex ea commodo consequat. Duis autem vel eum iriure dolor in hendrerit in vulputate velit esse molestie consequat, vel illum dolore eu feugiat nulla facilisis at vero eros et accumsan et iusto odio dignissim qui blandit praesent luptatum zzril delenit augue duis dolore te feugait nulla facilisi.

Lorem ipsum dolor sit amet, consectetuer adipiscing elit, sed diam nonummy nibh euismod tincidunt ut laoreet dolore magna aliquam erat volutpat. Ut wisi enim ad minim veniam, quis nostrud exerci tation ullamcorper suscipit lobortis nisl ut aliquip ex ea commodo consequat. Duis autem vel eum iriure dolor in hendrerit in vulputate velit esse molestie consequat, vel illum dolore eu feugiat nulla facilisis at vero eros et accumsan et iusto odio dignissim qui blandit praesent luptatum zzril delenit augue duis dolore te feugait nulla facilisi.

Lorem ipsum dolor sit amet, consectetuer adipiscing elit, sed diam nonummy nibh euismod tincidunt ut laoreet dolore magna aliquam erat volutpat. Ut wisi enim ad minim veniam, quis nostrud exerci tation ullamcorper suscipit lobortis nisl ut aliquip ex ea commodo consequat. Lorem ipsum dolor sit amet, consectetuer adipiscing elit, sed diam nonummy nibh euismod tincidunt.

Contact Trevor Example: 987 654 3210 or name@emailaddressz.com; More: http:// www.yourwebaddressz.com/articles/storyname.htm

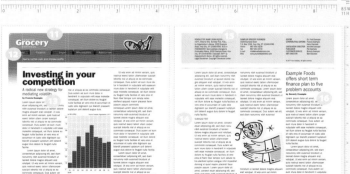

## Grocery

### Investing in your competition

A radical new strategy for mediating volatility

by Francis Example

Lorem ipsum dolor sit amet adipiscing elit, sed nibh euismod tincidunt ut laoreet dolore magna aliquam erat volutpat. Ut wisi enim ad minim veniam, quis nostrud exerci tation ullam corper suscipit lobortis nisl ut aliquip ex ea commodo consequat. Duis autem vel eum iriure dolor in hendrerit in vulputate velit esse molestie consequat, vel illum dolore eu feugiat nulla facilisis at vero eros et accumsan et iusto odio dignissim qui blandit praesent luptatum zzril delenit augue duis dolore te feugait nulla facilisi.

Lorem ipsum dolor sit amet, consectetuer adipiscing elit, sed diam nonummy nibh euismod tincidunt ut laoreet dolore magna aliquam erat volutpat. Ut wisi enim ad minim veniam, quis nostrud exerci tation ullamcorper suscipit lobortis nisl ut aliquip ex ea commodo consequat. Duis autem vel eum iriure dolor in hendrerit in vulputate velit esse molestie consequat, vel illum dolore eu feugiat

**SUBHEAD TEXT**

Lorem ipsum dolor sit amet, consectetuer adipiscing elit, sed diam nonummy nibh euismod tincidunt ut laoreet dolore magna aliquam erat volutpat. Ut wisi enim ad minim veniam, quis nostrud exerci tation ullamcorper suscipit lobortis nisl ut aliquip ex ea commodo consequat. Duis autem

Example Foods offers short term finance plan to five problem accounts

by Beverly Example

Lorem ipsum dolor sit amet, consectetuer adipiscing elit, sed nonummy nibh euismod tincidunt ut laoreet dolore magna aliquam erat volutpat.

**Grocery**
SAMPLER
BUSINESS

Welcome | Finance | Legal | Wholesalers | Resources

How to maximize good will and minimize liability

# The importance of accurate weights and measures

## How one small retailer learned the hard way

**by Simon Example**

Lorem ipsum dolor sit amet, consectetuer adipiscing elit, sed diam nonummy nibh euismod tincidunt ut laoreet dolore magna aliquam erat volutpat. Ut wisi enim ad minim veniam, quis nostrud exerci tation ullam corper suscipit lobortis nisl ut aliquip ex ea commodo consequat. Duis autem vel eum iriure dolor in hendrerit in vulputate velit esse molestie consequat, vel illum dolore eu feugiat nulla facilisis at vero eros et accumsan et iusto odio dignissim qui blandit praesent luptatum zzril delenit augue duis dolore te feugat nulla facilisi.

Lorem ipsum dolor sit amet, consectetuer adipiscing elit, sed diam nonummy nibh euismod tincidunt ut laoreet dolore magna aliquam erat volutpat. Ut wisi enim ad minim veniam, quis nostrud exerci tation ullamcorper suscipit lobortis nisl ut aliquip ex ea commodo consequat. Duis autem vel eum iriure dolor in hendrerit in vulputate velit esse molestie consequat, vel illum dolore eu feugiat nulla facilisis at vero eros et Nam liber tempor cum soluta nobis eleifend option congue nihil imperdiet doming id quod mazim placerat facer possim assum.

Lorem ipsum dolor sit amet, consectetuer adipiscing elit, sed diam nonummy nibh euismod tincidunt ut laoreet dolore magna aliquam erat volutpat. Ut wisi enim ad minim veniam,

suscipit lobortis nisl ut aliquip ex ea commodo consequat. Lorem ipsum dolor sit amet, consectetuer adipiscing elit, sed diam nonummy nibh euismod tincidunt ut laoreet dolore magna aliquam erat volutpat. Ut wisi enim ad minim veniam, quis nostrud exerci tation ullamcorper suscipit lobortis nisl ut aliquip ex ea commodo consequat. Duis autem vel elit, sed diam nonummy nibh euismod tincidunt ut laoreet dolore magna aliquam erat volutpat.

SUBHEAD TEXT

Ut wisi enim ad minim veniam, quis lobortis nisl ut aliquip ex ea commodo consequat. Duis autem vel eum iriure dolor in hendrerit in vulputate velit esseeum iriure dolor in hendrerit in vulputate velit esse molestie consequat, vel illum dolore eu feugiat nulla facilisis at vero eros et Nam liber tempor cum soluta nobis eleifend opquod mazim placerat facer possim assum commodo consequat. Lorem ipsum dolor sit amet, consectetuer adipiscing elit, sed diam nonummy nibh euismod tincidunt ut laoreet dolore magna aliquam erat volutpat.

Ut wisi enim ad minim veniam, VLorem ipsum dolor sit amet, consect etuer adipiscing elit, sed diam nonummy nibh euismod tincidunt ut laoreet dolore magna aliquam erat volutpat. Ut wisi enim ad minim veniam, quis nostrud exerci tation ullam corper suscipit lobortis nisl ut aliquip ex ea commodo consequat. Duis autem vel eum iriure dolor in hendrerit in vulputate velit esse molestie consequat, vel illum dolore eu feugiat nulla facilisis at vero eros et accumsan et iusto odio

dignissim qui blandit praesent luptatum. Lorem ipsum dolor sit amet, consectetuer adipiscing elit, sed diam nonummy nibh euismod tincidunt ut laoreet dolore magna aliquam erat volutpat. Ut wisi enim ad minim veniam, quis nostrud exerci tation ullam corper suscipit lobortis nisl ut aliquip ex ea commodo consequat.

Lorem ipsum dolor sit amet, consectetuer adipiscing elit, sed diam nonummy nibh euismod tincidunt ut laoreet dolore magna aliquam erat volutpat. Ut wisi enim ad minim veniam, quis nostrud exerci tation ullam corper suscipit lobortis nisl ut aliquip ex ea commodo consequat. Lorem ipsum.

Contact Simon Example: 987 654 3210 or name@emailaddressz.com; More: http://www.yourwebaddressz.com/articles/storyname.htm

## Law watch: Virginia Court prepares to rule

**By Diana Example**

Lorem ipsum dolor sit amet, consectetuer adipiscing elit, sed diam nonummy nibh euismod tincidunt ut laoreet dolore magna aliquam erat volutpat. Ut wisi enim ad minim veniam, quis nostrud exerci tation aliquip ex ea commodo consequat. Duis autem vel eum iriure dolor in hendrerit in vulputate velit esse molestie consequat, vel illum dolore eu feugiat nulla facilisis at vero eros et accumsan et iusto odio dignissim qui blandit praesent luptatum zzril delenit augue duis dolore te feugait nulla facilisi. Ut wisi enim ad minim veniam, quis nostrud exerci tation aliquip consequat.

Contact Diana Example: 987 654 3210 or name@emailaddressz.com; More: http://www.yourwebaddressz.com/articles/storyname.htm

STYLE 12 (20 PAGES)

# Tall

Think outside the box. Does a newsletter have to be 8.5 inches wide and 11 inches high? Does it have to have a nameplate at the top of the cover with an article below it? Does it have to present an 2.5 articles per page?

No, no, and no. The only thing your newsletter *must* do is communicate your message. How it does that is entirely up to you. It may, in fact, be to your advantage to make your newsletter look nothing like a newsletter. This recipe, for example, breaks the size barrier, features a magazine-like cover, and presents one article over multiple pages rather than multiple articles on a single page.

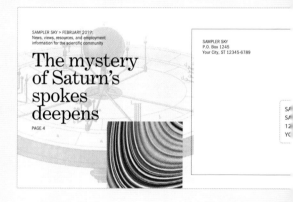

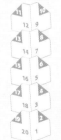

**Page flow**
Five 8.5 by 11 inch sheets (portrait) are folded to 4.25 by 11 inches and saddle-stitched.

**What you need**
General layout and design requires a desktop publishing program. Editing photographic images requires a digital imaging program. Dividing and reassembling the parts and pieces of vector clip art images and type requires a drawing program. (See *Step 7: Choose Your Tools*, page 176.)

SAMPLER SKY > FEBRUARY 20??:
News, views, resources, and employment
information for the scientific community

Sampler **SKY**

U.S. POSTAGE
PAID
YOUR CITY, ST
PERMIT NO. ???
ZIP CODE 98765

...ON
...ARD STE 200
...6789

3028 Example Road, P.O. Box 1245
Your City, ST 12345-6789
987 654 3210
987 654 3210 Fax
info@emailaddressz.com

EXECUTIVE DIRECTOR
Sarah Example
987 654 3210
name@emailaddressz.com

NEWSLETTER EDITOR
Charles Example
987 654 3210
name@emailaddressz.com

NEWSLETTER NAME (ISSN #1234-5678)
20??, Volume One, Number Five, Publis...
Organization's Name, 3028 Example R...
ST 12345-6789. $12/yr. POSTMASTER...
changes to Publication Name, 3028 E...
Your City, ST 12345-6789. Copyright...
Organization's Name. All rights rese...
Disclaimer. Copyright Clearance Ce...

## Sampler SKY

FEBRUARY 20??:
News, views, resources,
and employment information
for the scientific community

# The storm on Mars

PAGE 12

### The design grid

There are two single-column grids used—one for the cover and headline pages, one for the article text. The cover/headline page grid is narrower and has a wider left-hand margin. (See *Step 11.2: Establish the Page Size and Grid*, page 187.)

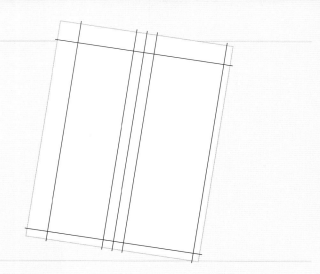

### The typefaces

As with many of the nameplates, the typeface used here, **Raleigh Gothic,** is used only in the nameplate. **Century Expanded** is used for the headlines and text, and **Franklin Gothic** is used for the contents, captions, contact links, and other supporting details.

Raleigh Gothic

# Typeface
AaBbEeGgKkMmQqRrSsWw!?

Century Expanded

# Typeface
AaBbEeGgKkMmQqRrSsW

Franklin Gothic Book Condensed

# Typeface
AaBbEeGgKkMmQqRrSsWw!?

Franklin Gothic Book Condensed

Text Lorem ipsum dolor sit amet, consectetuer adipiscing elit, sed diam nonummy nibh euismod tincidunt ut laoreet dolore magna aliquam erat volutpat. Ut wisi enim ad minim veniam, quis nostrud exerci tation ullamcorper suscipit lobortis nisl ut aliquip ex ea commodo consequat. Duis autem vel eum iriure dolor in hendrerit in vulputate velit esse molestie consequat, vel illum dolore eu feugiat nulla facilisis at vero eros.

### The illustrations

A subject that lends itself to as diverse a collection of photographic subjects as this one does can benefit from a secondary visual element—in this case, a series of beautifully complex antique scientific diagrams and illustrations. The images offer a subtle visual connection between pages.

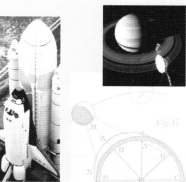

DISTINGUISHING FEATURES

### Learn from magazines

Just because your newsletter arrives in your reader's mailbox does not guarantee it will be read. You compete with everything in your reader's life that demands attention. This newsletter cover follows the magazine model; it previews the best of what's inside to persuade the reader to pick it up.

### Lead the reader into the text

Once you've got the reader inside, make your publication reader-friendly. One simple way of doing it is to begin the text of each article with a compelling statement—a paragraph or two of text that is more prominent and easier to read than the text—a technique demonstrated throughout this book.

### Be redundant and redundant

Few people will read your newsletter cover to cover. One thing Web sites do better than newsletters is ensure that no matter what page you see, you have a statement of or access to crucial information and what amounts to a table of contents. You can increase the odds of people taking the actions you prescribe by repeating your nameplate, defining phase, and key contact information several times throughout the pages of your newsletter.

20 1

20 1

SAMPLER SKY > FEBRUARY 20??:
News, views, resources, and employment
information for the scientific community

# The mystery of Saturn's spokes deepens

PAGE 4

SAMPLER SKY
P.O. Box 1245
Your City, ST 12345-6789

SANDRA EXAMPLE
SAMPLER CORPORATION
123 EXAMPLE BOULEVARD STE 200
YOUR CITY ST 12345 6789

U.S. POSTAGE
PAID
YOUR CITY, ST
PERMIT NO. ???
ZIP CODE 98765

# Sampler SKY

FEBRUARY 20??:
News, views, resources,
and employment information
for the scientific community

# The storm on Mars

PAGE 12

8.5 W
11 H

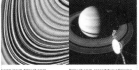

SAMPLER SKY > FEBRUARY 20??:
News, views, resources, and employment
information for the scientific community

# The mystery of Saturn's spokes deepens

BY ROBIN EXAMPLE

*Lorem ipsum dolor sit amet, consectetuer adipiscing elit, sed diam nonummy nibh euismod tincidunt ut laoreet dolore magna aliquam erat volutpat. Ut wisi enim ad minim veniam, quis nostrud exerci tation ullam corper suscipit lobortis nisl ut aliquip ex ea commodo consequat. Duis autem vel eum iriure dolor in hendrerit in vulputate velit esse molestie consequat.*

Lorem ipsum dolor sit amet, consectetuer adipiscing elit, sed diam nonummy nibh euismod tincidunt ut laoreet dolore magna aliquam erat volutpat. Ut wisi enim ad minim veniam, quis nostrud exerci tation ullam corper suscipit lobortis nisl ut aliquip ex ea commodo consequat. Duis autem vel eum iriure dolor in hendrerit in vulputate velit esse molestie consequat, vel illum dolore eu feugiat nulla facilisis at vero eros et accumsan et iusto odio dignissim qui blandit praesent luptatum zzril delenit augue duis dolore te feugait nulla facilisi.

Lorem ipsum dolor sit amet, consectetuer adipiscing elit, sed diam nonummy nibh euismod tincidunt ut laoreet dolore magna aliquam erat volutpat. Ut wisi enim ad minim veniam, quis nostrud exerci tation ullamcorper suscipit lobortis nisl ut aliquip ex ea commodo consequat. Duis autem vel eum iriure dolor in hendrerit in vulputate velit esse molestie consequat, vel illum dolore eu feugiat nulla facilisis at vero eros et Nam liber tempor cum soluta nobis eleifend option congue nihil imperdiet doming id quod mazim placerat facer possim assum.

Lorem ipsum dolor sit amet, consectetuer adipiscing elit, sed diam nonummy nibh euismod tincidunt ut laoreet dolore magna aliquam erat volutpat. Ut wisi enim ad minim veniam, quis nostrud exerci tation ullamcorper suscipit lobortis nisl ut aliquip ex ea commodo consequat. Lorem ipsum dolor sit amet, consectetuer adipiscing elit, sed diam nonummy nibh euismod tincidunt ut laoreet dolore erat volutpat. Sed diam nonummy nibh euismod tincidunt ut laoreet dolore magna aliquam erat volutpat. Ut wisi enim ad minim veniam, quis nostrud exerci tation ullam corper suscipit lobortis nisl ut aliquip ex ea commodo consequat. Duis autem vel eum iriure dolor.

Lorem ipsum dolor sit amet, consectetuer adipiscing elit, sed diam nonummy nibh euismod tincidunt ut laoreet dolore magna.

Dolor sit amet, consectetuer adipiscing elit, sed diam nonummy nibh euismod tincidunt ut laoreet dolore

Lorem ipsum dolor sit amet, consectetuer adipiscing elit, sed diam nonummy nibh euismod tincidunt ut laoreet dolore magna aliquam erat volutpat. Ut wisi enim ad minim veniam, quis nostrud exerci tation ullam corper suscipit lobortis nisl ut aliquip ex ea commodo consequat. Duis autem vel eum iriure dolor in hendrerit in vulputate velit esse molestie consequat, vel illum dolore eu feugiat nulla facilisis at vero eros et accumsan et iusto odio dignissim qui blandit praesent luptatum zzril delenit augue duis dolore te feugait nulla facilisi.

Contact Robin Example: 987 654 3210;
name@emailaddressz.com; More: http://www.yourwebaddressz.com/
articles/storyname.htm

## Cover & back cover (pages 1 & 20)

**1** "SAMPLER" Century Expanded, 24pt, align center; "SKY" Raleigh Gothic, 100pt, align center; Date/defining phrase Franklin Gothic Book Condensed, 9/10pt, align left; **2** Cover teaser Century Expanded, 40/30pt, align left; Page link Franklin Gothic Book Condensed, 8pt, align left; **3** Date/defining phrase Franklin Gothic Book Condensed, 8/9pt, align left; Back cover teaser Century Expanded, 30/32pt, align left; Page link Franklin Gothic Book Condensed, 8pt, align left; **4** Line .5pt; Return address Franklin Gothic Book Condensed, 8/8pt, align left; **5** Label address Arial, 10/10pt, align left; Postage indicia Franklin Gothic Book Condensed, 8/8pt, align center; Line .5pt

## Pages 2 & 3

**6** Line .5pt; Date/defining phrase Franklin Gothic Book Condensed, 8/9pt, align left; "SAMPLER" Century Expanded, 24pt, align center; "SKY" Raleigh Gothic, 100pt, align center; **7** Contents Franklin Gothic Book Condensed, 7/16pt, align left; Masthead Franklin Gothic Book Condensed, 7/8pt, align left; Copyright Franklin Gothic Book Condensed, 6pt, align left; **8** Headline, small Century Expanded, 18/18pt, align left; **9** Text Century Expanded, 10/12pt, align left; **10** Contact link Franklin Gothic Book Condensed, 7/8pt, align left; **11** Page number Franklin Gothic Book Condensed, 8pt, align right

## Pages 4 & 5

**12** Line .5pt; Date/defining phrase Franklin Gothic Book Condensed, 8/9pt, align left; Headline, large Century Expanded, 32/30pt, align left; Contributor Franklin Gothic Book Condensed, 8pt, align left; Lead-in text Century Expanded, 14/16pt, align left; **13** Page number Franklin Gothic Book Condensed, 8pt, align left; **14** Caption Franklin Gothic Book Condensed, 8/9pt, align left; **15** Text Century Expanded, 10/12pt, align left; **16** Contact link Franklin Gothic Book Condensed, 7/8pt, align left; Page number Franklin Gothic Book Condensed, 8pt, align left or right

SOURCE Illustrations: Mars photos from Hubble Space Telescope (pg. 1) (Credit: Material created with support to AURA/STScI from NASA contract NAS5-26555); Antique scientific diagrams and illustrations (pg. 20, 4) from *Antique Science and Technology* from Visual Language, 888-702-8777, www.visuallanguage.com, © Visual Language, all rights reserved; Planetary photographs (pg. 5, 20) from *ClickArt 200,000* from Broderbund, available from software retailers worldwide, © T/Maker, all rights reserved; Man (pg. 3) from *Faces 1* from RubberBall Productions 801-224-6886, www.rubberball.com. © RubberBall Productions, all rights reserved.

SOURCE Type Families: Century Expanded, Franklin Gothic, Adobe Systems, Inc. 800-682-3623, www.adobe.com/type; Raleigh Gothic, AGFA/Monotype, 888-988-2432, 978-658-0200, www.agfamonotype.com.

**Pages 8 & 9**

**17** Line .5pt; Date/defining phrase Franklin Gothic Book Condensed, 8/9pt, align left; Headline, large Century Expanded, 32pt, align left; Lead-in text Century Expanded, 14/16pt, align left; **18** Line .5pt; Listing text Century Expanded, 8/9pt, align left; **19** Contact link Franklin Gothic Book Condensed, 7/8pt, align left; Page number Franklin Gothic Book Condensed, 8pt, align left or right

**Pages 12 & 13**

**20** Line .5pt; Date/defining phrase Franklin Gothic Book Condensed, 8/9pt, align left; Headline, large Century Expanded, 32/30pt, align left; Contributor Franklin Gothic Book Condensed, 8pt, align left; Lead-in text Century Expanded, 14/16pt, align left; **21** "continued" Century Expanded, 8pt, align left; Caption Franklin Gothic Book Condensed, 8/9pt, align left; **22** Page number Franklin Gothic Book Condensed, 8pt, align left or right

**Pages 14 & 15**

**23** Caption Franklin Gothic Book Condensed, 8/9pt, align left; **24** Text Century Expanded, 10/12pt, align left; **24** Contact link Franklin Gothic Book Condensed, 7/8pt, align left; Page number Franklin Gothic Book Condensed, 8pt, align left or right

**Color**

Side one of the cover is printed in four-color process (Step 11.6) using values of cyan, magenta, yellow, and black (CMYK) as defined on the color palette below. Actual color will vary. The rest of the newsletter is printed in black and white.

SOURCE Illustrations: Antique scientific diagrams and illustrations (pg. 8, 12) from *Antique Science and Technology* from Visual Language, 888-702-8777, www.visuallanguage.com, © Visual Language, all rights reserved; Space Shuttle photographs (pg. 13, 14, 15) *ClickArt 200,000* from Broderbund, available from software retailers worldwide, © T/Maker, all rights reserved.

SOURCE Type Families: Century Expanded, Franklin Gothic, Adobe Systems, Inc. 800-682-3623, www.adobe.com/type.

2077:
employment
community

# by.
# money
# nts"
# e launch.

*dolor sit amet,*
*adipiscing elit, sed*
*my nibh euismod*
*aoreet dolore ma-*
*erat volutpat. Ut*
*minim veniam,*
*exerci tation ullam*
*it lobortis nisl ut*
*commodo*
*is autem vel eum*
*n hendrerit in*
*it esse molestie*

*continued on page 3*

orem ipsum dolor sit amet,
onsectetuer adipiscing elit, sed diam
onummy nibh euismod tincidunt ut
aoreet dolore magna.

Fig.17.

13

Lorem ipsum dolor sit amet,
consectetuer adipiscing elit, sed diam
nonummy nibh euismod tincidunt ut
laoreet dolore magna.

Ut wisi enim ad minim veniam, quis nostrud exerci tation ullam corper suscipit lobortis nisl ut aliquip ex ea commodo consequat. Duis autem vel eum iriure dolor in hendrerit in vulputate velit esse molestie consequat, vel illum dolore eu feugiat nulla facilisis at vero eros et accumsan et iusto odio dignissim qui blandit praesent luptatum zzril delenit augue duis dolore te feugait nulla facilisi.

Lorem ipsum dolor sit amet, consectetuer adipiscing elit, sed diam nonummy nibh euismod tincidunt ut laoreet dolore magna aliquam erat volutpat. Ut wisi enim ad minim veniam, quis nostrud exerci tation ullamcorper suscipit lobortis nisl ut aliquip ex ea commodo consequat. Duis autem vel eum iriure dolor in hendrerit in vulputate velit esse molestie consequat, vel illum dolore eu feugiat nulla facilisis at vero eros et Nam liber tempor cum soluta nobis eleifend option congue nihil imperdiet doming id quod mazim placerat facer possim assum.

Lorem ipsum dolor sit amet, consectetuer adipiscing elit, sed diam nonummy nibh euismod tincidunt ut laoreet dolore magna aliquam erat volutpat. Ut wisi enim ad minim veniam, quis nostrud exerci tation u rper suscipit lobortis nisl ut aliquip ex ea commodo consequat. Lorem ipsum dolor sit amet, consectetuer adipiscing elit, sed diam nonummy nibh euismod tincidunt ut laoreet dolore magna aliquam erat volutpat. Sed diam nonummy nibh euismod tincidunt ut laoreet dolore magna aliquam erat volutpat. Ut wisi enim ad minim veniam, quis nostrud exerci tation ullam corper suscipit lobortis nisl ut aliquip ex ea commodo consequat. Lorem ipsum dolor sit amet, consectetuer adipiscing elit, sed diam nonummy nibh euismod tincidunt ut laoreet dolore magna aliquam erat volutpat. Ut wisi enim ad minim veniam, quis nostrud exerci tation

Dolor sit amet, consectetuer adipiscing elit, sed diam nonummy nibh euismod tincidunt ut laoreet dolore

ullam corper suscipit lobortis nisl ut aliquip ex ea commodo consequat. Duis autem vel eum iriure dolor in hendrerit in vulputate velit esse molestie consequat, vel illum dolore eu feugiat nulla facilisis at vero eros et accumsan et iusto odio dignissim qui blandit praesent.

14

Lorem ipsum dolor sit amet, consectetuer adipiscing elit, sed diam nonummy nibh euismod tincidunt ut laoreet dolore magna aliquam erat volutpat. Ut wisi enim ad minim veniam, quis nostrud exerci tation ullamcorper suscipit lobortis nisl ut aliquip ex ea commodo consequat. Duis autem vel eum iriure dolor in hendrerit in vulputate velit esse molestie consequat, vel illum dolore eu feugiat nulla facilisis at vero eros et Nam liber tempor cum soluta nobis eleifend option congue nihil imperdiet doming id quod mazim placerat facer possim assum.

Lorem ipsum dolor sit amet, consectetuer adipiscing elit, sed diam nonummy nibh euismod tincidunt ut laoreet dolore magna aliquam erat volutpat. Ut wisi enim ad minim veniam, quis nostrud exerci tation ullamcorper suscipit lobortis nisl ut aliquip ex ea commodo consequat. Lorem ipsum dolor sit amet, consectetuer adipiscing elit, sed diam

Lorem ipsum dolor sit amet,
consectetuer adipiscing elit, sed diam
nonummy nibh euismod tincidunt ut
laoreet dolore magna.

nonummy nibh euismod tincidunt ut laoreet dolore erat volutpat. Ut wisi enim ad minim veniam, quis nostrud exerci tation ullamcorper suscipit lobortis nisl ut aliquip ex ea commodo consequat. Duis autem vel eum iriure dolor in hendrerit in vulputate velit esse molestie consequat, vel illum dolore eu feugiat nulla facilisis at vero eros et Nam liber tempor cum soluta nobis eleifend option congue nihil imperdiet doming id quod mazim placerat facer possim assum.

Lorem ipsum dolor sit amet, consectetuer adipiscing elit, sed diam nonummy nibh euismod tincidunt ut laoreet dolore magna aliquam erat volutpat. Ut wisi enim ad minim veniam, quis nostrud exerci tation ullamcorper suscipit lobortis nisl ut aliquip ex ea commodo consequat. Lorem ipsum dolor sit amet, consectetuer adipiscing elit, sed diam nonummy nibh euismod tincidunt ut laoreet dolore erat volutpat. Sed diam nonummy nibh euismod tincidunt ut laoreet dolore magna aliquam erat volutpat. Ut wisi enim ad minim veniam, quis nostrud exerci tation ullam corper suscipit lobortis nisl ut aliquip ex ea commodo consequat.

Contact Tamra Example: 987 654 3210;
name@emailaddressz.com; More: http://www.yourwebaddressz.com/
articles//storyname.htm

15

STYLE 13 (4 PAGES)

# Wing

Innovation is often the result of operating within constraints. This recipe is unique, practical, and easy to produce. A wind is folded into the cover to reveal the illustrations on the third page. The cover includes space for a lead article and a discussion of up to five separate topics—in this case music, academics, clubs, sports, and honors. The inside spread provides space for one article in each of the topic areas and the back cover features a comprehensive text calendar.

APRIL 20??: News, events, and resources for students, parents, and teachers

## Music

### Marching Band headed for statewide competition in Charlottesville
REPORTED BY MELVIN EXAMPLE

Lorem ipsum dolor sit amet, consectetuer adipiscing elit, sed diam nonummy nibh euismod tincidunt ut laoreet dolore magna aliquam erat volutpat. Ut wisi enim ad minim veniam, quis nostrud exerci tation ullam corper suscipit lobortis nisl ut aliquip ex ea commodo consequat.
Duis autem vel eum iriure dolor in hendrerit in vulputate velit esse molestie consequat, vel illum dolore eu feugiat nulla facilisis at vero eros et accumsan et iusto odio dignissim qui blandit praesent luptatum zzril delenit augue duis dolore

## Clubs

### Club leaders tackle rebuilding bylaws from the ground up
REPORTED BY ELISHA EXAMPLE

Lorem ipsum dolor sit amet, consectetuer adipiscing elit, sed diam nonummy nibh euismod tincidunt ut laoreet dolore magna aliquam erat volutpat. Ut wisi enim ad minim veniam, quis nostrud exerci tation ullam corper suscipit lobortis nisl ut aliquip ex ea commodo consequat.
Duis autem vel eum iriure dolor in hendrerit in vulputate velit esse molestie consequat, vel illum dolore eu feugiat nulla facilisis at vero eros et accumsan et iusto odio dignissim qui blandit praesent luptatum zzril delenit augue duis dolore

## Academics

### New courses: Public speaking, real-world marketing, and computer programming
REPORTED BY MURRAY EXAMPLE

Lorem ipsum dolor sit amet, consectetuer adipiscing elit, sed diam nonummy nibh euismod tincidunt ut laoreet dolore magna aliquam erat volutpat. Ut wisi enim ad minim veniam, quis nostrud exerci tation ullam corper suscipit lobortis nisl ut aliquip ex ea commodo consequat.
Duis autem vel eum iriure dolor in hendrerit in vulputate velit esse molestie consequat, vel illum dolore eu feugiat nulla facilisis at vero eros et accumsan et iusto odio dignissim qui blandit praesent luptatum zzril delenit augue duis dolore

## Sports

### Cross country training takes on a special meaning for Coach Example
REPORTED BY BRANDON EXAMPLE

Lorem ipsum dolor sit amet, consectetuer adipiscing elit, sed diam nonummy nibh euismod tincidunt ut laoreet dolore magna aliquam erat volutpat. Ut wisi enim ad minim veniam, quis nostrud exerci tation ullam corper suscipit lobortis nisl ut aliquip ex ea commodo consequat.
Duis autem vel eum iriure dolor in hendrerit in vulputate velit esse molestie consequat, vel illum dolore eu feugiat nulla facilisis at vero eros et accumsan et iusto odio dignissim qui blandit praesent luptatum zzril delenit augue duis dolore

## Honors

### National Honor Society ratchets up membership qualifications
REPORTED BY JEFFREY EXAMPLE

Lorem ipsum dolor sit amet, consectetuer adipiscing elit, sed diam nonummy nibh euismod tincidunt ut laoreet dolore magna aliquam erat volutpat. Ut wisi enim ad minim veniam, quis nostrud exerci tation ullam corper suscipit lobortis nisl ut aliquip ex ea commodo consequat.
Duis autem vel eum iriure dolor in hendrerit in vulputate velit esse molestie consequat, vel illum dolore eu feugiat nulla facilisis at vero eros et accumsan et iusto odio dignissim qui blandit praesent luptatum zzril delenit augue duis dolore

**Page flow**
One 11 by 17 inch sheet is folded to 8.5 by 11 inches then the cover is folded to form a 2.625-inch wing.

**What you need**
General layout and design requires a desktop publishing program. Editing photographic images requires a digital imaging program. Dividing and reassembling the parts and pieces of vector clip art images and type requires a drawing program. (See *Step 7: Choose Your Tools*, page 176.)

# Sampler High School
# NEWS

YELLOW JACKETS

APRIL 20??: News, events, and resources for students, parents, and teachers

## Expand your thinking about choosing a career and finding just the right college

REPORTED BY REBECCA EXAMPLE

Lorem ipsum dolor sit amet, consectetuer adipiscing elit, sed diam nonummy nibh euismod tincidunt ut laoreet dolore magna aliquam erat volutpat. Ut wisi enim ad minim veniam, quis nostrud exerci tation ullam corper suscipit lobortis nisl ut aliquip ex ea commodo consequat. Duis autem vel eum iriure dolor in hendrerit in vulputate velit esse molestie consequat, vel illum dolore eu feugiat nulla facilisis at vero eros et accumsan et iusto odio dignissim qui blandit praesent luptatum zzril delenit augue duis dolore te feugait nulla facilisi.

Lorem ipsum dolor sit amet, consectetuer adipiscing elit, sed diam nonummy nibh euismod tincidunt ut laoreet dolore magna aliquam erat volutpat. Ut wisi enim ad minim veniam, quis nostrud exerci tation ullamcorper suscipit lobortis nisl ut aliquip ex ea commodo consequat. Duis autem vel eum iriure dolor in hendrerit in vulputate velit esse molestie consequat, vel illum dolore eu feugiat nulla facilisis at vero eros et Nam liber tempor cum soluta nobis eleifend option congue nihil imperdiet doming id quod mazim placerat facer possim assum.

Lorem ipsum dolor sit amet, consectetuer adipiscing elit, sed diam nonummy nibh euismod tincidunt ut laoreet dolore magna Lorem ipsum dolor sit amet, consectetuer adipiscing elit, sed diam nonummy nibh euismod tincidunt ut laoreet dolore magna aliquam erat volutpat. Ut wisi enim ad minim veniam, quis nostrud exerci tation ullam corper suscipit lobortis nisl ut aliquip ex ea commodo consequat.

## Music IN BRIEF

Lorem ipsum dolor sit amet, consectetuer adipiscing elit, sed diam nonummy. > Nibh euismod tincidunt ut laoreet dolore magna aliquam erat volutpat. > Ut wisi enim ad minim veniam, quis nostrud exerci tation ullam corper suscipit lobortis nisl ut aliquip ex ea commodo consequat. > Duis autem vel eum iriure dolor in hendrerit in vulputate velit esse molestie consequat, vel illum dolore eu feugiat nulla.

## Clubs IN BRIEF

Lorem ipsum dolor sit amet, consectetuer adipiscing elit, sed diam nonummy. Nibh euismod tincidunt ut laoreet dolore magna aliquam erat volutpat. > Ut wisi enim ad minim veniam, quis nostrud exerci tation ullam corper suscipit lobortis nisl ut aliquip ex ea commodo consequat. > Duis autem vel eum iriure dolor in hendrerit in vulputate velit esse molestie consequat, vel illum dolore eu feugiat nulla.

## Academics IN BRIEF

Lorem ipsum dolor sit amet, consectetuer adipiscing elit. > Sed diam nonummy nibh euismod tincidunt ut laoreet dolore magna aliquam erat volutpat. > Ut wisi enim ad minim veniam, quis nostrud exerci tation ullam corper suscipit lobortis nisl ut aliquip ex ea commodo consequat. > Duis autem vel eum iriure dolor in hendrerit in vulputate velit esse molestie consequat, vel illum dolore eu feugiat nulla.

## Sports IN BRIEF

Lorem ipsum dolor sit amet, consectetuer adipiscing elit, sed diam nonummy. Nibh euismod tincidunt ut laoreet dolore magna aliquam erat volutpat. > Ut wisi enim ad minim veniam, quis nostrud exerci tation ullam corper suscipit lobortis nisl ut aliquip ex ea commodo consequat. > Duis autem vel eum iriure dolor in hendrerit in vulputate velit esse molestie consequat. > Vel illum dolore eu feugiat nulla.

## Honors IN BRIEF

Lorem ipsum dolor sit amet, consectetuer adipiscing elit, sed diam nonummy. > Nibh euismod tincidunt ut laoreet dolore magna aliquam erat volutpat. Ut wisi enim ad minim veniam, quis nostrud exerci tation ullam corper suscipit lobortis nisl ut aliquip ex ea commodo consequat. > Duis autem vel eum iriure dolor in hendrerit in vulputate velit esse molestie consequat, vel illum dolore eu feugiat nulla.

## The design grid

A basic three-column grid is divided top to bottom into five equal sections one for each topic area. (See *Step 11.2: Establish the Page Size and Grid*, page 187.)

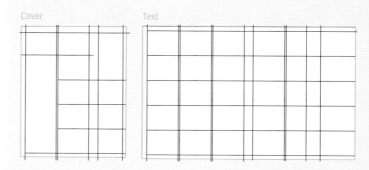

Cover

Text

## The typefaces

Two type families do all the work—**Impact** for the nameplate and the topic headings, and **Franklin Gothic** for everything else.

Impact

# Typeface
### AaBbEeGgKkMmQqRrSsWw!?

Minion Condensed

# Typeface
AaBbEeGgKkMmQqRrSsWw!?

Franklin Gothic Book Condensed

# Typeface
AaBbEeGgKkMmQqRrSsWw!?

Minion Condensed

Text Lorem ipsum dolor sit amet, consectetuer adipiscing elit, sed diam nonummy nibh euismod tincidunt ut laoreet dolore magna aliquam erat volutpat. Ut wisi enim ad minim veniam, quis nostrud exerci tation ullamcorper suscipit lobortis nisl ut aliquip ex ea commodo consequat. Duis autem vel eum iriure dolor in hendrerit in vulputate velit esse molestie consequat, vel illum dolore eu feugiat nulla facilisis at vero eros.

## The illustrations

This design recognizes the fact that, in many settings, it is necessary to use a patchwork of illustrations—some photographs, some artwork—from a variety of sources. To that end, the only other artwork used is that incorporated in the nameplate. Limiting the amount of visual information eliminates a potential visual tug-of-war.

DISTINGUISHING FEATURES

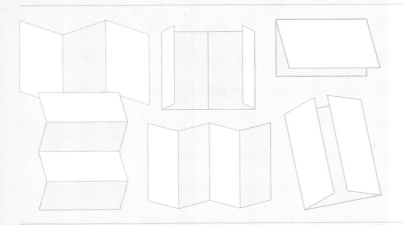

### Experiment with folds

This is just one of hundreds of ways to fold a newsletter. You can pick up a sheet of paper and start folding or investigate the topic through a book such as *How To Fold* by Laurence K. Withers (Art Direction Book Company, 1993). The challenge is to use folds to organize the message in a way that improves its communication.

## April Calendar

| DATE | DAY | TIME | EVENT | PLACE | CONTACT |
|------|-----|------|-------|-------|---------|
| 02 | Tuesday | 8:15 AM | Marching Band Practice | Football field | Sam Example |
| 02 | Tuesday | 9:00 AM | Pep rally | Field house | Marsha Example |
| 02 | Tuesday | 7:00 PM | Boys Volleyball (Home) | Gym | Harry Example |
| 00 | Day | 0:00 PM | Description lorem ipsum dolor | Place | Name Example |
| 00 | Day | 0:00 PM | Description lorem ipsum dolor | Place | Name Example |
| 00 | Day | 0:00 PM | Description lorem ipsum dolor | Place | Name Example |
| 00 | Day | 0:00 PM | Description lorem ipsum dolor | Place | Name Example |
| 00 | Day | 0:00 PM | Description Duis autem vel eum iriure | Place | Name Example |
| 00 | Day | 0:00 PM | Description lorem ipsum dolor | Place | Name Example |
| 00 | Day | 0:00 PM | Description lorem ipsum dolor | Place | Name Example |
| 00 | Day | 0:00 PM | Description lorem ipsum dolor | Place | Name Example |
| 00 | Day | 0:00 PM | Description Duis autem vel eum iriure | Place | Name Example |
| 00 | Day | 0:00 PM | Description lorem ipsum dolor | Place | Name Example |
| 00 | Day | 0:00 PM | Description lorem ipsum dolor | Place | Name Example |
| 00 | Day | 0:00 PM | Description lorem ipsum dolor | Place | Name Example |
| 00 | Day | 0:00 PM | Description lorem ipsum dolor | Place | Name Example |
| 00 | Day | 0:00 PM | Description Duis autem vel eum iriure | Place | Name Example |
| 00 | Day | 0:00 PM | Description lorem ipsum dolor | Place | Name Example |
| 00 | Day | 0:00 PM | Description lorem ipsum dolor | Place | Name Example |
| 00 | Day | 0:00 PM | Description lorem ipsum dolor | Place | Name Example |

### Create a space-saving text calendar

You can fit the dates, times, locations, and contact details for lots of events in a very small place using a simple text calendar like this. It is this type of useful, detailed information that earns your newsletter space at the office bulletin board or home on the refrigerator.

### Lead with news "in brief"

One technique common to many newspapers and magazines is to string together one-sentence news blurbs that, in brief, summarize a story. For a high school newsletter it might read something like this: "Basketball Coach Judy Example has been nominated for the state coach of the year. > The county has approved a $10,000 turf renovation for the football stadium to be completed by next August. > Scouts for three out-of-state universities were seen at the regional women's volleyball finals—University of Sampler, Sampler State, and Sampler College."

# Sampler High School NEWS

YELLOW JACKETS

APRIL 20??: News, events, and resources for students, parents, and teachers

## Expand your thinking about choosing a career and finding just the right college

REPORTED BY REBECCA EXAMPLE

Lorem ipsum dolor sit amet, consectetuer adipiscing elit, sed diam nonummy nibh euismod tincidunt ut laoreet dolore magna aliquam erat volutpat. Ut wisi enim ad minim veniam, quis nostrud exerci tation ullam corper suscipit lobortis nisl ut aliquip ex ea commodo consequat. Duis autem vel eum iriure dolor in hendrerit in vulputate velit esse molestie consequat, vel illum dolore eu feugiat nulla facilisis at vero eros et accumsan et iusto odio dignissim qui blandit praesent luptatum zzril delenit augue duis dolore te feugait nulla facilisi.

Lorem ipsum dolor sit amet, consectetuer adipiscing elit, sed diam nonummy nibh euismod tincidunt ut laoreet dolore magna aliquam erat volutpat. Ut wisi enim ad minim veniam, quis nostrud exerci tation ullamcorper suscipit lobortis nisl ut aliquip ex ea commodo consequat. Duis autem vel eum iriure dolor in hendrerit in vulputate velit esse molestie consequat, vel illum dolore eu feugiat nulla facilisis at vero eros et Nam liber tempor cum soluta nobis eleifend option congue nihil imperdiet doming id quod mazim placerat facer possim assum.

Lorem ipsum dolor sit amet, consectetuer adipiscing elit, sed diam nonummy nibh euismod tincidunt ut laoreet dolore magna Lorem ipsum dolor sit amet, consectetuer adipiscing elit, sed diam nonummy nibh euismod tincidunt ut laoreet dolore magna aliquam erat volutpat. Ut wisi enim ad minim veniam, quis nostrud exerci tation ullam corper suscipit lobortis nisl ut aliquip ex ea commodo consequat.

## Music IN BRIEF

Lorem ipsum dolor sit amet, consectetuer adipiscing elit, sed diam nonummy. > Nibh euismod tincidunt ut laoreet dolore magna aliquam erat volutpat. > Ut wisi enim ad minim veniam, quis nostrud exerci tation ullam corper suscipit lobortis nisl ut aliquip ex ea commodo consequat. > Duis autem vel eum iriure dolor in hendrerit in vulputate velit esse molestie consequat, vel illum dolore eu feugiat nulla.

## Clubs IN BRIEF

Lorem ipsum dolor sit amet, consectetuer adipiscing elit, sed diam nonummy. Nibh euismod tincidunt ut laoreet dolore magna aliquam erat volutpat. > Ut wisi enim ad minim veniam, quis nostrud exerci tation ullam corper suscipit lobortis nisl ut aliquip ex ea commodo consequat. > Duis autem vel eum iriure dolor in hendrerit in vulputate velit esse molestie consequat, vel illum dolore eu feugiat nulla.

## Academics IN BRIEF

Lorem ipsum dolor sit amet, consectetuer adipiscing elit. > Sed diam nonummy nibh euismod tincidunt ut laoreet dolore magna aliquam erat volutpat. > Ut wisi enim ad minim veniam, quis nostrud exerci tation ullam corper suscipit lobortis nisl ut aliquip ex ea commodo consequat. > Duis autem vel eum iriure dolor in hendrerit in vulputate velit esse molestie consequat, vel illum dolore eu feugiat nulla.

## Sports IN BRIEF

Lorem ipsum dolor sit amet, consectetuer adipiscing elit, sed diam nonummy. Nibh euismod tincidunt ut laoreet dolore magna aliquam erat volutpat. > Ut wisi enim ad minim veniam, quis nostrud exerci tation ullam corper suscipit lobortis nisl ut aliquip ex ea commodo consequat. > Duis autem vel eum iriure dolor in hendrerit in vulputate velit esse molestie consequat. > Vel illum dolore eu feugiat nulla.

## Honors IN BRIEF

Lorem ipsum dolor sit amet, consectetuer adipiscing elit, sed diam nonummy. > Nibh euismod tincidunt ut laoreet dolore magna aliquam erat volutpat. Ut wisi enim ad minim veniam, quis nostrud exerci tation ullam corper suscipit lobortis nisl ut aliquip ex ea commodo consequat. > Duis autem vel eum iriure dolor in hendrerit in vulputate velit esse molestie consequat, vel illum dolore eu feugiat nulla.

## PTA announces scholarships, academic programs, and senior Baccalaureate

REPORTED BY GLENN EXAMPLE

Lorem ipsum dolor sit amet, consectetuer adipiscing elit, sed diam nonummy nibh euismod tincidunt ut laoreet dolore magna aliquam erat volutpat. Ut wisi enim ad minim veniam, quis nostrud exerci tation ullam corper suscipit lobortis nisl ut aliquip ex ea commodo consequat. Duis autem vel eum iriure dolor in hendrerit in vulputate velit esse molestie consequat, vel illum dolore eu feugiat nulla facilisis at vero eros et accumsan et iusto odio dignissim qui blandit praesent luptatum zzril delenit augue duis dolore te feugait nulla facilisi.

Lorem ipsum dolor sit amet, consectetuer adipiscing elit, sed diam nonummy nibh euismod tincidunt ut volutpat. Ut wisi enim ad minim veniam, quis nostrud exerci tation ullamcorper suscipit lobortis nisl ut aliquip ex ea commodo consequat. Duis autem vel eum iriure dolor in hendrerit in vulputate velit esse molestie consequat, vel illum dolore eu feugiat nulla facilisis at vero eros et Nam liber tempor cum soluta nobis eleifend.

Contact Jody Example: 987 654 3210 or name@emailaddressz.com; More: http:// www.yourwebaddressz.com/articles/storyname.htm

SAMPLER HIGH SCHOOL NEWS
3028 Example Road, P.O. Box 1245
Your City, ST 12345-6789
987 654 3210
987 654 3210 Fax
info@emailaddressz.com
www.yourwebaddressz.org

PRINCIPAL
Roberta Example, name@emailaddressz.com

ASSISTANT PRINCIPAL
Eric Example, name@emailaddressz.com

GUIDANCE
Fran Example, name@emailaddressz.com

ACTIVITIES DIRECTOR
Dean Example, name@emailaddressz.com

PTA PRESIDENT
Louis Example, name@emailaddressz.com

SCA PRESIDENT
Mike Example, name@emailaddressz.com

8.5 W
11 H

## April Calendar

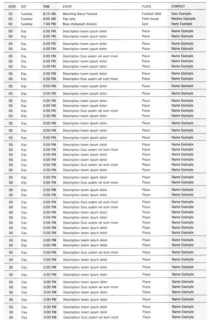

| DATE | DAY | TIME | EVENT | PLACE | CONTACT |
|---|---|---|---|---|---|
| 02 | Tuesday | 8:15 AM | Marching Band Practice | Football field | Sam Example |
| 02 | Tuesday | 9:00 AM | Pep rally | Field house | Martha Example |
| 02 | Tuesday | 7:00 PM | Boys Volleyball (Home) | Gym | Harry Example |
| 00 | Day | 0:00 PM | Description lorem ipsum dolor | Place | Name Example |
| 00 | Day | 0:00 PM | Description lorem ipsum dolor | Place | Name Example |
| 00 | Day | 0:00 PM | Description Duis autem vel eum irure | Place | Name Example |
| 00 | Day | 0:00 PM | Description lorem ipsum dolor | Place | Name Example |
| 00 | Day | 0:00 PM | Description Duis autem vel eum irure | Place | Name Example |
| 00 | Day | 0:00 PM | Description lorem ipsum dolor | Place | Name Example |
| 00 | Day | 0:00 PM | Description Duis autem vel eum irure | Place | Name Example |
| 00 | Day | 0:00 PM | Description lorem ipsum dolor | Place | Name Example |
| 00 | Day | 0:00 PM | Description Duis autem vel eum irure | Place | Name Example |
| 00 | Day | 0:00 PM | Description lorem ipsum dolor | Place | Name Example |
| 00 | Day | 0:00 PM | Description lorem ipsum dolor | Place | Name Example |
| 00 | Day | 0:00 PM | Description Duis autem vel eum irure | Place | Name Example |
| 00 | Day | 0:00 PM | Description lorem ipsum dolor | Place | Name Example |
| 00 | Day | 0:00 PM | Description lorem ipsum dolor | Place | Name Example |
| 00 | Day | 0:00 PM | Description lorem ipsum dolor | Place | Name Example |
| 00 | Day | 0:00 PM | Description Duis autem vel eum irure | Place | Name Example |
| 00 | Day | 0:00 PM | Description lorem ipsum dolor | Place | Name Example |
| 00 | Day | 0:00 PM | Description Duis autem vel eum irure | Place | Name Example |
| 00 | Day | 0:00 PM | Description lorem ipsum dolor | Place | Name Example |
| 00 | Day | 0:00 PM | Description lorem ipsum dolor | Place | Name Example |
| 00 | Day | 0:00 PM | Description Duis autem vel eum irure | Place | Name Example |
| 00 | Day | 0:00 PM | Description Duis autem vel eum irure | Place | Name Example |
| 00 | Day | 0:00 PM | Description lorem ipsum dolor | Place | Name Example |
| 00 | Day | 0:00 PM | Description Duis autem vel eum irure | Place | Name Example |
| 00 | Day | 0:00 PM | Description lorem ipsum dolor | Place | Name Example |
| 00 | Day | 0:00 PM | Description lorem ipsum dolor | Place | Name Example |
| 00 | Day | 0:00 PM | Description Duis autem vel eum irure | Place | Name Example |
| 00 | Day | 0:00 PM | Description lorem ipsum dolor | Place | Name Example |
| 00 | Day | 0:00 PM | Description Duis autem vel eum irure | Place | Name Example |
| 00 | Day | 0:00 PM | Description lorem ipsum dolor | Place | Name Example |
| 00 | Day | 0:00 PM | Description Duis autem vel eum irure | Place | Name Example |
| 00 | Day | 0:00 PM | Description lorem ipsum dolor | Place | Name Example |
| 00 | Day | 0:00 PM | Description lorem ipsum dolor | Place | Name Example |

Sampler High School

# NEWS

APRIL 20??: News, events, and resources for students, parents, and teachers

## Survey reveals where and how Sampler High students spend free time

REPORTED BY JODY EXAMPLE

Lorem ipsum dolor sit amet, consectetuer adipiscing elit, sed diam nonummy nibh euismod tincidunt ut laoreet dolore magna aliquam erat volutpat. Ut wisi enim ad minim veniam, quis nostrud exerci tation ullam corper suscipit lobortis nisl ut aliquip ex ea commodo consequat. Duis autem vel eum iriure dolor in hendrerit in vulputate velit esse molestie consequat, vel illum dolore eu feugiat nulla facilisis at vero eros et accumsan et iusto odio dignissim qui blandit praesent luptatum zzril delenit augue duis dolore te feugait nulla facilisi.

Lorem ipsum dolor sit amet, consectetuer adipiscing elit, sed diam nonummy nibh euismod tincidunt ut laoreet dolore magna aliquam erat volutpat. Ut wisi enim ad minim veniam, quis nostrud exerci tation ullamcorper suscipit lobortis nisl ut aliquip ex ea commodo consequat. Duis autem vel eum iriure dolor in hendrerit in vulputate velit esse molestie consequat, vel illum dolore eu feugiat nulla facilisis at vero eros et Nam liber tempor cum soluta nobis eleifend option congue nihil imperdiet doming id quod mazim placerat facer possim assum.

Lorem ipsum dolor sit amet, consectetuer adipiscing elit, sed diam nonummy nibh euismod tincidunt ut laoreet dolore magna aliquam erat volutpat. Ut wisi enim ad minim veniam, quis nostrud exerci tation ullamcorper suscipit lobortis nisl ut aliquip ex ea commodo consequat. Duis autem vel eum iriure dolor in hendrerit in vulputate velit esse molestie consequat, vel illum dolore eu feugiat nulla facilisis at vero eros et Nam liber tempor cum soluta nobis eleifend option congue nihil imperdiet doming id quod mazim placerat facer possim assum.

Contact Jody Example: 987 654 3210 or name@emailaddressz.com; More: http://www.youwebaddressz.com/articles/storyname.htm

## Cover (page 1)

**1** "SAMPLER" Franklin Gothic Book Condensed, 20/17pt, align left; "NEWS" Impact, 82pt, align left; "YELLOW" Franklin Gothic Book Condensed, 7/6pt, align left; Date/defining phrase Franklin Gothic Book Condensed, 8/8pt, align left; **2** Headline Franklin Gothic Book Condensed, 20/20pt, align left; Contributor Franklin Gothic Book Condensed, 8pt, align left; Text Minon Condensed, 10/11.5pt, align left; **3** Title Impact, 82pt, align left; Title tag Franklin Gothic Book Condensed, 14pt, align left; Text Minon Condensed, 10/11.5pt, align left; **4** Contact link Franklin Gothic Book Condensed, 8pt, align left; **5** Masthead Franklin Gothic Book Condensed, 9/10pt, align left; Copyright Franklin Gothic Book Condensed, 7pt, align left; **6** Line .5pt

## Back cover (page 4)

**1** "SAMPLER" Franklin Gothic Book Condensed, 20/17pt, align left; "NEWS" Impact, 82pt, align left; "YELLOW" Franklin Gothic Book Condensed, 7/6pt, align left; Date/defining phrase Franklin Gothic Book Condensed, 8/8pt, align left; **2** Headline Franklin Gothic Book Condensed, 20/20pt, align left; Contributor Franklin Gothic Book Condensed, 8pt, align left; Text Minon Condensed, 10/11.5pt, align left; **3** Title Impact, 32pt, align left; Title tag Franklin Gothic Book Condensed, 14pt, align left; Text Minon Condensed, 10/11.5pt, align left; **4** Contact link Franklin Gothic Book Condensed, 8pt, align left; **5** Masthead Franklin Gothic Book Condensed, 9/10pt, align left; Copyright Franklin Gothic Book Condensed, 7pt, align left; **6** Line .5pt; **7** Headline Franklin Gothic Book Condensed, 20pt, align left; Text calendar Franklin Gothic Book Condensed, 7/9pt, align left; **8** "SAMPLER" Franklin Gothic Book Condensed, 13/11pt, align left; "NEWS" Impact, 47pt, align left; "YELLOW" Franklin Gothic Book Condensed, 4/4pt, align left; Date/defining phrase Franklin Gothic Book Condensed, 8/8pt, align left

## Color
Printed in black.

**Pages 2 & 3**

**9** Title Impact, 30pt, align left; Headline Franklin Gothic Book Condensed, 20/20pt, align left; Contributor Franklin Gothic Book Condensed, 8pt, align left; Text Minon Condensed, 10/11.5pt, align left; **10** Line .5pt; **11** Caption Franklin Gothic Book Condensed, 7/8pt, align left; **12** Contact link Franklin Gothic Book Condensed, 8pt, align left

**Color**

Printed in black and white.

## Music

### Marching Band headed for statewide competition in Charlottesville
REPORTED BY MELVIN EXAMPLE

Lorem ipsum dolor sit amet, consectetuer adipiscing elit, sed diam nonummy nibh euismod tincidunt ut laoreet dolore magna aliquam erat volutpat. Ut wisi enim ad minim veniam, quis nostrud exerci tation ullam corper suscipit lobortis nisl ut aliquip ex ea commodo consequat. Duis autem vel eum iriure dolor in hendrerit in vulputate velit esse molestie consequat, vel illum dolore eu feugiat nulla facilisis at vero eros et accumsan et iusto odio dignissim qui blandit praesent luptatum zzril delenit augue duis dolore te feugait nulla facilisi. Lorem ipsum dolor sit amet, consectetuer adipiscing elit, sed diam nonummy nibh euismod tincidunt ut laoreet dolore magna aliquam erat volutpat. Ut wisi enim ad minim veniam, quis nostrud exerci tation ullamcorper suscipit lobortis nisl ut aliquip ex ea commodo consequat. Duis autem vel eum iriure dolor in hendrerit in vulputate velit esse molestie consequat, vel illum dolore eu feugiat nulla facilisis at vero eros et. Nam liber tempor cum soluta nobis eleifend option

## Clubs

### Club leaders tackle rebuilding bylaws from the ground up
REPORTED BY ELISHA EXAMPLE

Lorem ipsum dolor sit amet, consectetuer adipiscing elit, sed diam nonummy nibh euismod tincidunt ut laoreet dolore magna aliquam erat volutpat. Ut wisi enim ad minim veniam, quis nostrud exerci tation ullam corper suscipit lobortis nisl ut aliquip ex ea commodo consequat. Duis autem vel eum iriure dolor in hendrerit in vulputate velit esse molestie consequat, vel illum dolore eu feugiat nulla facilisis at vero eros et accumsan et iusto odio dignissim qui blandit praesent luptatum zzril delenit augue duis dolore te feugait nulla facilisi. Lorem ipsum dolor sit amet, consectetuer adipiscing elit, sed diam nonummy nibh euismod tincidunt ut laoreet dolore magna aliquam erat volutpat. Ut wisi enim ad minim veniam, quis nostrud exerci tation ullamcorper suscipit lobortis nisl ut aliquip ex ea commodo consequat. Duis autem vel eum iriure dolor in hendrerit in vulputate velit esse molestie consequat, vel illum dolore eu feugiat nulla facilisis at vero eros et. Nam liber tempor cum soluta nobis eleifend option

## Academics

### New courses: Public speaking, real-world marketing, and computer programming
REPORTED BY MURRAY EXAMPLE

Lorem ipsum dolor sit amet, consectetuer adipiscing elit, sed diam nonummy nibh euismod tincidunt ut laoreet dolore magna aliquam erat volutpat. Ut wisi enim ad minim veniam, quis nostrud exerci tation ullam corper suscipit lobortis nisl ut aliquip ex ea commodo consequat. Duis autem vel eum iriure dolor in hendrerit in vulputate velit esse molestie consequat, vel illum dolore eu feugiat nulla facilisis at vero eros et accumsan et iusto odio dignissim qui blandit praesent luptatum zzril delenit augue duis dolore te feugait nulla facilisi. Lorem ipsum dolor sit amet, consectetuer adipiscing elit, sed diam nonummy nibh euismod tincidunt ut laoreet dolore magna aliquam erat volutpat. Ut wisi enim ad minim veniam, quis nostrud exerci tation ullamcorper suscipit lobortis nisl ut aliquip ex ea commodo consequat. Duis autem vel eum iriure dolor in hendrerit in vulputate velit esse molestie consequat, vel illum dolore eu feugiat nulla facilisis at vero eros et. Nam liber tempor cum soluta nobis eleifend option

## Sports

### Cross country training takes on a special meaning for Coach Example
REPORTED BY BRANDON EXAMPLE

Lorem ipsum dolor sit amet, consectetuer adipiscing elit, sed diam nonummy nibh euismod tincidunt ut laoreet dolore magna aliquam erat volutpat. Ut wisi enim ad minim veniam, quis nostrud exerci tation ullam corper suscipit lobortis nisl ut aliquip ex ea commodo consequat. Duis autem vel eum iriure dolor in hendrerit in vulputate velit esse molestie consequat, vel illum dolore eu feugiat nulla facilisis at vero eros et accumsan et iusto odio dignissim qui blandit praesent luptatum zzril delenit augue duis dolore te feugait nulla facilisi. Lorem ipsum dolor sit amet, consectetuer adipiscing elit, sed diam nonummy nibh euismod tincidunt ut laoreet dolore magna aliquam erat volutpat. Ut wisi enim ad minim veniam, quis nostrud exerci tation ullamcorper suscipit lobortis nisl ut aliquip ex ea commodo consequat. Duis autem vel eum iriure dolor in hendrerit in vulputate velit esse molestie consequat, vel illum dolore eu feugiat nulla facilisis at vero eros et. Nam liber tempor cum soluta nobis eleifend option

## Honors

### National Honor Society ratchets up membership qualifications
REPORTED BY JEFFREY EXAMPLE

Lorem ipsum dolor sit amet, consectetuer adipiscing elit, sed diam nonummy nibh euismod tincidunt ut laoreet dolore magna aliquam erat volutpat. Ut wisi enim ad minim veniam, quis nostrud exerci tation ullam corper suscipit lobortis nisl ut aliquip ex ea commodo consequat. Duis autem vel eum iriure dolor in hendrerit in vulputate velit esse molestie consequat, vel illum dolore eu feugiat nulla facilisis at vero eros et accumsan et iusto odio dignissim qui blandit praesent luptatum zzril delenit augue duis dolore te feugait nulla facilisi. Lorem ipsum dolor sit amet, consectetuer adipiscing elit, sed diam nonummy nibh euismod tincidunt ut laoreet dolore magna aliquam erat volutpat. Ut wisi enim ad minim veniam, quis nostrud exerci tation ullamcorper suscipit lobortis nisl ut aliquip ex ea commodo consequat. Duis autem vel eum iriure dolor in hendrerit in vulputate velit esse molestie consequat, vel illum dolore eu feugiat nulla facilisis at vero eros et. Nam liber tempor cum soluta nobis eleifend option

SOURCE Illustrations: Marching band (pg. 3) from *Image Club ArtRoom Musicville* from Eyewire, 800-661-9410, 403-262-8008, www.eyewire.com. © Eyewire, Inc., all rights reserved; Students/hallway, Dictionary, Student/diploma (pg. 3) from *Photo-Objects 50,000, Vol II* from Hemera Technologies 819-772-8200, www.hemera.com, © Hemera Technologies Inc., all rights reserved; Runners (pg. 3) *ClickArt 200,000* from Broderbund, available from software retailers worldwide, © T/Maker, all rights reserved.

SOURCE Type Families: Franklin Gothic, Impact, Minion, Adobe Systems, Inc. 800-682-3623, www.adobe.com/type.

congue nihil imperdiet doming id quod mazim placerat facer possim assum.

Lorem ipsum dolor sit amet, consectetuer adipiscing elit, sed diam nonummy nibh euismod tincidunt ut laoreet dolore magna aliquam erat volutpat. Ut wisi enim ad minim veniam, quis nostrud exerci tation ullamcorper suscipit lobortis nisl ut aliquip ex ea commodo consequat praesent luptatum zzril delenit augue duis dolore te feugait nulla facilisi. Lorem ipsum dolor sit amet, consectetuer adipiscing elit, sed diam nonummy

nibh euismod tincidunt ut lao dolore magna aliquam erat volutpat. Suscipit lobortis nisl ut aliquip ex ea commodo consequat.

Contact Melvin Example: 987 654 3210 or name@emailaddressz.com; More: http://www.yourwebaddressz.com/articles/storyname.htm

Caption: Lorem ipsum dolor sit amet, consectetuer adipiscing elit, sed diam nonummy nibh euismod tincidunt consectetuer adipiscing elit, sed diam. Ut wisi enim ad minim veniam, quis nostrud exerci tation ullamcorper suscipit lobortis nisl ut aliquip ex ea commodo consequat praesent luptatum zzril.

---

congue nihil imperdiet doming id quod mazim placerat facer possim assum.

Lorem ipsum dolor sit amet, consectetuer adipiscing elit, sed diam nonummy nibh euismod tincidunt ut laoreet dolore magna aliquam erat volutpat. Ut wisi enim ad minim veniam, quis nostrud exerci tation ullamcorper suscipit lobortis nisl ut aliquip ex ea commodo consequat praesent luptatum zzril delenit augue duis dolore te feugait nulla facilisi. Lorem ipsum dolor sit amet, consectetuer adipiscing elit, sed diam nonummy

nibh euismod tincidunt ut lao dolore magna aliquam erat volutpat. Ut wisi enim.

Contact Elisha Example: 987 654 3210 or name@emailaddressz.com; More: http://www.yourwebaddressz.com/articles/storyname.htm

Caption: Lorem ipsum dolor sit amet, consectetuer adipiscing elit, sed diam nonummy nibh euismod tincidunt consectetuer adipiscing elit, sed diam. Ut wisi enim ad minim veniam, quis nostrud exerci tation ullamcorper suscipit lobortis nisl.

---

congue nihil imperdiet doming id quod mazim placerat facer possim assum.

Lorem ipsum dolor sit amet, consectetuer adipiscing elit, sed diam nonummy nibh euismod tincidunt ut laoreet dolore magna aliquam erat volutpat. Ut wisi enim ad minim veniam, quis nostrud exerci tation ullamcorper suscipit lobortis nisl ut aliquip ex ea commodo consequat praesent luptatum zzril delenit augue duis dolore te feugait nulla facilisi. Lorem ipsum dolor sit amet, consectetuer adipiscing elit, sed diam nonummy

nibh euismod tincidunt ut lao dolore magna aliquam erat volutpat. Ut wisi enim ad min im veniam, quis nostrud suscipit lobortis nisl ut aliquip ex ea commodo consequat.

Contact Murray Example: 987 654 3210 or name@emailaddressz.com; More: http://www.yourwebaddressz.com/articles/storyname.htm

Caption: Lorem ipsum sit amet, consectetuer adipiscing elit, sed diam nonummy nibh euismod tincidunt consectetuer adipiscing elit, sed diam. Ut wisi enim ad minim venia

---

congue nihil imperdiet doming id quod mazim placerat facer possim assum.

Lorem ipsum dolor sit amet, consectetuer adipiscing elit, sed diam nonummy nibh euismod tincidunt ut laoreet dolore magna aliquam erat volutpat. Ut wisi enim ad minim veniam, quis nostrud exerci tation ullamcorper suscipit lobortis nisl ut aliquip ex ea commodo consequat praesent luptatum zzril delenit augue duis dolore te feugait nulla facilisi. Lorem ipsum dolor sit amet, consectetuer adipiscing elit, sed diam nonummy

nibh euismod tincidunt ut lao dolore magna aliquam erat volutpat. Ut wisi enim ad min im veniam, quis nostrud exerci ea commodo consequat. Duis autem vel eum iriure do lor in hendrerit in vulputate velit esse molestie consequat.

Contact Brandon Example: 987 654 3210 or name@emailaddressz.com; More: http://www.yourwebaddressz.com/articles/storyname.htm

Caption: Lorem ipsum sit amet, consectetuer adipiscing elit, sed diam nonummy nibh euismod tincidunt consectetuer adipiscing elit, sed diam. Ut wisi enim ad minim veniam, quis nostrud exerci tation ullamcorper suscipit lobortis nisl ut aliquip ex ea commodo consequat praesent luptatum zzril delenit augue duis dolore te feugit nulla facilisi.

---

congue nihil imperdiet doming id quod mazim placerat facer possim assum.

Lorem ipsum dolor sit amet, consectetuer adipiscing elit, sed diam nonummy nibh euismod tincidunt ut laoreet dolore magna aliquam erat volutpat. Ut wisi enim ad minim veniam, quis nostrud exerci tation ullamcorper suscipit lobortis nisl ut aliquip ex ea commodo consequat praesent luptatum zzril delenit augue duis dolore te feugait nulla facilisi. Lorem ipsum dolor sit amet, consectetuer adipiscing elit, sed diam nonummy

nibh euismod tincidunt ut lao dolore magna aliquam erat volutpat. Ut wisi enim ad min im veniam, quis nostrud exerci tation ullamcorper suscipit lobortis nisl ut aliquip ex ea commodo.

Contact Jeffrey Example: 987 654 3210 or name@emailaddressz.com; More: http://www.yourwebaddressz.com/articles/storyname.htm

Caption: Consectetuer adipiscing elit. Ut wisi enim ad minim veniam, quis nostrud exerci tation ullamcorper suscipit lobortis nisl ut aliquip ex ea commodo consequat praesent luptatum zzril delenit augue duis dolore te feugait nulla facilisi.

8.5 W
11 H

# Glossary

**Bit-mapped graphics** *See* Paint graphics.

**Bleed** The layout image area that extends beyond the trim edge.

**CMYK** *See* Four-color process.

**Coated stock** Paper coated with a thin layer of clay-like substrate that creates a smooth, flat surface ideal for printing colored inks and superfine detail such as photographs. *See* Uncoated stock.

**Cropping** The act of eliminating certain parts of an illustration.

**Defining phrase** A five- to fifteen-word phrase that defines your market and expresses the most important benefits of using your product or service.

**Design** The process of arranging elements and information on a page in a way that improves its communication.

**Design grid** The invisible framework on which a page is designed.

**Draw graphics** Graphics created using objects such as lines, ovals, rectangles, and curves in a program such as Adobe Illustrator, CorelDRAW, or Macromedia FreeHand. Common draw file formats include: Encapsulated PostScript (EPS) and Windows Metafiles (WMF). Also referred to as "vector" or "object-oriented" graphics. *See* Paint graphics.

**Expert newsletter** Provides information, statistics, advice, or instruction for the price of a subscription.

**Eyebrow** Introductory/identifying text above a headline.

**Fill** The area within the stroke or outline of a shape or typeface character. In a drawing software program, strokes and fills can be assigned different colors. *See* Stroke.

**Font** There is disagreement over the current definition of this term. For the purposes of this book, a font is a typeface in digital form. *See* Typeface *and* Type family.

**Four-color process** A printing process that primarily uses cyan, magenta, yellow, and black (referred to as CMYK) to reproduce color photographs and other materials that contain a range of colors that cannot economically be reproduced using individual solid ink colors. *See* Solid color.

**Ghosting** A double or blurred image on the printed sheet typically caused by a misapplication of ink on the rollers.

**Hickey** A spot or other imperfection on the printed sheet caused by dirt or paper particles that adhere to the plate or rollers during printing.

**Hook** The combination of product or service benefits that establishes the important difference between an organization and its competition.

**Icon** An image that suggests its meaning—for example, an opened padlock represents the state of being unlocked.

**Kerning** The space between typeface characters.

**Leading** The amount of vertical space between the baselines of a typeface. Expressed as 12/18pt, which means the size of the specified type is 12 pt and the space between lines is 18 pt.

**Logo** The combination of a name, a symbol, and a short tag line. At a glance, identifies the nature of your product or service, transmits the benefit of using it, and defines your attitude about it.

**Lorem ipsum** Scrambled Latin text used by designers to demonstrate the approximate number of words it will take to fill an area of the layout before the actual text is specified.

**Masthead** The block of information that defines the publication, posts legal information, identifies the publisher and the key contributors, and provides contact information.

**Mottle** Uneven, spotty areas of ink coverage on a printed sheet.

**Nameplate** The logo-like banner that typically appears at the top of page one of a newsletter. May include the name of the publication, the name of the publisher, the defining phrase, and/or the issue date, volume, and issue numbers.

**Newsletter** A condensed periodical used to communicate specialized editorial information.

**Object-oriented graphics** *See* Draw graphics.

**Page flow** Diagram that shows the sequence of pages and how they are printed front to back.

**Paint graphics** Graphics created on a grid of tiny rectangles called pixels. Each pixel can be a different colors or shade of gray. Created in a program such as Adobe Photoshop or Jasc Software's Paint Shop Pro. Common paint files formats include Joint Photographic Experts Group (JPEG or JPG) and Tagged-Image File Format (TIFF or TIF) Also referred to as "raster" or "bit-mapped" graphics. *See* Draw graphics.

**Picture font** Collection of images that are installed like a font and produced by typing on the computer keyboard.

**Pinhole** A speck on a printed sheet caused by a hole in the printing plate negative.

**Preflight** The process of gathering together and reviewing all the elements necessary for translating the designer's information to a commercial printer's computer software and printing presses.

**Prepress process** The series of steps taken to prepare a project for printing.

**Press check** The process of reviewing a job on the printing press at the beginning of the press run. Provides an opportunity for slight color adjustments of process colors.

**Promotional newsletter** Used to educate readers about a certain area of interest and to provide solutions, some of which come in the form of the publisher's products, services, or way of thinking.

**Proof** A mock page or series of pages produced prior to printing by a commercial printer to demonstrate how a finished printed job will look.

**Raster graphics** *See* Paint graphics.

**Reader profile** A list of attributes that identifies the characteristics of the reader the publication is designed to attract.

**Registration** The process by which multiple printed images are aligned.

**Relationship newsletter** Used to inform the reader about a group to which they belong or might consider joining. It promotes the group's shared philosophy, a calendar of events, notices of meetings, individual or group milestones, member profiles, and so on.

**Royalty-free** In most cases, grants the buyer unlimited (within the vendor's license agreement) use of a photograph or illustration. *See* Stock.

**Running head** The text and graphics, typically located at the top or bottom of most pages, that reminds the reader where they are—the publication name, the page number, perhaps the subject of the publication or its defining phrase, and so on.

**Saddle stitch** Process of stapling two or more signatures on the fold.

**Sans serif** A type character that does not have an end stroke or "foot." *See* Serif.

**Serif** The end stroke, or "foot," of a type character.

**Service mark** The United States Patent and Trademark Office defines a service mark as "the same as a trademark except that it identifies and distinguishes the source of a service rather than a product." *See* Trademark.

**Sign** A shorthand device that stands for something else—for example, the @ sign, which stands for "at."

**Signature** A printed, folded sheet.

**Skew** A crooked image in a printed sheet caused by a misaligned plate or careless trimming.

**Solid color** A specific ink color produced by a specific manufacturer. Typically matched using a printed source book such as a PANTONE formula guide.

**Spread** Two facing pages.

**Stock** (1) In most cases, grants the buyer one-time use of a photograph or illustration for a specific project. See Royalty-free. (2) The substrate on which printing is applied—in most cases, paper.

**Stroke** The line that surrounds the solid area of a shape or typeface character. In a drawing software program, strokes can be widened or eliminated, and strokes and fills can be assigned different colors.

**Style** (1) The visual and emotional mood of your organization. It is the combination of the message, how it is presented, the images used to illustrate it, the stance of the layout, and the choices of typefaces and color. (2) Feature of a desktop publishing program used to apply multiple paragraph attributes to a paragraph of text with a single keystroke. May include attributes such as its typeface, its size, bold, italic, all caps, underline, and whether the paragraph is indented, has extra space above or below it, is hyphenated, and if it is aligned, right, left, centered, or justified.

**Symbol** A visible image of something that is invisible—for example, an hourglass represents the idea of time.

**Tint** A tone of a solid color expressed as a percentage.

**Trap** The hairline overlap between colors necessary to eliminate gaps between colors.

**Trim** The page dimensions on which a final printed sheet is cut.

**Type family** Two or more typefaces with a common design, including weights, widths, and slopes. *See* Typeface and Font.

**Typeface** One variation of a type family with a specific weight (i.e., light, regular, bold), width (i.e., condensed, narrow, extended), or slope (i.e., roman, italic). *See* Type family *and* Font.

**Trademark** The United States Patent and Trademark Office defines a trademark as a "word, phrase, symbol, or design, or combination of words, phrases, symbols, or designs, which identifies and distinguishes the source of the goods or services of one party from those of others." *See* Service mark.

**Uncoated stock** Paper with no applied surface. *See* Coated stock.

**Vector graphics** *See* Draw graphics.

# Index

# About the Author

**Chuck Green** is a graphic designer and principle of Logic Arts, a design and marketing firm. He is a frequent contributor to online and print publications, as well as the author of *The Desktop Publisher's Idea Book.* He has designed brochures, corporate identification, advertising, and presentation materials for hundreds of clients, ranging from small businesses to major corporations.